Frommer's

POSTCARDS FROM

Washington, D.C. 2003

P9-BZW-173

IN THIS TEMPLE
S IN THE HEARTS OF THE PEOPLE
OR WHOM HE SAVED THE UNION
E MEMORY OF ABRAHAM LINCOLN
IS ENSHRINED FOREVER

This moving testament to the nation's greatest president is a neoclassical temple-like structure, housing Daniel Chester French's timeless and powerful 19-foot-high seated statue of Lincoln. See chapter 7. © Robert Shafer/Folio, Inc.

The Supreme Court and the Capitol, two prime examples of Washington, D.C.'s grand neoclassical architecture. See chapter 7. © Kelly/Mooney Photography.

Viewing this stark memorial to America's Vietnam War dead is a powerful and poignant experience. See chapter 7. © Wolfgang Kaehler Photography.

Washington is at its most beautiful in the spring, when delicate pink and white blossoms from thousands of cherry trees burst into bloom along the Tidal Basin. The trees bloom for a little less than 2 weeks in late March or early April, an event that's heralded by a festival with a major parade. See chapter 7. © John Skowronski/Folio, Inc.

The Folger Shakespeare Library houses the world's largest collection of the Bard's printed works. See chapter 7. © Catherine Karnow Photography.

Painstakingly restored to its former glory, stunning Union Station is not only a gateway to D.C., but an attraction itself, with great dining and shopping. See chapters 6, 7, and 8. © Catherine Karnow Photography.

The dignified simplicity of Arlington National Cemetery. See chapter 7. © Christie Parker/
Houserstock, Inc.

The domed Main Reading Room of the Library of Congress is the epicenter of the world's largest library. Visit it to admire its exquisite architecture or to peruse one of its 113 million items. See chapter 7. © Jake Rajs/Tony Stone Images.

Lincoln was sitting in this box at Ford's Theatre when he was shot by John Wilkes Booth on April 14, 1865. See chapter 7.
© Catherine Karnow Photography.

The streets extending out from Dupont Circle are jumping with all-night bookstores, great restaurants and nightspots, movie theaters, and Washingtonians at play. See chapters 6 and 9. © Michael Ventura/Folio, Inc.

The memorial to America's third president and its original Renaissance man, Thomas Jefferson, is even more beautiful at night. See chapter 7. © Robert Shafer/Tony Stone Images.

A New Star-Rating System & Other Exciting News from Frommer's!

In our continuing effort to publish the savviest, most up-to-date, and most appealing travel guides available, we've added some great new features.

Frommer's guides now include a new **star-rating system.** Every hotel, restaurant, and attraction is rated from 0 to 3 stars to help you set priorities and organize your time.

We've also added **seven brand-new features** that point you to the great deals, in-the-know advice, and unique experiences that separate travelers from tourists. Throughout the guide, look for:

Finds	Special finds—those places only insiders know about
Fun Fact	Fun facts—details that make travelers more informed and their trips more fun
Kids	Best bets for kids—advice for the whole family
Moments	Special moments—those experiences that memories are made of
Overrated	Places or experiences not worth your time or money
Tips	Insider tips—some great ways to save time and money
Value	Great values—where to get the best deals

We've also added a **"What's New"** section in every guide—a timely crash course in what's hot and what's not in every destination we cover.

Here's what the critics say about Frommer's:

"Amazingly easy to use. Very portable, very complete."

—*Booklist*

"Detailed, accurate, and easy-to-read information for all price ranges."

—*Glamour Magazine*

"Hotel information is close to encyclopedic."

—*Des Moines Sunday Register*

"Frommer's Guides have a way of giving you a real feel for a place."

—*Knight Ridder Newspapers*

Other Great Guides for Your Trip:

Frommer's Memorable Walks in Washington, D.C.
Frommer's Washington, D.C., from $80 a Day
Frommer's Portable Washington, D.C.
The Unofficial Guide to Washington, D.C.

Frommer's®

Washington, D.C.

2003

by Elise Hartman Ford

Wiley Publishing, Inc.

About the Author

Elise Hartman Ford has been a freelance writer in the Washington, D.C., area since 1985. Her writing has appeared in *The Washington Post; Washingtonian magazine;* the London-based *Bradman's North America Guide, The Essential Guide to Business Travel; Ladies' Home Journal,* and other national, regional, and trade publications. In addition to this guide, she is the author of *Frommer's Washington, D.C., from $80 a Day, Frommer's Memorable Walks in Washington, D.C.,* and *Unique Meeting, Wedding, and Party Places in Greater Washington.*

Published by:

Wiley Publishing, Inc.

909 Third Ave.
New York, NY 10022

ISBN 0-7645-6683-0
ISSN 0899-3246

Editor: John Vorwald
Production Editor: M. Faunette Johnston
Cartographer: Roberta Stockwell
Photo Editor: Richard Fox
Production by Wiley Indianapolis Composition Services

For information on our other products and services or to obtain technical support, please contact our Customer Care Department within the U.S. at 800-762-2974, outside the U.S. at 317-572-3993 or fax 317-572-4002.

Wiley also publishes its books in a variety of electronic formats. Some content that appears in print may not be available in electronic formats.

Manufactured in the United States of America

5 4 3 2

Contents

List of Maps

This one's for the Groupies.

An Invitation to the Reader

In researching this book, we discovered many wonderful places—hotels, restaurants, shops, and more. We're sure you'll find others. Please tell us about them, so we can share the information with your fellow travelers in upcoming editions. If you were disappointed with a recommendation, we'd love to know that, too. Please write to:

Frommer's Washington, D.C. 2003
Wiley Publishing, Inc. • 909 Third Ave. • New York, NY 10022

An Additional Note

Please be advised that travel information is subject to change at any time—and this is especially true of prices. We therefore suggest that you write or call ahead for confirmation when making your travel plans. The authors, editors, and publisher cannot be held responsible for the experiences of readers while traveling. Your safety is important to us, however, so we encourage you to stay alert and be aware of your surroundings. Keep a close eye on cameras, purses, and wallets, all favorite targets of thieves and pickpockets.

New! Frommer's Star Ratings & Icons

Every hotel, restaurant, and attraction listing in this guide has been ranked for quality, value, service, amenities, and special features using a star-rating scale. In country, state, and regional guides, we also rate towns and regions to help you narrow down your choices and budget your time accordingly. Hotels and restaurants in the Very Expensive and Expensive categories are rated on a scale of one (highly recommended) to three stars (exceptional). Those in the Moderate and Inexpensive categories rate from zero (recommended) to two stars (very highly recommended). Attractions, towns, and regions are rated according to the following scale: zero stars (recommended), one star (highly recommended), two stars (very highly recommended), and three stars (must-see).

In addition to the rating system, we also use seven icons to highlight insider information, useful tips, special bargains, hidden gems, memorable experiences, kid-friendly venues, places to avoid, and other useful information:

(Finds   (Fun Fact   (Kids   (Moments   (Overrated   (Tips   (Value

The following abbreviations are used for credit cards:

AE American Express	DISC Discover	V Visa
DC Diners Club	MC MasterCard	

FROMMERS.COM

Now that you have the guidebook to a great trip, visit our website at **www.frommers.com** for travel information on nearly 2,500 destinations. With features updated regularly, we give you instant access to the most current trip-planning information available. At Frommers.com, you'll also find the best prices on airfares, accommodations, and car rentals—and you can even book travel online through our travel booking partners. At Frommers.com, you'll also find the following:

- Online updates to our most popular guidebooks
- Vacation sweepstakes and contest giveaways
- Newsletter highlighting the hottest travel trends
- Online travel message boards with featured travel discussions

What's New in Washington, D.C.

Washington, D.C., in the year 2003, is a city full of fresh promise, even as it maintains its standing as a bastion of cherished and established treasures. In the aftermath of the September 11, 2001, terrorist attacks, city and federal officials not only recognized that Washington must better secure its people and landmarks, but also, that the city's best response to such an attack was to prosper and renew itself. So, what's new in Washington are the safeguards you will encounter as you tour the city, as well as a proliferation of just-opened museums and exhibits, hotels, restaurants, shops, and other enterprises—including the huge new convention center—all shining hallmarks of a vital and inviting economy.

GETTING HERE If you are flying to Washington, D.C., you can expect increased security screening at your home airport, of course, including restrictions on carry-on items and the requirement of showing a photo ID at check-in. You should also know about certain security precautions in place on the Washington end. At none of Washington's three airports, Baltimore-Washington International, Washington Dulles International, or Ronald Reagan Washington National, are people without tickets allowed through the gates. This means that if someone is meeting you at the airport, you should arrange to rendezvous somewhere outside the gates; the baggage claim area designated for your flight makes the most sense. If you are flying into or out of

National, you should know that passengers are not permitted to leave their seats for the 30 minutes prior to landing and the first 30 minutes after the plane takes off from National.

GETTING AROUND Nothing is grandly new about the Metrorail system, which remains the easiest and most convenient mode of travel. What is new is a shuttle service that finally connects the Metro with transportation to Georgetown. Dubbed the **"Georgetown Metro Connection,"** these attractive, bright blue shuttle buses travel to Georgetown every 10 minutes from the Metro stations at Foggy Bottom, Dupont Circle, and Rosslyn. The buses run from 7am to midnight weekdays and until 2am weekends, and cost 50¢ one-way, or 25¢ with a Metrorail transfer.

ACCOMMODATIONS Boutique hotels are all the rage in Washington. In this edition, you will find the first three of five opening in rapid succession around town: the **Hotel Monaco,** 700 F St. NW (© 877/ 202-5411 or 202/628-7177; www. monaco-dc.com), the most upscale of the bunch; the **Hotel Rouge,** 1315 16th St. NW (© 800/368-5689 or 202/232-8000; www.hotelrouge. com), and the **Topaz Hotel,** 1733 N St. NW (© 800/424-2950 or 202/ 393-3000), the Rouge and the Topaz being hot and hip. Coming soon will be the **Hotel Madeira,** 1310 New Hampshire Ave. NW, and the **Hotel Helix,** 1430 Rhode Island Ave. NW, both of which you can expect to be as fun-filled in experience and as whimsical in design as the Rouge and Topaz.

Meanwhile, you should know about a couple of new high-end hotels. If you're a Francophile, check out the **Hotel Sofitel Lafayette Square,** 806 15th St. NW, at H Street (© **800/763-4835** or 202/737-8800; www.sofitel.com), a four-star luxury property and part of an upscale French hotel chain. The hotel sits at Lafayette Square across from the White House, and features a French staff, amenities, and restaurant.

A **Ritz-Carlton,** under construction for many years, was due to open in Georgetown at the end of 2002, at 31st and K streets NW (© **800/ 241-3333** or 202/835-0500; www. ritzcarlton.com). This Ritz is a luxury boutique hotel, with only 93 rooms; its design incorporates into the structure the 2-centuries-old former residence of Georgetown's first mayor.

DINING   Hotel restaurants may be convenient, but they aren't always the best places in town to eat. At least that's how it used to be. Lately, new hotels seem to be emphasizing their restaurants as much as their lodging, and getting credit for it. Worthy establishments include **15 ria,** at the Washington Terrace Hotel, 1515 Rhode Island Ave. NW (© **202/232-7000**), which serves contemporary American cuisine with a mid-Atlantic accent; **Poste,** inside the Hotel Monaco, 700 F St. NW (© **202/628-7177**), offering upscale modern American fare; and **Café 15,** at the Sofitel Lafayette Square, 806 15th St. NW (© **202/ 737-8800**), where a three-star Michelin chef creates au courant French dishes.

SIGHTSEEING   Security concerns have closed certain sites to public tours and altered touring procedures at others, because of the September 11, 2001, terrorist attacks. Unless policies have changed by the time you read this, you will not be able to tour the **White House** or the **Pentagon** as an individual (certain group tours are allowed; read write-ups in chapter 7). The **U.S. Capitol,** at the east end of the Mall (© **202/225-6827**), is open to public tours, but you can no longer go through self-guided, nor can you arrange reserve tickets ahead of time, as you could in the past.

Construction began in mid-2002 on a comprehensive underground **Capitol Visitor Center,** with completion scheduled for 2005. The new visitor center is being created directly beneath the plaza where people traditionally lined up for tours on the east side of the Capitol, which means that you must now stand in line at the southwest corner of the Capitol, the side facing the Mall, at the intersection of 1st St. and Independence Ave. SW.

At the Capitol, and at other attractions, including the Smithsonian museums, your bags are examined for prohibited items and you must pass through a metal detector. Prohibited items include liquids, cans, bottles, knives of any kind, and mace or pepper spray. At the Capitol, you won't be allowed on a tour if you're carrying an oversized backpack, duffel bag, or suitcase, since there's no place to check these items. If you're planning to visit the Capitol at any time in 2003, call ahead to find out the latest information about touring procedures, and whether the areas of the building you wish to visit are closed to tourists.

Attractions that are closed for renovations include the Smithsonian's **National Portrait Gallery,** Eighth and F streets NW (© **202/357-2700;** www.npg.si.edu), the **American Art Museum,** Eighth and G streets NW (© **202/357-2700;** http://american art.si.edu), and the **Newseum** (© **888/ NEWSEUM;** www.newseum.org) formerly located in Rosslyn, Virginia, but scheduled to open in larger digs on Pennsylvania Avenue downtown—but not until 2006.

You'll discover a new memorial on the Mall, the **George Mason Memorial** (© 202/426-6841) located between the Jefferson and the FDR Memorials, near the Tidal Basin, in West Potomac Park; and several wonderful new museums, including the **International Spy Museum,** 800 F St. NW (© 202/393-7798; www.spymuseum.org), which offers exhibits and hands-on activities to explore the history of espionage; and the **City Museum of Washington,** 800 Mount Vernon Square Place NW (© 202/785-2068; www.citymuseumdc.org), which covers the 200-year history of the city, as well as its neighborhoods and the people who helped shape the town.

1

The Best of Washington, D.C.

Even if you've never visited Washington, D.C., you know its images well: the stately White House, the Washington Monument with its pencil-point nose thrusting into the sky, the wedding-cake tiered dome atop the majestic Capitol, and the gleaming white columns of the Lincoln Memorial. When you get here, you will see for yourself that the capital's famous monuments stand strong and unswerving, where they were planted decades and centuries ago. The very presence of these and the many other significant landmarks in this white marble town remind us of the constancy of our government and the strength that lies within our country's history. Tour these sites and be reassured that democracy is alive and well in the land. Such an experience is reason enough to come to Washington, D.C.

The museums are another. Nowhere else in the world will you find such vast and diverse collections of art and inventions—and free to view, courtesy of the Smithsonian Institution. Within its city limits (67 square miles), Washington has more than 40 other museums besides the Smithsonian's, and these include the National Gallery of Art, the country's oldest modern art museum (the Phillips Collection), and the city's newest museums: the International Spy Museum and the City of Washington Museum.

And then there are Washington's performing arts venues, from the world-renowned John F. Kennedy Center for the Performing Arts to lively local nightclubs, its lovely parks and gardens, top-rated restaurants preparing every possible cuisine, charming neighborhoods, embassy-lined streets, awesome architecture: Acquaint yourself with any or all of these aspects of Washington and you will certainly be enjoying some of the best the city has to offer.

In the end, your personal-best list of favorite Washington experiences most likely will be a catalog, not just of places you've visited, but also of people you've met along the way. Try to allow for these chance encounters. In this cosmopolitan city, whose population is as culturally diverse as those who tour here, you may find yourself forging connections with people from halfway around the world—or from your own hometown—and these experiences may become your fondest memories of the city. As the nation's capital and the home of our democratic government, Washington, like no other city, holds a certain place in the world, as it represents all the freedoms and ideals that Americans hold dear. Against the backdrop of the White House, the Capitol, and the Supreme Court, a little small talk between strangers creates opportunities for understanding differences. Such moments, dear reader, are the best of the best that Washington has to offer.

1 Frommer's Favorite D.C. Experiences

- **Sipping Afternoon Tea at the Top of Washington National Cathedral.** On Tuesday and Wednesday afternoons at 1:30pm, you can tour the world's sixth largest cathedral, then indulge in tea, scones, and lemon tarts served on the seventh floor of the West tower, whose arched windows overlook the city and beyond to the Sugarloaf Mountains in Maryland. It's $18 per person; reserve as far in advance as possible (© 202/537-8993). See p. 209.

- **Visiting the Lincoln Memorial After Dark.** A must. During the day, be prepared to run interference with hordes of schoolchildren and tour groups; at night, the experience is amazing. See p. 179.

- **Taking a Monument and Memorials Walking Tour.** Have a hearty breakfast, then take the Metro to Foggy Bottom, and when you exit turn right on 23rd Street NW and follow it to Constitution Avenue NW. Cross the avenue, make a left, walk past Henry Bacon Drive, and follow the signs to the Vietnam and Lincoln memorials; cross Independence Avenue and follow the cherry tree-lined Tidal Basin path to the FDR Memorial and further to the Jefferson Memorial; and finish your tour at the Washington Monument. This is a long but beautiful hike; afterward, head up 15th Street NW for a strength-restoring meal at one of the many excellent downtown restaurants. See chapters 6 and 7.

- **Rambling Through Rock Creek Park.** A paved bike/walking path extends 11 miles from the Lincoln Memorial to the Maryland border. You can hop on the trail at many spots throughout the city—it runs past the National Zoo, behind the Omni Shoreham Hotel in Woodley Park, near Dupont Circle, and across from the Watergate/Kennedy Center complex. You can rent a bike from **Big Wheel Bikes** at 1034 33rd St. NW (© 202/337-0254) in Georgetown, and from **Thompson's**

Boat Center (© 202/333-4861), located on the path across from the Kennedy Center. For a really long bike ride, trek to the Lincoln Memorial, get yourself across the busy stretch that connects the parkway to the Arlington Memorial Bridge, and cross the bridge to the trail on the other side; this path winds 19 miles to Mount Vernon. See chapter 7.

- **Spending the Day in Alexandria.** Just a short distance (by Metro, car, or bike) from the District is George Washington's Virginia hometown. Roam the quaint cobblestone streets, browse charming boutiques and antiques stores, visit the 18th-century houses and other historic attractions, and dine in one of Alexandria's fine restaurants. See chapter 10.

- **Weighing in Judgment.** If you're in town when the Supreme Court is in session (Oct–late Apr; call © 202/479-3211 for details), you can observe a case argued; it's thrilling to see this august institution at work. See p. 171.

- **Admiring the Library of Congress.** The magnificent Italian Renaissance–style Thomas Jefferson Building of the Library of Congress—filled with murals, mosaics, sculptures, and allegorical paintings—is one of America's most notable architectural achievements. See p. 199.

- **Attending a Millennium Stage Performance at the Kennedy Center.** Every evening at 6pm, the Kennedy Center presents a free 1-hour concert performed by local, up-and-coming, or nationally known musicians. This is a winner. Call the Kennedy Center (© 800/444-1324 or 202/467-4600, or check its website at **www.kennedy-center.org**, to see the schedule of upcoming acts. See p. 245 .

- **Spending a Morning on the Mall.** Take the Metro to the Smithsonian station early in the morning (about 8:30am is early enough), when the Mall is magical and tourist-free. Walk toward the Capitol Building along Jefferson Drive to the Smithsonian Information Center (the Castle) and stroll through the magnolia-lined parterres of the beautiful Enid A. Haupt Garden. Return to Jefferson Drive, walk farther east to the Hirshhorn, ducking in, on your way, for a look at the lovely Ripley Garden, before crossing the street to tour the Hirshhorn's sunken Sculpture Garden. Climb back to street level and cross the Mall to the enchanting National Gallery Sculpture Garden, at Seventh Street and Madison Drive. See chapter 7.

- **Debarking at Union Station.** Noted architect Daniel H. Burnham's turn-of-the-20th-century beaux arts railway station is worth a visit even if you're not trying to catch a train. Dawdle and admire its coffered 96-foot-high ceilings, grand arches, and great halls, modeled after the Baths of Diocletian and the Arch of Constantine in Rome. Then shop and eat: The station's 1988 restoration filled the trilevel hall with everything from Ann Taylor and Crabtree & Evelyn to a high-quality food court and the refined B. Smith's restaurant. See chapters 7 and 8.

- **Enjoying an Artful Evening at the Phillips Collection.** Thursday evenings year-round, from 5 to 8:30pm, you pay $5 to tour the mansion-museum rooms filled with Impressionist, post-Impressionist, and modern art. Your tour ends up in the paneled Music Room, where you'll enjoy jazz, blues, or other musical combinations performed by fine local musicians, topped off by an artful lecture. It's a popular mingling spot for singles (there's a cash bar and sandwich fare). Call ✆ 202/387-2151 for information. See chapter 7 for complete details on the Phillips Collection. See chapter 9 for more nightlife.

- **Strolling Along Embassy Row.** Head northwest on Massachusetts Avenue from Dupont Circle. It's a gorgeous walk along tree-shaded streets lined with beaux arts mansions. Built by fabulously wealthy magnates during the Gilded Age, most of these palatial precincts are occupied today by foreign embassies.

- **People-Watching at Dupont Circle.** One of the few "living" circles, Dupont's is the all-weather hangout for mondo-bizarre biker-couriers, chess players, street musicians, and lovers. Sit on a bench and be astounded by the passing scene. See chapter 4.

- **Viewing Washington from the Water.** Cruise the Potomac River aboard one of several sightseeing vessels and relax from foot-weary travels. River cruises not only offer a pleasant interval for catching a second wind, they treat you to a marvelous perspective of the city. See chapter 7.

- **Cutting a Deal at the Georgetown Flea Market.** Pick up a latte and spend a pleasant Sunday browsing through the castoffs of wealthy Washingtonians,

---

Impressions

My God! What have I done to be condemned to reside in such a city!
*   —A French diplomat in the early days*

hand-painted furniture by local artists, and a hodgepodge of antiques and collectibles. Everybody shops here at one time or another, so you never know who you'll see or what you'll find. Wisconsin Avenue NW at S Street NW in Georgetown; open year-round, Sunday from 9am to 5pm. See chapter 8 for more shopping.

- **Shopping at Eastern Market.** Capitol Hill is home to more than government buildings; it's a community of old town houses, antiques shops, and the veritable institution, Eastern Market. Here, the locals barter and shop on Saturday mornings for fresh produce and baked goods, and on Sunday for flea-market bargains. At Seventh Street SE, between North Carolina Avenue and C Street SE. See chapter 8 for more shopping.

- **Ordering Drinks on the Sky Terrace of the Hotel Washington.** Posher bars exist, but none with this view. The experience is almost a cliché in Washington: When spring arrives, make a date to sit on this outdoor rooftop terrace, sip a gin and tonic, and gaze at the panoramic view of the White House, Treasury Building, and monuments. Open from the end of April to October for drinks and light fare, it's located at 515 15th St. NW, at Pennsylvania Ave. NW (© **202/347-4499**). See p. 93.

- **Chilling to the Sounds of Live Jazz in the Sculpture Garden.** Friday evenings in the summer at the National Gallery of Art Sculpture Garden, dip your toes in the fountain pool and chill, as live jazz groups serenade you, from 5 to 8pm. The garden's Pavilion Café sells tapas and wine and beer, by the way. See chapter 7.

- **Ice Skating on the Mall.** The National Gallery of Art Sculpture Garden pool turns into an ice-skating rink in winter. So visit the Gallery, finishing up at the Sculpture Garden, where you can rent skates and twirl around on the ice, admiring sculptures as you go. Treat yourself to hot chocolate and sandwiches at the Pavilion Café in the garden. Seventh Street and Madison Drive. See chapter 7.

2 Best Hotel Bets

- **Best Historic Hotel:** The grande dame of Washington hotels is the magnificent **Renaissance Mayflower,** 1127 Connecticut Ave. NW (© **800/228-7697** or 202/347-3000; www.renaissance hotels.com), which, when it was built in 1925, was considered not only the last word in luxury and beauty, but also "the second-best address" in town. Harry S. Truman preferred it to the White House. See p. 96.

- **Best Historic-into-Hip Hotel: The Hotel Monaco,** 700 F St. NW (© **877/202-5411** or 202/ 628-7177; www.monaco-dc.com), with its mid-19th-century neo-classical architecture, looks stately and historic. Step inside, though, and you'll marvel over the way the hotel cleverly marries contemporary decor with original, century-and-a-half-old features. See p. 89.

- **Best Location: Willard Inter-Continental,** 1401 Pennsylvania Ave. NW (© **800/327-0200** or 202/628-9100; www.washington. interconti.com), is within walking distance of the White House, museums, theaters, downtown offices, good restaurants, and the Metro. It's also a quick taxi ride to Capitol Hill. A top contender in the best historic hotel category, as well. See p. 91.

- **Best Place for Hipsters:** It's a tossup between the **Hotel Rouge,** 1315 16th St. NW (© **800/368-5689** or 202/232-8000; www.rougehotel.com), where the color red rules in the decor, bloody marys are complimentary in the morning, and Red Bull is found in the in-room minibar; and the **Topaz Hotel,** 1733 N St. NW (© **800/424-2950** or 202/393-3000; www.topazhotel.com), where the decor is all New Agey, the complimentary morning drinks are energy potions, and guest room offerings include "yoga" rooms, which come with yoga mat and instructional tapes, and "energy" rooms, which come with a piece of exercise equipment and fitness magazines. Each of the hotels has an exotically decorated bar that serves wild drinks and delicious food. See p. 98 and 104.

- **Best Place for a Romantic Getaway:** The posh **Jefferson Hotel,** 16th and M streets NW (© **800/235-6397** or 202/347-2200; www.thejeffersonhotel.com), is just enough off the beaten track, but still conveniently downtown, to feel like you've really escaped. Because the service, bar, and restaurant (see chapter 6) are outstanding, you have no need to leave the premises. The restaurant has one of the most romantic nooks in the city. Just up the street at 16th and K streets is another excellent choice, the **St. Regis Hotel** (© **800/526-5661** or 202/638-2626; www.stregis.com), with its luxurious guest rooms, an opulent lobby that resembles an Italian palazzo, a cozy paneled bar, and a good restaurant. See p. 96 and 97.

- **Best Moderately Priced Hotel: Lincoln Suites Downtown,** 1823 L St. NW (© **800/424-2970** or 202/223-4320; www.lincolnhotels.com), is located downtown, within easy walking distance of the White House, Dupont Circle, and Foggy Bottom. Its rates are outstanding for the clean, newly renovated, spacious suites, one-third of which have full kitchens. Free use of a nearby health spa and complimentary homemade cookies and milk each evening will win you over. See p. 99.

- **Best Inexpensive Hotel:** The **Jurys Normandy,** a boutique hotel at 2118 Wyoming Ave. NW (© **800/424-3729** or 202/483-1350; www.jurysdoyle.com), charges $79 to $175 for personable service and rooms that are small but charming. Extras like an exercise room, a pool, and a restaurant are available at its sister hotel around the corner. See p. 102.

- **Best Inn:** The stunning **Morrison-Clark Historic Inn,** Massachusetts Avenue and 11th Street NW (© **800/332-7898** or 202/898-1200; www.morrisonclark.com), housed in two beautifully restored Victorian town houses, has exquisite rooms and a good restaurant. See p. 94.

- **Best B&B: Swann House,** 1808 New Hampshire Ave. NW (© **202/265-4414;** www.swannhouse.com), is remarkably pretty and comfortable, and in a great neighborhood (Dupont Circle). See p. 104.

- **Best Service:** The staff at the **Ritz-Carlton,** 1150 22nd St. NW (© **800/241-3333** or 202/835-0500; www.ritzcarlton.com), is engaging but not overbearing; service is solicitous and quick, whether you've ordered a glass of wine in the lounge or room service. A 24-hour concierge will handle anything you request, and the nightly turndown maid places a freshly baked brownie upon your

Impressions

I know of no other capital in the world which stands on so wide and splendid a river. But the people and the mode of life are enough to take your hair off!

—Henry James

pillow instead of a mint. Likewise, the **Four Seasons,** 2800 Pennsylvania Ave. NW (© **800/332-3442** or 202/342-0444; www.fourseasons.com), pampers you relentlessly and greets you by name. The hotel also offers an "I Need It Now" program that delivers any of 100 or more left-at-home essentials (tweezers, batteries, cuff links, electric hair curlers, and so on) to you in 3 minutes, at no cost. See p. 108 and 110.

• **Best for Pets:** The two Loews properties, **The Jefferson,** 16th and M streets NW (© **800/235-6397** or 202/347-2200; www.thejeffersonhotel.com), and the **Loews L'Enfant Plaza,** 480 L'Enfant Plaza (© **800/23-LOEWS** or 202/484-1000; www.loewshotels.com), are known for their pet perks, which include pet place mats and toys and treats in the room, information about nearby dog-walking routes and veterinarians, and the availability of pet-walking and pet-sitting services. See p. 96 and 86.

• **Best Place to Hide If You're Embroiled in a Scandal:** Lovely as it is, the **Jurys Normandy,** 2118 Wyoming Ave. NW (© **800/424-3729** or 202/483-1350; www.jurysdoyle.com), remains unknown to many Washingtonians—a plus if you need to lay low. The neighborhood teems with embassies, in case your trouble is of the I-need-a-foreign-government-to-bail-me-out variety. (And it's a bargain to boot.) See p. 102.

• **Best for Business Travelers:** If money's no object, the **Four Seasons Hotel,** 2800 Pennsylvania Ave. NW (© **800/332-3442** or 202/342-0444; www.fourseasons.com), is a standout, offering complimentary sedan service weekdays within the District, high-speed Internet access in every room, and a special wing designed for executives: these rooms are soundproof and each has an office equipped with a fax machine and portable telephones. Transmitters installed throughout the entire hotel afford you wireless connection to the Internet on your laptop, wherever you go in the hotel. Finally, the hotel has started up a "Travel Light" program, which allows guests who stay there frequently to store personal belongings at the hotel; you then find your possessions waiting for you in your room, upon your return. See p. 110.

Business travelers on a budget should try the **Four Points Sheraton, Washington, D.C. Downtown,** 1201 K St. NW (© **800/481-7191** or 202/289-7600; www.fourpointswashingtondc.com). You'll get a great central downtown location near both convention centers, weekday rates as low as $99, and services that include high-speed Internet access in all rooms, a 24-hour fitness center, and an excellent on-site restaurant for business entertaining. See p. 95.

• **Best Hotel Restaurant:** My vote goes to **Michel Richard**

Citronelle, in the Latham Hotel, 3000 M St. NW (© 800/528-4261 or 202/726-5000; www.the latham.com), for creative French fare. Another top pick is the Melrose, in the Park Hyatt Hotel, 1201 24th St. NW (© 800/778-7477 or 202/789-1234; www.parkhyatt.com), for New American cuisine. See p. 153 and 151.

• **Best Health Club:** The Ritz-Carlton, 1150 22nd St. NW (© 800/241-3333 or 202/835-0500; www.ritzcarlton.com), has the best fitness center in the city. Its two-level, 100,000-square-foot Sports Club/LA boasts state-of-the-art weight-training equipment and free weights, two regulation-size basketball courts and four squash courts, an indoor heated swimming pool and aquatics pool with sun deck, exercise classes, personal trainers, the full-service Splash Spa and Salon, and its own restaurant and cafe. Second place goes to the Fitness Company West End, at the Monarch Hotel, 2401 M St. NW (© 877/222-2266 or 202/429-2400; www.monarchdc.com), a 17,500-square-foot center offering classes in yoga and aerobics; seminars in stress management and weight loss; and equipment that includes virtual-reality bike machines, stair climbers and exercise bikes with telephones and TV/VCR units, skiing and rowing machines, and more. The health club also has squash and racquetball courts, a swimming pool, a steam room, a whirlpool, saunas, and a minispa. Personal trainers, fitness evaluation, and workout clothes are available. See p. 108 and 107.

• **Best Views:** The Hay-Adams, 16th and H streets NW (© 800/424-5054 or 202/638-6600; www.hayadams.com), has such a great, unobstructed view of the White House that the Secret Service comes over regularly to do security sweeps of the place. See p. 95.

• **Best for Travelers with Disabilities:** The Omni-Shoreham Hotel, 2500 Calvert St. NW (© 800/843-6664 or 202/234-0700; www.omnihotels.com), has 41 specially equipped rooms for guests with disabilities, about half with roll-in showers; vibrating door knockers and pillows, TTYs, and flashing lights to alert guests when fire alarms are sounding (all of these devices are available, but you must ask for them); and the hotel carries copies of disabilityguide.org's *Access Entertainment* guide, which offers detailed information about how to travel around and enjoy D.C., if you have disabilities. See p. 114.

• **Best for Packages:** The St. Gregory Hotel and Suites, 2033 M St. NW (at 21st St.; © 800/829-5034 or 202/530-3600; www.stgregoryhotelwdc.com), is distinctly lovely, which makes its packages distinctly good values. One example: posted on its website in 2002 was the One Dollar Summer Sale, which offered you an overnight stay for $169, with the second night for $1. The package was available on Friday and Saturday nights, or Saturday and Sunday nights, in summer. (If this package is no longer available, look for others on the website.) See p. 104.

3 Best Dining Bets

• **Best Spot for a Romantic Dinner:** Just ask for the "snug" (tables 39 and 40) at The Restaurant at

the Jefferson, 1200 16th St. NW, at M Street (© 202/833-6206). Two cozy banquette areas in alcoves are secluded from the main dining room. Follow your sumptuous dinner with drinks in front of the fireplace in the adjoining lounge. Another option: **Butterfield 9,** 600 14th St. NW (© **202/BU-9-8810**), woos you with its award-winning cuisine and its romantic, stylized black-and-white photos of handsome men and women dressed in fashions of the 1930s, '40s, and '50s. See p. 136 and 123.

• **Best Spot for a Business Lunch: La Colline,** 400 N. Capitol St. NW (© **202/737-0400**), conveniently located near Capitol Hill, has a great bar, four private rooms, high-backed leather booths that allow for discreet conversations, and, last but not least, consistently good food. A perfect spot for the Washington breakfast meeting or fundraiser. And then there's **The Caucus Room,** 401 Ninth St. NW (© **202/393-0777**), where there's always a whole lot of handshaking going on. See p. 122 and 126.

• **Best Spot for a Celebration: Café Atlantico,** 405 Eighth St. NW (© **202/393-0812**), will give you reason to celebrate even if you didn't arrive with one. The restaurant is pure fun, with charming waiters, seating on three levels, colorful wall-size paintings by Latin and Caribbean artists, fantastic cocktails, and unusual but not trendy South American food. Other good choices: **Teatro Goldoni,** 1909 K St. NW (© **202/955-9494**); and **Kinkead's,** 2000 Pennsylvania Ave. NW (© **202/296-7700**). See p. 129 and 139.

• **Best Decor:** The **Willard Room** (© **202/637-7440**), in the Willard Inter-Continental, 1401 Pennsylvania Ave. NW, at 14th Street, has such grand decor—with paneling, velvet, and silk—that it's been used more than once

for a movie shoot. (Consider this another contender in the "Most Romantic" category.) See p. 128.

• **Best View:** The awning-covered sidewalk at **Les Halles,** 1201 Pennsylvania Ave. NW (© **202/347-6848**), is open in summer, enclosed in winter—a fine spot for viewing the sights along Pennsylvania Avenue all year-round. See p. 130.

• **Best Wine List:** At **Michel Richard Citronelle,** in the Latham Hotel, 3000 M St. NW (© **202/625-2150**), the extensive, 8,000-bottle wine cellar is on display behind glass in the dining room. If you're serious about wine, come here; but check your wallet first. Citronelle is one of the city's most expensive restaurant and wines with three-digit prices predominate. The food is excellent. See p. 153.

• **Best for Kids: Luigi's,** 1132 19th St. NW (© **202/331 7574**), not only serves up some of the best pizza in town, but also has the best prices for kids' portions of pasta dishes (all under $5). Plus, the place is loud and indestructible. See p. 141.

• **Best American Cuisine: Cashion's Eat Place,** 1819 Columbia Rd. NW (© **202/797-1819**), is as welcoming as can be. Chef-owner Ann Cashion serves creative American food with a homey touch—she's unafraid to put onion rings next to something like a finely grilled black bass filet. Desserts are prepared with care. See p. 142.

• **Best Chinese Cuisine: Full Kee,** 509 H St. NW (© **202/371-2233**), in the heart of Chinatown, is consistently good and a great value—but don't expect much in the way of decor. If you want to enjoy your surroundings as well as the food, head to Dupont Circle's

Site Seeing: The Best Washington Websites

- **www.washingtonpost.com**: This is the *Washington Post*'s site, a most helpful source for up-to-date information on restaurants, attractions, shopping, and nightlife (as well as world news).

- **www.washington.org**: The Washington Convention and Tourism Corporation operates this site, which gives a broad overview of what to see and do in D.C., and provides travel updates on security issues. Click on "Plan a Vacation" for tips on where to stay, dine, shop, and sightsee.

- **www.washingtonian.com**: The print magazine of the same name posts some of its articles here, including "What's Happening," a monthly guide to what's on at museums, theaters, and other cultural showplaces around town, and a directory of reviews of Washington restaurants. The magazine really wants you to buy the print edition, though—for sale at bookstores, drugstores, and grocery stores throughout the area.

- **www.washingtonflyermag.com**: In addition to its extensive information about airline travel in and out of Washington (and ground transportation from each airport), this site also offers fun articles about restaurants and things to do in D.C.

- **www.opentable.com**: This site allows you to make reservations at some of the capital's finest restaurants.

- **www.dcaccommodations.com**: This nicely designed site recommends hotels suited for families, women, sightseers, or business travelers.

- **www.hotelsdc.com**: Capitol Reservations, a 19-year-old company, represents more than 100 hotels in the Washington area, each of which has been screened for cleanliness, safety, and other factors. You can book your room online.

- **www.bnbaccom.com**: For those who prefer to stay in a private home, guesthouse, inn, or unfurnished apartment, this service offers more than 80 for you to consider.

- **www.si.edu**: This is the Smithsonian Institution's home page, which provides information about visiting Washington and leads you to the individual websites for each Smithsonian museum.

- **www.kennedy-center.org**: Find out what's playing at the Kennedy Center and listen to live broadcasts through the Net.

- **www.mountvernon.org**: Click on "Visitor's Guide" for daily attractions at Mount Vernon and a calendar of events, as well as information on

---

City Lights of China, 1731 Connecticut Ave. NW (© 202/265-6688). See p. 134 and 148.

- **Best French Cuisine:** Top of the line and extremely expensive is **Gerard's Place,** 915 15th St. NW (© 202/737-4445), which boasts the only Michelin two-star chef in the United States: Gerard Pangaud, whose cooking expertise is considered an art form (p. 126). Also consider **Michel Richard** dining, shopping, and school programs. For a sneak preview, click on "Mount Vernon Tour" to see images of the master bedroom, dining room, slave memorial, and the Washingtons' tomb.

- **www.nps.gov/nacc**: This National Park Service site includes links to some dozen memorials and monuments. Among the links: the Washington Monument, Jefferson Memorial, National Mall, Ford's Theatre, FDR Memorial, Lincoln Memorial, and Vietnam Veterans Memorial.

- **www.house.gov**: Once you're in the U.S. House of Representatives site, click on "Visiting the Nation's Capital" to learn more about touring the Capitol building. From here, click on "The House Chamber," where you can get a view of the chamber where the House meets and learn whether the House is in session. The site also connects you with the Web pages for each of the representatives; you can use this site to e-mail your representative (especially valuable if you want VIP tickets too.

- **www.senate.gov**: In the U.S. Senate site, click on "Visiting the Senate" for an online virtual tour of the Capitol building and information about touring the actual Senate Gallery. It takes a few seconds for the images to download, but it's worth the wait to enjoy the panoramic video tour. Also, find out when the Senate is in session. The site connects you with the Web pages for each of the senators; you can use this site to e-mail your senator.

- **www.whitehouse.gov**: Click on "Tour Information" to learn about visiting the White House and upcoming public events. You'll find all sorts of links here, from a history of the White House, to archived White House documents, to an e-mail page you can use to contact the president or vice president.

- **www.metwashairports.com**: Ground transport, terminal maps, flight status, and airport facilities for Washington Dulles International and Ronald Reagan Washington National airports.

- **www.bwiairport.com**: Ground transport, terminal maps, flight status, and airport facilities for Baltimore-Washington International Airport.

- **www.wmata.com**: Timetables, maps, fares, and more for the Metro buses and subways that serve the Washington, D.C., metro area.

Citronelle, in the Latham Hotel in Georgetown, 3000 M St. NW (© **202/625-2150**), where Richard ebulliently works in his open kitchen, creating sumptuous, constantly changing dishes (p. 153). For French classics and Parisian atmosphere, dine at **Bistrot Lepic,** at 1736 Wisconsin Ave. NW (© **202/333-0111**); and for bistro food and spirit, try

Bistrot du Coin, 1738 Connecticut Ave. NW (© **202/234-6969**). See p. 156 and 148.

- **Best Italian Cuisine:** Roberto Donna's **Galileo,** 1110 21st St. NW (© **202/293-7191**), does fine Italian cuisine best, preparing exquisite pastas, fish, and meat dishes with savory ingredients. Also see listing below for "Best of the Best." **Tosca,** 1112 F St. NW (© **367-1990**), is another winner, serving fine and unusual dishes derived from the chef's northern Italian upbringing. At **Obelisk,** 2029 P St. NW (© **202/872-1180**), chef-owner Peter Pastan crafts elegantly simple and delicious food in a pleasantly spare room. See p. 135, 132, and 146, respectively.
- **Best Seafood:** You could eat at **Kinkead's,** 2000 Pennsylvania Ave. NW (© **202/296-7700**), every day and never go wrong. See p. 152.
- **Best Southern Cuisine:** At **Vidalia,** 1990 M St. NW (© **202/659-1990**), chef Jeff Buben calls his cuisine "provincial American"—it's a euphemism for fancy fare that includes cheese grits and biscuits in cream gravy. See p. 139.
- **Best Mexican Cuisine: Lauriol Plaza,** 1835 18th St. NW (© **202/387-0035**), isn't completely Mexican (it's also Salvadoran and Cuban). But it's all delicious and well priced, and worth standing in line for, since the restaurant does not take reservations. For more contemporary, more sophisticated Mexican cuisine, try **Andale,** 401 7th St. NW (© **202/783-3133**). See p. 144 and 128.
- **Best Steakhouse: The Palm,** 1225 19th St. NW (© **202/293-9091**), going strong after 31 years, is still a classy joint that serves some of the best beef in town, despite some awesome competition. Also

consider **The Caucus Room,** 401 Ninth St. NW (© **202/393-0777**). See p. 139 and 126.

- **Best Spanish Cuisine:** No contest here. The elegant **Taberna del Alabardero,** 1776 I St. NW (© **202/429-2200**), is famous for its paellas, as well as tapas. See p. 136.
- **Best Pizza:** At **Pizzeria Paradiso,** 2029 P St. NW (© **202/223-1245**), peerless chewy-crusted pies are baked in an oak-burning oven and crowned with delicious toppings; you'll find great salads and sandwiches on fresh-baked focaccia here, too. If you like thick, old-fashioned pizzas, head to **Luigi's,** 1132 19th St. NW (© **202/331-7574**). See p. 149 and 141.
- **Best for Vegetarians:** The chef's wife is vegetarian, so **Equinox,** 818 Connecticut Ave. NW (© **202/331-8118**), always offers at least one fine vegetarian entree each evening, and accompanies meat and seafood entrees with absurdly delicious vegetable side dishes. Also consider the **Bombay Club,** 815 Connecticut Ave. NW (© **202/659-3727**), whose menu features one whole page of vegetarian main courses. See p. 137 and 140.
- **Best Healthy Meal:** At **Legal Sea Foods,** 2020 K St. NW (© **202/496-1111**), follow up a cup of light clam chowder (made without butter, cream, or flour) with an entree of grilled fresh fish and vegetables and a superb sorbet for dessert. It's fabulous guilt-free dining. The restaurant has several other locations throughout the area. See p. 140.
- **Best Late-Night Dining:** To satisfy a yen for Chinese food, go to **Full Kee,** 509 H St. NW, in Chinatown (© **202/371-2233**), open until 3am on weekends. For more

comfortable surroundings and good old American cuisine, try the **Old Ebbitt Grill,** 675 15th St. NW (© **202/347-4801**), whose kitchen stays open until 1am on weekends. Also consider **Les Halles,** 1201 Pennsylvania Ave. NW (© **202/347-6848**). See p. 134, 133, and 130.

- **Best for a Bad Mood:** At **Al Tiramisu,** 2014 P St. NW (© **202/467-4466**), the waiters, the owner, the conviviality, and the Italian food gently coax that smile back onto your face. See p. 146.
- **Best Brunch:** Go to **Georgia Brown's,** 950 15th St. NW (© **202/393-4499**), Sunday from 10:30am to 2:30pm to enjoy live jazz and a part buffet/part a la carte menu featuring such dishes as biscuit-batter French toast with maple-pecan syrup, country ham, buttermilk-fried chicken, omelets made to order, and a host of other items. This brunch ($22.95 per person) is popular, so be sure to make a reservation. See p. 130.
- **Best for Pretheater Dinner:** Head for **701,** at 701 Pennsylvania Ave. NW (© **202/393-0701**). How could you do better than 701's $24.95 three-course bargain and its prime location (right around the corner from the Shakespeare Theatre and a few blocks from the National and Warner theaters)? More expensive, but still a deal, is **Marcel's,** 2401 Pennsylvania Ave. NW (© **202/296-1166**), pretheater dinner: For $42 you might dine on arugula salad, pan-seared salmon, and crème brûlée. Marcel's even throws in free shuttle service to the Kennedy Center. See p. 131 and 150.

- **Best for "Taste of Washington" Experience:** Eat lunch at **The Monocle,** 107 D St. NE (© **202/546-4488**), and you're bound to see a Supreme Court justice, congressman, or senator dining here, too. For some down-home and delicious Washington fun, sit at the counter at **Ben's Chili Bowl,** 1213 U St. NW (© **202/667-0909**), and chat with the owners and your neighbor over a chili dog or plate of blueberry pancakes; the place is an institution, and open for breakfast, lunch, and dinner. See p. 122 and 142.
- **Best of the Best:** Few can deny that Roberto Donna's **Laboratorio del Galileo,** inside the restaurant Galileo, 1110 21st St. NW (© **202/331-0880**), is a sublime experience. In this private dining area enclosed by glass, Donna prepares a 10- to 12-course tasting menu and entertains the 30 diners lucky enough to have snagged a table. See p. 135.

2

Planning Your Trip to Washington, D.C.

As you prepare to visit the nation's capital, you'll want to make sure you pack certain essentials. Got your curiosity about American history? Good. How about your appreciation of our democratic society and for the government that ensures our freedoms? Great. OK, now do you have your interest in beautiful art and architecture? That's terrific. And an enthusiasm for the peoples, food, music, crafts, inventions, and theater, not just of the United States, but of the world? Yes? Well, then, Washington, D.C., in all its glory, awaits you. You're good to go.

Wait a second. It might help if you do a little practical planning, as well. Read on for tips to help make your trip here hassle-free.

1 Visitor Information

Before you leave, contact the **Washington, D.C. Convention and Tourism Corporation,** 1212 New York Ave. NW, Washington, DC 20005 (© **800/422-8644** or 202/789-7000; www.washington.org), and ask for a free copy of the *Washington, D.C. Visitors Guide,* which details hotels, restaurants, sights, shops, and more. The staff will also be happy to answer specific questions.

For the latest information about specific tourist spots, check out the National Park Service's website, **www.nps.gov/nacc** (the Park Service maintains Washington's monuments, memorials, and other sites), and the Smithsonian Institution's **www.si.edu.**

Also helpful is the *Washington Post* site, **www.washingtonpost.com**, which gives you up-to-the-minute news, weather, visitor information, restaurant reviews, and nightlife insights. Another good site is *Washington Flyer* magazine. You can pick up the magazine for free at the airports, but you may want to browse it online in advance (at **www.fly2dc.com**), since it often covers airport and airline news and profiles upcoming events in Washington—things you might want to know before you travel. The Metropolitan Washington Airports Authority publishes the magazine, which carries a comprehensive flight guide for National and Dulles airports in each issue. If you don't have access to the Internet, you can subscribe to the bimonthly by calling © **202/331-9393;** the rate is $15 for six issues, or $3 for one.

2 Money

Perhaps because so many of Washington's attractions (the Smithsonian museums, the monuments, even nightly concerts at the Kennedy Center) are either free or inexpensive, it may come as a shock to see the high price of lodging or a meal at a fine restaurant.

Tips **Small Change**

When you change money, ask for some small bills or loose change. Petty cash will come in handy for tipping and public transportation. Consider keeping the change separate from your larger bills, so it's readily accessible and you'll be less of a target for theft.

It makes sense to have some cash on hand to pay for incidentals, but it's not necessary to carry around large sums. After all, even some Metro farecard machines accept credit cards now.

ATMS

ATMs (automated teller machines) are everywhere, from the National Gallery of Art gift shop, to Union Station, to the bank at the corner. ATMs link local banks to a network that most likely includes your bank at home. **Cirrus** (✆ **800/424-7787;** www.mastercard.com) and **PLUS** (✆ **800/843-7587;** www.visa.com) are the two most popular networks in the United States; call or check online for ATM locations at your destination. Be sure you know your four-digit PIN before you leave home and be sure to find out your daily withdrawal limit before you depart. You can also get cash advances on your credit card at an ATM. Keep in mind that credit card companies try to protect themselves from theft by limiting the funds someone can withdraw away from home. It's therefore best to call your credit card company before you leave and let them know where you're going and how much you plan to spend. You'll get the best exchange rate if you withdraw money from an ATM, but keep in mind that many banks impose a fee, usually $1.50 to $2, every time you use a card at an ATM in a different city or bank. On top of this, the bank from which you withdraw cash may charge its own fee.

TRAVELER'S CHECKS

ATMs have made traveler's checks all but obsolete. But if you still prefer the security of traveler's checks over carrying cash (and you don't mind showing identification every time you want to cash one), you can get them at almost any bank, paying a service charge that usually ranges from 1% to 7%. **American Express** offers denominations of $20, $50, $100, $500, and (for card-holders only) $1,000. You can also get **American Express** traveler's checks online at www.americanexpress.com, or over the phone by calling ✆ **800/221-7282;** by using this number, Amex gold and platinum cardholders are exempt from the 1% fee.

Visa offers traveler's checks at Citibank locations nationwide, as well as at several other banks. The service charge ranges between 1.5% and 2%; checks come in denominations of $20, $50, $100, $500, and $1,000. Call ✆ **800/732-1322** for information. **MasterCard** also offers traveler's checks. Call ✆ **800/223-9920** for a location near you.

AAA members can obtain checks without a fee at most AAA offices. (AAA has a downtown Washington office at 701 15th St. NW, not far from the White House.)

CREDIT CARDS

Credit cards are invaluable when traveling. They are a safe way to carry money and provide a convenient record of all your expenses. You can also withdraw cash advances from your credit cards at any bank (though you'll start paying hefty interest on the advance the moment you receive the cash). At most banks, you don't even need to go to a teller; you can get a cash advance at the ATM if you know

ⓒ Destination: Washington, D.C.—Red Alert Checklist

- Have you packed a photo ID? You'll need one to board a plane, of course, but even if you are not flying, you may find yourself being asked for a photo ID, once you're here. As a result of the September 11 terrorist attacks, many hotels, the St. Regis and certain Hilton hotels among them, require some type of photo ID at check in. Government buildings that you may want to visit may also require photo IDs for entry.

- And while we're on the subject of IDs: Did you bring your ID cards that could entitle you to discounts such as AAA and AARP cards, student IDs, etc.? If you are 65 or older, or have disabilities, you can apply in advance (allow at least 3 weeks) to Metro for an ID card that entitles you to discounted travel on the Metro system; see sections on travelers with disabilities and seniors later in this chapter for more information.

- Have you booked theater and restaurant reservations? If dining at a hot new restaurant or an old favorite is important, or if you're keen on catching a performance scheduled during your stay, why not play it safe by calling in advance (2 weeks is realistic) to reserve a table, and as soon as possible for the theater tickets.

- Have you checked to make sure your favorite attraction is open? Some sites, such as the Pentagon, remain closed indefinitely to public tours, for security reasons. Other attractions, such as the National Portrait Gallery, are closed for renovations. Call ahead for opening and closing hours, and call again on the day you plan to visit an attraction, to confirm that it is open.

- Would you like to avoid the wait of a long line or the ultimate disappointment of missing a tour altogether? A number of sightseeing attractions permit you to reserve a tour slot in advance. The Supreme Court, the Library of Congress, the Washington National Cathedral, and the Kennedy Center all direct you to your senator or representative's office to request advance reservations for "congressional" tours

---

your PIN. If you've forgotten yours, or didn't even know you had one, call the number on the back of your credit card and ask the bank to send it to you. It usually takes 5 to 7 business days, though some banks will provide the number over the phone if you tell them your mother's maiden name or pass some other security clearance.

WHAT TO DO IF YOUR WALLET GETS STOLEN

Be sure to block charges against your account the minute you discover a card has been lost or stolen. Then be sure to file a police report.

Almost every credit card company has an emergency 800-number to call if your card is stolen. They may be able to wire you a cash advance off your credit card immediately, and in many places, they can deliver an emergency credit card in a day or two. The issuing bank's 800-number is usually on the back of your credit card—though, of course, if your card has been stolen, that won't help you unless you recorded the number elsewhere.

at each of their sites. (Advance tickets for congressional tours are not necessary to tour an attraction, they just preclude a long wait.) Specify the dates you plan to visit and the number of tickets you need. Your member's allotment of tickets for each site is limited, so there's no guarantee you'll secure them. In the past, it was possible also to reserve advance tickets for tours of the Capitol, the White House, and the FBI; this policy still holds at the FBI but was canceled after September 11 at the Capitol and the White House. It may have been reinstated by the time you read this—it's worth a call to your senator or representative.

The switchboard for the Senate is ✆ 202/224-3121; for the House switchboard, call ✆ 202/225-3121. You can also correspond by e-mail; check out the websites www.senate.gov and www.house.gov for e-mail addresses, individual member information, legislative calendars, and much more. Or you can write for information. Address requests to representatives as follows: name of your congressperson, U.S. House of Representatives, Washington, DC 20515; or name of your senator, U.S. Senate, Washington, DC 20510. Don't forget to include the exact dates of your Washington trip.

- If you purchased traveler's checks, have you recorded the check numbers, and stored the documentation separately from the checks?
- Did you pack your camera and an extra set of camera batteries, and purchase enough film? If you packed film in your checked baggage, did you invest in protective pouches to shield film from airport X-rays?
- Do you have a safe, accessible place to store money?
- Did you bring emergency drug prescriptions and extra glasses and/or contact lenses?
- Do you have your credit card PIN?
- If you have an E-ticket, do you have documentation?
- Did you leave a copy of your itinerary with someone at home?

Citicorp Visa's U.S. emergency number is ✆ 800/336-8472. American Express cardholders and traveler's check holders should call ✆ 800/221-7282. MasterCard holders should call ✆ 800/307-7309. Otherwise, call the toll-free number directory at ✆ 800/555-1212.

Odds are that if your wallet is gone, the police won't be able to recover it for you. However, it's still worth informing the authorities. Your credit card company or insurer may require a police report number or record of the theft.

If you choose to carry traveler's checks, be sure to keep a record of their serial numbers separate from your checks. You'll get a refund faster if you know the numbers.

If you need emergency cash over the weekend when all banks and American Express offices are closed, you can have money wired to you from **Western Union** (✆ 800/325-6000; www.westernunion.com/). You must present valid ID to pick up the cash at the Western Union office. However, in most countries, you can pick up a money transfer even if you don't have valid identification, as long as you can answer a test question provided by the sender. Be sure to let the sender know in advance that you don't have ID. If you need to use a test question instead of ID, the sender must take cash to his or her local Western Union office, rather than transferring the money over the phone or online.

3 When to Go

The city's peak seasons generally coincide with two activities: the sessions of Congress and springtime, starting with the appearance of the cherry blossoms along the Potomac. Specifically, when Congress is "in," from about the second week in September until Thanksgiving, and again from about mid-January through June, hotels are full with guests whose business takes them to Capitol Hill or to conferences. Mid-March through June traditionally is the most frenzied season, when families and school groups descend upon the city to see the cherry blossoms and enjoy Washington's sensational spring. This is also the season for protest marches. Hotel rooms are at a premium and airfares tend to be higher.

If crowds turn you off, consider visiting Washington at the end of August/early September, when Congress is still "out," and families return home to get their children back to school, or between Thanksgiving and mid-January, when Congress leaves again and many people are ensconced in their own holiday-at-home celebrations. Hotel rates are cheapest at this time, too, and many places offer attractive packages.

If you're thinking of visiting in July and August, be forewarned: The weather is very hot and humid. Many of Washington's stages go dark in summer, although outdoor arenas and parks pick up some of the slack by featuring concerts, festivals, parades, and more (see chapter 9 for details about performing arts schedules). There's something doing almost every night and day. And, of course, Independence Day (July 4th) in the capital is a spectacular celebration.

THE WEATHER

Check the *Washington Post*'s website (**www.washingtonpost.com**) for weather forecasts.

Season by season, here's what you can expect of the weather in Washington:

Fall: This is my favorite season. The weather is often warm during the day—in fact, if you're here in early fall, it may seem entirely *too* warm. But it cools off, getting even a bit crisp, at night. All the greenery that Washington is famous for dons the brilliant colors of fall foliage, and the stream of tourists tapers off.

Winter: People like to say that Washington winters are mild—and sure, if you're from Minnesota, you'll find Washington warmer, no doubt. But D.C. winters can be unpredictable: bitter cold one day, an ice storm the next, followed by a couple of days of sun and higher temperatures. Pack for all possibilities.

Spring: Spring weather is delightful, and, of course, there are those cherry blossoms. Along with autumn, it's the nicest time to enjoy D.C.'s outdoor attractions, to visit museums in comfort, and to laze away an afternoon or evening at an outdoor cafe. But this is when the city is most crowded with visitors and school groups, and, often, protesters.

Summer: Throngs remain in summer, and anyone who's ever spent August in D.C. will tell you how hot and steamy it can be. Though the buildings are air-conditioned, many of Washington's attractions, like the memorials, monuments, and organized tours, are outdoors and unshaded, and the heat can quickly get to you. Make sure you stop frequently for drinks (vendors are everywhere), and wear a hat and/or sunscreen.

Average Temperatures (°F/C) & Rainfall (in inches) in Washington, D.C.

	Jan	Feb	Mar	Apr	May	June	July	Aug	Sept	Oct	Nov	Dec
Avg. High	42/5	46/8	57/12	67/19	76/25	85/29	89/32	87/31	80/26	70/20	59/14	47/8
Avg. Low	27/-1	29/-1	38/2	46/8	57/14	67/19	71/20	70/20	63/16	50/10	41/4	32/0
Rainfall	2.72	2.71	3.17	2.71	3.66	3.38	3.8	3.91	3.31	3.2	3.12	3.12

WASHINGTON CALENDAR OF EVENTS

Washington's most popular annual events are the Cherry Blossom Festival in spring, the Fourth of July celebration in summer, the Taste of D.C. food fair in the fall, and the lighting of the National Christmas Tree in winter. But there's some sort of special event almost daily. Check www.washington.org for the latest schedules.

In the calendar below, I've done my best to accurately list phone numbers for more information, but they seem to change constantly. If the number you try doesn't get you the details you need, call the Washington, D.C. Convention and Tourism Corporation at ℂ 202/789-7000.

Once you're in town, grab a copy of the *Washington Post,* especially the Friday "Weekend" section. The Smithsonian Information Center, 1000 Jefferson Dr. SW (ℂ 202/357-2700), is another good source of information.

For annual events in Alexandria, see p. 273.

January

Martin Luther King, Jr.'s, Birthday. Events include speeches by prominent civil rights leaders and politicians; readings; dance, theater, and choral performances; prayer vigils; a wreath-laying ceremony at the Lincoln Memorial (call ℂ 202/0619-7222); and concerts. Many events take place at the Martin Luther King Memorial Library, 901 G St. NW (ℂ 202/727-0321). Third Monday in January.

February

Black History Month. Features numerous events, museum exhibits, and cultural programs celebrating the contributions of African Americans to American life, including a celebration of abolitionist Frederick Douglass's birthday. For details, check the *Washington Post* or call ℂ 202/357-2700. For additional activities at the Martin Luther King Library, call ℂ 202/727-0321.

Chinese New Year Celebration. A friendship archway, topped by 300 painted dragons and lighted at night, marks Chinatown's entrance at 7th and H streets NW. The celebration begins the day of the Chinese New Year and continues for 10 or more days, with traditional firecrackers, dragon dancers, and colorful street parades. Some area restaurants offer special menus. For details, call ℂ 202/789-7000. Early February.

Abraham Lincoln's Birthday. Marked by the laying of a wreath at the Lincoln Memorial and a reading of the Gettysburg Address at noon. Call ℂ 202/619-7222. February 12.

George Washington's Birthday. Similar celebratory events to Lincoln's birthday, centered around the Washington Monument. Call ℂ 202/619-7222 for details. Both presidents' birthdays also bring annual citywide sales. February 22. Mount Vernon also marks Washington's birthday with free admission and activities that include music and military performances on the bowling green. Call ✆ 703/780-2000. The town of Alexandria holds the nation's largest parade celebrating Washington's birthday; call ✆ 703/838-4200. Third Monday in February.

International Tourist Guide Day. Two-hour motor-coach and walking tours of Washington during this 12th annual event, departing from a downtown location. Tickets are cheap (last year's were $2), but they're sold on a first-come, first-served basis, on the day of the event. Call ✆ 202/298-9425. Late February.

March

Women's History Month. Various institutions throughout the city stage celebrations of women's lives and achievements. For the Smithsonian's schedule of events, call ✆ 202/357-2700; for other events, check the *Washington Post.*

St. Patrick's Day Parade, on Constitution Avenue NW from 7th to 17th streets. A big parade with floats, bagpipes, marching bands, and the wearin' o' the green. For parade information, call ✆ 202/789-7000. The Sunday before March 17.

Smithsonian Kite Festival. A delightful event if the weather cooperates—an occasion for a trip in itself. Throngs of kite enthusiasts fly their unique creations on the Washington Monument grounds and compete for ribbons and prizes. To compete, just show up with your kite and register between 10am and noon. Call ✆ 202/357-2700 or 202/357-3030 for details. A Saturday in mid- or late March, or early April.

April

Cherry Blossom Events. Washington's best-known annual event: the blossoming of the 3,700 famous Japanese cherry trees by the Tidal Basin in Potomac Park. Festivities include a major parade (marking the end of the festival) with floats, concerts, celebrity guests, and more. There are also special ranger-guided tours departing from the Jefferson Memorial. For information, call ✆ 202/547-1500. See p. 215 for more information about the cherry blossoms. Early April (national news programs monitor the budding).

White House Easter Egg Roll. The biggie for little kids. This year's is the White House's 124th Easter Egg Roll (and before that, it took place on the Capitol grounds—until Congress banned it). In past years, entertainment on the White House South Lawn and the Ellipse has included clog dancers, clowns, Ukrainian egg-decorating exhibitions, puppet and magic shows, military drill teams, an egg-rolling contest, and a hunt for 1,000 or so wooden eggs, many of them signed by celebrities, astronauts, or the president. *Note:* Attendance is limited to children ages 3 to 6, who must be accompanied by an adult. Hourly timed tickets are issued at the National Parks Service Ellipse Visitors Pavilion just behind the White House at 15th and E streets NW beginning at 7am. Call ✆ 202/208-1631 for details. Easter Monday between 10am and 2pm; enter at the southeast gate on East Executive Avenue, and arrive early, to make sure you get in, and also to allow for increased security procedures. One such new rule: Strollers are not permitted.

African-American Family Day at the National Zoo. This tradition extends back to 1889, when the zoo opened. The National Zoo celebrates African-American families the day after Easter with music, dance, Easter egg rolls, and other activities. Free. Easter Monday.

Thomas Jefferson's Birthday. Celebrated at the Jefferson Memorial with wreaths, speeches, and a military ceremony. Call ℂ **202/619-7222** for time and details. April 13.

White House Spring Garden Tours. These beautifully landscaped creations are open to the public for free afternoon tours. Call ℂ **202/208-1631** for details. Two days only, in mid-April.

Shakespeare's Birthday Celebration. Music, theater, children's events, food, and exhibits are all part of the afternoon's hail to the bard at the Folger Shakespeare Library. Call ℂ **202/544-7077.** Free admission. Mid-April.

Filmfest DC. This annual international film festival presents as many as 75 works by filmmakers from around the world. Screenings are staged throughout the festival at movie theaters, embassies, and other venues. Tickets are usually $8 per movie and go fast; some events are free. Call ℂ **202/789-7000** or check the website, www.filmfestdc. org. Two weeks in early to mid-April.

Taste of the Nation. An organization called Share Our Strength (SOS) sponsors this fundraiser, for which 100 major restaurants and many wineries set up tasting booths and offer some of their finest fare. In 2002, the event was staged at the Ritz-Carlton Hotel. For the price of admission, you can do the circuit, sampling everything from barbecue to bouillabaisse. Wine flows freely, and there are dozens of great desserts. The evening also includes a silent auction. Tickets are $125 if purchased in advance, $150 at the door, and 100% of the profits go to

feed the hungry. To obtain tickets and information, call ℂ **202/478-6578** or check out www.strength. org. Late April/early May.

Smithsonian Craft Show. Held in the National Building Museum, 401 F St. NW, this juried show features one-of-a-kind limited-edition crafts by more than 100 noted artists from all over the country. There's an entrance fee of about $12 per adult, free for children under 12, each day. For details, call ℂ **202/357-4000** (TDD 202/357-1729). Four days in late April.

May

Georgetown Garden Tour. View the remarkable private gardens of one of the city's loveliest neighborhoods. Admission (about $25) includes light refreshments. Some years there are related events such as a flower show at a historic home. Call ℂ **202/789-7000** or browse the website, www.gtowngarden.org for details. Early to mid-May.

Washington National Cathedral Annual Flower Mart. Now in its 64th year, the flower mart takes place on cathedral grounds, featuring displays of flowering plants and herbs, decorating demonstrations, ethnic food booths, children's rides and activities (including an antique carousel), costumed characters, puppet shows, and other entertainment. Admission is free. Call ℂ **202/537-6200** for details. First Friday and Saturday in May.

Memorial Day. At 11am, a wreath-laying ceremony takes place at the Tomb of the Unknowns in Arlington National Cemetery, followed by military band music, a service, and an address by a high-ranking government official (sometimes the president); call ℂ **202/685-2851** for details. There's also a ceremony at 1pm at the Vietnam Veterans

Memorial, including a wreath-laying, speakers, and the playing of taps (© **202/619-7222** for details), and activities at the U.S. Navy Memorial (© **202/737-2300**). On the Sunday before Memorial Day, the National Symphony Orchestra performs a free concert at 8pm on the West Lawn of the Capitol to officially welcome summer to Washington; call © **202/619-7222** for details.

June

Dupont-Kalorama Museum Walk Day. This is an annual celebration of collections by six museums and historic houses in this charming neighborhood. Free food, music, tours, and crafts demonstrations. Call © **202/667-0441.** Early June.

Shakespeare Theatre Free For All. This free theater festival presents a different Shakespeare play each year for a 2-week run at the Carter Barron Amphitheatre in upper northwest Washington. Tickets are required, but they're free. Call © **202/334-4790.** Evenings in mid-June.

Smithsonian Festival of American Folklife. A major event with traditional American music, crafts, foods, games, concerts, and exhibits, staged the length of the National Mall. All events are free; most events take place outdoors. Call © **202/357-2700,** or check the listings in the *Washington Post* for details. For 5 to 10 days, always including July 4.

July

Independence Day. There's no better place to be on the Fourth of July than in Washington, D.C. The festivities include a massive National Independence Day Parade down Constitution Avenue, complete with lavish floats, princesses, marching groups, and military bands. There are also celebrity entertainers and concerts. (Most events take place on the Washington Monument grounds.) A morning program in front of the National Archives includes military demonstrations, period music, and a reading of the Declaration of Independence. In the evening, the National Symphony Orchestra plays on the west steps of the Capitol with guest artists (for example, Leontyne Price). And big-name entertainment also precedes the fabulous fireworks display behind the Washington Monument. You can also attend a free 11am organ recital at Washington's National Cathedral. Consult the *Washington Post* or call © **202/789-7000** for details. July 4, all day.

Bastille Day. This Washington tradition honors the French Independence Day with live entertainment and a race by tray-balancing waiters and waitresses from Les Halles Restaurant to the U.S. Capitol and back. Free, *mais bien sur.* Twelfth Street and Pennsylvania Avenue NW. Call © **202/296-7200.** July 14.

September

National Frisbee Festival. Washington Monument grounds. See world-class Frisbee champions and their disk-catching dogs at this noncompetitive event. Labor Day weekend.

Labor Day Concert. West Lawn of the Capitol. The National Symphony Orchestra closes its summer season with a free performance at 8pm; call © **202/619-7222** for details. Labor Day. (Rain date: Same day and time at Constitution Hall.)

Kennedy Center Open House Arts Festival. A day-long festival of the performing arts, featuring local and national artists on the front plaza and river terrace (which overlooks the Potomac), and throughout the stage halls of the Kennedy Center. Past festivals have featured the likes of Los Lobos, Mary Chapin Carpenter, and Washington Opera soloists. Kids' activities usually include a National Symphony Orchestra "petting zoo," where children get to bow, blow, drum, or strum a favorite instrument. Admission is free, although you may have to stand in a long line for the inside performances. Check the *Washington Post* or call ℂ **800/ 444-1324** or 202/467-4600 for details. A Sunday in early to mid-September, noon to 6pm.

Black Family Reunion. Performances, food, and fun are part of this celebration of the African-American family and culture, held on the Mall. Free. Call ℂ **202/737-0120.** Mid-September.

Hispanic Heritage Month. Various museums and other institutions host activities celebrating Hispanic culture and traditions. Call ℂ **202/ 789-7000.** Mid-September to mid-October.

Washington National Cathedral's Open House. Celebrates the anniversary of the laying of the foundation stone in 1907. Events include demonstrations of stone carving and other crafts utilized in building the cathedral; carillon and organ demonstrations; and performances by dancers, choirs, strolling musicians, jugglers, and puppeteers. This is the only time visitors are allowed to ascend to the top of the central tower to see the bells; it's a tremendous climb, but you'll be rewarded with a spectacular view. For details, call ℂ **202/ 537-6200.** A Saturday in late September or early October.

October

Taste of D.C. Festival. Pennsylvania Avenue, between 9th and 14th streets NW. Dozens of Washington's restaurants offer food tastings, along with live entertainment, dancing, storytellers, and games. Admission is free; purchase tickets for tastings. Call ℂ **202/789-7000** for details. Three days, including Columbus Day weekend.

White House Fall Garden Tours. For 2 days, visitors have an opportunity to see the famed Rose Garden and South Lawn. Admission is free. A military band provides music. For details, call ℂ **202/208-1631.** Mid-October.

Marine Corps Marathon. More than 16,000 runners compete in this 26.2-mile race (the 4th-largest marathon in the United States). It begins at the Marine Corps Memorial (the Iwo Jima statue) and passes major monuments. Call ℂ **800/ RUN-USMC** or 703/784-2225 for details. Anyone can enter; register online at www.marinemarathon. com. Fourth Sunday in October.

Halloween. There's no official celebration, but costumed revels seem to get bigger every year. Giant block parties take place in the Dupont Circle area and Georgetown. Check the *Washington Post* for special parties and activities. October 31.

November

Veterans Day. The nation's war dead are honored with a wreath-laying ceremony at 11am at the Tomb of the Unknowns in Arlington National Cemetery followed by a memorial service. The president of the United States or a very high-ranking government personage officiates. Military music is provided by a military band. Call ℂ **202/ 685-2951** for information. At the Vietnam Veterans Memorial (ℂ **202/619-7222**), observances include speakers, wreath placement, a color guard, and the playing of taps. November 11.

December

Christmas Pageant of Peace/ National Tree Lighting. At the northern end of the Ellipse, the president lights the national Christmas tree to the accompaniment of orchestral and choral music. The lighting inaugurates the 3-week Pageant of Peace, a tremendous holiday celebration with seasonal music, caroling, a nativity scene, 50 state trees, and a burning yule log.

Call ℂ **202/208-1631** for details. A select Wednesday or Thursday in early December at 5pm.

White House Candlelight Tours. On 3 evenings between Christmas and New Year's from 5 to 7pm, visitors can see the president's Christmas holiday decorations by candlelight. String music enhances the tours. Lines are long; arrive early. Call ℂ **202/208-1631** for dates and details.

4 Insurance, Health & Safety

TRAVEL INSURANCE AT A GLANCE

Check your existing insurance policies before you buy travel insurance to cover trip-cancellation, lost luggage, medical expenses, or car-rental insurance. You're likely to have partial or complete coverage. But if you need some, ask your travel agent about a comprehensive package. The cost of travel insurance varies widely, depending on the cost and length of your trip, your age and overall health, and the type of trip you're taking.

For information, contact one of the following popular insurers:

- **Access America** (ℂ 800/284-8300; www.accessamerica.com)
- **Travel Guard International** (ℂ 800/826-1300; www.travel guard.com)
- **Travel Insured International** (ℂ 800/243-3174; www.travel insured.com)
- **Travelex Insurance Services** (ℂ 800/228-9792; www.travelex-insurance.com).

TRIP-CANCELLATION INSURANCE (TCI)

There are three major types of trip-cancellation insurance—one, in the event that you prepay for a package tour that gets canceled, and you can't get your money back; a second when you or someone in your family gets sick or dies, and you can't travel (but beware that you may not be covered for a pre-existing condition); and a third, when bad weather makes travel impossible. Some insurers provide coverage for events like jury duty; natural disasters close to home, like floods or fire; even the loss of a job. A few have added provisions for cancellations due to terrorist activities. Always check the fine print before signing on, and don't buy trip-cancellation insurance from the tour operator that may be responsible for the cancellation; buy it only from a reputable travel insurance agency. Don't overbuy. You won't be reimbursed for more than the cost of your trip.

MEDICAL INSURANCE

Most health insurance policies cover you if you get sick away from home—but check, particularly if you're insured by an HMO. Members of **Blue Cross/Blue Shield** can now use their cards at select hospitals in most major cities worldwide (ℂ **800/810-BLUE** or www.bluecares.com for a list of hospitals).

Some credit cards (American Express and certain gold and platinum Visa and MasterCards, for example) offer automatic flight insurance against death or dismemberment in case of an airplane crash if you charged the cost of your ticket.

If you require additional insurance, try one of the following companies:

- **MEDEX International,** 9515 Deereco Rd., Timonium, MD 21093-5375 (© **888/MEDEX-00** or 410/453-6300; fax 410/453-6301; www.medexassist.com)
- **Travel Assistance International** (© **800/821-2828;** www.travelassistance.com), 9200 Keystone Crossing, Suite 300, Indianapolis, IN 46240 (for general information on services, call the company's Worldwide Assistance Services, Inc., at © **800/777-8710**).

The cost of travel medical insurance varies widely. Check your existing policies before you buy additional coverage. Also, check to see if your medical insurance covers you for emergency medical evacuation: If you have to buy a one-way same-day ticket home and forfeit your nonrefundable round-trip ticket, you may be out big bucks.

LOST-LUGGAGE INSURANCE

On domestic flights, checked baggage is covered up to $2,500 per ticketed passenger. On international flights (including U.S. portions of international trips), baggage is limited to approximately $9.05 per pound, up to approximately $635 per checked bag. If you plan to check items more valuable than the standard liability, you may purchase "excess valuation" coverage from the airline, up to $5,000. Be sure to take any valuables or irreplaceable items with you in your carry-on luggage. If you file a lost luggage claim, be prepared to answer detailed questions about the contents of your baggage, and be sure to file a claim immediately, as most airlines enforce a 21-day deadline. Before you leave home, compile an inventory of all packed items and a rough estimate of the total value to ensure you're properly compensated if your luggage is lost. You will only be reimbursed for what you lost, no more. Once you've filed a complaint, persist in securing your reimbursement; there are no laws governing the length of time it takes for a carrier to reimburse you. If you arrive at a destination without your bags, ask the airline to forward them to your hotel or to your next destination; they will usually comply. If your bag is delayed or lost, the airline may reimburse you for reasonable expenses, such as a toothbrush or a set of clothes, but the airline is under no legal obligation to do so.

Your homeowner's or renter's policy may cover lost luggage. Many platinum and gold credit cards cover you as well. If you choose to purchase additional lost-luggage insurance, be sure not to buy more than you need. Buy in advance from the insurer or a trusted agent (prices will be much higher at the airport).

CAR-RENTAL INSURANCE (LOSS/DAMAGE WAIVER OR COLLISION DAMAGE WAIVER)

If you hold a private auto insurance policy, you probably are covered in the United States for loss or damage to the car and liability in case a passenger is injured. The credit card you used to rent the card also may provide some coverage.

Car-rental insurance probably does not cover liability if you caused the accident. Check your own auto insurance policy, the rental company policy, and your credit card coverage for the extent of coverage: Is your destination covered? Are other drivers covered? How much liability is covered if a passenger is injured? (If you rely on your credit card for coverage, you may

---

> **(Tips Quick I.D.**
>
> Tie a colorful ribbon or piece of yarn around your luggage handle, or slap a distinctive sticker on the side of your bag. This makes it less likely that someone will mistakenly appropriate it. And if your luggage gets lost, it will be easier to find.

---

want to bring a 2nd credit card with you, as damages may be charged to your card and you may find yourself stranded with no money.)

Car-rental insurance costs about $20 a day.

THE HEALTHY TRAVELER
WHAT TO DO IF YOU GET SICK AWAY FROM HOME

If you worry about getting sick away from home, consider purchasing **medical travel insurance** and carry your ID card in your purse or wallet. In most cases, your existing health plan will provide the coverage you need. See "Medical Insurance," above for more information.

If you suffer from a chronic illness, consult your doctor before your departure. For conditions like epilepsy, diabetes, or heart problems, wear a **Medic Alert Identification Tag** (© **800/825-3785;** www.medicalert. org), which will immediately alert doctors to your condition and give them access to your records through Medic Alert's 24-hour hot line.

Pack **prescription medications** in your carry-on luggage, and carry prescription medications in their original containers. Also bring along copies of your prescriptions in case you lose your pills or run out. And don't forget sunglasses and an extra pair of contact lenses or prescription glasses.

If you need medical care, see the entry for "Hospitals" in "Fast Facts: Washington, D.C." on p. 80.

THE SAFE TRAVELER

If, following the terrorist attack on the Pentagon on September 11, 2001,

you are nervous about visiting the capital, you should know that the government has increased security, not just at airports, but around the city, especially at government buildings. You will notice vehicle barriers in place at a wider radius around the Capitol building and the White House, and new vehicle barriers and better lighting installed at the Washington Monument and at the Lincoln and Jefferson memorials. E Street, south of the White House, and certain streets near the Capitol are closed to car traffic. Self-guided tours of the Capitol are no longer possible, and public guided tours are less comprehensive than they used to be. Greater numbers of police and security officers are on duty around and inside government buildings, the monuments, and the Metro. Twenty-four-hour video surveillance cameras, long in use at the Capitol and the White House, may be in place, by the time you read this, in public areas at the Washington Monument, and at the Jefferson, Lincoln, Franklin Delano Roosevelt, Vietnam Veterans, and Korean War memorials.

On the other hand, Washington, like any urban area, has a criminal element, so it's important, generally, to stay alert and take normal safety precautions.

Ask your hotel front-desk staff or the city's tourist office if you're in doubt about which neighborhoods are safe.

For more safety tips, see "General Safety Suggestions," in chapter 3.

5 Tips for Travelers with Special Needs

TRAVELERS WITH DISABILITIES

Washington, D.C., is one of the most accessible cities in the world for travelers with disabilities. The best overall source of information about accessibility at specific Washington hotels, restaurants, shopping malls, and attractions is the nonprofit organization Access Information. You can read the information (including restaurant reviews) online at www.disability guide.org, or order a free copy of *The Access Entertainment Guide for the Greater Washington Area* by calling © 301/528-8591, or by writing to Access Information, dba Disability Guide.org, 21618 Slidell Rd., Boyds, MD 20841.

The **Washington Metropolitan Transit Authority** publishes accessibility information on its website **www.wmata.com**, or you can call © 202/962-1245 with questions about Metro services for travelers with disabilities, including how to obtain a Disabled ID card that entitles you to discounted fares. (Make sure you call at least 3 weeks ahead to allow enough time to obtain an ID card.) For up-to-date information about how Metro is operating on the day you're using it, for instance, to verify that the elevators are operating at the stations you'll be traveling to, call © 202/962-6464.

Each Metro station is equipped with an elevator (complete with Braille number plates) to train platforms, and rail cars are fully accessible. Metro has installed 24-inch sections of punctuated rubber tiles leading up to the granite-lined platform edge to warn visually impaired Metro riders that they're nearing the tracks. Unfortunately, a 1- to 3-inch gap between the train platform and the subway car makes it difficult for those in powered wheelchairs to board the train. Train operators make station and on-board announcements of train destinations and stops. Most of the District's Metrobuses have wheelchair lifts and kneel at the curb (the number will increase as time goes on). The TDD number for Metro information is © 202/638-3780. Regular **Tourmobile** trams (p. 221) are accessible to visitors with disabilities. The company also operates special vans for immobile travelers, complete with wheelchair lifts. Tourmobile recommends that you call a day ahead to ensure that the van is available for you when you arrive. For information, call © 703/979-0690, or go to www.tourmobile.com.

All **Smithsonian museum buildings** are accessible to wheelchair visitors. A comprehensive free publication called "Smithsonian Access" lists all services available to visitors with disabilities, including parking, building access, sign-language interpreters, and more. To obtain a copy, call © 202/357-2700 or TTY 202/357-1729, or find the information online, at www.si.edu/resource/faq/access.htm. You can also use the TTY number to get information on all Smithsonian museums and events.

If tours of **the White House** have resumed by the time you read this, then so will its tour accessibility policy: Visitors in wheelchairs should come to the East Visitors' Gate (along East Executive Ave.) between 10am and noon, and they will be allowed to go to the head of the line. Visitors arriving in wheelchairs and their companions do not need tickets. For details, call © 202/456-2322, TDD 202/456-2121.

The **Lincoln, Jefferson,** and **Vietnam memorials** and the **Washington Monument** are also equipped to accommodate visitors with disabilities and keep wheelchairs on the premises. There's limited parking for visitors with disabilities on the south side of the Lincoln Memorial. Call ahead to other sightseeing attractions for accessibility information and special services: ℂ 202/426-6842.

Call your senator or representative to arrange wheelchair-accessible tours of **the Capitol;** they can also arrange special tours for the blind or deaf. For further information, call ℂ 202/224-4048.

Union Station, the Shops at National Place, the Pavilion at the Old Post Office, and Georgetown Park Mall are **well-equipped shopping spots** for visitors with disabilities.

Washington theaters are handily equipped. Among the most accessible are the following three.

The **John F. Kennedy Center for the Performing Arts** provides headphones to hearing-impaired patrons at no charge. A wireless, infrared listening-enhancement system is available in all theaters. Some performances offer sign language and audio description. A public TTY is located at the Information Center in the Hall of States. Large-print programs are available at every performance; a limited number of Braille programs are available from the house manager. All theaters in the complex are wheelchair accessible. To reserve a wheelchair, call ℂ 202/416-8340. For other questions regarding patrons with disabilities, including information about half-priced tickets (you will need to submit a letter from your doctor stating that your disability is permanent), access the center's website, www.kennedy-center.org, or call ℂ 202/416-8727. The TTY number is ℂ 202/416-8728.

The **Arena Stage** (ℂ 202/554-9066; www.arenastage.org) has a wheelchair lift, offers audio description and sign interpretation at designated performances as well as infrared and audio loop assisted-listening devices for the hearing impaired, plus

program books in Braille and large print. The TTY box office line is ℂ 202/484-0247. You can also call ahead to reserve handicapped parking spaces for a performance.

The **National Theatre** is wheelchair accessible and features special performances of its shows for visually and hearing-impaired theatergoers. To obtain amplified-sound earphones for narration, simply ask an usher before the performance (you'll need to provide an ID). The National also offers a limited number of half-price tickets to patrons with disabilities, who have obtained a Special Patron card from the theater, or who can provide a letter from a doctor certifying disability; seating is in the orchestra section and you may receive no more than two half-price tickets. For details, call ℂ 202/628-6161, or go the website, www.nationaltheatre.org.

AGENCIES/OPERATORS

- **Flying Wheels Travel** (ℂ 800/535-6790; www.flyingwheels travel.com) offers escorted tours and cruises that emphasize sports and private tours in minivans with lifts.
- **Access Adventures** (ℂ 716/889-9096), a Rochester, New York–based agency, offers customized itineraries for a variety of travelers with disabilities.
- **Accessible Journeys** (ℂ 800/TINGLES or 610/521-0339; www.disabilitytravel.com) caters specifically to slow walkers and wheelchair travelers and their families and friends.

ORGANIZATIONS

- **The Moss Rehab Hospital** (ℂ 215/456-9603; www.moss resourcenet.org) provides friendly, helpful phone assistance through its **Travel Information Service.**
- **The Society for Accessible Travel and Hospitality** (ℂ 212/447-7284; fax 212/725-8253;

www.sath.org) offers a wealth of travel resources for all types of disabilities and informed recommendations on destinations, access guides, travel agents, tour operators, vehicle rentals, and companion services. Annual membership costs $45 for adults; $30 for seniors and students.

- **The American Foundation for the Blind** (℃ 800/232-5463; www.afb.org) provides information on traveling with Seeing Eye dogs.

PUBLICATIONS

- **Mobility International USA** (℃ 541/343-1284; www.miusa. org) publishes *A World of Options*, a 658-page book of resources, covering everything from biking trips to scuba outfitters, and a biannual newsletter, *Over the Rainbow*. Annual membership is $35.
- **Twin Peaks Press** (℃ 360/694-2462) publishes travel-related books for travelers with special needs.
- *Open World for Disability and Mature Travel* magazine, published by the Society for Accessible Travel and Hospitality (see above), is full of good resources and information. A year's subscription is $13 ($21 outside the U.S.).

GAY & LESBIAN TRAVELERS

Washington, D.C., has a strong gay and lesbian community, and clearly welcomes gay and lesbian visitors, as evidenced by the fact that the Washington Convention and Tourism Corporation publishes a guide, "The Gay and Lesbian Traveler's Guide to Washington, D.C.," which you can download from its website, www.washington.org, or order by calling ℃ 202/789-7000.

While in Washington, you'll want to get your hands on the *Washington Blade*, a comprehensive weekly newspaper distributed free at about 1,000 locations in the District. Every issue provides an extensive events calendar and a list of hundreds of resources, such as crisis centers, health facilities, switchboards, political groups, religious organizations, social clubs, and student activities; it puts you in touch with everything from groups of lesbian bird-watchers to the Asian Gay Men's Network. Gay restaurants and clubs are, of course, also listed and advertised. You can subscribe to the *Blade* for $45 a year, check out **www.washingtonblade.com**, or pick up a free copy at Olsson's Books/Records, 1307 19th St. NW; Borders, 18th and L streets; and Kramerbooks, 1517 Connecticut Ave. NW, at Dupont Circle. Call the *Blade* office at ℃ 202/797-7000 for other locations.

Washington's gay bookstore, **Lambda Rising**, 1625 Connecticut Ave. NW (℃ 202/462-6969), also informally serves as an information center for the gay community, which centers in the Dupont Circle neighborhood.

The **International Gay & Lesbian Travel Association** (IGLTA) (℃ 800/448-8550 or 954/776-2626; fax 954/776-3303; www.iglta.org) links travelers with gay-friendly hoteliers, tour operators, and airline and cruise-line representatives. It offers monthly newsletters, marketing mailings, and a membership directory that's updated once a year. Membership is $150 yearly, plus a $100 administration fee for new members.

AGENCIES/OPERATORS

- **Above and Beyond Tours** (℃ 800/397-2681; www.abovebeyondtours.com) offers gay and lesbian tours worldwide and is the exclusive gay and lesbian tour operator for United Airlines.
- **Now, Voyager** (℃ 800/255-6951; www.nowvoyager.com) is a San Francisco–based gay-owned and -operated travel service.

PUBLICATIONS

- *Out and About* (© 800/929-2268 or 415/644-8044; www.outandabout.com) offers guidebooks and a newsletter 10 times a year packed with solid information on the global gay and lesbian scene.
- *Spartacus International Gay Guide* and *Odysseus* are good, annual English-language guidebook focused on gay men, with some information for lesbians. You can get them from most gay and lesbian bookstores, or order them from **Giovanni's Room** bookstore, 1145 Pine St., Philadelphia, PA 19107 (© 215/923-2960; www.giovannisroom.com).
- *Gay Travel A to Z: The World of Gay & Lesbian Travel Options at Your Fingertips,* by Marianne Ferrari (Ferrari Publications), is a very good gay and lesbian guidebook series.

SENIOR TRAVEL

Mention the fact that you're a senior citizen when you first make your travel reservations. All major airlines and many hotels offer discounts for seniors. Major airlines also offer coupons for domestic travel for seniors over sixty. Typically, a book of four coupons costs less than $700, which means you can fly anywhere in the continental United States for under $350 round-trip.

Washington, like most cities, offers discounted admission to seniors at theaters, at those few museums that charge for entry, and for discounted travel on Metro, although the designated "senior" age differs slightly from place to place. For instance, discount eligibility requires that you must be 60 or older at Arena Stage, older than 62 at the Phillips Collection, and 65 or older for the Metro. Some places, such as Arena Stage, take you at your word that you qualify for a discount, so you

may order your tickets over the phone, without showing proof of your age. To obtain discounted fare cards to ride the Metro, you must first apply for a Senior ID card, well in advance of your trip; call © 202/962-2136 for more information.

Members of **AARP** (formerly known as the American Association of Retired Persons), 601 E St. NW, Washington, DC 20049 (© 800/424-3410 or 202/434-2277; www.aarp.org), get discounts on hotels, airfares, and car rentals. AARP offers members a wide range of benefits, including *Modern Maturity* magazine and a monthly newsletter. Anyone over 50 can join.

The **Alliance for Retired Americans**, 8403 Colesville Rd., Suite 1200, Silver Spring, MD 20910 (© 301/578-8422; www.retiredamericans.org), offers a newsletter six times a year and discounts on hotel and auto rentals; annual dues are $13 per person or couple. *Note:* Members of the former National Council of Senior Citizens receive automatic membership in the Alliance.

AGENCIES/OPERATORS

- **Elderhostel** (© 877/426-8056; www.elderhostel.org) arranges study programs for those aged 55 and over (and a spouse or companion of any age) in the United States and in more than 80 countries around the world. Most courses last 5 to 7 days in the United States (2–4 weeks abroad), and many include airfare, accommodations in university dormitories or modest inns, meals, and tuition.

PUBLICATIONS

- *The Book of Deals* is a collection of more than 1,000 senior discounts on airlines, lodging, tours, and attractions around the country; it's available for $9.95 by calling © 800/460-6676.

- *101 Tips for the Mature Traveler* is available from Grand Circle Travel (© **800/221-2610** or 617/350-7500; fax 617/346-6700).
- *The 50+ Traveler's Guidebook* (St. Martin's Press).
- *Unbelievably Good Deals and Great Adventures That You Absolutely Can't Get Unless You're Over 50* (Contemporary Publishing Co.).

FAMILY TRAVEL

Field trips during the school year and family vacations during the summer keep Washington, D.C., crawling with kids all year long. More than any other city, perhaps, Washington is crammed with historic buildings, arts and science museums, parks, and recreational sites to interest young and old alike. Some museums, like the National Museum of Natural History and the Daughters of the American Revolution (DAR) Museum, have hands-on exhibits for children. Many more sponsor regular, usually free, family oriented events, such as the Corcoran Gallery of Art's "Family Days" and the Folger Shakespeare Library's seasonal activities. It's worth calling or checking websites in advance for schedules from the attractions you're thinking of visiting (see chapter 7 for phone numbers and Web addresses). The fact that so many attractions are free is a boon to the family budget.

Hotels, more and more, are doing their part to make family trips affordable, too. At many lodgings, children under a certain age (usually 12) sleep free in the same room with their parents (I've noted these policies in all the listings in chapter 5). Hotel weekend packages often offer special family rates. See the "Family-Friendly Hotels" box on p. 87 for a rundown of the hotels that are most welcoming to young travelers.

Restaurants throughout the Washington area are growing increasingly family friendly as well. Many provide kids' menus or charge less for children's portions. The best news, though, is that families are welcome at all sorts of restaurants these days and need no longer stick only to burger joints. See the "Family-Friendly Restaurants" box on p. 134 for a list of places kids will especially love.

Washington, D.C., is easy to navigate with children. The Metro covers the city and it's safe. Children under 4 ride free.

Once you arrive, get your hands on a copy of the most recent *Washington Post* "Weekend" section, published each Friday. The section covers all possible happenings in the city, with a weekly feature, "Saturday's Child," and a column, "Carousel," devoted to children's activities.

AGENCIES/OPERATORS

Familyhostel (© **800/733-9753**; www.learn.unh.edu/familyhostel) takes the whole family on moderately priced domestic and international learning vacations. All trip details are handled by the program staff, and lectures, fields trips, and sightseeing are guided by a team of academics. For kids ages 8 to 15 accompanied by their parents and/or grandparents.

PUBLICATIONS

- *How to Take Great Trips with Your Kids* (The Harvard Common Press) is full of good general advice that can apply to travel anywhere.

WEBSITES

- **Family Travel Forum** (© **888/383-6786**; www.familytravelforum.com), whose motto is "Have Family, Still Travel," is another helpful source of information and travel discounts for families planning trips. At last count, the website listed six articles on different family trips to Washington, D.C. A comprehensive annual membership is $48, or you can subscribe to the online service for $3.95 monthly.

- **Family Travel Network** (www.familytravelnetwork.com) offers travel tips and reviews of family friendly destinations, vacation deals, and thoughtful features such as "What to Do When Your Kids Are Afraid to Travel."
- **Travel with Your Children** (www.travelwithyourkids.com) is a comprehensive site offering sound advice for traveling with children.

STUDENT TRAVEL

When it comes to theater and museum admission discounts in Washington, students rule. The one caveat: You must have a valid ID, although your current school ID should be good enough. For benefits that extend beyond reduced admission to D.C. attractions, you may want to consider obtaining an International Student Identity Card (ISIC).

STA Travel (℃ 800/781-4040; www.statravel.com) is the largest student travel agency in the world, catering especially to young travelers, although their bargain-basement prices are available to people of all ages. From STA, you can purchase the $22 ISIC, good for cut rates on rail passes, plane tickets, and other discounts. It also provides you with basic health and life insurance, and a 24-hour help line. If you're no longer a student but are still under 26, you can get a **GO 25 card** from the same people, which entitles you to insurance and some discounts (but not on museum admissions). In Washington, STA has an office in Georgetown, at 3301 M St. NW (℃ 202/337-6464).

In Canada, **Travel CUTS** (℃ 800/667-2887 or 416/614-2887; www.travelcuts.com), offers similar services. In London, **Campus Travel** (℃ 0171/730-3402; www.campustravel.co.uk), opposite Victoria Station, is Britain's leading specialist in student and youth travel.

WEBSITE

Studentuniverse.com (www.studentuniverse.com) is an online student travel agency in partnership with Orbitz.com. that consistently offers great discounts on airfares to students and faculty.

6 Getting There

BY PLANE

All three of Washington, D.C.'s airports, Washington Dulles International Airport (Dulles), Ronald Reagan Washington National Airport (National), and Baltimore-Washington International Airport (BWI), are operating up to speed once again, though with added security procedures, following the terrorist attacks of September 11, 2001.

Note: At these three airports, as at all American airports now, only ticketed passengers are permitted to go through security to the gates, which means that if people are meeting you at the airport they will no longer be allowed to greet you at the gate; you should agree beforehand on some other designated rendezvous site. Don't have your party wait just outside the security clearance areas to greet you, since this section gets pretty crowded, and you may have trouble spotting each other; you may not even be sure that you are both at the same security clearance gates. Your best plan is to arrange to rendezvous at the baggage claim area. Monitors always post the designated baggage claim carousel for each arriving flight, so, for the time being, at least, this zone remains the best spot for reunions—even if you haven't checked your luggage. Eventually, airports may provide waiting rooms.

THE MAJOR AIRLINES

Domestic airlines with scheduled flights into all three airports include **American** (© 800/433-7300; www.aa.com), **Continental** (© 800/525-0280; www.continental.com), **Delta** (© 800/221-1212; www.delta.com), **Northwest** (© 800/225-2525; www.nwa.com), **United** (© 800/241-6522; www.united.com), and **US Airways** (© 800/428-4322; www.usairways.com). United Airlines, which uses Washington Dulles International Airport as one of its hubs, boasts that it offers more nonstops from more destinations to Washington than any other airline: 350 flights a day.

For a list of international airlines with scheduled flights into all three area airports, see chapter 3, "For International Visitors."

Low-fare airlines are on the rise and offer great deals. If you can do without frills, find out whether any of the following low-fare airlines fly from your city to Washington: **Delta Express** (© 800/325-5205; www.flydlx.com), **AirTran** (© 800/247-8726; www.airtran.com), **Southwest Airlines** (© 800/435-9792; www.southwest.com), **Frontier** (© 800/432-1359; www.frontierairlines.com), **JetBlue** (© 800/538-2583; www.jetblue.com), and **American Trans Air** (**ATA;** © 800/435-9282; www.ata.com). Delta Express flies into Dulles and, by the time you read this, may have resumed flights to National; AirTran flies into Dulles and BWI; Southwest flies into BWI; Frontier flies into National and BWI; JetBlue flies into Dulles; and American Trans Air flies into National.

SHUTTLE SERVICE FROM NEW YORK, BOSTON & CHICAGO

Delta and US Airways continue to dominate the lucrative D.C.–East Coast shuttle service. Between the two of them, the airlines operate hourly or almost hourly shuttle service between Boston's Logan Airport and Washington, and New York's La Guardia Airport and Washington. The **Delta Shuttle** (© **800/221-1212**) travels daily between New York and Washington, while the **US Airways Shuttle** (© **800/428-4322**) operates weekdays, between Boston and Washington, and New York and Washington. Both airlines fly into and out of Ronald Reagan Washington National Airport. Southwest Airlines, known for its low fares, offers nearly hourly service daily between BWI and Chicago's Midway Airport, Providence, Hartford, and Nashville.

D.C.'S AREA AIRPORTS

All together, Ronald Reagan Washington National, Washington Dulles International, and Baltimore–Washington International offer a total of about 2,500 passenger flights daily. General information follows that should help you determine which airport is your best bet; for details about individual airport services, see "Visitor Information," in chapter 4.

Ronald Reagan Washington National Airport (everyone still calls it simply "National") lies across the Potomac River in Virginia, a few minutes by car, 15 to 20 minutes by Metro from downtown in non-rush-hour traffic. Its proximity to the District and its direct access to the Metro rail system are reasons why you might want to fly into National. The word is, however, that proximity to the District is also what makes flying into and out of National the most inconvenient, because security procedures are more intense and take more time. There's also the matter of the "30-minute rule": Passengers must stay in their seats for the 30 minutes prior to landing at National, and for the 30 minutes after their plane takes off from National.

As you know, the airport was closed completely from September 11 to October 4, 2001. Service resumed in stages, returning to normal operation on April 15, 2002. Approximately 22 major airlines and shuttles serve this airport. Nearly all nonstop flights are to and from cities located 1,250 miles from Washington. An aviation bill passed in 1999 allows for a few exceptions and currently, the flights that National offers beyond the 1,250-mile standard fly to and from Denver, Phoenix, Las Vegas, and Seattle.

While Washington's two other airports are in the midst of extensive renovations, National's own vast renovation was completed in 1997, and so the airport is able to offer certain enhancements that may still be in the works at Dulles and BWI: a new terminal; ticket counters that provide access to passengers with disabilities; more than 100 restaurants and shops; more parking space; and climate-controlled pedestrian bridges that connect the terminal directly to the Metro station, whose Blue and Yellow lines stop here. The Metropolitan Washington Airports Authority oversees both National and Dulles airports, so the main information numbers and websites are the same for the two facilities: For airport information, call © **703/572-2700** or go to www.metwashairports.com. For Metro information, call © **202/ 637-7000.**

Washington Dulles International Airport (Dulles) lies 26 miles outside the capital, in Chantilly, Virginia, a 35- to 45-minute ride to downtown in non-rush-hour traffic. Of the three airports, Dulles handles more daily flights—about 1,000, although by the time you read this, the number may have returned to its pre-September 11 average of 1,200—and its airlines fly to more destinations, about 69 U.S. and 23 foreign cities. And though the airport is not as convenient to the heart of Washington as National, it's more convenient than BWI, thanks to an uncongested airport access road that travels half the distance toward Washington. A decades-long expansion has so far added two new concourses and a parking garage; eventually, the airport will more than double its annual passenger traffic to 55 million, add a runway, pedestrian walkways, and an underground airport train system that will replace the inconvenient and unwieldy mobile lounges that, for now, transport travelers to and from the main and midfield terminals. Fifteen major domestic, 8 regional, and 20 international carriers use Dulles. The airport's information line and website are the same as National's: © **703/572-2700;** www. metwashairports.com.

Last but not least is **Baltimore– Washington International Airport** (BWI), which is located about 45 minutes from downtown, a few miles outside of Baltimore. Two factors especially recommend BWI to travelers: Southwest Airlines, with its bargain fares, commands a major presence here, pulling in about one-third of BWI's business. BWI destinations via Southwest total at least 32, and you should find out whether your city is one of them, if you want to save some money. (A couple of other low-fare airlines operate here as well; see the "Major Airlines" section earlier in this chapter.)

The other big benefit to using BWI concerns security. The airport is the primary screening site for the Transportation Security Administration's field testing of possible new security measures; the best and brightest security procedures will be tried here first. If you're extremely anxious about traveling, you may want to choose to fly into and out of BWI. Call © **800/ 435-9294** for airport information, or point your browser to www.bwi airport.com.

GETTING INTO TOWN FROM THE AIRPORT

All three airports provide the following options for getting into the city. In each case, you simply follow the signs to "ground transportation" in your airport, and look there for signs or a staff representative of the service you desire.

Taxi service: For a trip to downtown D.C., you can expect a taxi to cost anywhere from $8 to $15 for the 10- to 15-minute ride from National Airport; $35 to $47 for the 30- to 40-minute ride from Dulles Airport; and $55 for the 45-minute ride from BWI.

SuperShuttle buses (ℂ 800/258-3826; www.supershuttle.com) offer shared-ride, door-to-door service between the airport and your destination, whether in the District or in a suburban location. No need to reserve seats; however, if you arrive after midnight, call the toll-free number above to summon a van. This 24-hour service bases its fares on ZIP code, so, to reach downtown, expect to pay about $10, plus $8 for each additional person, from National; $22, plus $10 per additional person, from Dulles; and $26 to $32, plus $8 per additional person, from BWI.

Limousine service is the most costly of all options, with prices starting at $25 at National, $42 at Dulles, and $70 at BWI, for private car transportation to downtown D.C. For pickup from BWI, call ℂ 202/737-2600; for pickup from National or Dulles, try **Red Top Executive Sedan** (ℂ 800/296-3300 or 202/882-3300—see "When You Want to Travel in Style," below) or consult the yellow pages.

Hotel/motel shuttles operate from all three airports to certain nearby properties. Best to inquire about such transportation when you book a room at your hotel.

Individual transportation options at each airport are as follows:

FROM RONALD REAGAN WASHINGTON NATIONAL AIRPORT If you are not too encumbered with luggage, you should take **Metrorail** (ℂ 202/637-7000) into the city. Metro's Yellow and Blue lines stop at the airport and connect via an enclosed walkway to level two, the concourse level, of the main terminal, adjacent to terminals B and C. If yours is one of the airlines that still uses the "old" terminal A (Midway, Northwest, Alaska, and ATA), you

---

⌒Tips When You Want to Travel in Style

So you don't want to wait in line for a cab at the airport, or share a ride with fellow passengers aboard a shuttle van? You can call in advance to reserve a **Red Top Executive Sedan** (ℂ 800/296-3300 or 202/882-3300; www.redtopcab.com), which will be waiting for you at the curb outside your airline's baggage-claim area. Your chauffeur tracks the status of your flight to know of delays or early arrivals so he can be there when you are. It's more expensive than regular cab service (for instance, from National Airport to downtown you'll pay about $25, plus 15% tip, versus cab fare of about $15, plus gratuity), but the relief of being able to step right into a comfortable and spacious private car after a tiring trip may be worth the extra money to you. The service is available 24 hours daily. The company also offers special transportation for seniors and passengers with disabilities.

will have a longer walk to reach the Metro station, and signs pointing the way can be confusing; ask an airport employee if you're headed in the right direction; or, better yet, head out to the curb and hop a shuttle bus to the station, but be sure to ask the driver to let you know when you've reached the Metro (it may not be obvious, and drivers don't always announce the stops). **Metrobuses** (© **202/637-7000**) also serve the area, should you be going somewhere off the Metro route. But Metrorail is fastest, a 15- to 20-minute non-rush-hour ride to downtown. It is safe, convenient, and cheap, costing $1.10 during non-rush hours, $1.40 during rush hour.

If you're renting a car from on-site **car-rental agencies, Avis** (© 703/ 419-5815), **Budget** (© 703/419-1021), **Dollar** (© 703/519-8701), **Hertz** (© 703/419-6300), or **National** (© 703/419-1032), go to level two, the concourse level, follow the pedestrian walkway to the parking garage, find garage A, and descend one flight. You can also take the complimentary Airport Shuttle (look for the sign posted at the curb outside the terminal) to parking garage A. If you've rented from off-premises agencies **Alamo** (© 703/684-0086), **Enterprise** (© 703/553-7744), or **Thrifty** (© 703/838-6895), head outside the baggage claim area of your terminal, and catch the shuttle bus marked for your agency. See appendix B at the back of this book for toll-free numbers and websites.

To get downtown by car, follow the signs out of the airport for the George Washington Parkway. Stay on the GW Parkway until you see signs for I-395 north to Washington. Take the I-395 north exit to the 12th Street exit, which puts you at 12th Street and Constitution Avenue NW; ask your hotel for directions from that point. Or, take the more scenic route, always staying to the left on the GW Parkway

as you follow the signs for Memorial Bridge; you'll be driving alongside the Potomac River, with the monuments in view across the river; then, as you cross over Memorial Bridge, you're greeted by the Lincoln Memorial. Stay left coming over the bridge, swoop around to the left of the Memorial, take a left on 23rd Street NW, a right on Constitution Avenue, and then left again on 15th Street NW (the Washington Monument will be to your right), if you want to be in the heart of downtown.

FROM WASHINGTON DULLES INTERNATIONAL AIRPORT

The **Washington Flyer Express Bus** runs between Dulles and the West Falls Church Metro station, where you can board a train for D.C. Buses to the West Falls Church Metro station run daily, every 30 minutes, and cost $8 one way. (By the way, "**Washington Flyer**" is also the name under which the taxi service operates at Dulles.)

More convenient is the fairly new **Metrobus** service that runs between Dulles and the L'Enfant Plaza Metro station, located near Capitol Hill and within walking distance of the National Mall and Smithsonian museums. The bus departs hourly, daily, costs only $1.10, and takes about 45 to 50 minutes.

If you are renting a car at Dulles, head down the ramp near your baggage claim area, and walk outside to the curb to look for your rental car's shuttle bus stop. The buses come by every 5 minutes or so en route to nearby rental lots. These include **Alamo** (© 703/260-0182), **Avis** (© 703/661-3505), **Budget** (© 703/437-9373), **Dollar** (© 703/661-6630), **Enterprise** (© 703/661-8800), **Hertz** (© 703/471-6020), **National** (© 703/471-5278), and **Thrifty** (© 703/481-3599). See appendix B at the back of this book for these companies' toll-free numbers and websites.

To reach downtown Washington from Dulles by car, exit the airport and stay on the Dulles Access Road, which leads right into I-66 east. Follow I-66 east to exit 73, Rosslyn/Key Bridge. Ask your hotel for directions from this point.

FROM BALTIMORE–WASHINGTON INTERNATIONAL AIRPORT

In late 2001, BWI initiated an Express Metro Bus service that runs between the Greenbelt Metro station and the airport. The service operates daily, departs every 40 minutes, and costs $2. At the Greenbelt Metro station, you purchase a Metro fare card and board a Metro train, which takes you into the city.

You also have the choice of taking either an **Amtrak** (© **800/872-7245**) or a **Maryland Rural Commuter** (**MARC;** © **800/325-7245**) train into the city. Both trains travel between the BWI Railway Station and Washington's Union Station, about a 30-minute ride. Amtrak's service is daily (starting at about $23 per person, one way, depending on time and train type), while MARC's is weekdays only ($5 per person, one-way). A courtesy shuttle runs every 10 minutes or so between the airport and the train station; stop at the desk near the baggage-claim area to check for the next departure time of both the shuttle bus and the train. Trains depart about every 30 minutes during rush hours, about every 50 minutes the rest of the day.

For most of 2003, BWI will continue to offer the most convenient **car-rental** arrangement of the three area airports, with reservation desks located inside the airport, near baggage claim carousels. Upon confirming your reservation and obtaining your key, you simply walk from the terminal a few yards to the on-site lot, where all rental cars are held. In late 2003, this procedure will change; BWI plans to move its car-rental lots to an off-site location, and you will have to board a shuttle bus at the airport to transport you to the lot. On-site rental agencies include **Avis** (© 410/859-1680), **Alamo** (© 410/850-5011), **Budget** (© 410/859-0850), **Dollar** (© 410/859-5600), **Hertz** (© 410/850-7400), **National** (© 410/859-8860), and **Thrifty** (© 410/859-1136). For these companies' 800-numbers and websites, consult appendix B at the back of this book.

Here's how you reach Washington: Look for signs for I-195 and follow I-195 west until you see signs for Washington and the Baltimore–Washington Parkway (I-295); head south on I-295. Get off I-295 when you see the signs for Route 50/New York Avenue, which lead right into the District. New York Avenue will take you right into downtown; ask your hotel for specific directions from New York Avenue NE.

NEW AIR TRAVEL SECURITY MEASURES

In the wake of the terrorist attacks of September 11, 2001, the airline industry began implementing sweeping security measures in airports. Expect a lengthy check-in process and extensive delays. Although regulations vary from airline to airline, you can expedite the process by taking the following steps:

- **Arrive early.** Arrive at the airport at least 2 hours before your scheduled flight.
- **Try not to drive your car to the airport.** Parking and curbside access to the terminal may be limited. Call ahead and check.
- **Don't count on curbside check-in.** Some airlines and airports have stopped curbside check-in altogether, whereas others offer it on a limited basis. For up-to-date information on specific regulations and implementations, check with the individual airline.

> **Tips What You Can Carry On—And What You Can't**
>
> The Federal Aviation Administration (FAA) has devised new restrictions on carry-on baggage, not only to expedite the screening process but to prevent potential weapons from passing through airport security. Passengers are now limited to bringing just one carry-on bag and one personal item onto the aircraft (previous regulations allowed two carry-on bags and one personal item, like a briefcase or a purse). For more information, go to the FAA's website www.faa.gov. The agency has released a new list of items passengers are not allowed to carry onto an aircraft:
>
> **Not permitted:** knives and box cutters, corkscrews, straight razors, metal scissors, metal nail files, golf clubs, baseball bats, pool cues, hockey sticks, ski poles, ice picks.
>
> **Permitted:** nail clippers, tweezers, eyelash curlers, safety razors (including disposable razors), syringes (with documented proof of medical need), walking canes and umbrellas (must be inspected first).
>
> The airline you fly may have **additional restrictions** on items you can and cannot carry on board. Call ahead to avoid problems.

- **Be sure to carry plenty of documentation.** A government-issued photo ID (federal, state, or local) is now required. You may need to show this at various checkpoints. With an E-ticket, you may be required to have with you printed confirmation of purchase, and perhaps even the credit card with which you bought your ticket (see the box "All about E-Ticketing," below). This varies from airline to airline, so call ahead to make sure you have the proper documentation. And be sure that your ID is **up-to-date:** An expired driver's license, for example, may keep you from boarding the plane altogether. *Note:* Airlines specify that the photo ID requirement applies to those 18 and older, but if your teenager, though younger than 18, looks older, save yourself a possible hassle by having the teen carry a photo ID, too. (A student photo ID will do fine, in this case, and also qualify the teen for possible

discounts at theaters and elsewhere in the city.)

- **Know what you can carry on—and what you can't.** Travelers in the United States are now limited to one carry-on bag, plus one personal bag (such as a purse or a briefcase). The FAA has also issued a list of newly restricted carry-on items; see the box "What You Can Carry On—And What You Can't," below.

- **Prepare to be searched.** Expect spot-checks. Electronic items, such as a laptop or cellphone, should be readied for additional screening. Limit the metal items you wear on your person. If you're carrying wrapped presents, you can count on having to unwrap them.

- **It's no joke.** When a check-in agent asks if someone other than you packed your bag, don't decide that this is the time to be funny. The agents will not hesitate to call an alarm.

- **No ticket, no gate access.** Only ticketed passengers will be allowed beyond the screener checkpoints, except for those people with specific medical or parental needs.

FLYING FOR LESS: TIPS FOR GETTING THE BEST AIRFARE

Passengers within the same airplane cabin are rarely paying the same fare. Business travelers who need to purchase tickets at the last minute, change their itinerary at a moment's notice, or get home for the weekend pay the premium rate. Passengers who can book their ticket long in advance, who can stay over Saturday night, or who are willing to travel on a Tuesday, Wednesday, or Thursday after 7pm, will pay a fraction of the full fare. On many flights, even the shortest hops, the full fare is close to $1,000 or more, while a 7- or 14-day advance purchase ticket may cost less than half that amount. Here are a few other easy ways to save.

- Airlines periodically lower prices on their most popular routes. Check the travel section of your Sunday newspaper for advertised discounts or call the airlines

directly and ask if any **promotional rates** or special fares are available. You'll almost never see a sale during the peak summer vacation months of July and August, or during the Thanksgiving or Christmas seasons; but in periods of low-volume travel, you should pay no more than $400 for a domestic cross-country flight. If your schedule is flexible, say so, and ask if you can secure a cheaper fare by staying an extra day, by flying midweek, or by flying at less-trafficked hours. If you already hold a ticket when a sale breaks, it may even pay to exchange your ticket, which usually incurs a $100 to $150 charge.

  Note: The lowest-priced fares are often nonrefundable, require advance purchase of 1 to 3 weeks and a certain length of stay, and carry penalties for changing dates of travel.

- **Consolidators,** also known as bucket shops, are a good place to find low fares. Consolidators buy seats in bulk from the airlines and then sell them back to the public

---

⌒Tips All About E-Ticketing

Only yesterday **electronic tickets** (E-tickets) were the fast and easy ticket-free alternative to paper tickets. E-tickets allowed passengers to avoid long lines at airport check-in, all the while saving the airlines money on postage and labor. With the increased security measures in airports, however, an E-ticket no longer guarantees an accelerated check-in. You often can't go straight to the boarding gate, even if you have no bags to check. You'll probably need to show your printed E-ticket receipt or confirmation of purchase, as well as a photo ID, and sometimes even the credit card with which you purchased your E-ticket. That said, buying an E-ticket is still a fast, convenient way to book a flight; instead of having to wait for a paper ticket to come through the mail, you can book your fare by phone or on the computer, and the airline will immediately confirm by fax or e-mail. In addition, airlines often offer frequent flier miles as incentive for electronic bookings.

at prices usually below even the airlines' discounted rates. Their small ads usually run in Sunday newspaper travel sections. And before you pay, request a confirmation number from the consolidator and then call the airline to confirm your seat. Be aware that bucket shop tickets are usually nonrefundable or rigged with stiff cancellation penalties, often as high as 50% to 75% of the ticket price. Protect yourself by paying with a credit card rather than cash. Keep in mind that if there's an airline sale going on, or if it's high season, you can often get the same or better rates by contacting the airlines directly, so do some comparison shopping before you buy. Also check out the name of the airline; you may not want to fly on some obscure Third World airline, even if you're saving $10. And check whether you're flying on a charter or a scheduled airline; the latter is more expensive but more reliable.

STA Travel (© 800/781-4040; www.statravel.com) caters especially to young travelers, but their bargain-basement prices are available to people of all ages. The TravelHub (© 888/AIR-FARE; www.travelhub.com) represents nearly 1,000 travel agencies, many of whom offer consolidator and discount fares. Other reliable consolidators include 1-800-FLY-CHEAP (www.1800flycheap.com); TFI Tours International (© 800/745-8000 or 212/736-1140; www.lowestprice.com), which serves as a clearinghouse for

unused seats; or "rebators" such as Travel Avenue (© 800/333-3335; www.travelavenue.com) and the Smart Traveller (© 800/448-3338 or 305/448-3338), which rebate part of their commissions to you.

• Search the Internet for cheap fares. Great last-minute deals are available through free weekly e-mail services provided directly by the airlines. See "Planning Your Trip Online," later in this chapter, for more information.

• Book a seat on a charter flight. Discounted fares have pared the number available, but they can still be found. Most charter operators advertise and sell their seats through travel agents, thus making these local professionals your best source of information for available flights. Before deciding to take a charter flight, however, check the restrictions on the ticket: You may be asked to purchase a tour package, to pay in advance, to be amenable if the day of departure is changed, to pay a service charge, to fly on an airline you're not familiar with (this usually is not the case), and to pay harsh penalties if you cancel—but be understanding if the charter doesn't fill up and is canceled up to 10 days before departure. Summer charters fill up more quickly than others and are almost sure to fly, but if you decide on a charter flight, seriously consider buying cancellation and baggage insurance. Also be prepared for late departure hours and long airport delays, as charters usually do not have priority.

Tips Canceled Plans

If your flight is canceled, don't book a new fare at the ticket counter. Find the nearest phone and call the airline directly to reschedule. You'll be relaxing while other passengers are still standing in line.

- Look into **courier flights**—though they are usually not available on domestic flights. These companies hire couriers to hand-deliver packages or mail, and use your luggage allowance for themselves; in return, you get a deeply discounted ticket—for example, $300 round-trip to Europe in winter. Flights often become available at the last minute, so check in often. **Halbart Express** has offices in New York (☏ **718/656-8189**), Los Angeles (☏ **310/417-9790**), and Miami (☏ **305/593-0260**). **Jupiter Air** (www.jupiterair.com) has offices in New York (☏ **718/656-6050**), Los Angeles (☏ **310/670-5123**), and San Francisco (☏ **650/697-1773**).
- Join a travel club such as **Moment's Notice** (☏ **718/234-6295**; www.moments-notice.com) or **Sears Discount Travel Club** (☏ **800/433-9383,** or 800/255-1487 to join; www.travelers advantage.com), which supply unsold tickets at discounted prices. You pay an annual membership fee to get the club's hot line number. Of course, you're limited to what's available, so you have to be flexible.
- Join **frequent-flier clubs.** It's best to accrue miles on one program, so you can rack up free flights and achieve elite status faster. But it makes sense to open as many accounts as possible, no matter how seldom you fly a particular airline. It's free, and you'll get the best choice of seats, faster response to phone inquiries, and prompter service if your luggage is stolen, your flight is canceled or delayed, or if you want to change your seat.

BY CAR

Major highways approach Washington, D.C., from all parts of the country. Specifically, these are I-270, I-95, and I-295 from the north; I-95 and I-395, Route 1, and Route 301 from the south; Route 50/301 and Route 450 from the east; and Route 7, Route 50, I-66, and Route 29/211 from the west.

No matter which road you take, there's a good chance you will have to navigate some portion of the **Capital Beltway** (I-495 and I-95) to gain entry to D.C. The Beltway girds the city, 66 miles around, with 56 interchanges or exits, and is nearly always congested, but especially during weekday morning and evening rush hours, roughly between 7 to 9am and 3 to 7pm. Commuter traffic on the Beltway now rivals that of major L.A. freeways, and drivers can get a little crazy, weaving in and out of traffic.

If you're planning to drive to Washington, get yourself a good map before you do anything else. The **American Automobile Association** (**AAA;** ☏ **800/222-4357** for emergency road service, or 703/222-6000 for the mid-Atlantic office; www.aaa.com) provides its members with maps and detailed Trip-Tiks that give precise directions to a destination, including up-to-date information about areas of construction. AAA also provides towing services should you have car trouble during your trip. If you are driving to a hotel in D.C. or its suburbs, contact the establishment to find out the best route to the hotel's address and other crucial details concerning parking availability and rates. See "Getting Around," in chapter 4 for information about driving in D.C.

The District is 240 miles from New York City, 40 miles from Baltimore, 700 miles from Chicago, nearly 500 miles from Boston, and about 630 miles from Atlanta.

BY TRAIN

Amtrak (☏ **800/USA-RAIL;** www.amtrak.com) offers daily service to Washington from New York, Boston, Chicago, and Los Angeles (you change trains in Chicago). Amtrak also travels daily from points south of Washington, including Raleigh, Charlotte, Atlanta, cities in Florida, and to New Orleans.

Metroliner service—which costs a little more but provides faster transit and roomier, more comfortable seating than regular trains—is available between New York and Washington, D.C., and points in between. *Note:* Metroliner fares are substantially reduced on weekends. The most luxurious way to travel is First Class Club Service, available on all Metroliners as well as some other trains. For a hefty additional fee, passengers enjoy more spacious and refined seating in a private car; complimentary meals and beverage service; and Metropolitan Lounges (in New York, Chicago, Philadelphia, and Washington), where travelers can wait for trains in a comfortable setting while enjoying free snacks and coffee.

Even faster, roomier, and more expensive than Metroliner service are Amtrak's high-speed **Acela** trains. The trains, which travel as fast as 150 miles per hour, navigate the Northeast Corridor, linking Boston, New York, and Washington. With relatively new cars boasting comfortable seats and plenty of leg space, the Acela wins justified praise for its genuinely smooth—as well as fast—ride. Weeknight trains are packed, though, and the din of cellphone chatter can be difficult to ignore. So grab a seat on the "Quiet Car" at the front of the train for a more relaxing trip.

Two types of service are available: the Acela Express, which travels between New York and Washington in 2 hours and 43 minutes, and between Boston and Washington in about 6 hours and 30 minutes; and the Acela Regional, which travels between New York and Washington in 3 hours and 40 minutes, and between Boston and Washington in about 8 hours.

Amtrak's goal is to run a total of 19 Acela round-trips daily between New York and Washington, eventually replacing Metroliner service between those two cities.

Amtrak trains arrive at historic **Union Station,** 50 Massachusetts Ave. NE (✆ **202/371-9441;** www.union stationdc.com), a short walk from the Capitol, across the circle from several hotels, and a short cab or Metro ride from downtown. Union Station is a turn-of-the-20th-century beaux arts masterpiece that was magnificently restored in the late 1980s. Offering a three-level marketplace of shops and restaurants, this stunning depot is conveniently located and connects with Metro service. There are always taxis available there. (For more on Union Station, see chapters 4, 7, and 8.)

Like the airlines, Amtrak offers several discounted fares; although not all are based on advance purchase, you have more discount options by reserving early. The discount fares can be used only on certain days and hours of the day; be sure to find out exactly what restrictions apply. Tickets for children ages 2 to 15 cost half the price of a regular coach fare when the children are accompanied by a fare-paying adult. Amtrak's website features a bargain fares service, Rail SALE, which allows you to purchase tickets for one-way designated coach seats at great discounts. This program is only available on **www.amtrak.com** when you charge your tickets by credit card.

Also inquire about money-saving packages that include hotel accommodations, car rentals, tours, and so on with your train fare. Call ✆ **800/321-8684** for details.

Note: Amtrak requires that passengers 18 and older show a valid photo ID when buying tickets or checking baggage.

D.C. Metropolitan Area

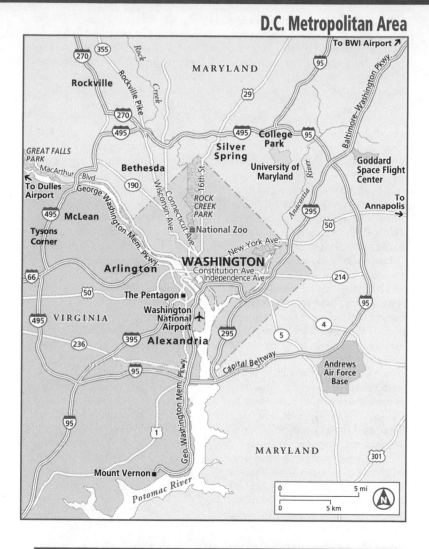

7 Planning Your Trip Online

Researching and booking your trip online can save time and money. Then again, it may not. It is simply not true that you always get the best deal online. Most booking engines do not include schedules and prices for budget airlines, and from time to time you'll get a better last-minute price by calling the airline directly, so it's best to call the airline to see if you can do better before booking online.

On the plus side, Internet users today can tap into the same travel-planning databases that were once accessible only to travel agents—and do it at the same speed. Sites such as **Frommers.com**, **Travelocity.com**, **Expedia.com**, and **Orbitz.com** allow consumers to comparison shop for airfares, access special bargains, book flights, and reserve hotel rooms and rental cars.

But don't fire your travel agent just yet. Although online booking sites offer tips and hard data to help you bargain shop, they cannot endow you with the hard-earned experience that makes a seasoned, reliable travel agent an invaluable resource, even in the Internet age. And for consumers with a complex itinerary, a trusty travel agent is still the best way to arrange the most direct flights to and from the best airports.

Still, there's no denying the Internet's emergence as a powerful tool in researching and plotting travel time. The benefits of researching your trip online can be well worth the effort.

Last-minute specials, such as weekend deals or Internet-only fares, are offered by airlines to fill empty seats. Most of these are announced on Tuesday or Wednesday and must be purchased online. They are only valid for travel that weekend, but some can be booked weeks or months in advance. Sign up for weekly e-mail alerts at airline websites or check megasites that compile comprehensive lists of last-minute specials, such as **Smarter Living** (smarterliving.com) or **WebFlyer** (www.webflyer.com).

Some sites, such as Expedia.com, will send you **e-mail notification** when a cheap fare becomes available to your favorite destination. Some will also tell you when fares to a particular destination are lowest.

TRAVEL PLANNING & BOOKING SITES

Keep in mind that because several airlines are no longer willing to pay commissions on tickets sold by online travel agencies, these agencies may either add a $10 surcharge to your bill if you book on that carrier—or neglect to offer those carriers' schedules.

The list of sites below is selective, not comprehensive. Some sites will have evolved or disappeared by the time you read this.

- **Travelocity** (www.travelocity.com or www.frommers.travelocity.com) and **Expedia** (www.expedia.com) are among the most popular sites, each offering an excellent range of options. Travelers search by destination, dates and cost.
- **Orbitz** (www.orbitz.com) is a popular site launched by United, Delta, Northwest, American, and Continental airlines. (Stay tuned: At press time, travel-agency associations were waging an antitrust battle against this site.)
- **Qixo** (www.qixo.com) is another powerful search engine that allows you to search for flights and accommodations from some 20 airline and travel-planning sites (such as Travelocity) at once. Qixo sorts results by price.
- **Priceline** (www.priceline.com) lets you "name your price" for airline tickets, hotel rooms, and rental cars. For airline tickets, you can't say what time you want to fly—you have to accept any flight between 6am and 10pm on the dates you've selected, and you may have to make one or more stopovers. Tickets are nonrefundable, and no frequent-flyer miles are awarded.

SMART E-SHOPPING

The savvy traveler is armed with insider information. Here are a few tips to help you navigate the Internet successfully and safely.

- **Know when sales start.** Last-minute deals may vanish in minutes. If you have a favorite booking site or airline, find out when last-minute deals are released to the public. (For example, Southwest's specials are posted every Tuesday at 12:01am central time.)
- **Shop around.** If you're looking for bargains, compare prices on different sites and airlines—and

Tips   Easy Internet Access Away from Home

There are a number of ways to get your e-mail on the Web, using any computer.

- Your **Internet Service Provider (ISP)** may have a Web-based interface that lets you access your e-mail on computers other than your own. Just find out how it works before you leave home. The major ISPs maintain local access numbers around the world so that you can go online by placing a local call. Check your ISP's website or call its toll-free number and ask how you can use your current account away from home, and how much it will cost. Also ask about the cost of the service before you leave home.

- You can open an account on a free, Web-based **e-mail provider** before you leave home, such as Microsoft's **Hotmail** (hotmail.com) or **Yahoo! Mail** (mail.yahoo.com). Your home ISP may be able to forward your home e-mail to the Web-based account automatically.

- Check out **www.mail2web.com**. This amazing free service allows you to type in your regular e-mail address and password and retrieve your e-mail from any Web browser, anywhere, so long as your home ISP hasn't blocked it with a firewall.

- Call your hotel in advance to see whether Internet connection is possible from your room.

against a travel agent's best fare. Try a range of times and alternative airports before you make a purchase.

- **Stay secure.** Book only through secure sites (some airline sites are not secure). Look for a key icon (Netscape) or a padlock (Internet Explorer) at the bottom of your Web browser before you enter credit card information or other personal data.

- **Avoid online auctions.** Sites that auction airline tickets and frequent-flier miles are the number-one perpetrators of Internet fraud, according to the National Consumers League.

- **Maintain a paper trail.** If you book an E-ticket, print out a confirmation, or write down your confirmation number, and keep it safe and accessible—or your trip could be a virtual one!

8 Tips on Accommodations

The challenge for anyone trying to book a hotel reservation in Washington is not finding a hotel with vacancies, but finding a hotel that is affordable. The capital has at least 100 hotels, with more opening all the time. Unfortunately, most of them cater to the business crowd and charge accordingly—the average daily room rate in 2002 ranged from about $140 to $157, and you can expect to pay upward of $250 at the best hotels. Chain hotels predominate here, with Marriott owned or managed properties in the lead with at least 12 hotels. Those who prefer only-in-Washington lodging will find happiness in choosing from historic hotels, unique boutique hotels, and a small but worthy number of bed-and-breakfasts. On the rise are all-suites (or mostly suites) hotels, the better to accommodate business travelers, who stay for weeks at a time, as well as families, who appreciate the space and homey facilities.

TIPS FOR SAVING ON YOUR HOTEL ROOM

The **rack rate** is the maximum rate that a hotel charges for a room. It's the rate you'd get if you walked in off the street and asked for a room for the night. Hardly anybody pays these prices, however, and there are many ways around them.

- **Don't be afraid to bargain.** Most rack rates include commissions of 10% to 25% for travel agents, which some hotels may be willing to reduce if you make your own reservations and haggle a bit. Always ask whether a room less expensive than the first one quoted is available, or whether any special rates apply to you. You may qualify for corporate, student, military, senior citizen, or other discounts. Be sure to mention membership in AAA, AARP, frequent-flier programs, or trade unions, which may entitle you to special deals as well. Find out the hotel policy on children—do kids stay free in the room or is there a special rate?
- **Rely on a qualified professional.** Certain hotels give travel agents discounts in exchange for steering business their way, so if you're shy about bargaining, an agent may be better equipped to negotiate discounts for you.
- **Dial direct.** When booking a room in a chain hotel, compare the rates offered by the hotel's local line with that of the toll-free number. Also check with an agent and online. A hotel makes nothing on a room that stays empty, so the local hotel reservation desk may be willing to offer a special rate unavailable elsewhere.

- **Remember the law of supply and demand.** Resort hotels are most crowded and therefore most expensive on weekends, so discounts are usually available for midweek stays. Business hotels in downtown locations are busiest during the week, so you can expect big discounts over the weekend. Avoid high-season stays whenever you can: planning your vacation just a week before or after official peak season can mean big savings.
- **Look into group or long-stay discounts.** If you come as part of a large group, you should be able to negotiate a bargain rate, since the hotel can then guarantee occupancy in a number of rooms. Likewise, if you're planning a long stay (at least 5 days), you might qualify for a discount. As a general rule, expect 1 night free after a 7-night stay.
- **Avoid excess charges.** When you book a room, ask whether the hotel charges for parking. Many hotels charge a fee just for dialing out on the phone in your room. Find out whether your hotel imposes a surcharge on local and long-distance calls. A pay phone, however inconvenient, may save you money, although many calling cards charge a fee when you use them on pay phones. Finally, ask about local taxes and service charges, which could increase the cost of a room by 25% or more.
- **Watch for coupons and advertised discounts.** Scan ads in your local Sunday newspaper travel section, an excellent source for up-to-the-minute hotel deals.
- **Consider a suite.** If you are traveling with your family or another couple, you can pack more people into a suite (which usually comes with a sofa bed), and thereby reduce your per-person rate.

Remember that some places charge for extra guests.

- **Book an efficiency.** A room with a kitchenette allows you to shop for groceries and cook your own meals. This is a big money saver, especially for families on long stays.
- Join hotel **frequent-visitor clubs,** even if you don't use them much. You'll be more likely to get upgrades and other perks.
- Many hotels offer **frequent-flier points.** Don't forget to ask for yours when you check in.
- **Investigate reservations services.** These outfits usually work as consolidators, buying up or reserving rooms in bulk, and then dealing them out to customers at a profit. You can get 10% to 50% off; but remember, these discounts apply to inflated rack rates that savvy travelers rarely end up paying. You may get a decent rate, but always call the hotel as well to see if you can do better.

Among the more reputable reservations services, offering both telephone and online bookings, are: **Accommodations Express** (✆ **800/950-4685;** www.accommodationsexpress.com); **Hotel Reservations Network** (✆ **800/715-7666;** www.hoteldiscounts.com or www.180096HOTEL.com);

Quikbook (✆ **800/789-9887,** includes fax on demand service; www.quikbook.com). Online, try booking your hotel through **Arthur Frommer's Budget Travel** (www.frommers.com). **Microsoft Expedia** (www.expedia.com) features a "Travel Agent" that will also direct you to affordable lodgings.

LANDING THE BEST ROOM

Somebody has to get the best room in the house. It might as well be you.

Always ask about a corner room. They're often larger and quieter, with more windows and light, and they often cost the same as standard rooms.

When you make your reservation, ask if the hotel is renovating; if it is, request a room away from the construction. Ask about nonsmoking rooms, rooms with views, rooms with twin, queen- or king-size beds. If you're a light sleeper, request a quiet room away from vending machines, elevators, restaurants, bars, and discos. Ask for one of the rooms that have been most recently renovated or redecorated. If you aren't happy with your room when you arrive, talk to the front desk. If they have another room, they may be willing to accommodate you. Join the hotel's frequent visitor club; you may qualify for upgrades.

9 Recommended Reading

You can put yourself in the mood for a visit to Washington by reading some great novels set in Washington, memoirs and histories by some of the city's more famous residents, and other guidebooks whose topics supplement what you've learned in these pages.

Fiction-lovers might pick up books by Ward Just, including his collection of stories *The Congressman Who Loved Flaubert;* Ann Berne's *A Crime in the Neighborhood;* Marita Golden's *The Edge of Heaven;* Allen Drury's *Advise and Consent;* or one of the growing number of mysteries whose plot revolves around the capital, such as Margaret Truman's series (*Murder at the Smithsonian, Murder at the Kennedy Center,* and so on), or hardcore thrillers by George Pelecanos: *Hell to Pay* and *King Suckerman,* to name just two.

If you're keen on learning more about the history of the nation's capital and about the people who have lived here, try Arthur Schlesinger's *The Birth of the Nation,* F. Cary's *Urban Odyssey,* David Brinkley's *Washington at War,* and Paul Dickson's *On This Spot,* which traces the history of the city by revealing exactly what took place at specific locations—"on this spot"—in years gone by, neighborhood by neighborhood.

Two memoirs are musts for finding out how the powerful operate in Washington: *Personal History,* by the late Katharine Graham, who for many years was publisher of the *Washington Post,* and *Washington,* by Graham's close friend and colleague, Meg Greenfield, a columnist and editor at the *Washington Post* for more than 30 years.

Finally, to find out more about the architecture of Washington, pick up a copy of the *AIA Guide to the Architecture of Washington, D.C.,* by Christopher Weeks; to discover information about Washington's parks, hiking trails, and other green spaces, look for *Natural Washington* by Richard Berman and Deborah Gerhard; for a humorous read, put your hands on Dave Barry's *Dave Barry Hits Below the Beltway,* and for a book that may send chills up your spine, purchase a copy of *Ghosts: Washington's Most Famous Ghost Stories* by John Alexander.

For International Visitors

Washington, D.C., annually welcomes more than a million visitors from outside the United States. If you are planning to be one of them in 2003, you should find the information in this chapter helpful as you prepare for your trip.

1 Preparing for Your Trip

ENTRY REQUIREMENTS

Check at any U.S. embassy or consulate for current information and requirements. You can also obtain a visa application and other information online at the **U.S. State Department's** website, at **www.travel.state.gov**.

VISAS The U.S. State Department has a **Visa Waiver Program** allowing citizens of certain countries to enter the United States without a visa for stays of up to 90 days. At press time these included Andorra, Australia, Austria, Belgium, Brunei, Denmark, Finland, France, Germany, Iceland, Ireland, Italy, Japan, Liechtenstein, Luxembourg, Monaco, the Netherlands, New Zealand, Norway, Portugal, San Marino, Singapore, Slovenia, Spain, Sweden, Switzerland, the United Kingdom, and Uruguay. Citizens of these countries need only a valid passport and a round-trip air or cruise ticket in their possession upon arrival. If they first enter the United States, they may also visit Mexico, Canada, Bermuda, and/or the Caribbean islands and return to the United States without a visa. Further information is available from any U.S. embassy or consulate. Canadian citizens may enter the United States without visas; they need only proof of residence.

Citizens of all other countries must have (1) a valid passport that expires at least 6 months later than the scheduled end of their visit to the United States, and (2) a tourist visa, which may be obtained without charge from any U.S. consulate.

To obtain a visa, the traveler must submit a completed application form (either in person or by mail) with a 1½-inch-square photo, and must demonstrate binding ties to a residence abroad. Usually you can obtain a visa at once or within 24 hours, but it may take longer during the summer rush from June through August. If you cannot go in person, contact the nearest U.S. embassy or consulate for directions on applying by mail. Your travel agent or airline office may also be able to provide you with visa applications and instructions. The U.S. consulate or embassy that issues your visa will determine whether you will be issued a multiple- or single-entry visa and whether you will encounter any restrictions regarding the length of your stay.

British subjects can obtain up-to-date passport and visa information by calling the **U.S. Embassy Visa Information Line** (© 0891/200-290), or the **London Passport Office** (© 0990/210-410 for recorded information), or they can find the visa information on the U.S. Embassy Great Britain website (**www.usembassy.org.uk/cons_web/visa/visaindex.htm**).

Irish citizens can obtain up-to-date passport and visa information through the **Embassy of USA Dublin,** 42 Elgin Rd., Dublin 4, Ireland (ⓒ **353/ 1-668-8777;** or by checking the visa website at **www.usembassy.ie/ consulate/applications.html**).

Australian citizens can obtain up-to-date passport and visa information by calling the **U.S. Embassy Canberra,** Moonah Place, Yarralumla, ACT 2600 (ⓒ **02/6214-5600**) or check the website's visa page (**www. usisaustralia.gov/consular/niv.html**).

Citizens of **New Zealand** can obtain up-to-date passport and visa information by calling the **U.S. Embassy New Zealand,** 29 Fitzherbert Terr., Thorndon, Wellington, New Zealand; ⓒ **644/472-2068** or get the information directly from the website (**http://usembassy.org.nz/ nzservices/visas/**).

MEDICAL   REQUIREMENTS

Unless you're arriving from an area known to be suffering from an **epidemic** (particularly cholera or yellow fever), inoculations or vaccinations are not required for entry into the United States. If you have a medical condition that requires **syringe-administered medications,** carry a valid signed prescription from your physician—the Federal Aviation Administration (FAA) no longer allows airline passengers to pack syringes in their carry-on baggage without documented proof of medical need. If you have a disease that requires treatment with **narcotics,** you should also carry documented proof with you—smuggling narcotics aboard a plane is a serious offense that carries severe penalties in the United States.

For **HIV-positive visitors,** requirements for entering the United States are somewhat vague and change frequently. According to the latest publication of *HIV and Immigrants: A Manual for AIDS Service Providers,* the Immigration and Naturalization Service (INS) doesn't require a medical exam for entry into the United States, but INS officials may stop individuals because they look sick or because they are carrying AIDS/HIV medicine.

If an HIV-positive noncitizen applies for a nonimmigrant visa, the question on the application regarding communicable diseases is tricky no matter which way it's answered. If the applicant checks "no," INS may deny the visa on the grounds that the applicant committed fraud. If the applicant checks "yes" or if INS suspects the person is HIV-positive, it will deny the visa unless the applicant asks for a special waiver for visitors. This waiver is for people visiting the United States for a short time, to attend a conference, for instance, to visit close relatives, or to receive medical treatment. It can be a confusing situation. For further up-to-the-minute information, contact the Centers for Disease Control's **National Center for HIV** (ⓒ **404/332-4559;** www.hivatis.org) or the **Gay Men's Health Crisis** (ⓒ **212/367-1000;** www.gmhc.org).

DRIVER'S   LICENSES Foreign driver's licenses are mostly recognized in the United States, although you may want to get an international driver's license if your home license is not written in English.

PASSPORT INFORMATION

Safeguard your passport in an inconspicuous, inaccessible place like a money belt. Make a copy of the critical pages, including the passport number, and store it in a safe place, separate from the passport itself. If you lose your passport while in Washington, visit your country's embassy or consulate as soon as possible for a replacement. Passport applications are downloadable from the Internet sites listed below.

Note that the International Civil Aviation Organization (ICAO) has recommended a policy requiring that *every* individual who travels by air have his or her own passport. In response, many countries are now requiring that children must be issued their own passport to travel internationally, where before those under 16 or so may have been allowed to travel on a parent or guardian's passport.

FOR RESIDENTS OF CANADA

You can pick up a passport application at one of 28 regional passport offices or most travel agencies. As of December 11, 2001, Canadian children who travel will need their own passport. However, if you hold a valid Canadian passport issued before December 11, 2001, that bears the name of your child, the passport remains valid for you and your child until it expires. Passports cost C$85 for those 16 years and older (valid 5 years), C$35 children 3 to 15 (valid 5 years), and C$20, children under 3 (valid for 3 years). Applications, which must be accompanied by two identical passport-size photographs and proof of Canadian citizenship, are available at travel agencies throughout Canada or from the central **Passport Office, Department of Foreign Affairs and International Trade,** Ottawa, Ont. K1A 0G3 (© **800/567-6868;** www. dfait-maeci.gc.ca/passport). Processing takes 5 to 10 days if you apply in person, or about 3 weeks by mail.

FOR RESIDENTS OF THE UNITED KINGDOM

As a member of the European Union, you need only an identity card, not a passport, to travel to other EU countries. However, if you already possess a passport, it's always useful to carry it. To pick up an application for a regular 10-year passport (the Visitor's Passport has been abolished), visit your nearest passport office, major post office, or travel agency. You can also contact the **London Passport Office** at © **0171/271-3000** or search its website at **www.open.gov. uk/ukpass/ukpass.htm**. Passports are £21 for adults and £11 for children under 16.

FOR RESIDENTS OF IRELAND

You can apply for a 10-year passport, costing IR£45, at the **Passport Office,** Setanta Centre, Molesworth Street, Dublin 2 (© **01/671-1633;** www.irl gov.ie/iveagh/foreignaffairs/services). Those under age 18 and over 65 must apply for a IR£10 3-year passport. You can also apply at 1A South Mall, Cork (© **021/272-525**) or over the counter at most main post offices.

FOR RESIDENTS OF AUSTRALIA

Apply at your local post office or passport office or search the government website at **www.dfat.gov.au/ passports/**. Passports for adults are A$126 and for those under 18 are A$63.

FOR RESIDENTS OF NEW ZEALAND

You can pick up a passport application at any travel agency or Link Centre. For more info, contact the **Passport Office,** P.O. Box 805, Wellington (© **0800/225-050**). Passports for adults are NZ$80 and for those under 16 they're NZ$40.

CUSTOMS
WHAT YOU CAN BRING IN

Every visitor more than 21 years of age may bring in, free of duty, the following: (1) 1 liter of wine or hard liquor; (2) 200 cigarettes, 100 cigars (but not from Cuba), or 3 pounds of smoking tobacco; and (3) $100 worth of gifts. These exemptions are offered to travelers who spend at least 72 hours in the United States and who have not claimed them within the preceding 6 months. It is altogether forbidden to bring into the country foodstuffs (particularly fruit, cooked meats, and canned goods) and plants (vegetables, seeds, tropical plants, and the like). Foreign tourists may bring in or take out up to $10,000 in U.S. or foreign currency with no formalities; larger sums must be declared to U.S. Customs on entering or leaving, which includes filing form CM 4790. For more specific information regarding U.S. Customs, call your nearest U.S. embassy or consulate, or the **U.S. Customs** office at © **202/927-1770** or www.customs.ustreas.gov.

WHAT YOU CAN TAKE HOME

U.K. citizens returning from a non-EC country have a Customs allowance of: 200 cigarettes; 50 cigars; 250g of smoking tobacco; 2 liters of still table wine; 1 liter of spirits or strong liqueurs (over 22% volume); 2 liters of fortified wine, sparkling wine or other liqueurs; 60cc (ml) perfume; 250cc (ml) of toilet water; and £145 worth of all other goods, including gifts and souvenirs. People under 17 cannot have the tobacco or alcohol allowance. For more information, contact HM Customs & Excise, Passenger Enquiry Point, 2nd Floor Wayfarer House, Great South West Road, Feltham, Middlesex, TW14 8NP (© **0181/910-3744;** from outside the U.K. 44/181-910-3744), or consult their website at www.open.gov.uk.

For a clear summary of **Canadian** rules, write for the booklet *I Declare,* issued by **Revenue Canada,** 2265 St. Laurent Blvd., Ottawa K1G 4KE (© **506/636-5064**). Canada allows its citizens a C$750 exemption, and you're allowed to bring back duty-free 1 carton of cigarettes, 1 can of tobacco, 40 imperial ounces of liquor, and 50 cigars. In addition, you're allowed to mail gifts to Canada valued at less than C$60 a day, provided they're unsolicited and don't contain alcohol or tobacco (write on the package "Unsolicited gift, under C$60 value"). All valuables should be declared on the Y-38 form before departure from Canada, including serial numbers of valuables you already own, such as expensive foreign cameras. *Note:* The C$750 exemption can only be used once a year and only after an absence of 7 days.

The duty-free allowance in **Australia** is A$400 or, for those under 18, A$200. Personal property mailed back from England should be marked "Australian goods returned" to avoid payment of duty. Upon returning to Australia, citizens can bring in 250 cigarettes or 250 grams of loose tobacco, and 1,125ml of alcohol. If you're returning with valuable goods you already own, such as foreign-made cameras, you should file form B263. A helpful brochure, available from Australian consulates or Customs offices, is *Know Before You Go.* For more information, contact **Australian Customs Services,** GPO Box 8, Sydney NSW 2001 (© **02/9213-2000**).

The duty-free allowance for **New Zealand** is NZ$700. Citizens over 17 can bring in 200 cigarettes, or 50 cigars, or 250 grams of tobacco (or a mixture of all 3 if their combined weight doesn't exceed 250g); plus 4.5 liters of wine and beer, or 1.125 liters of liquor. New Zealand currency does not carry import or export restrictions. Fill out a certificate of export, listing the valuables you are taking out of the country; that way, you can bring them back without paying duty. Most questions are answered in a free pamphlet available at New Zealand consulates and Customs offices: *New Zealand Customs Guide for Travellers, Notice no. 4.* For more information, contact New Zealand Customs, 50 Anzac Ave., P.O. Box 29, Auckland (© **09/359-6655**).

HEALTH INSURANCE

Although it's not required of travelers, health insurance is highly recommended. Unlike many European countries, the United States does not usually offer free or low-cost medical care to its citizens or visitors. Doctors and hospitals are expensive, and in most cases will require advance payment or proof of coverage before they render their services. Policies can cover everything from the loss or theft of your baggage and trip cancellation to the guarantee of bail in case you're arrested. Good policies will also cover the costs of an accident, repatriation, or death. See "Insurance, Health & Safety," in chapter 2 for more information. Packages such as **Europ Assistance** in Europe are sold by automobile clubs and travel agencies at attractive rates. **Worldwide Assistance Services,** Inc. (© **800/821-2828;** www.worldwideassistance.com), is the agent for Europ Assistance in the United States.

Though lack of health insurance may prevent you from being admitted to a hospital in nonemergencies, don't worry about being left on a street corner to die: The American way is to fix you now and bill the living daylights out of you later.

INSURANCE FOR BRITISH TRAVELERS Most big travel agents offer their own insurance, and will probably try to sell you their package when you book a holiday. Think before you sign. **Britain's Consumers' Association** recommends that you insist on seeing the policy and reading the fine print before buying travel insurance. **The Association of British Insurers** (© **0171/600-3333;** www.abi.org.uk/) gives advice by phone and publishes *Holiday Insurance,* a free guide to policy provisions and prices. You might also shop around for better deals: Try **Columbus Direct** (© **0171/375-0011;** www.columbusdirect.net/) or, for students, **Campus Travel** (© **0171/730-2101;** www.campustravel.co.uk).

INSURANCE FOR CANADIAN TRAVELERS Canadians should check with their provincial health plan offices or call **Health Canada** (© **613/957-2991;** www.he-sc.gc.ca/) to find out the extent of their coverage and what documentation and receipts they must take home in case they are treated in the United States.

MONEY
CURRENCY The U.S. monetary system is very simple: The most common **bills** are the $1 (colloquially, a "buck"), $5, $10, and $20 denominations. There are also $2 bills (seldom encountered), $50 bills, and $100 bills (the last 2 are usually not welcome as payment for small purchases). All the paper money was recently redesigned, making the famous faces adorning them disproportionately large. The old-style bills are still legal tender.

There are seven denominations of coins: 1¢ (1 cent, or a penny); 5¢ (5 cents, or a nickel); 10¢ (10 cents, or a dime); 25¢ (25 cents, or a quarter); 50¢ (50 cents, or a half dollar); the new gold "Sacagawea" coin worth $1; and, prized by collectors, the rare, older silver dollar.

CURRENCY EXCHANGE It's best to change money before you arrive in the United States, but if you do need to exchange currency, you can go to the currency-exchange desk at any of the three airports, or to one of the following locations: the Thomas Cook currency exchange office (© **800/CURRENCY**) at Union Station, opposite Gate G on the train concourse; the Sun Trust Bank, 1445 New York Ave. NW (© **202/879-6000**); and the Riggs Bank, 800 17th St. NW (© **301/887-6000**).

TRAVELER'S CHECKS Though traveler's checks are widely accepted, make sure that they're denominated in U.S. dollars, as foreign-currency checks are often difficult to exchange. The three traveler's checks that are most widely recognized—and least likely to be denied—are **Visa,**

American Express, and **Thomas Cook.** Be sure to record the numbers of the checks, and keep that information in a separate place in case they get lost or stolen. Most businesses are pretty good about taking traveler's checks, but you're better off cashing them in at a bank (in small amounts, of course) and paying in cash. Remember: You'll need identification, such as a driver's license or passport, to change a traveler's check.

CREDIT CARDS & ATMs Credit cards are the most widely used form of payment in the United States: **Visa** (BarclayCard in Britain), **MasterCard** (EuroCard in Europe, Access in Britain, Chargex in Canada), **American Express, Diners Club, Discover,** and **Carte Blanche.** Most Washington establishments accept Visa, Master-Card, and American Express, and many also accept Diners Club, Discover, and Carte Blanche. A handful of stores and restaurants do not take credit cards at all, so be sure to ask in advance. Most businesses display a sticker near their entrance to let you know which cards they accept. (*Note:* Businesses may require a minimum purchase, usually around $10, to use a credit card.)

You should bring at least one major credit card. You must have a credit or charge card to rent a car. Hotels and airlines usually require a credit-card imprint as a deposit against expenses, and in an emergency a credit card can be priceless.

You'll find **automated teller machines (ATMs)** on just about every block—at least in almost every town—across the country. Some ATMs will allow you to draw U.S.

currency against your bank and credit cards. Check with your bank before leaving home, and remember that you will need your personal identification number (PIN) to do so. Most accept Visa, MasterCard, and American Express, as well as ATM cards from other U.S. banks. Expect to be charged up to $3 per transaction, however, if you're not using your own bank's ATM.

One way around these fees is to ask for cash back at grocery stores that accept ATM cards and don't charge usage fees. Of course, you'll have to purchase something first.

ATM cards with major credit card backing, known as "debit cards," are now a commonly acceptable form of payment in most stores and restaurants. Debit cards draw money directly from your checking account. Some stores enable you to receive "cash back" on your debit-card purchases as well.

SAFETY
GENERAL SAFETY SUGGESTIONS Although tourist areas are generally safe, U.S. urban areas tend to be less safe than those in Europe or Japan. You should always stay alert. Ask your hotel front-desk staff or call the Washington Convention and Tourism Corporation (© **202/789-7000**) to find out which neighborhoods are safe.

Avoid deserted areas, especially at night, and don't go into public parks at night unless there's a concert or similar occasion that will attract a crowd.

Avoid carrying valuables with you on the street, and don't display expensive cameras or electronic equipment.

Tips **Travel Tip**

Be sure to keep a copy of all your travel papers separate from your wallet or purse, and leave a copy with someone at home should you need it faxed in an emergency.

If you're using a map, consult it inconspicuously—or better yet, try to study it before you leave your room. In general, the more you look like a tourist, the more likely someone will try to take advantage of you. If you're walking, pay attention to who is near you as you walk. If you're attending a convention or event where you wear a name tag, remove it before venturing outside. Hold onto your purse, and place your billfold in an inside pocket. In theaters, restaurants, and other public places, keep your possessions in sight.

Remember also that hotels are open to the public, and in a large hotel, security may not be able to screen everyone entering. Always lock your room door.

Be careful crossing streets, especially in the downtown area, especially at rush hour. Though this may seem like obvious and silly advice, it's worth a mention here, as there's been an alarming increase lately in the number of pedestrians being hit by cars. Drivers in a hurry run red lights, turn corners too quickly, and so on, so be sure to take your time and check for oncoming traffic when crossing streets, and to use the crosswalks. If you're from Great Britain, you'll need to pay special attention, looking to your left, rather than to your right, on two-way streets.

DRIVING SAFETY Question your rental agency about personal safety and ask for a traveler-safety brochure when you pick up your car. Obtain written directions—or a map with the route clearly marked—from the agency showing how to get to your destination. (Many agencies now offer the option of renting a cellular phone for the duration of your car rental; check with the rental agent when you pick up the car.) And, if possible, arrive and depart during daylight hours.

If you drive off a highway and end up in a dodgy-looking neighborhood, leave the area as quickly as possible. If you have an accident, even on the highway, stay in your car with the doors locked until you assess the situation or until the police arrive. If you're bumped from behind on the street or are involved in a minor accident with no injuries, and the situation appears to be suspicious, motion to the other driver to follow you. Never get out of your car in such situations. Go directly to the nearest police precinct, well-lit service station, or 24-hour store. You may want to look into renting a cellphone on a short-term basis. One recommended wireless rental company is **InTouch USA** (✆ **800/872-7626**; www.in touchusa.com).

Park in well-lit and well-traveled areas whenever possible. Always keep your car doors locked, whether the vehicle is attended or unattended. Never leave any packages or valuables in sight. If someone attempts to rob you or steal your car, don't try to resist the thief/carjacker. Report the incident to the police department immediately by calling ✆ **911.**

2 Getting to the United States

Most international flights to the Washington, D.C., area land at Washington Dulles International Airport, with Baltimore-Washington International Airport handling some, and Ronald Reagan Washington National Airport offering service to only one international carrier. Specific information follows.

The one international airline with scheduled flights into Ronald Reagan Washington National Airport is **Air Canada** (✆ 888/247-2262; www.air canada.ca).

International airlines with scheduled flights into Baltimore–Washington International airport include **Air Canada** (see above),

British Airways (© 0345/222-111 or 0845/77-333-77 in the U.K., or 800/247-9297; www.british-airways.com), and Icelandair (© 800/223-5500; www.icelandair.com).

International airlines with scheduled flights into Washington Dulles International Airport include Aeroflot (© 888/340-6400; www.aeroflot.com), Air Canada (see above), Air France (© 800/321-4538; www.airfrance.com), ANA Airways (© 800/235-9262; http://svc.ana.co.jp/eng), British Airways (see above), KLM (© 800/225-2525; http://en.nederland.klm.com), Lufthansa (© 800/645-3880; www.lufthansa.com), Saudi Arabian Airlines (© 800/472-8342; www.saudiairlines.com), and Virgin Atlantic (© 01293/747-747 in the U.K., or 800/8628621 in the U.S.; www.virgin-atlantic.com).

AIRLINE DISCOUNTS The smart traveler can find numerable ways to reduce the price of a plane ticket simply by taking time to shop around. For example, overseas visitors can take advantage of the APEX (Advance Purchase Excursion) reductions offered by all major U.S. and European carriers. For more money-saving airline advice, see "Getting There," in chapter 2. For the best rates, compare fares and be flexible with the dates and times of travel.

IMMIGRATION & CUSTOMS CLEARANCE Visitors arriving by air, no matter what the port of entry, should cultivate patience and resignation before setting foot on U.S. soil. Getting through immigration control can take as long as 2 hours on some days, especially on summer weekends, so be sure to carry this guidebook or something else to read. This is especially true in the aftermath of the September 11, 2001 terrorist attacks, when security clearances have been considerably beefed up at U.S. airports.

People traveling by air from Canada, Bermuda, and certain countries in the Caribbean can sometimes clear Customs and Immigration at the point of departure, which is much quicker.

3 Getting Around the United States

BY PLANE Some large airlines (for example, Northwest and Delta) offer travelers on their transatlantic or transpacific flights special discount tickets under the name Visit USA, allowing mostly one-way travel from one U.S. destination to another at very low prices. These discount tickets are not on sale in the United States and must be purchased abroad in conjunction with your international ticket. This system is the best, easiest, and fastest way to see the United States at low cost. You should obtain information well in advance from your travel agent or the office of the airline concerned, since the conditions attached to these discount tickets can be changed without advance notice.

BY TRAIN International visitors (excluding Canada) can also buy a USA Railpass, good for 15 or 30 days of unlimited travel on Amtrak (© 800/USA-RAIL; www.amtrak.com). The pass is available through many foreign travel agents. Prices in 2002 for a 15-day pass were $295 off-peak, $440 peak; a 30-day pass costs $385 off-peak, $550 peak. With a foreign passport, you can also buy passes at Amtrak stations and at travel agencies in the United States, including locations in San Francisco, Los Angeles, Chicago, New York, Miami, Boston, and Washington, D.C. Reservations are generally required and should be made for each part of your trip as early as possible. Regional rail passes are also available.

FAST FACTS: For the International Traveler

Automobile Organizations Auto clubs will supply maps, suggested routes, guidebooks, accident and bail-bond insurance, and emergency road service. The **American Automobile Association (AAA)** is the major auto club in the United States. If you belong to an auto club in your home country, inquire about AAA reciprocity before you leave. You may be able to join AAA even if you're not a member of a reciprocal club; to inquire, call AAA (℃ **800/763-9900;** www.aaa.com). AAA is actually an organization of regional auto clubs. In the Washington, D.C., area, AAA's emergency road service telephone number is ℃ 800/AAA-HELP.

Business Hours Offices are usually open weekdays from 9am to 5pm. Banks are open weekdays from 9am to 3pm or later and sometimes Saturday mornings. Stores typically open between 9 and 10am and close between 5 and 6pm from Monday through Saturday. Stores in shopping complexes or malls tend to stay open late: until about 9pm on weekdays and weekends, and many malls and larger department stores are open on Sundays.

Currency & Currency Exchange See "Entry Requirements" and "Money" under "Preparing for Your Trip," earlier in this chapter.

Electricity Like Canada, the United States uses 110 to 120 volts AC (60 cycles), compared to 220 to 240 volts AC (50 cycles) in most of Europe, Australia, and New Zealand. If your small appliances use 220 to 240 volts, you'll need a 110-volt transformer and a plug adapter with two flat parallel pins to operate them here. Downward converters that change 220–240 volts to 110–120 volts are difficult to find in the United States, so bring one with you.

Embassies & Consulates All embassies are located in the nation's capital, Washington, D.C. On the Internet, you will find a complete listing, with links to each embassy, at www.embassy.org/embassies/index.html.

Here are several embassy addresses: **Australia,** 1601 Massachusetts Ave. NW (℃ 202/797-3000; www.austemb.org); **Canada,** 501 Pennsylvania Ave. NW (℃ 202/682-1740; www.canadianembassy.org); **France,** 4101 Reservoir Rd. NW (℃ 202/944-6000; www.amba-france-us.org); **Germany,** 4645 Reservoir Rd. NW (℃ 202/298-4000; www.germany-info.org); **Ireland,** 2234 Massachusetts Ave. NW (℃ 202/462-3939; www.irelandemb.org); **Japan,** 2520 Massachusetts Ave. NW (℃ 202/238-6700; www.embjapan. org); the **Netherlands,** 4200 Linnean Ave. NW (℃ 202/244-5300; www.netherlands-embassy.org); **New Zealand,** 37 Observatory Circle NW (℃ 202/328-4800; www.nzemb.org); and the **United Kingdom,** 3100 Massachusetts Ave. NW (℃ 202/588-6500; www.britainusa.com/consular/ embassy/embassy.asp). You can also obtain the telephone numbers of other embassies and consulates by calling information in Washington, D.C. (℃ **411** within D.C. and its metropolitan area), or consult the phone book in your hotel room.

Emergencies Call ℃ **911** to report a fire, call the police, or get an ambulance anywhere in the United States. This is a toll-free call. (No coins are required at public telephones.)

If you encounter serious problems, contact the **Traveler's Aid Society International** (*(C)* 202/546-1127; www.travelersaid.org), a nationwide, nonprofit, social-service organization geared to helping travelers in difficult straits, from reuniting families separated while traveling, to providing food and/or shelter to people stranded without cash, to emotional counseling. Traveler's Aid operates help desks at Washington Dulles International Airport (*(C)* 703/572-8296), Ronald Reagan Washington National Airport (*(C)* 703/417-3975), and Union Station (*(C)* 202/371-1937).

Gasoline (Petrol) Petrol is known as gasoline (or simply "gas") in the United States, and petrol stations are known as both gas stations and service stations. Gasoline costs about half as much here as it does in Europe (about $1.65 per gallon at press time), and taxes are already included in the printed price. One U.S. gallon equals 3.8 liters or .85 Imperial gallons.

Holidays Banks, government offices, post offices, and many stores, restaurants, and museums are closed on the following legal national holidays: January 1 (New Year's Day), the third Monday in January (Martin Luther King Jr. Day), the third Monday in February (Presidents' Day, Washington's Birthday), the last Monday in May (Memorial Day), July 4 (Independence Day), the first Monday in September (Labor Day), the second Monday in October (Columbus Day), November 11 (Veterans' Day/Armistice Day), the fourth Thursday in November (Thanksgiving Day), and December 25 (Christmas). Also, the Tuesday following the first Monday in November is Election Day and is a federal government holiday in presidential-election years (held every 4 years, and next in 2004).

Language Aid **Meridian International Center** provides language assistance via a telephone bank of volunteers who, together, speak 42 different languages. Meridian also publishes maps and tourist brochures in French, Spanish, German, Japanese, and Chinese. Best of all, these services are free. Call the Center at *(C)* **202/939-5552** or 202/939-5554, preferably a day or two in advance. You will probably hear a recorded voice asking you to leave a message; you can hit "0" for the operator and explain why you are calling, or leave a message, and someone from Meridian will call you back with the assistance you need. Or you can go to Meridian's website at **www.meridian.org** and e-mail the center from there. Meridian also runs an **information desk at Washington Dulles International Airport** (*(C)* 703/572-2536). In addition, most Washington museums, hotels restaurants, and other attractions boast multilingual staff. Many sights, like the White House, the Kennedy Center, the Library of Congress, and the Smithsonian Institution, offer free brochures in several languages; the Smithsonian also welcomes international visitors at its Information Center with a multilingual slide show and audio phones. The city's Metro system provides maps in French, German, Japanese, Korean, and Spanish (obtain them in advance by calling *(C)* **202/637-7000**), and the Washington Convention and Tourism Corporation's website, **www.washington.org**, displays visitor information in French, Spanish, and German (not available in printed material, unfortunately).

Legal Aid If you are "pulled over" for a minor infraction (such as speeding), never attempt to pay the fine directly to a police officer; this could be construed as attempted bribery, a much more serious crime. Pay fines by mail, or directly into the hands of the clerk of the court. If accused of a more serious offense, say and do nothing before consulting a lawyer. Here the burden is on the state to prove a person's guilt beyond a reasonable doubt, and everyone has the right to remain silent, whether he or she is suspected of a crime or actually arrested. Once arrested, a person can make one telephone call to a party of his or her choice. Call your embassy or consulate.

Liquor Laws The legal age for purchase and consumption of alcoholic beverages is 21; proof of age is required and often requested at bars, nightclubs, and restaurants, so it's always a good idea to bring ID when you go out. Liquor stores are closed on Sunday. District gourmet grocery stores, mom-and-pop grocery stores, and 7-11 convenience stores often sell beer and wine, even on Sunday.

Do not carry open containers of alcohol in your car or any public area that isn't zoned for alcohol consumption. The police can fine you on the spot. And nothing will ruin your trip faster than getting a citation for DUI (driving under the influence), so don't even think about driving while intoxicated.

Mail Generally found at intersections, mailboxes are blue with a red-and-white stripe and carry the inscription U.S. MAIL. If your mail is addressed to a U.S. destination, don't forget to add the five-digit postal code (or ZIP code), after the two-letter abbreviation of the state to which the mail is addressed. This is essential to prompt delivery.

At press time, domestic postage rates were 20¢ for a postcard and 34¢ for a letter. For international mail, a first-class letter of up to one-half ounce costs 60¢ (46¢ to Canada and 40¢ to Mexico); a first-class postcard costs 50¢ (40¢ to Canada and 35¢ Mexico); and a preprinted postal aerogramme costs 50¢.

Measurements See the chart on the inside front cover of this book for details on converting metric measurements to U.S. equivalents.

Taxes The United States has no value-added tax (VAT) or other indirect tax at the national level. Every state, county, and city has the right to levy its own local tax on all purchases, including hotel and restaurant checks, airline tickets, and so on.

The sales tax on merchandise is 5.75% in the District, 5% in Maryland, and 4.5% in Virginia. The tax on restaurant meals is 10% in the District, 5% in Maryland, and 4.5% in Virginia.

In the District, you pay 14.5% hotel tax. The hotel tax in Maryland varies by county but averages 12%. The hotel tax in Virginia also varies by county, averaging about 9.75%.

Telephone, Telegraph, Telex & Fax The telephone system in the United States is run by private corporations, so rates, especially for long-distance service and operator-assisted calls, can vary widely. Generally, hotel surcharges on long-distance and local calls are astronomical, so you're usually better off using a **public pay telephone,** which you'll find clearly marked in most public buildings and private establishments as well as on the street. Convenience grocery stores and gas stations always have them. Many convenience groceries and packaging services sell **prepaid calling**

cards in denominations up to $50; these can be the least expensive way to call home. Many public phones at airports now accept American Express, MasterCard, and Visa credit cards. **Local calls** made from public pay phones in most locales cost either 25¢ or 35¢. Pay phones do not accept pennies, and few will take anything larger than a quarter.

You may want to look into leasing a cellphone for the duration of your trip.

Most long-distance and international calls can be dialed directly from any phone. **For calls within the United States and to Canada,** dial 1 followed by the area code and the seven-digit number. **For other international calls,** dial 011 followed by the country code, city code, and the telephone number of the person you are calling.

Calls to area codes **800, 888,** and **877** are toll-free. However, calls to numbers in area codes **700** and **900** (chat lines, bulletin boards, "dating" services, and so on) can be very expensive—usually a charge of 95¢ to $3 or more per minute, and they sometimes have minimum charges that can run as high as $15 or more.

For **reversed-charge or collect calls,** and for person-to-person calls, dial 0 (zero, not the letter O) followed by the area code and number you want; an operator will then come on the line, and you should specify that you are calling collect, or person-to-person, or both. If your operator-assisted call is international, ask for the overseas operator.

For **local directory assistance** (information), dial 411; for long-distance information, dial 1, then the appropriate area code and 555-1212.

Telegraph and telex services are provided primarily by Western Union. You can bring your telegram into the nearest Western Union office (there are hundreds across the country) or dictate it over the phone (✆ 800/ 325-6000). You can also telegraph money, or have it telegraphed to you, very quickly over the Western Union system, but this service can cost as much as 15% to 20% of the amount sent.

Most hotels have **fax machines** available for guest use (be sure to ask about the charge to use it). Many hotel rooms are even wired for guests' fax machines. A less expensive way to send and receive faxes may be at stores such as Mail Boxes Etc., a national chain of packing service shops. (Look in the Yellow Pages directory under "Packing Services.")

There are two kinds of telephone directories in the United States. The so-called **White Pages** list private households and business subscribers in alphabetical order. The inside front cover lists emergency numbers for police, fire, ambulance, the Coast Guard, poison-control center, crime-victims hot line, and so on. The first few pages will tell you how to make long-distance and international calls, complete with country codes and area codes. Government numbers are usually printed on blue paper within the White Pages. Printed on yellow paper, the so-called **Yellow Pages** list all local services, businesses, industries, and houses of worship according to activity with an index at the front or back. (Drugstores/pharmacies and restaurants are also listed by geographic location.) The Yellow Pages also include city plans or detailed area maps, postal ZIP codes, and public transportation routes.

Time The continental United States is divided into **four time zones:** eastern standard time (EST), central standard time (CST), mountain standard time (MST), and Pacific standard time (PST). Alaska and Hawaii have their own zones. For example, noon in Washington, D.C. (EST), is 11am in Chicago (CST), 10am in Denver (MST), 9am in Los Angeles (PST), 8am in Anchorage (AST), and 7am in Honolulu (HST).

Daylight saving time is in effect from 1am on the first Sunday in April through 1am on the last Sunday in October, except in Arizona, Hawaii, part of Indiana, and Puerto Rico. Daylight saving time moves the clock 1 hour ahead of standard time. At 1am on the last Sunday in October, clocks are set back 1 hour.

For the correct time, call © 202/844-2525.

Tipping Tipping is so ingrained in the American way of life that the annual income tax of tip-earning service personnel is based on how much they should have received in light of their employers' gross revenues. Accordingly, they may have to pay tax on a tip you didn't actually give them.

Here are some rules of thumb:

In hotels, tip **bellhops** at least $1 per bag ($2–$3 if you have a lot of luggage) and tip the **chamber staff** $1 to $2 per day (more if you've left a disaster area for him or her to clean up, or if you're traveling with kids and/or pets). Tip the **doorman** or **concierge** only if he or she has provided you with some specific service (for example, calling a cab for you or obtaining difficult-to-get theater tickets). Tip the **valet-parking attendant** $1 every time you get your car.

In restaurants, bars, and nightclubs, tip **service staff** 15% to 20% of the check, tip **bartenders** 10% to 15%, tip **checkroom attendants** $1 per garment, and tip **valet-parking attendants** $1 per vehicle. Tip the **doorman** only if he has provided you with some specific service (such as calling a cab for you). Tipping is not expected in cafeterias and fast-food restaurants.

Tip **cab drivers** 15% of the fare.

As for other service personnel, tip **skycaps** at airports at least $1 per bag ($2–$3 if you have a lot of luggage) and tip **hairdressers** and **barbers** 15% to 20%.

Tipping ushers at movies and theaters, and gas-station attendants, is not expected.

Toilets You won't find public toilets or "restrooms" on the streets in most U.S. cities, but they can be found in hotel lobbies, bars, restaurants, museums, department stores, railway and bus stations, and service stations. Large hotels and fast-food restaurants are probably the best bet for good, clean facilities. If possible, avoid the toilets at parks and beaches, which tend to be dirty; some may be unsafe. Restaurants and bars in resorts or heavily visited areas may reserve their restrooms for patrons. Some establishments display a notice indicating this. You can ignore this sign or, better yet, avoid arguments by paying for a cup of coffee or a soft drink, which will qualify you as a patron.

4

Getting to Know
Washington, D.C.

It doesn't take long for a visitor to discover that Washington is really two destinations: the nation's capital and a city in its own right. As you make your way to and from the capital's famous and historic buildings and landmarks, you may come upon a charming neighborhood, an intriguing-looking restaurant, a museum whose name is unfamiliar to you. My advice? Follow your inclination to incorporate D.C. experiences into your capital tour, and you'll leave with a better sense of the city.

Plan on visiting the Capitol, but make sure you get there by Metro. Tour the White House in the morning, but then follow it up with a stroll through the nearby Corcoran Gallery of Art, the city's oldest art museum. Climb to the top of a high landmark (say, the Washington Monument or Washington National Cathedral) and gaze at the city laid out before you, then climb back down and explore one of the neighborhoods you saw from above. Take in the zoo, and then find a sidewalk cafe where you can watch the passersby. Jog on the National Mall. Join a school tour in progress in the National Gallery. Flirt with a fellow browser in Kramerbooks, at Dupont Circle. Stay out until 2am carousing the clubs along Connecticut Avenue. Visit your senator or representative, then hang out in a bar on Capitol Hill, eavesdropping on "Hill" staffers. You get the picture: Do the tourist thing, then go native.

It might help to know how to get around, hmmm? That's what this chapter's about—how to navigate the city.

1 Orientation

On the one hand, Washington, D.C., is an easy place to get to know. It's a small city, where walking will actually get you places, but also with a model public transportation system that travels throughout D.C.'s neighborhoods, and to most tourist spots. A building height restriction creates a landscape in which the lost tourist can get his bearings from tall landmarks—the Capitol, the Washington Monument—that loom into view from different vantage points.

On the other hand, when you do need help, it's hard to find. The city lacks a single, large, comprehensive, and easily found visitor center. Signage to tourist attractions and Metro stations, even street signs, are often missing or frustratingly inadequate. In the wake of September 11, touring procedures at individual sightseeing attractions are constantly changing, as new security precautions take effect, and these changes can be disorienting.

The District is always in the process of improving the situation, it seems. But in the meantime, you can turn to the following small visitors and information centers, helpful publications, and information phone lines.

VISITOR INFORMATION
INFORMATION CENTERS

AT THE AIRPORTS If you are arriving by plane, you may as well think of your airport as a visitor information center, since all three Washington area airports offer all sorts of visitor services. See chapter 2 for specific information about each airport's location, flights, designated place to rendezvous when someone is meeting you at the airport, and transportation options into town.

BALTIMORE–WASHINGTON INTERNATIONAL AIRPORT BWI (© 800/435-9294; www.bwiairport.com) services include two information desks (© 800/435-9294 for information and paging) located on the upper level near the ticket counters and a Maryland Welcome Center (© 410/691-2878) at Pier C on the lower level near the international arrival gates; foreign-language assistance in French, Italian, Spanish, and German (you just pick up one of the white courtesy phones located throughout the airport and request assistance); several locations for buying insurance and exchanging currency (© 410/859-5997); two ATMs near the ticket counters on the upper level; plenty of public phones throughout the airport, including 108 with dataports and some with TDD services and voice-relay phones; many restrooms, restaurants, shops, and bars; a playroom for kids; and a small aviation museum.

Other useful phone numbers are lost and found (© 410/859-7387), police (© 410/859-7040), and parking lots and garage (© 410/859-9230).

RONALD REAGAN WASHINGTON NATIONAL AIRPORT National (© 703/417-8000; www.mwaa.com/national). You'll arrive on the second level; ticket counters are on the third level, baggage claim and ground transportation on the first level. The second, or concourse, level is where you'll get your questions answered: At either end of the main concourse are both a general information desk and a customer service center (© 703/417-3200 or 703/417-3201), where you can exchange currency, purchase insurance, and recharge batteries. Some pay phones equipped with dataports are located throughout terminals B and C. An enclosed passageway connects the main concourse to "historic terminal A," where a **Traveler's Aid** desk operates (© 703/417-3972). You should seek Traveler's Aid assistance if you need foreign-language or crisis help or to page someone; a second Traveler's Aid desk (© 703/417-3974) operates on the baggage-claim level of the main concourse. You'll find ATMs located near the customer-service centers on the concourse level and next to the Traveler's Aid desk on the baggage-claim level. National Airport has more than 100 shops and restaurants.

Other useful phone numbers are lost and found (© 703/417-8560), parking lots and garage (© 703/417-4300), and police (© 703/417-8560).

WASHINGTON DULLES INTERNATIONAL AIRPORT Dulles (© 703/572-2700; www.mwaa.com/Dulles) is the most chaotic airport at which to arrive, with an ongoing major renovation and heavy traffic. Most flights arrive at midfield terminals, where you follow the crowd to the mobile lounges, which you ride for 7 minutes to the main terminal. In time, the plan is for an underground rail system to replace these lounges. The satellite terminals are actually rather attractive and offer decent shopping; the main terminal is another story. You can count on getting help from the **Traveler's Aid** folks (© 703/572-8296, or 703/260-0175 for TDD service). Phone numbers for other help desks include © 703/572-2536 or 703/572-2537 for the international visitors information desk; ☏ **703/572-2963** or 703/572-2969 for general service, foreign currency exchange, and insurance purchases. There are about 40 eateries, 35 retail shops, 7 currency exchanges, and plentiful ATMs, restrooms, stamp vending machines, and phones.

Other useful numbers: police ☏ **703/572-2952;** lost and found ☏ **703/572-2954;** and skycap and wheelchair services ☏ **703/661-8151** or 703/661-6239. Baggage claim areas are at ground level in the main terminal.

AT THE TRAIN STATION
Historic Union Station (☏ **202/371-9441;** www.unionstationdc.com), 50 Massachusetts Ave. NE, offers a visitor a pleasant introduction to the capital. The building is both an architectural beauty and a useful stopping place. Here you'll find a three-level marketplace of shops and restaurants, direct access to Metro service (you'll see signs directing you to the Metro's Red Line station even before you reach the main hall of Union Station), and, when you proceed through the grand arcade straight out through the station's front doors, a stellar view of the Capitol Building.

The central information desk is in the main hall at the front of the building. You'll find ATMs in the gate area, another near the side doors of the building (near the outdoor escalator to the Metro), and on the lower level, at the end of the Food Court. In the gate area are a Thomas Cook Currency Exchange office (☏ **202/371-9220**) across from gate G, and a Traveler's Aid desk (☏ **202/371-1937**) near the McDonald's and gate L. A number of car-rental agencies operate lots here (see "Getting Around," later in this chapter for specific names and phone numbers). For security, lost and found, and other help or information, call the main number, which is ☏ **202/371-9441.**

AROUND TOWN
The Washington, D.C., Visitor Information Center (☏ **202/328-4748;** www.dcvisit.com) is a small visitors center inside the immense Ronald Reagan Building and International Trade Center, at 1300 Pennsylvania Ave. NW. To enter the federal building, you need to show a picture ID. The visitor center lies on the ground floor of the building, a little to your right as you enter from the Wilson Plaza, near the Federal Triangle Metro. It's open Monday through Friday, 8am to 6pm and on Saturday from 11am to 5pm. For other information, see the accompanying sidebar box describing the visitor center and the building in which it resides.

The **White House Visitor Center,** on the first floor of the Herbert Hoover Building, Department of Commerce, 1450 Pennsylvania Ave. NW (between 14th and 15th sts.; ☏ **202/208-1631,** or 202/456-7041 for recorded information), is open daily from 7:30am to 4pm.

The **Smithsonian Information Center,** in the "Castle," 1000 Jefferson Dr. SW (☏ **202/357-2700,** or TTY 202/357-1729; www.si.edu), is open every day but Christmas from 9am to 5:30pm. Call for a free copy of the Smithsonian's "Planning Your Smithsonian Visit," which is full of valuable tips, or stop at the Castle for a copy. A calendar of Smithsonian exhibits and activities for the coming month appears the third Friday of each month in the *Washington Post's* "Weekend" section.

See chapter 7 for more information about these two centers.

The **American Automobile Association (AAA)** has a large central office near the White House, at 701 15th St. NW, Washington, DC 20005-2111 (☏ **202/331-3000**). Hours are 8:30am to 5:30pm Monday through Friday.

PUBLICATIONS

At the airport, pick up a free copy of *Washington Flyer* magazine (www.fly2dc. com), which is handy as a planning tool (see chapter 2).

Washington has two daily newspapers: the *Washington Post* (www. washingtonpost.com) and the *Washington Times* (www.washingtontimes. com). The Friday "Weekend" section of the *Post* is essential for finding out what's going on, recreation-wise. *City Paper,* published every Thursday and available free at downtown shops and restaurants, covers some of the same material but is a better guide to the club and art gallery scene.

Also on newsstands is *Washingtonian,* a monthly magazine with features, often about the "100 Best" this or that (doctors, restaurants, and so on) in Washington; the magazine also offers a calendar of events, restaurant reviews, and profiles of Washingtonians.

HELPFUL TELEPHONE NUMBERS & WEBSITES

- **National Park Service** (© 202/619-7222; www.nps.gov/nacc). You reach a real person and not a recording when you call the phone number with questions about the monuments, the National Mall, national park lands, and activities taking place at these locations. National Park Service information kiosks are located near the Jefferson, Lincoln, Vietnam Veterans, and Korean War memorials, and at several other locations in the city.
- **Dial-A-Park** (© 202/619-7275). This is a recording of information regarding park-service events and attractions.
- **Dial-A-Museum** (© 202/357-2020; www.si.edu). This recording informs you about the locations of the 14 Washington Smithsonian museums and of their daily activities.

CITY LAYOUT

Pierre Charles L'Enfant designed Washington's great sweeping avenues, which are crossed by numbered and lettered streets. At key intersections he placed spacious circles. Although the circles are adorned with monuments, statuary, and fountains, L'Enfant also intended them to serve as strategic command posts to ward off invaders or marauding mobs. (After what had happened in Paris during the French Revolution—and remember, that was current history at the time—his design views were quite practical.)

The U.S. Capitol marks the center of the city, which is divided into quadrants: **northwest (NW), northeast (NE), southwest (SW),** and **southeast (SE).** Almost all the areas of interest to tourists are in the northwest. If you look at your map, you'll see that some addresses—for instance, the corner of G and 7th streets—appear in all quadrants. Hence you must observe the quadrant designation (NW, NE, SW, or SE) when looking for an address.

MAIN ARTERIES & STREETS   From the Capitol, North Capitol Street and South Capitol Street run north and south, respectively. East Capitol Street divides the city north and south. The area west of the Capitol is not a street at all, but the National Mall, which is bounded on the north by Constitution Avenue and on the south by Independence Avenue.

The primary artery of Washington is **Pennsylvania Avenue,** scene of parades, inaugurations, and other splashy events. Pennsylvania runs northwest in a direct line between the Capitol and the White House—if it weren't for the Treasury Building, the president would have a clear view of the Capitol—before continuing on a northwest angle to Georgetown, where it becomes M Street.

Washington, D.C., at a Glance

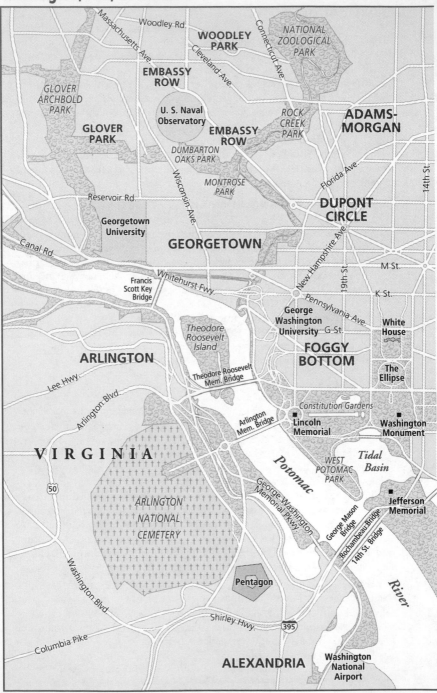

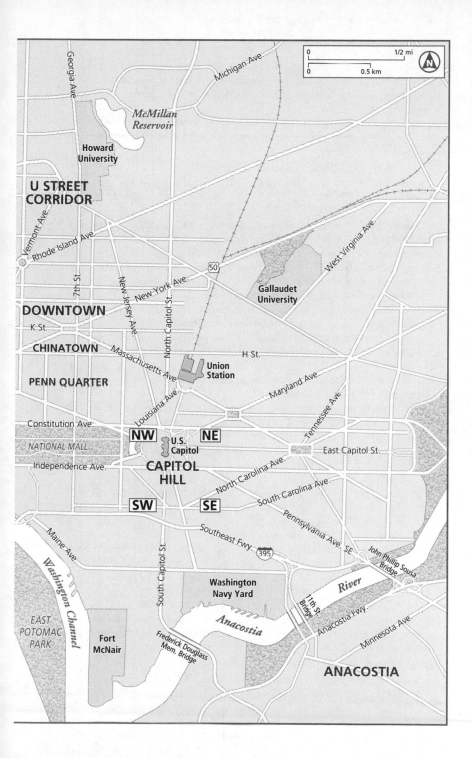

Impressions

If Washington should ever grow to be a great city, the outlook from the Capitol will be unsurpassed in the world. Now at sunset I seemed to look westward far into the heart of the continent from this commanding position.

—Ralph Waldo Emerson

Since May 1995, Pennsylvania Avenue between 15th and 17th streets NW has been closed to cars for security reasons. H Street is now one-way eastbound between 19th and 13th streets NW; I Street is one-way westbound between 11th and 21st streets NW.

Constitution Avenue, paralleled to the south most of the way by Independence Avenue, runs east-west, flanking the Capitol and the Mall. If you hear Washingtonians talk about the "House" side of the Hill, they're referring to the southern half of the Capitol, the side closest to Independence Avenue, and home to Congressional House offices and the House Chamber. Conversely, the Senate side is the northern half of the Capitol, where Senate offices and the Senate Chamber are found, closer to Constitution Avenue.

Washington's longest avenue, **Massachusetts Avenue,** runs parallel to Pennsylvania (a few avenues north). Along the way, you'll find Union Station and then Dupont Circle, which is central to the area known as Embassy Row. Farther out are the Naval Observatory (the vice president's residence is on the premises), Washington National Cathedral, American University, and, eventually, Maryland.

Connecticut Avenue, which runs more directly north (the other avenues run southeast to northwest), starts at Lafayette Square, intersects Dupont Circle, and eventually takes you to the National Zoo, on to the charming residential neighborhood known as Cleveland Park, and into Chevy Chase, Maryland, where you can pick up the Beltway to head out of town. Downtown Connecticut Avenue, with its posh shops and clusters of restaurants, is a good street to stroll.

Wisconsin Avenue originates in Georgetown; its intersection with M Street forms Georgetown's hub. Antiques shops, trendy boutiques, nightclubs, restaurants, and pubs all vie for attention. Wisconsin Avenue basically parallels Connecticut Avenue; one of the few irritating things about the city's transportation system is that the Metro does not connect these two major arteries in the heart of the city. (Buses do, and, of course, you can always walk or take a taxi from one avenue to the other. In 2001, Metro inaugurated its Georgetown Metro Connection shuttle, which travels between Georgetown and the Foggy Bottom, Dupont Circle, and Rosslyn Metro stations, and costs only 50¢, or 25¢ with a Metrorail transfer.) Metrorail's first stop on Wisconsin Avenue is in Tenleytown, a residential area. Follow the avenue north, and you land in the affluent Maryland cities of Chevy Chase and Bethesda.

FINDING AN ADDRESS   Once you understand the city's layout, it's easy to find your way around. As you read this, have a map handy.

Each of the four corners of the District of Columbia is exactly the same distance from the Capitol dome. The White House and most government buildings and important monuments are west of the Capitol (in the northwest and southwest quadrants), as are major hotels and tourist facilities.

Numbered streets run north-south, beginning on either side of the Capitol with First Street. Lettered streets run east-west and are named alphabetically, beginning with A Street. (Don't look for a B, a J, an X, a Y, or a Z Street, however.) After W Street, street names of two syllables continue in alphabetical order, followed by street names of three syllables; the more syllables in a name, the farther the street is from the Capitol.

Avenues, named for U.S. states, run at angles across the grid pattern and often intersect at traffic circles. For example, New Hampshire, Connecticut, and Massachusetts avenues intersect at Dupont Circle.

With this in mind, you can easily find an address. On lettered streets, the address tells you exactly where to go. For instance, 1776 K St. NW is between 17th and 18th streets (the 1st 2 digits of 1776 tell you that) in the northwest quadrant (NW). *Note:* I Street is often written Eye Street to prevent confusion with 1st Street.

To find an address on numbered streets, you'll probably have to use your fingers. For instance, 623 8th St. SE is between F and G streets (the 6th and 7th letters of the alphabet; the 1st digit of 623 tells you that) in the southeast quadrant (SE). One thing to remember: You count B as the second letter of the alphabet even though no B Street exists today (Constitution and Independence aves. were the original B sts.), but since there's no J Street, K becomes the 10th letter, L the 11th, and so on.

THE NEIGHBORHOODS IN BRIEF

Capitol Hill Everyone's heard of "the Hill," the area crowned by the Capitol. When people speak of Capitol Hill, they refer to a large section of town, extending from the western side of the Capitol to the D.C. Armory going east, bounded by H Street to the north and the Southwest Freeway to the south. It contains not only the chief symbol of the nation's capital, but the Supreme Court building, the Library of Congress, the Folger Shakespeare Library, Union Station, and the U.S. Botanic Garden. Much of it is a quiet residential neighborhood of tree-lined streets and Victorian homes. There are a number of restaurants in the vicinity and a smattering of hotels, mostly close to Union Station.

The Mall This lovely, tree-lined stretch of open space between Constitution and Independence avenues, extending for 2½ miles from the Capitol to the Lincoln Memorial, is the hub of tourist attractions. It includes most of the Smithsonian Institution museums and many other visitor attractions. The 300-foot-wide Mall is used by natives as well as tourists—joggers, food vendors, kite-flyers, and picnickers among them. As you can imagine, hotels and restaurants are located on the periphery.

Downtown The area roughly between 7th and 22nd streets NW going east to west, and P Street and Pennsylvania Avenue going north to south, is a mix of the Federal Triangle's government office buildings, K Street (Lawyer's Row), Connecticut Avenue restaurants and shopping, historic hotels, the city's poshest small hotels, **Chinatown,** and the White House. You'll also find the historic **Penn Quarter,** a part of downtown that continues to flourish, since the opening of the MCI Center, trendy restaurants, boutique hotels, and art galleries. The total downtown area takes in so many blocks and attractions that

I've divided discussions of accommodations (chapter 5) and dining (chapter 6) into two sections: "Downtown, 16th Street NW and West," and "Downtown, East of 16th Street NW." 16th Street and the White House form a natural point of separation.

U Street Corridor D.C.'s avant-garde nightlife neighborhood between 12th and 15th streets NW is rising from the ashes of nightclubs and theaters frequented decades ago by African Americans. At two renovated establishments, the Lincoln Theater and the Bohemian Caverns jazz club, where Duke Ellington, Louis Armstrong, and Cab Calloway once performed, patrons today can enjoy performances by leading artists. The corridor offers many nightclubs and several restaurants (see chapter 9 for details). Go here to party, not to sleep—there are no hotels along this stretch.

Adams-Morgan This ever-trendy, multiethnic neighborhood is about the size of a postage stamp, though crammed with boutiques, clubs, and restaurants. Everything is located on either 18th Street NW or Columbia Road NW. You won't find any hotels here, although there are a couple of B&Bs; nearby are the Dupont Circle and Woodley Park neighborhoods, each of which has several hotels (see below). Parking during the day is okay, but forget it at night. But you can easily walk (be alert—the neighborhood is edgy) to Adams-Morgan from the Dupont Circle or Woodley Park Metro stops, or taxi here. Weekend nightlife rivals that of Georgetown and Dupont Circle.

Dupont Circle My favorite part of town, Dupont Circle is fun day or night. It takes its name from the traffic circle minipark, where

Massachusetts, New Hampshire, and Connecticut avenues collide. Washington's famous **Embassy Row** centers on Dupont Circle, and refers to the parade of grand embassy mansions lining Massachusetts Avenue and its side streets. The streets extending out from the circle are lively with all-night bookstores, really good restaurants, wonderful art galleries and art museums, nightspots, movie theaters, and Washingtonians at their loosest. It is also the hub of D.C.'s gay community. There are plenty of hotels.

Foggy Bottom The area west of the White House and southeast of Georgetown, Foggy Bottom was Washington's early industrial center. Its name comes from the foul fumes emitted in those days by a coal depot and gasworks, but its original name, Funkstown (for owner Jacob Funk), is perhaps even worse. There's nothing foul (and not much funky) about the area today. This is a low-key part of town, enlivened by the presence of the Kennedy Center, George Washington University, small and medium-size hotels, and a mix of restaurants on the main drag, Pennsylvania Avenue, and residential side streets.

Georgetown This historic community dates from colonial times. It was a thriving tobacco port long before the District of Columbia was formed, and one of its attractions, the Old Stone House, dates from pre-Revolutionary days. Georgetown action centers on M Street and Wisconsin Avenue NW, where you'll find the luxury Four Seasons hotel and less expensive digs, numerous boutiques (see chapter 8 for details), chic restaurants, and popular pubs (lots of nightlife here). But get off the main drags and see the quiet, tree-lined streets of restored colonial row houses; stroll through the beautiful gardens of Dumbarton Oaks; and check out the C&O Canal. Georgetown is also home to Georgetown University. Note that the neighborhood gets pretty raucous on the weekends, which won't appeal to everyone.

Glover Park Mostly a residential neighborhood, this section of town, just above Georgetown and just south of the Washington National Cathedral, is worth mentioning because of the increasing number of good restaurants opening along its main stretch, Wisconsin Avenue

NW, and because the few hotels here tend to offer lower rates than you might expect for its location. Glover Park sits between the campuses of Georgetown and American universities, so there's a large student presence here.

Woodley Park Home to Washington's largest hotel (the Marriott Wardman Park), Woodley Park boasts the National Zoo, many good restaurants, and some antiques stores. Washingtonians are used to seeing conventioneers wandering the neighborhood's pretty residential streets with their name tags still on.

2 Getting Around

Washington is one of the easiest U.S. cities to navigate. Only New York rivals its comprehensive transportation system; but even with their problems, Washington's clean, efficient subways put the Big Apple's underground nightmare to shame. A complex bus system covers all major D.C. arteries as well, and it's easy to hail a taxi anywhere at any time. But because Washington is of manageable size and marvelous beauty, you may find yourself shunning transportation and choosing to walk.

BY METRORAIL

After 27 years in operation, Metrorail has begun to show its age. This is most apparent at rush hour (Mon–Fri 5:30–9:30am and 3–7pm), when delays are frequent, lines at fare-card machines are long, and trains are overcrowded. An increasing ridership is overloading the system, maintenance problems are cropping up, and the Washington Metropolitan Transit Authority (WMATA; **www.wmata.com**) is struggling just to keep pace, much less prevent future crises. Among the solutions are the addition of new trains and the installation of passenger information display boxes on station platforms reporting the number of minutes before the arrival of the next train and any delays or irregularities.

Though it's true that service has deteriorated, Washingtonians were spoiled to begin with. Stations are cool, clean, and attractive. Cars are air-conditioned and comfortable, fitted with upholstered seats; rides are quiet. You can expect to get

---

Tips Metro Etiquette 101

To avoid risking the ire of commuters, be sure to follow these guidelines: Stand to the right on the escalator so that people in a hurry can get past you on the left; and when you reach the train level, don't puddle at the bottom of the escalator blocking the path of those coming behind you, but move down the platform. Eating, drinking, and smoking are strictly prohibited on the Metro and in stations.

Major Metro Stops

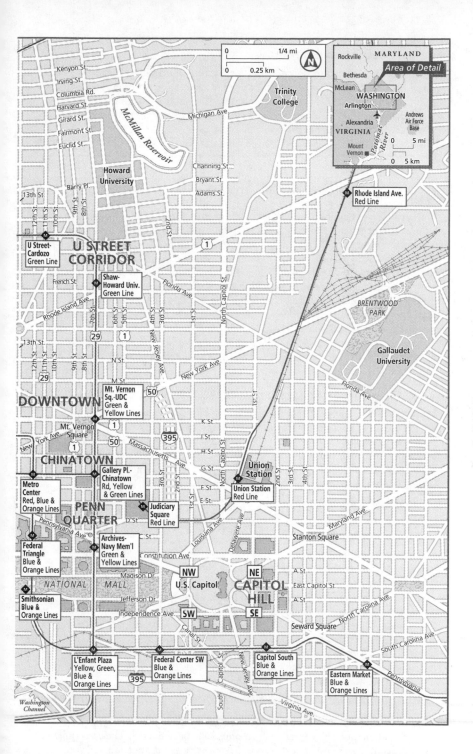

> ⌒ *Tips* **Getting to Georgetown**
>
> Metrorail doesn't go to Georgetown but a special shuttle bus, called the Georgetown Metro Connection, links three Metro stations, Rosslyn, Foggy Bottom, and Dupont Circle, to Georgetown. The shuttle travels between the 3 stations and Georgetown every 10 minutes from 7am to midnight weekdays and until 2am weekends. One-way fares cost 50¢, or 25¢ with a Metrorail transfer.

a seat during off-peak hours (basically weekdays 10am–3pm, weeknights after 7pm, and all day weekends).

Metrorail's system of 83 stations and 103 miles of track includes locations at or near almost every sightseeing attraction and extends to suburban Maryland and northern Virginia. (Construction underway now will add 3 miles and 3 stations by late 2004.) There are five lines in operation—Red, Blue, Orange, Yellow, and Green—with extensions planned for the future. The lines connect at several points, making transfers easy. All but Yellow and Green Line trains stop at Metro Center; all except Red Line trains stop at L'Enfant Plaza; all but Blue and Orange Line trains stop at Gallery Place/Chinatown. See the color map on the inside cover of this book.

Metro stations are indicated by discreet brown columns bearing the station's name and topped by the letter M. Below the M is a colored stripe or stripes indicating the line or lines that stop there. When entering a Metro station for the first time, go to the kiosk and ask the station manager for a free **"Metro System Pocket Guide."** It contains a map of the system, explains how it works, and lists the closest Metro stops to points of interest. The station manager can also answer questions about routing or purchase of fare cards.

To enter or exit a Metro station, you need a computerized **fare card,** available at vending machines near the entrance. The minimum fare to enter the system is $1.10, which pays for rides to and from any point within 7 miles of boarding during nonpeak hours; during peak hours (Mon–Fri 5:30–9:30am and 3–7pm), $1.10 takes you only 3 miles. The machines take nickels, dimes, quarters, and bills from $1 to $20; they can return up to $4.95 in change (coins only). If you plan to take several Metrorail trips during your stay, put more value on the farecard to avoid having to purchase a new card each time you ride. Up to two children under 5 can ride free with a paying passenger. Senior citizens (65 and older) and people with disabilities (with valid proof) ride Metrorail and Metrobus for a reduced fare.

Discount passes, called "One-Day Rail passes," cost $5 per person and allow you unlimited passage for the day, after 9:30am weekdays, and all day on Saturday, Sunday, and holidays. You can buy them at most stations; at WMATA headquarters, 600 5th St. NW (ⓒ **202/637-7000;** www.wmata.com), and at its sales office at Metro Center, 12th and G streets NW; or at retail stores, like Giant or Safeway grocery stores. Other passes are available—check out the website or call the main number for further information.

When you insert your card in the entrance gate, the time and location are recorded on its magnetic tape, and your card is returned. Don't forget to snatch it up and keep it handy; *you have to reinsert your farecard in the exit gate at your destination,* where the fare will automatically be deducted. The card will be returned if there's any value left on it. If you arrive at a destination and your fare card doesn't have enough value, add what's necessary at the Exitfare machines near the exit gate.

Metrorail opens at 5:30am weekdays and 8am Saturday and Sunday, operating until midnight Sunday through Thursday, and until 2am Friday and Saturday. Call ℭ 202/637-7000, or visit www.wmata.com, for holiday hours and for information on Metro routes.

BY BUS

While a 10-year-old can understand the Metrorail system, the **Metrobus** system is considerably more complex. The 12,490 stops on the 1,489-square-mile route (it operates on all major D.C. arteries as well as in the Virginia and Maryland suburbs) are indicated by red, white, and blue signs. However, the signs tell you only what buses pull into a given stop, not where they go. Furthermore, the bus schedules posted at bus stops are often way out of date, so don't rely on them. Instead, for routing information, call ℭ 202/637-7000. Calls are taken Monday through Friday from 6am to 10:30pm, weekends and holidays from 8am to 10:30pm. This is the same number you call to request a free map and time schedule, information about parking in Metrobus fringe lots, and for locations and hours of the places where you can purchase bus tokens.

Base fare in the District is $1.10; bus transfers are free and valid for 2 hours from boarding. There may be additional charges for travel into the Maryland and Virginia suburbs. Bus drivers are not equipped to make change, so be sure to carry exact change or tokens. If you'll be in Washington for a while and plan to use the buses a lot, consider buying a 1-week pass ($10), also available at the Metro Center station and other outlets.

Most buses operate daily almost around the clock. Service is quite frequent on weekdays, especially during peak hours. On weekends and late at night, service is less frequent.

Up to two children under 5 ride free with a paying passenger on Metrobus, and there are reduced fares for senior citizens (ℭ **202/637-7000**) and people with disabilities (ℭ **202/962-1245** or 202/962-1100; see "Tips for Travelers with Special Needs," in chapter 2 for transit information for travelers with disabilities). If you should leave something on a bus, a train, or in a station, call Lost and Found at ℭ **202/962-1195.**

BY CAR

More than half of all visitors to the District arrive by car; but once you get here, my advice is to park your car and either walk or use Metrorail for getting around. If you must drive, be aware that traffic is always thick during the week, parking spaces are often hard to find, and parking lots are ruinously expensive.

Watch out for **traffic circles.** The law states that traffic already in the circle has the right of way. No one pays any attention to this rule, however, which can

---

Tips **Transit Tip**

If you're on the subway and plan to continue your travel via Metrobus, pick up a free transfer at the station when you enter the system (not your destination station). Transfer machines are on the mezzanine levels of most stations. With the transfer, you pay 25¢ to board a bus upon exiting your Metrorail station. There are no bus-to-subway transfers.

be frightening (cars zoom into the circle without a glance at the cars already there). The other thing you will notice is that while some circles are easy to figure out (Dupont Circle, for example), others are nerve-wrackingly confusing (Thomas Circle, where 14th St. NW, Vermont Ave. NW, and Massachusetts Ave. NW come together, is to be avoided at all costs).

Sections of certain streets in Washington become **one-way** during rush hour: Rock Creek Parkway, Canal Road, and 17th Street NW are three examples. Other streets during rush hour change the direction of some of their traffic lanes: Connecticut Avenue NW is the main one. In the morning, traffic in four of its six lanes travels south to downtown, and in late afternoon/early evening, downtown traffic in four of its six lanes heads north; between the hours of 9am and 3:30pm, traffic in either direction keeps to the normally correct side of the yellow line. Lit-up traffic signs alert you to what's going on, but pay attention. Unless a sign is posted prohibiting it, a right-on-red law is in effect.

To keep up with street closings and construction information, grab the day's *Washington Post,* pull out the Metro section, and turn to page 3, where the column "Metro, In Brief" tells you about potential traffic and routing problems in the District and suburban Maryland and Virginia. The paper also publishes a regular column in the Metro section called "Dr. Gridlock," which addresses traffic questions.

CAR RENTALS

Outside of the city, you'll want a car to get to most attractions in Virginia and Maryland. All the major car-rental companies are represented here, including Alamo, Avis, Budget, Dollar, Enterprise, Hertz, National, and Thrifty. Consult appendix B at the back of this book for each rental company's toll-free number and website, and refer to the information about area airports at the beginning of this chapter for phone numbers for each of these companies' airport locations. Within the District, car-rental locations include **Avis,** 1722 M St. NW (© 202/467-6585) and 4400 Connecticut Ave. NW (© 202/686-5149); **Budget,** Union Station (© 202/289-5374); **Enterprise,** 3307 M St. NW (© 202/338-0015); **Hertz,** 901 11th St. NW (© 202/628-6174); **National,** Union Station (© 202/842-7454); and **Thrifty,** 12th and K streets NW (© 202/371-0485).

Car-rental rates can vary even more than airfares. Taking the time to shop around and asking a few key questions could save you hundreds of dollars:

- Are weekend rates lower than weekday rates? Ask if the rate is the same for pickup Friday morning, for instance, as it is for Thursday night.
- Is the weekly rate cheaper than the daily rate? Even if you need the car for only 4 days, it may be cheaper to keep it for 5.
- Does the agency assess a drop-off charge if you don't return the car to the same location where you picked it up? Is it cheaper to pick up the car at the airport or at a downtown location?
- Are special promotional rates available? If you see an advertised price in your local newspaper, be sure to ask for that specific rate; otherwise, you may be charged the standard cost. Terms change constantly.
- Are discounts available for members of AARP, AAA, frequent-flyer programs, or trade unions?
- How much tax will be added to the rental bill? Local tax? State use tax? Local taxes and surcharges can vary from location to location, even within the same car company, which can add quite a bit to your costs.

- What is the cost of adding an additional driver's name to the contract?
- How many free miles are included in the price? Free mileage is often negotiable, depending on the length of your rental.

Some companies offer "refueling packages," in which you pay for an entire tank of gas up front. The price is usually fairly competitive with local gas prices, but you don't get credit for any gas remaining in the tank. If a stop at a gas station on the way to the airport will make you miss your plane, then by all means take advantage of the fuel purchase option. Otherwise, skip it.

As for **insurance,** see chapter 2.

BY TAXI

At the time of this writing, District cabs continue to operate on a zone system instead of using meters, and the cabbies hope to keep it that way. By law, basic rates are posted in each cab. If you take a trip from one point to another within the same zone, you pay just $5 (during non-rush hour) regardless of the distance traveled. So it would cost you $5 to travel a few blocks from the U.S. Capitol to the National Museum of American History, but the same $5 could take you from the Capitol all the way to Dupont Circle. They're both in Zone 1, as are most other tourist attractions: the White House, most of the Smithsonian, the Washington Monument, the FBI, the National Archives, the Supreme Court, the Library of Congress, the Bureau of Engraving and Printing, the Old Post Office, and Ford's Theatre. If your trip takes you into a second zone, the price is $8.40, $9.60 for a third zone, $10.10 for a fourth, and so on. These rates are based on the assumption that you are hailing a cab. If you telephone for a cab, you will be charged an additional $1.50. During rush hour, between 7 and 9:30am and 4 and 6:30pm weekdays, you pay a surcharge of $1 per trip, plus a surcharge of $1 when you telephone for a cab, which brings that surcharge to $2.50.

Other charges might apply, as well: There's a $1.50 charge for each additional passenger after the first, so a $5 Zone 1 fare can become $10.50 for a family of four (though 1 child under 5 can ride free). Surcharges are also added for luggage (from 50¢ to $2 per piece, depending on size). Try **Diamond Cab Company** (© **202/387-6200**), **Yellow Cab** (© **202/544-1212**), or **Capitol Cab** (© **202/546-2400**).

The zone system is not used when your destination is an out-of-District address (such as an airport); in that case, the fare is based on mileage—$2.65 for the first half-mile or part thereof and 80¢ for each additional half-mile or part. You can call © **202/331-1671** to find out the rate between any point in D.C. and an address in Virginia or Maryland. Call © **202/645-6018** to inquire about fares within the District.

It's generally easy to hail a taxi, although even taxis driven by black cabbies often ignore African Americans to pick up white passengers. Unique to the city is the practice of allowing drivers to pick up as many passengers as they can comfortably fit, so expect to share (unrelated parties pay the same as they would if they were not sharing). To register a complaint, note the cab driver's name and cab number and call © **202/645-6010.** You will be asked to file a written complaint either by fax (© **202/889-3604**) or mail (Commendations/Complaints, District of Columbia Taxicab Commission, 2041 Martin Luther King Jr. Ave. SE, Room 204, Washington, DC 20020).

FAST FACTS: **Washington, D.C.**

American Express There's an American Express Travel Service office at 1150 Connecticut Ave. NW (✆ **202/457-1300**) and another in upper northwest Washington at 5300 Wisconsin Ave. NW, in the Mazza Gallerie (✆ **202/362-4000**).

Area Codes Within the District of Columbia, it's 202. In suburban Virginia, it's 703. In suburban Maryland, it's 301. You must use the area code when dialing any number, even local calls within the District or to nearby Maryland or Virginia suburbs.

Business Hours See "Fast Facts: For the International Traveler," chapter 3.

Car Rentals See section 2, "Getting Around," earlier in this chapter.

Climate See section 3, "When to Go," in chapter 2.

Congresspersons To locate a senator or congressional representative, call the Capitol switchboard (✆ **202/225-3121**). Point your Web browser to www.senate.gov and www.house.gov to contact individual senators and congressional representatives by e-mail, find out what bills are being worked on, the calendar for the day, and more.

Driving Rules See section 2, "Getting Around," earlier in this chapter.

Drugstores **CVS,** Washington's major drugstore chain (with more than 40 stores), has two convenient 24-hour locations: 14th Street and Thomas Circle NW, at Vermont Avenue (✆ **202/628-0720**), and at Dupont Circle (✆ **202/785-1466**), both with round-the-clock pharmacies. Check your phone book for other convenient locations.

Emergencies See "Fast Facts: For the International Traveler," in chapter 3.

Hospitals In case of a life-threatening emergency, call ✆ **911.** If you don't require immediate ambulance transportation but still need emergency-room treatment, call one of the following hospitals (and be sure to get directions): **Children's Hospital National Medical Center,** 111 Michigan Ave. NW ✆ **202/884-5000); George Washington University Hospital,** 23rd St. NW at Washington Circle ✆ **202/715-4000; Georgetown University Medical Center,** 3800 Reservoir Rd. NW ✆ **202/784-2000;** or **Howard University Hospital,** 2041 Georgia Ave. NW (✆ **202/865-6100**).

Hot Lines To reach a 24-hour poison-control hot line, call ✆ **800/222-1222;** to reach a 24-hour crisis line, call ✆ **202/561-7000;** and to reach the drug and alcohol abuse hot line, which operates from 8am to midnight daily, call ✆ **888/294-3572.**

Internet Access You have free Internet access at the **Martin Luther King Jr. Memorial Library,** 901 G St. NW (✆ **202/727-1111;** www.dclibrary.org), where you choose either a computer limited to 15 minutes' use or one limited to 1 hour's use; these are in high demand. Or try **Cyberstop Cafe,** 1513 17th St. NW (✆ **202/234-2470**), where you can get a bite to eat while you surf one of nine computers for $6 per half hour, $8 per hour; the cafe is open from 7am to midnight daily. In Dupont Circle, the bookstore **Kramerbooks and Afterwords,** 1517 Connecticut Ave. NW (✆ **202/387-1400**), has one computer available for free Internet access, 15 minute-limit.

Legal Aid See "Fast Facts: For the International Traveler," in chapter 3.

Liquor Laws See "Fast Facts: For the International Traveler," in chapter 3.

Maps Free city maps are often available at hotels and throughout town at tourist attractions. You can also contact the **Washington, D.C. Convention and Tourism Corporation,** 1212 New York Ave. NW, Washington, DC 20005 (© **202/789-7000**).

Newspapers & Magazines See section 1 "Visitor Information," earlier in this chapter.

Police In an emergency, dial © **911.** For a nonemergency, call © **202/ 727-1010.**

Safety See "Insurance, Health & Safety," in chapter 2.

Taxes See "Fast Facts: For the International Traveler," in chapter 3.

Time See "Fast Facts: For the International Traveler," in chapter 3.

Weather Call © **202/936-1212.**

5

Where to Stay

Most of Washington's 100-plus hotels center on the downtown and Dupont Circle neighborhoods, with a handful scattered in Georgetown, on Capitol Hill, and northward on Connecticut Avenue. Each of these communities has a distinct personality, which you should consider in choosing a location in which to base yourself. See the "Neighborhoods in Brief" section of chapter 4 and peruse the following descriptions to help you decide which location best suits you.

If proximity to the capital's major attractions is most important to you, consider hotels near Capitol Hill and the National Mall. Convenient for sightseeing and in the thick of things during the day, these hotels may feel isolated at night and on weekends, when Hill staff and office workers go home. With the exception of Capitol Hill Suites, the hotels are not located near residential areas, and restaurants and shops are few.

To take the pulse of the city as it goes about its business, stay in a downtown hotel. This is also where you should bunk if you want to be able to walk to good restaurants, bars, and nightclubs. Divided into two sections here, between 7th and 16th streets NW ("Downtown, East of 16th Street NW") and between 16th and 22nd streets NW ("Downtown, 16th Street NW & West"), Washington's downtown is bustling day and night during the week; it's quieter on weekends, but still fairly lively. Hotels in the downtown segment east of 16th Street are close to theaters; properties located on or near Pennsylvania Avenue, like the Willard and the Hotel Washington, are within walking distance of Smithsonian museums and the White House. Downtown hotels west of 16th Street are also within a stroll of the White House, as well as some of the smaller museums, like the National Geographic, Decatur House, and the Renwick and Corcoran galleries.

If you prefer the feel of being in a residential neighborhood, look to hotels in the Dupont Circle and Woodley Park areas. For a taste of campus life, you might choose lodging in Foggy Bottom; the accommodations near Pennsylvania Avenue and Washington Circle border George Washington University's widening campus. And if you're a serious shopper, Georgetown should be your top choice, with Dupont Circle as your second pick.

Within each neighborhood heading, this chapter further organizes hotels by rate categories, based on their lowest high-season rates for double rooms: Very Expensive (from about $250 and up), Expensive (from about $185), Moderate (from about $120), and Inexpensive (anything under $100). But these categories are intended as a general guideline only— rates can rise and fall dramatically, depending on how busy the hotel is. It's often possible to obtain a special package or a better rate; see "Tips for Saving on Your Hotel Room," in chapter 2 for specific information.

And if you suffer from information overload and would rather someone else do the research and bargaining, you can always turn to a national reservations service (listed in chapter 2's "Tips for Saving") or to one of the following reputable—and free!—local reservations services:

- **Capitol Reservations** (© 800/VISIT-DC or 202/452-1270; www.hotelsdc.com) will find you a hotel that meets your specific requirements and is within your price range. The 19-year-old service works with about 100 area hotels, all of which have been screened for cleanliness, safe locations, and other desirability factors; you can check rates and book online.
- **Washington D.C. Accommodations** (© 800/554-2220 or 202/289-2220; www.dcaccommodations.com) has been in business for 18 years, and, in addition to finding lodgings, can advise you about transportation and general tourist information and even work out itineraries.
- **U.S.A. Groups** (© 800/872-4777) can help you plan a meeting, convention, or other group function requiring 10 rooms or more; it's a free service representing

hotel rooms at almost every hotel in the District and the suburban Virginia-Maryland region, in all price categories.

- **Bed and Breakfast League/Sweet Dreams and Toast** (© 202/363-7767; bedandbreakfast-washington dc@erols.com), represents more than 60 B&Bs in the District, from private homes, to apartments, to small inns. The accommodations are screened and guest reports are given serious consideration. All listings are convenient to public transportation. There's a 2-night minimum-stay requirement and a booking fee of $10 (per reservation). American Express, Diners Club, MasterCard, and Visa are accepted.
- **Bed & Breakfast Accommodations Ltd.** (© 202/328-3510; www.bnbaccom.com), in business since 1978, works with more than 80 homes, inns, guesthouses, and unhosted furnished apartments to find visitors lodging. American Express, Diners Club, MasterCard, Visa, and Discover are accepted.

1 Capitol Hill/The Mall

VERY EXPENSIVE

Hotel George ★★ Until the boutique hotels Rouge and Topaz came along (see reviews on p. 98 and p. 104 respectively) the Hotel George was Washington's hippest place to stay. Well, it's still pretty rad. The hotel's facade is of stainless steel, limestone, and glass; the lobby is done in a sleek white, splashed with red, blue, and black furnishings; posters throughout the hotel depict a modern-day George Washington, sans wig; and clientele tends toward celebs (everyone from Christina Aguilera to Muhammad Ali). The oversize guest rooms sport a minimalist look, all creamy white and modern. Fluffy vanilla-colored comforters rest on oversize beds; slabs of granite top the desks and bathroom counters; and nature sounds (of the ocean, forest, and wind) emanate from the stereo CD/clock radios. A speaker in the spacious, mirrored, marble bathroom broadcasts TV sounds from the other room; other amenities include cordless phones, umbrellas, and terry-cloth robes. All rooms have high-speed Internet access; eighth-floor rooms also have fax machines, at no extra cost. The hotel has three one-bedroom suites.

Contributing to the hotel's hipness is the presence of its restaurant, **Bistro Bis,** which serves (duh) French bistro food to hungry lobbyists and those they are lobbying. (Capitol Hill is a block away.) See chapter 6 for a full review.

Washington, D.C., Accommodations

EMBASSY ROW

U.S. Naval Observatory

See "Adams-Morgan, Dupont Circle & West End Accommodations" Map

DUMBARTON OAKS PARK

MONTROSE PARK

ROCK CREEK PARK

NATIONAL ZOOLOGICAL PARK

ADAMS-MORGAN

Columbia Heights Green Line

1

2 Woodley Park-Zoo/ Adams Morgan Red Line

3

4

5

6

7 **8**

9

Georgetown University

GEORGETOWN

17

19 **20**

18

21

16 **15**

14

13

12

11

10 Dupont Circle Red Line

DUPONT CIRCLE

Scott Circle

Logan Circle

Thomas Circle

25 **26**

27 **28**

29

30 Farragut North Red Line

24

31

32 McPherson Square Blue & Orange Lines

22 Foggy Bottom-GWU Blue & Orange Lines

23

Washington Circle

George Washington University

Farragut Square

Farragut West Blue & Orange Lines

33

34

35

36 **37**

38

White House

Theodore Roosevelt Island

Kennedy Center

FOGGY BOTTOM

Rosslyn Blue & Orange Lines

VIRGINIA

Arlington Cemetery Blue Line

ARLINGTON NATIONAL CEMETERY

Lincoln Memorial

WEST POTOMAC PARK

Washington Monument

Tidal Basin

Jefferson Memorial

Potomac

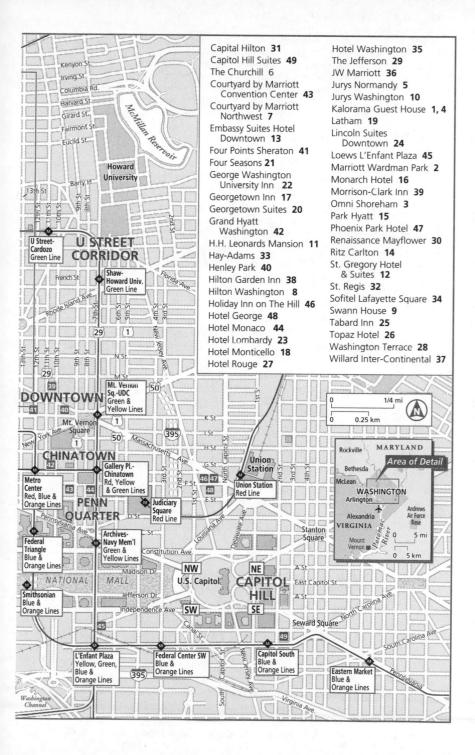

Capital Hilton **31**
Capitol Hill Suites **49**
The Churchill **6**
Courtyard by Marriott
  Convention Center **43**
Courtyard by Marriott
  Northwest **7**
Embassy Suites Hotel
  Downtown **13**
Four Points Sheraton **41**
Four Seasons **21**
George Washington
  University Inn **22**
Georgetown Inn **17**
Georgetown Suites **20**
Grand Hyatt
  Washington **42**
H.H. Leonards Mansion **11**
Hay-Adams **33**
Henley Park **40**
Hilton Garden Inn **38**
Hilton Washington **8**
Holiday Inn on The Hill **46**
Hotel George **48**
Hotel Monaco **44**
Hotel Lombardy **23**
Hotel Monticello **18**
Hotel Rouge **27**

Hotel Washington **35**
The Jefferson **29**
JW Marriott **36**
Jurys Normandy **5**
Jurys Washington **10**
Kalorama Guest House **1, 4**
Latham **19**
Lincoln Suites
  Downtown **24**
Loews L'Enfant Plaza **45**
Marriott Wardman Park **2**
Monarch Hotel **16**
Morrison-Clark Inn **39**
Omni Shoreham **3**
Park Hyatt **15**
Phoenix Park Hotel **47**
Renaissance Mayflower **30**
Ritz Carlton **14**
St. Gregory Hotel
  & Suites **12**
St. Regis **32**
Sofitel Lafayette Square **34**
Swann House **9**
Tabard Inn **25**
Topaz Hotel **26**
Washington Terrace **28**
Willard Inter-Continental **37**

15 E St. NW (at N. Capitol St.), Washington, DC 20001. ℂ 800/576-8331 or 202/347-4200. Fax 202/347-4213. www.hotelgeorge.com. 139 units. Weekdays $265–$350 double; weekends from $149 double; $950 suite. Ask about seasonal and corporate rates. Extra person $25. Children under 16 stay free in parents' room. AE, DC, DISC, MC, V. Parking $24. Metro: Union Station. **Amenities:** Restaurant (French bistro); small 24-hr. fitness center with steam rooms; cigar-friendly billiard room; 24-hr. concierge; business services; room service (7am–11pm); same-day laundry/dry cleaning; VCR rentals; 4 rooms for guests with disabilities. In room: A/C, TV w/pay movies, 2-line phone w/dataport, minibar, coffeemaker, hair dryer, iron, safe.

EXPENSIVE

Loews L'Enfant Plaza 𝒦   This is the hotel closest to the Smithsonian museums. It lies within a large complex (L'Enfant Plaza) of government office buildings, just off of Independence Avenue. In fact, the hotel building is primarily office space, with the hotel lobby on the first floor, and guest rooms occupying only the 11th, 12th, 14th, and 15th floors. Because of its setting, the hotel and the entire plaza, inside and out, bustle with the comings and goings of office workers. Conversely, at night, the complex shuts down, and you may feel isolated. This is not a place to stroll after dark. Most people visit a more lively part of town in the evening (easy to do, since the hotel has direct access to the Metro, and cabs are always waiting at the front door).

Because of its proximity to the Smithsonian and to Capitol Hill, the Loews L'Enfant Plaza is very popular, often booking solid in April and at other peak times. For best rates, call directly to the hotel way in advance.

Because the hotel is located right next to the freeway, you may hear sounds of traffic. Try to get an "outside" room on the 14th or 15th floors (although you may pay a little more), since these rooms distance you farther from traffic noise and have balconies and views. Rooms, generally, are of standard size and unremarkable decor. Bathrooms are small, but each includes a tiny TV, phone, and scale. Club rooms are on the 15th floor and are a little nicer, with king beds, a small sitting area, and extra amenities.

The Loews chain is very pet friendly and this location is no exception: Perks include pet place mats, toys and treats, and information about nearby dog-walking routes, veterinarians, and the availability of pet-walking and pet-sitting services.

480 L'Enfant Plaza SW (off Independence Ave.), Washington, DC 20024. ℂ 800/23-LOEWS or 202/484-1000. Fax 202/646-4456. www.loewshotels.com. 370 units. Weekdays $199–$329 double; weekends $129–$199 double; from $395 suite. Extra person $25. Children under 18 stay free in parents' room. AE, DC, DISC, MC, V. Parking $22. Metro: L'Enfant Plaza. Pets welcomed and pampered. **Amenities:** Restaurant (casual American); lobby lounge; pub; pool snack bar (seasonal); rooftop pool; full-service fitness center with Cybex equipment, personal trainers, and aerobics room; children's program (welcome kits, child-proof kits, and supply of games and videos); concierge (7am–9:30pm); business center; shopping arcade; 24-hr. room service; same-day laundry/dry cleaning; executive rooms; 8 rooms for guests with disabilities. In room: A/C, TV w/pay movies, 2-line phone w/dataport, minibar, fridge, coffeemaker, hair dryer, iron, safe.

Phoenix Park Hotel 𝒦   The Phoenix Park is one of a cluster of hotels across from Union Station and 2 blocks from the Capitol. It's distinguished by its popular and authentic Irish pub, The Dubliner, which attempts to set the tone for the entire property. Because of this well-worn, wood-paneled pub, which offers Irish fare, ale, and nightly entertainment (p. 261), the hotel attracts numerous sons and daughters of Erin, stages a number of Ireland-related events in its Connemara marble-accented ballroom, and generally conveys an air of Irish hospitality. The rooms are attractive but rather cramped with furnishings. Reserve a "superior" room (only about $10 more than a standard) to stay in a room with a view (Union Station, Smithsonian museums, or congressional buildings). Or book a one- or two-story suite, some of which have balconies, working fireplaces, and spiral staircases. The last major renovation was in 1997, when marble was installed in all the bathrooms; more recently, bathroom scales and heat lamps were added. Irish decorative accents include linens and bathrobes, artwork, toiletries, and carpeting.

520 N. Capitol St. NW (at Massachusetts Ave.), Washington, DC 20001. © **800/824-5419** or 202/638-6900. Fax 202/393-3236. www.phoenixparkhotel.com. 150 units. Weekdays $199–$289 double; weekends $119–$189 double; $299–$699 suite. Extra person $20. Children under 16 stay free in parents' room. AE, DC, DISC, MC, V. Valet parking $21, self-parking $10. Metro: Union Station. **Amenities:** Irish pub; small exercise room; concierge; secretarial services; room service (7am–11pm); same-day dry cleaning; 7 rooms for guest with disabilities. *In room:* A/C, TV w/pay movies, 2-line phone w/dataport, minibar, coffeemaker, hair dryer, iron, robe, umbrella.

MODERATE

Capitol Hill Suites ✦ Hotels frequently undergo refurbishments, though the changes may be barely noticeable to guests. But the $3 million renovation completed at this well-run, all-suite property in spring 2000 produced remarkable results. The old, outmoded decor has been replaced with panache. Bedroom walls are painted cobalt blue, heavy velvet drapes keep out morning sun, lamps and mirrors are from Pottery Barn, desks are long, desk chairs are ergonomically correct, and beds are firm. Bathrooms are tiny, but sparkling. The lobby, which features an enclosed fireplace, leather chairs, and an antique credenza where

---

⟮Kids⟯ Family-Friendly Hotels

Embassy Suites Hotel Downtown (p. 105)   You're close to both a Red line and a Blue line Metro station (the zoo is on the Red line; the Smithsonian museums are on the Blue line) and within walking distance of Georgetown. Your kids can sleep on the pullout sofa in the separate living room. You've got some kitchen facilities, but you might not use them, since the complimentary breakfast in the atrium is unbelievable. And there's an indoor pool and a free game room.

Holiday Inn on the Hill (p. 88)   Children receive a free toy and a book on arrival during summer promotions. Kids 12 and under eat free in the restaurant with an adult dining. The hotel is near Union Station, Capitol Hill, and the Mall and Smithsonian museums, and the kitchen will pack a picnic for you to enjoy on the Mall. Connecting rooms are available. Kids ages 4 to 14 can participate in the hotel's Discovery Zone program of activities 4 to 10pm daily in summer ($5 per child). The hotel has a rooftop outdoor pool.

Omni Shoreham (p. 114)   Adjacent to Rock Creek Park, the Omni is also within walking distance of the zoo and Metro and is equipped with a large outdoor pool and kiddie pool. The hotel gives children a goodie bag on check-in and the concierge has a supply of board games at the ready (no charge to borrow, just remember to return).

Hilton Washington (p. 100)   A large heated outdoor pool, a wading pool, three tennis courts, shuffleboard, and a goodie bag at check-in—what more does a kid need?

self-serve coffee is laid out, is inviting enough for lingering. (Sit here long enough and you might spy a congressman or senator—a number of members reserve suites for 100 days at a time.)

The location is another plus: Capitol Hill Suites is the only hotel truly *on* the Hill (on the House side of the Capitol). It stands on a residential street across from the Library of Congress, a short walk from the Capitol and Mall attractions, a food market, and more than 20 restaurants (many of which deliver to the hotel).

The term *suite* denotes the fact that every unit has a kitchenette with coffeemaker, toaster oven, microwave, refrigerator, flatware, and glassware. Most units are efficiencies, with the kitchenette, bed, and sofa all in the same room. The best choices are one-bedroom units, in which the kitchenette and living room are separate from the bedroom. A third option is a "studio double," with two queen beds and a kitchenette, but no living room area. Some rooms in each category have pullout sofas.

Guests have privileges to dine at the Capitol Hill Club, a members-only club for Republicans, and can charge their meals and drinks to their hotel bill.

200 C St. SE (at 2nd St.), Washington, DC 20003. (C) **800/424-9165** or 202/543-6000. Fax 202/547-2608. www.capitolhillsuites.com. 152 units. $119–$239 double. Weekend and long-term rates may be available. Extra person $22. Rates include continental breakfast. Children under 18 stay free in parents' room. AE, DC, DISC, MC, V. Valet parking $20. Metro: Capitol South. **Amenities:** Breakfast room, dining privileges at Capitol Hill Club; free use of nearby Washington Sports and Health Club; business services; coin-op washer/dryers; same-day laundry/dry cleaning; 10 rooms for visitors with disabilities, all with roll-in showers. *In room:* A/C, TV w/pay movies, 2-line phone w/dataport, refrigerator, coffeemaker, hair dryer, iron.

INEXPENSIVE

Holiday Inn on the Hill *(Kids (Value*   Business travelers without bottomless expense accounts and families on a budget will likely find this hotel's rates the most reasonable on Capitol Hill. Several labor union headquarters are nearby, making the hotel a popular choice among the "labor" folks doing business with one of them. Amenities, like the free 24-hour fitness center, seasonal (outdoor) pool, and the "kids 12 and under eat free" restaurant policy, increase the value of a stay here. Best of all for families is the Discovery Zone—available from 4 to 10pm daily in summer for a charge of $5 per kid per day—a supervised program offering fun but educational activities for children ages 4 to 14. (See the Holiday Inn entry in the "Family-Friendly Hotels" box on p. 87 for more details on their perks for kids.)

A major renovation completed in 1999 added new bedspreads, drapes, shower curtains, 25-inch TVs with Nintendo, and individually controlled thermostats. The staff aims to make you feel at home here. Rooms are standard size, though bathrooms are larger than expected, with a small vanity ledge just outside the bathroom for overflow counter space.

To get the best deals and perks, ask about summer promotions, the "Great Rates" package, and the hotel's "Priority Club" frequent guest membership.

415 New Jersey Ave. NW (between D and E sts.). (C) **800/638-1116** or 202/638-1616. Fax 202/638-0707. www.basshotels.com/was-onthehill. 343 units. $109–$225 double (Mon and Tues are the most expensive days). Extra person $20. Children under 19 stay free in parents' room. Ask about special promotions and packages. AE, DC, DISC, MC, V. Parking $18. Metro: Union Station. **Amenities:** Restaurant (American), where kids ages 12 and under eat free with an adult; bar; outdoor (unheated) rooftop pool; 24-hr. fitness room; children's program and game room in summer; concierge; business center; room service (6am–11pm); same-day laundry/dry cleaning service; large ballroom; ATM in the lobby; 8 rooms for guests with disabilities, including 4 with roll-in showers. *In room:* A/C, TV w/pay movies, 2-line phone w/dataport, coffeemaker, hair dryer, iron.

2 Downtown, East of 16th Street NW

VERY EXPENSIVE

Grand Hyatt Washington ✦ Hotel as circus—that's the Grand Hyatt. There's always something going on in the vast lobby, whose atrium is 12 stories high and enclosed by a glass, mansard-style roof. A baby grand piano floats on its own island in the 7,000-square-foot "lagoon"; waterfalls, catwalks, 22-foot-high trees, and an array of bars and restaurants on the periphery will keep you permanently entertained. Should you get bored, head to the nearby nightspots and restaurants, or hop on the Metro, to which the Hyatt has direct access. The hotel is across from the Convention Center, between Capitol Hill and the White House, and 2 blocks from the MCI Center.

Guest rooms underwent a renovation in 2001, replacing furniture and artwork, and overhauling bathrooms, to give each unit an updated, clean, modern look. Suites were redone in 2000 to individualize designs along certain themes, such as "The Orient."

Among the potpourri of special plans and packages available is one for business travelers: Pay an extra $20 and you stay in an eighth- or ninth-floor room equipped with a large desk, fax machine, computer hookup, and coffeemaker; have access to printers and other office supplies on the floor; and are entitled to complimentary continental breakfast and access to the health club. Always ask about seasonal and special offers, and check the website for the best deals.

1000 H St. NW, Washington, DC 20001. ℂ 800/233-1234 or 202/582-1234. Fax 202/637-4781. www. washington.grand.hyatt.com. 900 units. Weekdays $350 double; weekends $125–$139 double; $300–$1,700 suite. Extra person $25. Children under 18 stay free in parents' room. Ask about special promotions and packages. AE, DC, DISC, MC, V. Valet parking $26; self-parking $20. Metro: Metro Center. **Amenities:** 3 restaurants (Italian/Asian, continental, deli); 3 bars; health club with whirlpool, lap pool, steam and sauna rooms, aerobics, and spa services (hotel guests pay $10 for club use); concierge; courtesy car available on a first-come, first-served basis to nearby destinations; business center; room service (6am–1am); in-room and health-club massage; same-day dry cleaning; concierge-level rooms; 22 rooms for guests with disabilities, some with roll-in showers. *In room:* A/C, TV w/pay movies, 2-line phone w/dataports, minibar, coffeemaker, hair dryer, iron.

Hotel Monaco Washington, DC ✦✦✦ You may mistake this hotel for a museum. The Monaco occupies a four-story, all marble mid-19th-century building, half of which was designed by Robert Mills, the architect for the Washington Monument, the other half designed by Thomas Walter, one of the architects for the U.S. Capitol. The two halves connect seamlessly, enclosing a large interior, landscaped courtyard—picture a square within a square. (As a matter of fact, this is the same design as that of the two Smithsonian museums directly across the street from the Monaco; the Smithsonian American Art Museum and the National Portrait Gallery, both closed for renovations until 2005, join to form a central courtyard, too.) The hotel takes up an entire block, between 7th and 8th streets, and E and F streets. Superlatives are in order: The hotel is truly magnificent.

Constructed originally as the General Post Office, and later used to house the Tariff Commission, the building is a designated National Historic Landmark, and it remains a federal building. The Kimpton Hotel and Restaurant Group has leased the building for 60 years, performing an extensive renovation, which retains many original features, as required by its historic status, that blend creatively with the hotel's humming, hip, upscale decor. So you've got 19th-century columns uplit by Italian chrome and alabaster torchieres in the lobby, grand spiral staircases at each of the four corners, and high vaulted ceilings along corridors lit with whimsical, lantern-like red lamps.

The spacious guest rooms, similarly, combine historic and hip. Their vaulted ceilings are high (12 ft.–18 ft.) and windows are long, hung with charcoal and white patterned drapes. Each guest room has a removable bathroom module (its modular status is only apparent when you stand in your guest room and note that the bathroom ceiling lies a couple of feet below the overall ceiling of the room). A stand-alone headboard, upholstered in a funky black and white bull's-eye pattern, also screens a door behind the bed, which, in the building's former life, led to the next office. Eclectic furnishings include neoclassic armoires and three-legged desks. A color scheme successfully marries creamy yellow walls with periwinkle blue lounge chairs, with orange damask pillows. Interior rooms overlook the courtyard and the restaurant; you'll see the charming arched passageway through which horse and carriage came a century ago. Exterior rooms view the MCI Center and the Smithsonian's National Portrait Gallery on the north side, and downtown sights on the south side. This is a great location.

Need more? The Hotel Monaco gives you a complimentary goldfish at check-in; offers specially designed "Tall Rooms" with 18-foot-high ceilings, 96-inch-long beds, and raised shower heads, for tall guests. Its restaurant, **Poste,** is gaining attention. Though it only just opened in summer 2002, the Hotel Monaco is already a winner.

700 F St. NW (at 7th St.), Washington, DC 20004. © 877/202-5411 or 202/628-7177. Fax 202/628-7277. www.monaco-dc.com. 184 units. Weekdays $295 double; weekends $199 double; suites from $825 weekdays, $469 weekends. Extra person $20. Children under 18 stay free in parents' room. Rates include complimentary Starbucks coffee in morning and wine receptions in evening. AE, DC, DISC, MC, V. Parking $27. Pets allowed with $50 deposit: gets VIP treatment, with its own registration card at check-in, maps of neighborhood fire hydrants and parks, gourmet puppy and kitty treats. Metro: Gallery Place. **Amenities:** Restaurant (modern American); bar; spacious fitness center with flat screen TVs; 24-hr. concierge; full-service business center; 24-hr. room service; same-day laundry/dry cleaning; 9 rooms for guests with disabilities, 4 with roll-in showers. *In room:* A/C, TV w/pay movies and Nintendo, CD player, 2-line phones w/high-speed Internet access and dataports, minibar, hair dryer, iron, safe, robes.

JW Marriott Hotel on Pennsylvania Avenue *⟨⟩*   The best thing about this hotel is its prime location on Pennsylvania Avenue. It's adjacent to the National Theatre, 1 block from the Warner Theater, 2 blocks from the White House, and within walking distance of the Washington Monument, the Smithsonian museums, and lots of restaurants. The best rooms on the 7th to 12th, 14th, and 15th floors overlook Pennsylvania Avenue and the monuments (floors 12, 14, and 15 are concierge levels). Corporate types and conventioneers make up much of the clientele, with tourists (including families) filling in the rest on weekends. Guest rooms are looking patriotic these days, decorated in hues of red, white, and blue. They are furnished with desks and armoires, many of them cherry-wood pieces.

For the best value, book around the Christmas holidays, in late summer, or on weekends. You're more likely to hear about special promotions by calling direct to the hotel, than by browsing the hotel's website.

1331 Pennsylvania Ave. NW (at E St.), Washington, DC 20004. © 800/228-9290 or 202/393-2000. Fax 202/626-6991. www.marriott.com. 772 units. Weekdays $289–$359 double, weekends $159–$259 double; suite from $1,500. Extra person free. AE, DC, DISC, MC, V. Parking $25. Metro: Metro Center. **Amenities:** 2 restaurants (both upscale American); complete health club (with indoor swimming pool and whirlpool); concierge (6am–11pm); business center; connecting mall with 80 shops and restaurants; 24-hr. room service; in-room massage; same-day laundry/dry cleaning; concierge-level rooms; 15 rooms for guests with disabilities, some with roll-in showers. *In room:* A/C, TV w/pay movies, 2-line phones w/dataports, minibar, coffeemaker, hair dryer, iron, safe, robe.

Sofitel Lafayette Square, Washington, D.C. *⟨⟩⟨⟩*   The Hay-Adams faces some competition with the summer 2002 opening of this luxury hotel, which,

like the Hay-Adams, borders Lafayette Square and is just minutes from the White House. The Hay-Adams offers White House views, and the Sofitel does not, it's true, but the Sofitel's other appealing features may make up for that.

This handsome, 12-story limestone building was erected in the early 20th century, and its distinctive facade includes decorative bronze corner panels, bas-relief sculptural panels at ground-floor level, and a 12th-floor balcony that travels the length of both the H and 15th street-sides of the structure (decorative, not accessible, alas). Inside, hotel staff dressed in designer uniforms greet you with *"Bonjour!,"* small hints that a French company (Accor Hotels) owns the Sofitel. Noted French designer Pierre-Yves Rochon styled the interior; a Michelin three-star chef is behind the contemporary French cuisine served in Café 15, the hotel's restaurant; and the gift shop sells such specialty items as French plates and porcelain dolls.

Because of its corner location and exceptionally large windows, guest rooms are bright with natural light; second- and third-floor rooms facing 15th or H street bring in more light still, because their windows extend nearly from floor to ceiling. Each room sports an elegantly modern decor that includes a long desk, creamy duvet with a colorful throw on a king-size bed (about 17 rooms have 2 double beds instead of kings), a much-marbled bathroom with tub separate from the shower stall, fresh flowers, and original artwork, including dramatic photographs of Washington landmarks. The 11th floor has been designed with visiting heads of state in mind, and can be easily secured. In each of the 17 suites, the bedroom is separate from the living room.

806 15th St. NW (at H St.), Washington, DC 20005. ✆ 800/763-4835 or 202/737-8800. Fax 202/639-4677. www.sofitel.com. 254 units. Weekdays $275–$480 double; weekends, call for rates, which can start as low as $199 for a double; from $495 suite. For lowest rates at any time, call directly to the hotel and ask about specials or packages; also check out the website. Extra person $25. Children under 12 stay free in parents' room. AE, DC, DISC, MC, V. Parking $24. Pets allowed. Metro: McPherson Square, Farragut West, or Farragut North. **Amenities:** Restaurant (contemporary French); bar; fitness center with 14 pieces of state-of the art equipment; 24-hr. concierge; business services; 24-hr. room service; same-day laundry/dry cleaning; 8 rooms for guests with disabilities, all with roll-in showers. *In room:* A/C, TV with pay movies and Nintendo, CD player, 2-line phones w/high-speed Internet access and dataports, minibar, hair dryer, iron, safe, robes and slippers.

Willard Inter-Continental ✮✮✮

If you're lucky enough to stay here, you'll be a stone's throw from the White House and the Smithsonian museums, in the heart of downtown near plenty of excellent restaurants, down the block from the National Theatre, and down the avenue from the Capitol. The Willard is definitely the classiest hotel in this neighborhood, among the best in the city, and also, naturally, one of the most expensive. Heads of state favor the Willard (the hotel offers 1 floor as "Secret Service–cleared"), as do visitors from other countries (the gift shop sells newspapers from around the world) and movie directors (who like to shoot scenes in the famously ornate lobby and restaurant).

A renovation completed in late 2000 spruced up the guest rooms' handsome, if staid, decor, which is heavy on reproduction Federal- and Edwardian-style furnishings. The rooms with the best views are the oval suites overlooking Pennsylvania Avenue to the Capitol and the rooms fronting Pennsylvania Avenue. Rooms facing the courtyard are the quietest. Best of all is the "Jenny Lind" suite, perched in the curve of the 12th floor's southeast corner; its round bull's-eye window captures glimpses of the Capitol.

The Willard's designation as a National Historic Landmark in 1974 and magnificent restoration in the 1980s helped revitalize Pennsylvania Avenue and this part of town. Stop in at the Round Robin Bar for a mint julep (introduced here), and listen to bartender and manager Jim Hewes spin tales about the history of the 1901 Willard and its predecessor, the City Hotel, built on this site in 1815.

Always inquire about off-season and weekend packages, when rates are sometimes halved and come with one of five complimentary options, including an upgrade to a suite, valet parking, or a second room at half price.

1401 Pennsylvania Ave. NW (at 14th St.), Washington, DC 20004. ℂ **800/327-0200** or 202/628-9100. Fax 202/637-7326. www.washington.interconti.com. 341 units. Weekdays $480 double, weekends from $199; $850–$4,200 suite. Extra person $30. Children under 18 stay free in parents' room. Ask about special promotions and packages. AE, DC, DISC, MC, V. Parking $23. Metro: Metro Center. Small pets allowed if guest signs waiver. **Amenities:** Restaurant (Willard Room, p. 128); cafe; bar; modest-size but state-of-the-art fitness center; children's programs; concierge; business center; 24-hr. room service; babysitting; same-day laundry/dry cleaning; currency exchange; airline/train ticketing. *In-room:* A/C, TV, 2-line phone w/dataport, minibar, hair dryer, iron, safe, robes.

EXPENSIVE

Courtyard by Marriott Convention Center ⍟   Downtown Washington needs more places like this—a conveniently situated, reasonably priced, medium-size property with a better-than-average restaurant on site. The hotel itself is only a few years old, but the eight-story building, with its handsome stonework and many arches, is a historic landmark, constructed in 1891 to house a bank. The bank's safe-deposit vault, with its original 2-foot-thick circular door, now holds a boardroom, and the marble-floored, columned space that was once the bank's lobby has been reincarnated as the upscale brewery restaurant, Gordon Biersch. Rooms have firm mattresses, chairs and ottomans, large desks, good-size bathrooms, and lots of windows with views of downtown. (The best views—including glimpses of the Washington Monument and the Capitol—are on the Ninth Street side, the higher up the better.) Rooms 715 and 1015 are especially recommended; each is exceptionally large and has a sofa and many oval-shaped windows. You'll be across the street from the MCI Center, around the corner from Ford's Theatre, 1 block from the FBI, and 2½ blocks from the convention center. Lots of really good restaurants are nearby, and if you don't feel like going out, they'll deliver.

900 F St. NW (at 9th St. NW), Washington, DC 20004. ℂ **800/321-2211** or 202/638-4600. Fax 202/638-4601. www.courtyard.com/wascn. 188 units. Weekdays $219 double, weekends $129–$189 double; from $265 suite. No charge for extra person in room. AE, DC, DISC, MC, V. Parking $22. Metro: Gallery Place or Metro Center. **Amenities:** Restaurant (American) and brewery; small fitness center with pool and whirlpool; small business center; room service (during dinner hours only); coin-op washer/dryers; same-day dry cleaning; 6 rooms for guests with disabilities, some with roll-in showers. *In room:* A/C, TV w/pay movies, 2-line phone w/dataport, coffeemaker, hair dryer, iron.

Henley Park ⍟   This intimate English-style hotel with 119 gargoyles on its facade was originally an apartment house. Built in 1918, the stunning building retains many of its Tudor-style features, including the lobby's exquisite ceiling, archways, and leaded windows. The hotel's popular restaurant, bar, and parlor received facelifts in late 2000, while an ongoing renovation recently replaced wallpaper, linens, and other items in all the guest rooms. Luxurious appointments make this a good choice for upscale romantic weekends, although these lodgings fill up with corporate travelers on weekdays. Rooms are decorated in the English country house mode, with Hepplewhite-, Chippendale-, and Queen Anne–style furnishings, including lovely period beds. Rooms and bathrooms are of standard size. A handful of suites are either one-bedroom or junior (combined living room and bedroom). Look in the Sunday *New York Times* "Travel" section for ads posting low rates.

926 Massachusetts Ave. NW (at 10th St.), Washington, DC 20001. ⓒ **800/222-8474** or 202/638-5200. Fax 202/638-6740. www.henleypark.com. 96 units. Weekdays $185–$245 double, summer and weekends $99–159 double; suites from $325 weekdays, look for much lower rates on weekends. Extra person $20. Children under 14 stay free in parents' room. AE, DC, DISC, MC, V. Parking $16. Metro: Metro Center, Gallery Place, or Mt. Vernon Square. Very small pets allowed; you must call in advance. **Amenities:** Restaurant (New American); pub (with pianist Tues–Thurs evenings, live jazz and dancing on weekends); afternoon tea (daily 4–6pm); access to a fitness room in the Morrison-Clark Historic Inn (see listing below) across the street; 24-hr. concierge; complimentary weekday-morning sedan service to downtown and Capitol Hill; business services; room service during restaurant hours; same-day laundry/dry cleaning. *In room:* A/C, TV, 2-line speaker phone w/dataport, minibar, coffeemaker, hair dryer, iron, safe, robes.

Hotel Washington 🐾 Built in 1918, this hotel is the oldest continuously operating hotel in Washington. Renovations throughout the years play up the historic angle. The wooden moldings, crystal chandeliers, and marble floors in the two-story lobby are reconstructed originals. A remodeling done in 2001 added overstuffed chairs and lots of plants to make the lobby more comfortable. Decor in the small guest rooms is traditional, with lots of mahogany furnishings and historically suggestive print fabrics and wall coverings. Bathrooms are in marble and include telephones.

With at least four theaters nearby, the Hotel Washington is often home to cast members in current shows. But most of the clientele is a mix of business and leisure travelers, who are attracted to the hotel for its location and views, as well as its rates, which are among the more reasonable in this part of town. From its corner perch at Pennsylvania Avenue and 15th Street, the 12-story hotel surveys the avenue, monuments, the Capitol, and the White House. Ask for a room facing Pennsylvania Avenue for your own private view (these rooms also tend to be a little more spacious). The hotel has 14 suites, all one-bedroom, most with the capability of turning into two-bedroom suites.

No other hotel in town provides a more panoramic spectacle than the Hotel Washington's rooftop Sky Terrace, where from late April through October you can have drinks and light fare. The more formal Sky Room restaurant is also on the top floor, but doesn't have the views.

515 15th St. NW (at Pennsylvania Ave. NW), Washington, DC 20004. ⓒ **800/424-9540** or 202/638-5900. Fax 202/638-1595. www.hotelwashington.com. 340 units. Weekdays $185–$275 double, weekends $145–$185 double; $495–$725 suite. Family and other discount packages available. Extra person $20. Children under 14 stay free in parents' room. AE, DC, MC, V. Parking $20. Metro: Metro Center. Pets under 25 lb. allowed; inquire about policies when you reserve. **Amenities:** 2 restaurants (both American, 1 seasonal); bar; fitness center with sauna; tour desk; business center; salon; room service (6:30am–11pm); same-day laundry/dry cleaning; 12 rooms for guests with disabilities, 2 with roll-in showers. *In room:* A/C, TV w/pay movies, 2-line phone w/dataport, refrigerator, coffeemaker, hair dryer, iron, robes.

MODERATE

Hilton Garden Inn, Washington, DC, Franklin Square Located downtown between H and I streets, the Hilton Garden Inn is across the street from Metro's Blue Line McPherson Square station (and 3 stops from the Smithsonian museums station) and within walking distance of the White House, the convention centers (both the mammoth new one and the old one), and the MCI Center. Rooms are spacious with either king-size or double beds, and are designed for comfort—each room has a cushiony chair with ottoman and a large desk with an ergonomic chair and adjustable lighting. The business crowd is onto the 3-year-old hotel, but it seems that few tourists have discovered it, although its location and perks make it a good choice for both business and leisure travelers. The hotel's 20 suites are almost apartment size, with a small pullout sofa in the living room, and the bathroom separating the bedroom from the living room.

815 14th St. NW (between H and I sts.), Washington, DC 20005. © **800/HILTONS** or 202/783-7800. Fax 202/783-7801. www.washingtondcfranklinsquare.gardeninn.com. 300 units. Weekdays $139–$289 double, weekends $109–$179 double; $239–$375 suite. Extra person $20. No more than 4 people per room. Children under 18 stay free in parents' room. AE, DC, DISC, MC, V. Parking $21.95. Metro: McPherson Square. **Amenities:** Restaurant (American); bar with fireplace; small fitness center with indoor pool, StairMaster, and weight machines; business center; room service (6am–10pm); same-day laundry/dry cleaning; 16 rooms for guests with disabilities, 6 with roll-in showers. *In room:* A/C, TV w/pay movies, 2-line phone w/dataport, fridge, microwave, coffeemaker, hair dryer, iron.

Morrison-Clark Historic Inn 🛱

This property offers the homey ambience and personable service of an inn, coupled with hotel amenities, such as a first-rate restaurant, phones and TV, and a fitness center. The inn occupies twin 1864 Victorian brick town houses (with a newer wing in converted stables across an interior courtyard) and is listed on the National Register of Historic Places. Guests enter via a turn-of-the-20th-century parlor, with Victorian furnishings and lace-curtained bay windows. Beyond the parlor lies a suite of lovely public spaces including the inn's restaurant. Its slightly off-track location might deter some, but the truth is, that several of the best of Washington's restaurants and nightlife are only a few blocks away.

High-ceilinged guest rooms are individually decorated with original artworks, sumptuous fabrics, and antique or reproduction 19th-century furnishings, and are graced with fresh flowers. Most popular are the grand Victorian-style rooms, with new chandeliers and bedspreads. Four Victorian rooms have private porches; many others have plant-filled balconies. Guests enjoy a complimentary breakfast served daily in the Victorian parlor.

1015 L St. NW (at 11th St. and Massachusetts Ave. NW), Washington, DC 20001. © **800/332-7898** or 202/898-1200. Fax 202/289-8576. www.morrisonclark.com. 54 units. Weekdays $175–$245 double, weekends $99–$159 double. Extra person $20. Rates include continental breakfast. Children under 16 stay free in parents' room. AE, DC, DISC, MC, V. Parking $16. Metro: Metro Center or Mt. Vernon Square. Very small pets allowed with advance notice. **Amenities:** Restaurant (New American); tiny fitness center; concierge; business services; room service during restaurant hours; same-day laundry/dry cleaning. *In room:* A/C, TV, dataport, minibar, hair dryer, iron, robes.

Washington Terrace Hotel 🛱

For all intents and purposes, this is a new hotel, the transformation of the former Doubletree property being so utterly complete. Beautifully landscaped terraces front and back help create a buffer for this urban hotel. The flow of the public spaces leading back to the garden court-yard, and abundant use of earth tones and sandstone in decor accentuate the hotel's theme of "bringing the outdoors in." This theme resonates in the guest rooms, whose light golden wallcoverings feature an abstract botanical pattern, and whose windows are larger than the hotel norm, delivering lots of natural light. Ask for a room at the front of the house for a view of Scott Circle, the park across the street, and the city; request a room at the back for a view of the gar-den terrace. Best rooms are those on floors six through eight, all of which are spacious suites and have small wet bars, a dining table and sleeper sofa, high-speed Internet access, and larger bathrooms. Though the Washington Terrace calls itself an "upscale boutique hotel," I think its large size and its practical amenities, like ergonomic chairs in the guest rooms and extensive conference and party facilities, disqualify it. Still, the guest rooms do have a boutiquey feel, thanks to imaginative touches such as granite-topped desks, circular nightstands, and a blueberry toned wall behind the bed (the suites feature other colors: aubergine, nectar, and sienna), contrasting with the light toned coverings on the other walls.

1515 Rhode Island Ave. NW (at Scott Circle), Washington, DC 20005. © **866/984-6835** or 202/232-7000. Fax 202/332-8436. www.washingtonterracehotel.com. 220 units. Weekdays $139–$189, weekends $119–$149 double and suite. Extra person $30. Children 16 and under stay free in parents' room. AE, DC, DISC, MC, V. Parking $22. Metro: Dupont Circle or McPherson Square. **Amenities:** Restaurant (contemporary American with Southern flair); bar; fitness center with universal gym, free weights, treadmills, and life cycles; 24-hr. concierge; full-service business center; 24-hr. room service; same-day laundry/dry cleaning; 10 rooms for guests with disabilities, 2 with roll-in showers. *In room:* A/C, TV w/pay movies, radio/CD player, 2-line phones w/dataport, minibar, hair dryer, iron, safe, robes.

INEXPENSIVE

Four Points Sheraton, Washington, D.C. Downtown ★ *Value*   This for-mer Days Inn has been totally transformed into a contemporary property that offers all the latest gizmos, from high-speed Internet access in all the rooms to a 2,000-square-foot fitness center. A massive renovation undertaken by a new owner essentially gutted the old building, but the location is still as terrific as ever (close to the Convention Center, MCI Center, and downtown). Best of all, the rates are reasonable, and spectacular hotel amenities make this a good choice for both business and leisure visitors.

Five types of rooms are available: units with two double beds, with one queen bed, or with one king bed; junior suites; or one-bedroom suites. Corner rooms (there are only about 10) are a little more spacious than others, which are of standard size. While guest rooms offer city views, the rooftop pool and lounge boasts a sweeping vista of the city that includes the Capitol. Under separate ownership from the hotel is a recommended restaurant, Corduroy.

1201 K St. NW (at 12th St.), Washington, DC 20005. © **888/481-7191** or 202/289-7600. Fax 202/289-3310. www.fourpointswashingtondc.com. 265 units. In season $99–$275 double, off-season $99–$245 double; from $400 suite. Extra person $20. Children under 18 stay free in parents' room. AE, DC, DISC, MC, V. Park-ing $22. Metro: McPherson Square or Metro Center. **Amenities:** Restaurant (seasonal American); bar; indoor heated pool on rooftop; fitness center; business center; room service (6am–midnight); same-day laundry/dry cleaning; executive-level rooms; 5 rooms for guests with disabilities, 3 with roll-in showers. *In room:* A/C, TV w/pay movies, 2-line phone w/dataport, minibar, coffeemaker, hair dryer, iron, safe.

3 Downtown, 16th Street NW & West

VERY EXPENSIVE

Hay-Adams Hotel ★★   An extensive $18 million renovation completed in spring 2002 was the Hay-Adams's first major refurbishment in its 75 year his-tory. Some improvements, like the new heating and air-conditioning system and structural changes that make the hotel accessible to guests with disabilities, were long overdue. Other improvements, like the modernized kitchen, will be invisi-ble to guests. Most of the changes will be obvious to anyone who has visited the hotel in the past: the custom-fitted staff uniforms; an elegant decor of sage green, off-white, beige, and gold tones; and CD players, high-speed Internet access, custom European linens, new furnishings (the hotel donated its old fur-niture to local homeless shelters), and thermostats in each room.

But the best of the Hay-Adams remains much the same. The hotel still offers the best views in town. Reserve a room on the sixth through eighth floors on the H Street side of the hotel (or as low as the 2nd floor in winter, when the trees are bare), pull back the curtains from the windows, and *voilà!*—you get a full frontal view of Lafayette Square, the White House, and the Washington Monu-ment in the background. (You'll pay more for rooms with these views.) The view from rooms facing 16th Street isn't bad, either: Windows overlook the yellow-painted exterior of St. John's Episcopal Church, built in 1815, and known as the "church of the presidents."

The Hay-Adams is one in the triumvirate of exclusive hotels built by Harry Wardman in the 1920s (the Jefferson and the St. Regis are the other two). Its architecture is Italian Renaissance and much of the original features, such as ornate plaster moldings and ornamental fireplaces, the walnut-paneled lobby, and high-ceilinged guest rooms, are still in place. The hotel has about 15 one-bedroom suites (the living room and bedroom are separate) and seven junior suites (living room and bedroom are together in one space).

One Lafayette Square (at 16th and H sts. NW), Washington, DC 20006. ✆ **800/424-5054** or 202/638-6600. Fax 202/638-2716. www.hayadams.com. 145 units. Weekdays $345–$545 double, weekends $259–$425 double; from $1,000 suite. Extra person $30. Children under 17 stay free in parents' room. AE, DC, DISC, MC, V. Valet parking $28. Metro: Farragut West or McPherson Square. Small dogs accepted. **Amenities:** Restaurant (American); bar; access to local health club ($15 per day); 24-hr. concierge; complimentary morning car service; secretarial and business services; 24-hr. room service; same-day laundry/dry cleaning, 9 rooms for guests with disabilities. *In-room:* A/C, TV with pay movies, 2-line phone w/dataport, minibar, hair dryer, iron, safe, umbrella, robes.

The Jefferson, a Loews Hotel 🌟🌟
Opened in 1923 just 4 blocks from the White House, the Jefferson is one of the city's three most exclusive hotels (along with the Hay-Adams and the St. Regis). Those looking for an intimate hotel, with excellent service, a good restaurant, sophisticated but comfortable accommodations, inviting public rooms (should you want to hang out), and proximity to attractions and restaurants (should you not want to hang out) will find that the Jefferson satisfies on all scores. About one-third of the lodgings are suites: junior, one- and two-bedroom size. The hotel's largest rooms are located in the "carriage house," an attached town house with its own elevator, which you reach by passing through the pub/lounge in the main building. Guest rooms were last upgraded in 2000 and are individually decorated with antiques and lovely fabrics, evoking a European feel.

The lobby was refurbished in 2001; a fine art collection, including original documents signed by Thomas Jefferson, graces the public areas as well as the guest rooms. Many local foodies like to dine at the hotel's acclaimed **Restaurant at the Jefferson** 🌟🌟 (see the full review on p. 136). And the paneled pub/lounge is another popular stopping place for Washingtonians; here you can sink into a red-leather chair and enjoy a marvelous high tea or cocktails.

1200 16th St. NW (at M St.), Washington, DC 20036. ✆ **800/235-6397** or 202/347-2200. Fax 202/331-7982. www.loewshotels.com. 100 units. Weekdays $319–$339 double, $350–$1,200 suite; weekends from $199 double, from $289 suite. Extra person $25. Children under 12 stay free in parents' room. AE, DC, DISC, MC, V. Parking $20. Metro: Farragut North. Pets welcomed and pampered. **Amenities:** Restaurant (American); bar/lounge (serving high tea 3–5pm); access to nearby health club (with pool) at the University Club across the street ($20 per visit); children's program (care package at check-in); 24-hr. concierge; 24-hr. room service; 24-hr. butler service; in-room massage; babysitting; same-day laundry/dry cleaning; 2 rooms for guests with disabilities, both with roll-in showers; video and CD rentals. *In room:* A/C, TV w/pay movies and VCR, CD player, 2-line phone w/dataport, minibar, hair dryer, safe, robes.

Renaissance Mayflower 🌟
Superbly located in the heart of downtown, the Mayflower is the hotel of choice for guests as varied as Monica Lewinsky and Wynton Marsalis. The lobby, which extends an entire block from Connecticut Avenue to 17th Street, is always bustling—read chaotic, at check-in/check-out times—since Washingtonians tend to use it as a shortcut in their travels.

The Mayflower is steeped in history: When it opened in 1925, it was the site of Calvin Coolidge's inaugural ball (though Coolidge didn't attend—he was mourning his son's death from blood poisoning). President-elect FDR and family lived in rooms 776 and 781 while waiting to move into the White House, and this is where he penned the words, "The only thing we have to fear is fear itself." A major restoration in the 1980s uncovered large skylights and renewed the lobby's pink marble bas-relief frieze and spectacular promenade.

Each graciously appointed guest room has its own marble foyer, a high ceiling, and mahogany reproduction furnishings (Queen Anne, Sheraton, Chippendale, and Hepplewhite). You'll find more Italian marble in the bathroom; about half of the guest rooms also have a small color TV in the bathroom.

In the hotel's lovely Café Promenade, lawyers and lobbyists gather for weekday power breakfasts, and a full English tea is served Monday through Saturday afternoons. The clubby, mahogany-paneled Town and Country is the setting for light buffet lunches and complimentary hors d'oeuvres during cocktail hour. Bartender Sambonn Lek has quite a following, as much for his conversation as for his magic tricks.

1127 Connecticut Ave. NW (between L and M sts.), Washington, DC 20036. ℂ 800/228-7697 or 202/347-3000. Fax 202/776-9182. www.renaissancehotels.com. 660 units. Weekdays $289–$340 double, weekends $159–$209 double; from $329 suite. No charge for extra person in room. AE, DC, DISC, MC, V. Parking $26. Metro: Farragut North. **Amenities:** Restaurant (Mediterranean); lobby lounge; bar; fitness center; concierge; 24-hr. business center; 24-hr. room service; same-day laundry/dry cleaning; 15 rooms for guests with disabilities. *In room:* A/C, TV w/pay movies, 2-line phone w/dataport, minibar, hair dryer, iron, robes.

St. Regis ⭐⭐   If all goes according to plan, by the time you read this the St. Regis will be the most technologically advanced hotel on the East Coast. Think plasma televisions (the flat-screen TVs that are set in the wall), which you can program to play tomorrow's scheduled shows today, or to pick up a movie where you left off when you last stayed at the hotel. The hotel is undergoing a top-to-bottom renovation that will make it a marvel of technology, while enhancing its palace-like accommodations. The decor specifics are still being decided at this writing, but you can be sure that luxury will be the order of the day. Some St. Regis amenities that will carry on include the concierge level (called the "Astor Floor"), where a butler unpacks and packs your suitcase, presses two items upon your arrival, and generally sees to your needs. The best rooms (other than those on the Astor Floor) probably will still be the grand deluxe units, which are oversize traditional rooms with a sitting area. The number of one-bedroom suites most likely will increase to about 26. The hotel will continue to offer a top-notch restaurant, as well as its Library Lounge, a contender for the title of best hotel bar in Washington, with a working fireplace and paneled walls lined with bookcases.

923 16th St. NW (at K St.), Washington, DC 20006. ℂ 800/562-5661 or 202/638-2626. Fax 202/638-4231. www.stregis.com. 193 units. Weekdays $220–$460 double, weekends $189–$405 double; from $600 suite. For best rates, check the website or call the hotel directly to ask about special promotions. Children under 16 stay free in parents' room. AE, DC, DISC, MC, V. Parking $24. Metro: Farragut West or McPherson Square. Small pets allowed for $25 per night. **Amenities:** Restaurant (American); bar/lounge; 24-hr. state-of-the-art fitness room (plus access, for $25 fee, to either of 2 nearby health clubs, 1 of which has an indoor lap pool); bike rentals; concierge; complimentary 1-way transportation within 6 blocks of hotel (7–9:30am weekdays); business center; 24-hr. room service; in-room massage; babysitting; same-day laundry/dry cleaning; concierge-level rooms; 8 rooms for guests with disabilities, all with roll-in showers. *In room:* A/C, TV w/pay movies, fax, 2-line phone w/dataport, minibar, coffeemaker, hair dryer, iron, safe, robes.

EXPENSIVE

Capital Hilton ⭐   This longtime Washington hotel is crowing about the success of its brand-new Capital City Club fitness center and full-service day spa. The club fronts on K Street, so you can work your buns off while watching the downtown Washington scene. The club doesn't have a pool but does have 60 pieces of exercise equipment, from LifeCycle to treadmills; facials, massages, and other spa services; and personal trainers. Use of the club is free to certain Hilton

HHonors guests and $10 per day ($25 maximum, no matter how long your stay) for all others.

The hotel has hosted every American president since FDR, and the annual Gridiron Club Dinner and political roast takes place in its ballroom. The Hilton's central location (2 blocks from the White House) makes it convenient for tourists, and business travelers appreciate the Tower's concierge floors (10, 11, 12, and 14) and extensive facilities.

The rooms are decorated in Federal-period motif with Queen Anne– and Chippendale-style furnishings. Corner rooms on the 16th Street side are the most spacious and offer the best city views. A number of suites are available, including three with outdoor patios.

Most of the rooms are on the high end of the price range given below. But always ask about the "Hilton bounce-back" weekend rate, which includes full buffet breakfast for two, and discounts for AAA members, senior citizens, military, and families.

1001 16th St. NW (between K and L sts.), Washington, DC 20036. © 800/HILTONS or 202/393-1000. Fax 202/639-5784. www.capital.hilton.com. 543 units. Weekdays $169–$399 double, $30 more for Tower units; weekends from $119; from $339 minisuite, $439 1-bedroom suite. Extra person $25. Children under 18 stay free in parents' room. Weekend packages and other discounts available. AE, DC, DISC, MC, V. Parking $26. Metro: Farragut West, Farragut North, or McPherson Square. **Amenities:** 2 restaurants (steakhouse, American); 2 bars; 10,000-square-foot health club and spa; concierge (6:30am–11pm); tour and ticket desk; ATM with foreign currency; airline desks (American, Continental, Northwest); business center; salon; room service (until 2am); massage; babysitting; same-day laundry/dry cleaning; concierge floors; 13 rooms for guests with disabilities. *In room:* A/C, TV w/pay movies, 2-line phone w/dataport, minibar, coffeemaker, hair dryer, iron.

Hotel Rouge 🔔 High-energy rock music dances out onto the sidewalk. A red awning extends from the entrance. A guest with sleepy eyes and brilliant blue hair sits diffidently upon the white tufted leather sofa in the small lobby. Attractive, casually dressed patrons come and go, while an older couple roosts at a table just inside the doorway of the adjoining Bar Rouge sipping martinis at 2 in the afternoon. Shades of red are everywhere: in the staff's funky shiny shirts, in the accent pillows on the retro furniture, and in the artwork. This used to be a Quality Hotel: It's come a long way, baby.

The Kimpton Hotel Group (known for its offbeat but upscale boutique accommodations) has transformed five old D.C. buildings into these cleverly crafted and sexy hotels (see the Topaz and Hotel Monaco reviews on p. 104 and p. 89 respectively; hotels Helix and Madeira were expected to open in late 2002). In the case of Rouge, this means that your guest room will have deep crimson drapes at the window, a floor-to-ceiling red "pleather" headboard for your comfortable, white-with-red piping duvet-covered bed, and, in the dressing room, an Orange Crush–colored dresser, whose built-in minibar holds all sorts of red items, such as Hot Tamales candies, rex wax lips, and Red Bull. Guest rooms in most boutique hotels are notoriously cramped; not so here, where the rooms are spacious enough to easily accommodate several armchairs and a large ottoman (in shades of red and gold), a number of funky little lamps, a huge, mahogany framed mirror leaning against a wall, and a 10-foot-long mahogany desk. The Rouge has no suites but does offer 15 specialty guest rooms, including "Chill Rooms," which have DVD players and Sony PlayStation, "Chat Rooms," which have high-speed Internet access and computer/printers, and "Chow Rooms," which have a microwave and refrigerator. If you look at Rouge's website, you'll see that the hotel embraces the idea of "indulgence," a theme born out in the complimentary morning bloody mary bar set up in the lobby 10am to 11am, and in the Bar Rouge, where you can settle into thronelike armchairs and order drinks like "Sin on the Rocks" (blackberry schnapps, passion fruit Alize, and lime juice) and the Love Gun (ingredients a secret), as well as seductive bar food. See p. 260 for more info about Bar Rouge.

1315 16th St. NW (at Massachusetts Ave. NW and Scott Circle), Washington, DC 20036. © 800/368-5689 or 202/232-8000. Fax 202/667-9827. www.rougehotel.com. 137 units. Weekdays $220–$255 double, weekends $125 double; weekdays. $260 for specialty rooms weekdays, $165 specialty rooms weekends. Best rates available by calling the 800-number and asking for promotional rate. Extra person $20. Rates include complimentary bloody marys from 10–11am. Children under 16 stay free in parents' room. AE, DC, DISC, MC, V. Parking $20. Metro: Dupont Circle. Refundable security deposit of $50 with pets, who are pampered here. **Amenities:** Bar/restaurant (innovative American, with a Latin flair); modest size fitness center with treadmill, stationary bikes; 24-hr. concierge; business center; room service (7am–11pm); same-day laundry/dry cleaning; 6 rooms for guests with disabilities, 1 with roll-in showers; *In room:* A/C, 27-in. flat-screen TV with pay movies, CD player, 2-line cordless phones w/dataport, minibar, coffeemaker (with Starbucks coffee), hair dryer, iron, robes.

MODERATE

Lincoln Suites Downtown 🐾🐾 *Value*   This is a little hotel with a big heart. It tries hard to do right by its guests and, judging from feedback I've received from readers who've stayed here, I would say it succeeds. (Check out the website, where the hotel's can-do personality shines through.) Key elements include the hotel's location, in the heart of downtown, near Metro stops, restaurants, and the White House; a congenial staff; the complimentary milk and homemade cookies served each evening; and daily complimentary continental breakfast in the lobby. Lincoln Suites also has direct access to **Mackey's,** an Irish pub right next door (a second on-site restaurant is expected to open by the time you read this), and room service for lunch and dinner is delivered from **Luigi's** 🐾, an Italian restaurant and veritable Washington institution (see p. 141), which is right around the corner.

The all-suite 10-story hotel is quite nice, in a nothing-fancy sort of way. Lots of long-term guests bunk here. Suites are large and comfortable; about 28 offer full kitchens, while the rest have kitchenettes. An ongoing renovation has slowly but surely overhauled the hotel, replacing all the furniture, appliances, carpeting, and wall coverings. Most recently, the previously cramped lobby was transformed into a hip two-story lobby/lounge.

1823 L St. NW, Washington, DC 20036. © 800/424-2970 or 202/223-4320. Fax 202/223-8546. www. lincolnhotels.com. 99 suites. Weekdays $129–$199, weekends $99–$139. Rates include continental breakfast. Discounts available for long-term stays. Children under 16 stay free in parents' room. AE, DC, DISC, MC, V. Parking $16 (in adjoining garage). Metro: Farragut North or Farragut West. Pets under 25 lb. accepted, second floor only, for $15 a day. **Amenities:** Bar/restaurant (Irish); free passes to the well-equipped Bally's Holiday Spa nearby; 24-hr. front desk/concierge; room service (11am–11pm); coin-op washer/dryers; same-day laundry/dry cleaning; 2 rooms for guests with disabilities, 1 with roll-in showers. *In room:* A/C, TV w/pay movies, dataport, kitchen or kitchenette, refrigerator, coffeemaker, microwave, wet bar, hair dryer, iron.

4 Adams-Morgan

Note: The hotels listed here are situated just north of Dupont Circle, more at the mouth of Adams-Morgan than within its actual boundaries.

EXPENSIVE

The Churchill 🐾   This 1906 building, a registered historic property, sits on a hill a short walk from lively Dupont Circle; its elevated position allows for great city views from upper-floor rooms. You're also just a short walk from trendy Adams-Morgan (just cross Connecticut and walk up Columbia Rd.). The former Sofitel hotel underwent a thorough renovation in 2001–02 to emphasize its historic qualities and replaced all furnishings with custom-made pieces, including five-layer feather beds in every guest room. You can still count on the rooms being spacious, each with a breakfast/study alcove and many with sitting areas. You can choose from one of 84 regular guest rooms, each with a study but no parlor; 24 suites, with bedroom and parlor in one room, study separate; and 36 deluxe suites, in which the bedroom, study, and parlor are all separate rooms. The hotel welcomes an international clientele of diplomats, foreign delegations, and corporate travelers.

1914 Connecticut Ave. NW (between Wyoming Ave. and Leroy Place), Washington, DC 20009. ℂ 800/424-2464 or 202/797-2000. Fax 202/462-0944. www.thechurchillhotel.com. 144 units. Weekdays $199–$249 double, $279–$329 suite, $319–$369 deluxe suite; weekends $129–$149 double, $209–$229 suite, $249–$269 deluxe suite. Extra person $30. Children under 12 stay free in parents' room. AE, DISC, DC, MC, V. Valet parking $19 plus tax ($9 plus tax just for the day). Metro: Dupont Circle. **Amenities:** Restaurant (Continental); lounge/bar; fitness center; concierge; room service (5:30am–11pm); same-day laundry/dry cleaning; 3 rooms for guests with disabilities. *In room:* A/C, TV with pay movies, 3 phones, dataport, hair dryer, iron, robes.

Hilton Washington 🕺 (Kids) This sprawling hotel, built in 1965, occupies 7 acres and calls itself a "resort"—mostly on the basis of having landscaped gardens and tennis courts on its premises, unusual amenities for a D.C. hotel. The Hilton caters to corporate groups, which may have their families in tow (there's a kiddie pool and, from Memorial Day to Labor Day, children receive a goodie bag at check-in), and is accustomed to coordinating meetings for thousands of attendees. Its vast conference facilities include one of the largest hotel ballrooms on the East Coast (it accommodates nearly 4,000). By contrast, guest rooms are on the small side. A renovation of all guest rooms will be complete in 2003, installing elegant dark wood furnishings in every room. From the fifth floor up, city-side, you'll have panoramic views of Washington (as well as the Olympic-size pool).

The two designated concierge level rooms usually go for about $30 more than the standard room rate. The hotel has 53 suites, in all kinds of configurations, from the junior executive (in which parlor and bedroom are combined) to the huge Presidential suite.

The Hilton puts you within an easy stroll of embassies, great restaurants, museums, and the charming neighborhoods of Adams-Morgan, Kalorama, and Woodley Park (all up the hill), and Dupont Circle (down the hill).

1919 Connecticut Ave. NW (at T St.), Washington, DC 20009. ℂ 800/HILTONS or 202/483-3000. Fax 202/797-5755. www.washington-hilton.com. 1,119 units. Weekdays $169–$374 double, weekends (and some weekdays and holidays) $119–$314 double; $300–$1,500 suite. Look for deals on the website or by calling Hilton's 800-number. Extra person $20. Children 18 and under stay free in parents' room. AE, DISC, MC, V. Self-parking $15. Metro: Dupont Circle. **Amenities:** 2 restaurants (both American); deli; 2 bars (lobby bar featuring a pianist nightly and a pub); Olympic-size heated outdoor pool, children's pool; 3 lighted tennis courts; shuffleboard; extensive health-club facilities; concierge; transportation/sightseeing desk; comprehensive business center; lobby shops; room service (until 2am); same-day laundry/dry cleaning; concierge-level rooms; 28 rooms for guests with disabilities, some with roll-in showers. *In room:* A/C, TV w/pay movies; 2-line phone w/dataport, coffeemaker, hair dryer, iron.

MODERATE

Courtyard by Marriott Northwest This hotel isn't much to look at from the outside, but inside it has a European feel and a well-heeled appearance. Waterford crystal chandeliers hang in the lobby and in the restaurant, and you may hear an Irish lilt from time to time (the hotel is 1 of 3 in Washington owned by Jurys, an Irish management company). Guests tend to linger in the comfortable lounge off the lobby, where coffee is available all day.

Adams-Morgan, Dupont Circle & West End Accommodations

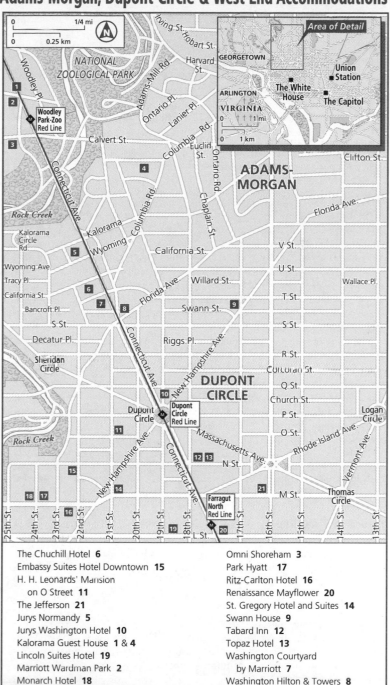

The Chuchill Hotel **6**
Embassy Suites Hotel Downtown **15**
H. H. Leonards' Mansion
   on O Street **11**
The Jefferson **21**
Jurys Normandy **5**
Jurys Washington Hotel **10**
Kalorama Guest House **1** & **4**
Lincoln Suites Hotel **19**
Marriott Wardman Park **2**
Monarch Hotel **18**

Omni Shoreham **3**
Park Hyatt **17**
Ritz-Carlton Hotel **16**
Renaissance Mayflower **20**
St. Gregory Hotel and Suites **14**
Swann House **9**
Tabard Inn **12**
Topaz Hotel **13**
Washington Courtyard
   by Marriott **7**
Washington Hilton & Towers **8**

Guest rooms are very comfortable and bright. Accommodations facing the street on the sixth to ninth floors provide panoramic views. Especially nice are the 15 "executive king" rooms, which are a little larger and are equipped with marble bathrooms, trouser presses, and robes.

Look for the best deals in summer, when a "two for breakfast" promotion often runs.

1900 Connecticut Ave. NW (at Leroy Place), Washington, DC 20009. © 800/842-4211 or 202/332-9300. Fax 202/328-7039. www.jurysdoyle.com. 147 units. $99–$235 double. Extra person $15. Children under 18 stay free in parents' room. Ask about discount packages. AE, DC, DISC, MC, V. Parking $12. Metro: Dupont Circle. **Amenities:** Restaurant (American, open for breakfast and dinner); bar; outdoor pool (seasonal); small exercise room; business center; room service (5–10pm); coin-operated laundry; same-day laundry and dry cleaning; 18 rooms for guests with disabilities, 2 with roll-in showers. *In room:* A/C, TV w/pay movies, 2-line phone w/dataports, coffeemaker, hair dryer, iron, safe.

INEXPENSIVE

Jurys Normandy *Finds*   This gracious hotel is a gem—a small gem, but a gem nonetheless. Situated in a neighborhood of architecturally impressive embassies, the hotel hosts many embassy-bound guests. You may discover this for yourself on a Tuesday evening, when guests gather in the charming Tea Room to enjoy complimentary wine and cheese served from the antique oak sideboard. This is also where you'll find daily continental breakfast (for about $6), complimentary coffee and tea after 10am, and cookies after 3pm. You can lounge or watch TV in the conservatory, or, in nice weather, you can move outside to the garden patio.

The six-floor Normandy has small but pretty twin and queen guest rooms (all remodeled in 1998), with tapestry-upholstered mahogany and cherry-wood furnishings in 18th-century style, and pretty floral-print bedspreads covering firm beds. Rooms facing Wyoming Avenue overlook the tree-lined street, while other rooms mostly offer views of apartment buildings. The Normandy is an easy walk from both Adams-Morgan and Dupont Circle, where many restaurants and shops await you.

2118 Wyoming Ave. NW (at Connecticut Ave.), Washington, DC 20008. © 800/424-3729 or 202/483-1350. Fax 202/387-8241. www.jurysdoyle.com. 75 units. $79–$175 double. Extra person $10. Children under 12 stay free in parents' room. AE, DC, DISC, MC, V. Metro: Dupont Circle. **Amenities:** Access to the neighboring Courtyard by Marriott's pool and exercise room; room service at breakfast; coin-op washer/dryers; same-day laundry/dry cleaning (Mon–Sat); 4 rooms for guests with disabilities, 1 with roll-in shower. *In room:* A/C, TV with pay movies, 2-line phone w/dataport, minibar, coffeemaker, hair dryer, iron, safe.

Kalorama Guest House   This San Francisco–style B&B has two locations: in Adams Morgan, where a Victorian town house at 1854 Mintwood Place NW is the main dwelling, with three other houses on the same street providing additional lodging; and in nearby Woodley Park (© **202/328-0860;** fax 202/328-8730), where two houses on Cathedral Avenue NW offer a total of 19 guest rooms (see "Woodley Park," later in this chapter for more information about this location).

The cozy common areas and homey guest rooms are furnished with finds from antique stores, flea markets, and auctions. The town house at 1854 Mintwood Place houses a cheerful breakfast room with plant-filled windows. There's a garden behind the house with umbrella tables.

Rooms in all the houses generally offer either double or queen-size beds, but 1854 Mintwood offers larger units in a greater variety of configurations: There's an efficiency apartment with a kitchen, telephone, and TV; one small two-room apartment with a kitchen, cable TV, and telephone; and four suites (2 two-bedroom and 2 "executive" suites, in which the living room and bedroom are together).

All locations serve a complimentary breakfast of juice, coffee, fruit, bagels, croissants, and English muffins. They also give guests access to laundry and ironing facilities, a refrigerator, a seldom-used TV, and a phone (local calls are free; incoming calls are answered around the clock, so people can leave messages for you). It's customary for the innkeepers to put out sherry, crackers, and cheese on Friday and Saturday afternoons. Magazines, games, and current newspapers are available. Some of the houses are nonsmoking. At both locations, your fellow guests are likely to be students, Europeans, and conferees.

The Mintwood Place location is near Metro stations, dozens of restaurants, nightspots, and shops. The Cathedral Avenue houses, which are even closer to the Woodley Park–Zoo Metro, offer proximity to Rock Creek Park and the National Zoo.

1854 Mintwood Place NW (between 19th St. and Columbia Rd.), Washington, DC 20009. ✆ **202/667-6369.** Fax 202/319-1262. http://yp.washingtonpost.com/yp/kgh. 30 units, 16 with bathroom (6 with shower only). $55–$75 double with shared bathroom, $75–$100 double with bathroom; $105–$145 suite or apt. Extra person $5. Rates include continental breakfast. AE, DC, DISC, MC, V. Limited parking $7. Metro: Woodley Park–Zoo or Dupont Circle. Kids 6 and older. **Amenities:** Coin-op washer/dryer; nonsmoking rooms; common refrigerator; common TV. *In room:* A/C, no phone.

5 Dupont Circle

EXPENSIVE

H. H. Leonards' Mansion on O Street 👯👯 *(Finds)*   A legend in her own time, H. H. Leonards operates this Victorian property, made up of four interconnecting, five-story town houses, as a museum with rotating exhibits, an event space, a private club, an art gallery, an antiques emporium, and—oh, yeah—a B&B. If you stay here, you may find yourself buying a sweater, a painting, or (who knows?) an antique bed. Everything's for sale.

Guest rooms are so creative they'll blow you away; they're expensive, but simply outrageous. Most breathtaking is a log cabin loft suite, with a bed whose headboard encases an aquarium. The Art Deco–style penthouse takes up an entire floor (with a large living room, a bedroom, and a kitchen) and has its own elevator, 10 phones, and 7 televisions. The International Room (1 room with a queen bed and sitting area) has a nonworking fireplace and four TVs, a combination of Victorian antiques and contemporary furnishings, a sunny sitting area, hand-made prism-glass windows, and a bright bathroom with two-person Jacuzzi. The simplest of the bunch is the "Country Room," decorated in blue and white, and with French doors leading to a porch overlooking O Street. All rooms have either king-size or queen-size beds and computer-activated telephones that can hook you up to the Internet; most have a whirlpool and a few have kitchens. Elsewhere on the property, there's an outdoor pool, eight office/conference spaces, 28 far-out bathrooms, art and antiques everywhere, and a thousand or so books. Full business services are available.

2020 O St. NW (between 20th and 21st sts.), Washington, DC 20036. ✆ **202/496-2000.** Fax 202/659-0547. www.omansion.com. 18 units, all with private bathrooms (2 have shower only). $150–$1,000; Summer $100–$750. Nonprofit, group, and long-term rates available. Rates include breakfast. AE, MC, V. Parking $15 by reservation. Metro: Dupont Circle. **Amenities:** Small outdoor pool; concierge; state-of-the-art business center; self-operated laundry service at no charge. *In room:* A/C, TV, dataport, hair dryer, iron, robes.

St. Gregory Hotel and Suites ⊛⊛   The St. Gregory, open since June 2000, is an affordable luxury property, with marble floors and chandeliers. The hotel is well situated at the corner of 21st and M streets, not far from Georgetown, Dupont Circle, Foggy Bottom, and the White House, and with many good restaurants within a literal stone's throw.

Most of the guest rooms are one-bedroom suites, with a separate living room and bedroom, and with a pullout sofa in the living room. The best rooms are the 16 "sky" suites on the ninth floor, each with terrace and city views. All of the 100 suites have fully appointed kitchens, including microwaves, ovens, and full-size refrigerators. The remaining units are deluxe double rooms. Decor throughout the hotel is an attractive mélange of olive green and gold, with un-hotel-like lamps, mirror frames, and fabrics. Three whole floors of the hotel are reserved for club-level rooms.

The St. Gregory offers special rates to long-term and government guests, and to those from the diplomatic community. If you don't fall into one of those categories, check the hotel's website for great deals like the "One Dollar Summer Clearance Sale" posted in 2002: You pay $169 the first night and only $1 for the second night, for Friday and Saturday, or Saturday and Sunday stays.

2033 M St. NW (at 21st St.), Washington, DC 20036. ℂ 800/829-5034 or 202/530-3600. Fax 202/466-7353. www.stgregoryhotelwdc.com. 154 units. Weekdays $189–269 double or suite, weekends $149–$249 double or suite. Extra person $20. Children under 16 stay free in parents' room. Ask about discounts, long-term stays, and packages. AE, DC, MC, V. Parking $12 weekends, $19 weekdays. Metro: Dupont Circle or Farragut North. **Amenities:** Cafe and coffee bar (American) with sidewalk seating seasonally; state-of-the-art fitness center, as well as access to the nearby and larger Sports Club/LA (p. 109 for full description); concierge; tour desk; business center; room service (6:30am–10:30pm); massage; babysitting; coin-op laundry room; same-day laundry/dry cleaning; concierge-level rooms; 6 rooms for guests with disabilities, 2 with roll-in showers. *In room:* A/C, TV w/pay movies, CD player, 2-line phone w/dataport, refrigerator, coffeemaker, hair dryer, iron.

Swann House ⊛ *(Finds)*   This stunning 1883 mansion, poised prominently on a corner 4 blocks north of Dupont Circle, has nine exquisite guest rooms, two with private entrances. The coolest unit is the Blue Sky Suite, which has the original rose-tiled working fireplace, a queen-size bed and sofa bed, a gabled ceiling, and its own roof deck. The most romantic room is probably Il Duomo, with Gothic windows, a cathedral ceiling, a working fireplace, and a turreted bathroom with angel murals. The Jennifer Green Room has a queen-size bed, a working fireplace, an oversize marble steam shower, and a private deck overlooking the pool area and garden. The Regent Room also has a private deck overlooking the pool, as well as a king-size bed in front of a carved working fireplace and a whirlpool. There are three suites. You'll want to spend some time on the main floor of the mansion, which has 12-foot ceilings, fluted woodwork, inlaid wood floors, a turreted living room, a columned sitting room, and a sunroom (where breakfast is served) leading through three sets of French doors to the garden and pool. No smoking.

1808 New Hampshire Ave. NW (between S and Swann sts.), Washington, DC 20009. ℂ 202/265-4414. Fax 202/265-6755. www.swannhouse.com. 9 units, all with private bathroom (3 with shower only, 1 with tub only). $140–$295 depending on unit and season. 2-night minimum weekends, 3-night minimum holiday weekends. Extended-stay and government rates available. Extra person $35. Rates include expanded continental breakfast. Limited off-street parking $12. AE, MC, V. Metro: Dupont Circle. No children under age 12. **Amenities:** Outdoor pool; access to nearby health club; business services; same-day dry cleaning; in-room massage. *In room:* A/C, TV, dataport, hair dryer.

Topaz Hotel ⊛   Like the Hotel Rouge (see p. 98 for review), the Topaz is an upscale boutique hotel for those who think young. This hotel seems tamer than the Rouge, but it still has a buzz about it, a pleasant, interesting sort of buzz. The reception area, lobby and bar flow together, so if you arrive in the evening, you may feel like you've arrived at a party: The Topaz Bar and the Bar Rouge have fast become favorite hangouts for the after-work crowd. At the Topaz, they're liking drinks called "Blue Nirvana" (champagne mixed with vodka and blueberry liqueur) and "Pop" (6-oz. single servings of Pommery champagne), the better-than-bar-food cuisine with an Asian accent, and the decor of velvety settees, zebra-patterned ottomans, and a lighting system that fades in and out. (See p. 266 for more information about the Topaz Bar.)

Upstairs are guest rooms appealingly, whimsically decorated with striped lime green wallpaper; a polka dot padded headboard for the down-comforter-covered bed; a bright blue, curved-back settee; a big, round mirror set in a sunburst frame; a light green and yellow painted armoire with fabric panels; and a red, with gold star-patterned cushioned chair. The rooms are unusually large (in its former life as the Canterbury Hotel, these were "junior suites" and held kitchenettes), and each has an alcove where the desk is placed, and a separate dressing room that holds a dressing table and cube-shaped ottoman. The Topaz pursues a sort of New Age wellness motif; do note the spill of smooth stones arranged just so upon your bed ("Through time people have carried special stones called totems to bring them energy and empowerment . . ." reads a little card accompanying the stones.) You also have the option to book a specialty room: one of four "energy" guest rooms, which include a piece of exercise equipment (either a treadmill or a stationary bike), and fitness magazines; or one of three "yoga" rooms, which come with an exercise mat, an instructional tape, padded pillows, special towels, and yoga magazines.

The Topaz lies on a quiet residential street, whose front-of-the-house windows overlook picturesque town houses.

1733 N St. NW (right next to the Tabard Inn, see below, between 17th and 18th sts.), Washington, DC 20036. © **800/424-2950** or 202/393-3000. Fax 202/785-9581. www.topazhotel.com. 99 units. Weekdays $240–$275 double, $280 specialty room; weekends $145 double; $185 specialty rooms. Extra person $20. Children under 16 stay free in parents' room. Rates include complimentary morning energy potions. AE, DC, DISC, MC, V. Parking $20. Pets welcome. Metro: Dupont Circle. **Amenities:** Bar/restaurant (innovative American with an Asian influence); access to nearby health club ($5 per guest); 24-hr. concierge; business services; room service (7am–11pm); same-day laundry/dry cleaning; 5 rooms for guests with disabilities, 2 with roll-in showers. *In room:* A/C, TV w/pay movies, 2-line cordless phones w/dataports, minibar, teapot with exotic teas, hair dryer, iron, safe, robes.

MODERATE

Embassy Suites Hotel Downtown ☆ *Kids*   This hotel offers unbelievable value and a convenient location, within walking distance of Foggy Bottom, Georgetown, and Dupont Circle. You enter into a tropical and glassy eight-story atrium with two waterfalls constantly running. This is where you'll enjoy an ample complimentary breakfast—not your standard cold croissant and coffee, but stations from which you can choose omelets made to order, waffles, bacon, fresh fruit, juices, bagels, and pastries. Tables are scattered in alcoves throughout the atrium to allow for privacy. Each evening, the atrium is the setting for complimentary beverages (including cocktails) and light cold snacks.

The accommodations are nicer than your average hotel room, with better amenities. Every unit is a two-room suite, with a living room that closes off completely from the rest of the suite. The living room holds a queen-size sofa bed, TV, easy chair, and large table with four comfortable chairs around it. The bedroom lies at the back of the suite, overlooking a quiet courtyard of brick walkways or the street. A king-size bed or two double beds, TV, sink, easy chair, and chest of drawers furnish this space. Between the living room and the bedroom are the bathroom, small closet, and a kitchenette. It's worth requesting one of the eighth- or ninth-floor suites with views of Georgetown and beyond, as far as Washington National Cathedral (the hotel will note your request, but won't be able to guarantee you such a suite). For the roomiest quarters, ask for an "executive corner suite," the slightly larger, slightly more expensive suites situated in the corners of the hotel.

1250 22nd St. NW (between M and N sts.), Washington, DC 20037. © 800/EMBASSY or 202/857-3388. Fax 202/293-3173. www.embassysuitesdcmetro.com. 318 suites. $169–$309 double. Rates include full breakfast and evening reception. Ask for AAA discounts or check the website for best rates. Extra person $25. Children 18 under stay free in parents' room. AE, DC, DISC, MC, V. Parking $19. Metro: Foggy Bottom. **Amenities:** Restaurant (northern Italian); state-of-the-art fitness center with indoor pool, whirlpool, sauna; game room; concierge; business center; room service (11am–11pm); coin-op washer/dryers; same-day laundry/dry cleaning; 8 rooms for guests with disabilities, 2 with roll-in showers. *In room:* A/C, TV w/pay movies, 2-line phone w/dataport, kitchenette with fridge and microwave, coffeemaker, hair dryer, iron.

Jurys Washington Hotel 𝒜 *Value* This hotel gets high marks for convenience (it's located right on Dupont Circle), service, and comfort. Open since 2000, the hotel is favored by business groups especially, who like its reasonable rates. Each of the large rooms is furnished with two double beds with firm mattresses, an armoire with TV, a desk, a wet-bar alcove, and a tiny but attractive bathroom. Decor is Art Deco-ish, with lots of light-wood furniture. All guest rooms offer free, high-speed Internet access. Despite its prime location in a sometimes raucous neighborhood, the hotel's rooms are insulated from the noise. Rooms on higher floors offer the best views of the city and of Dupont Circle. An Irish management company owns this hotel (along with 2 other properties in Washington), which explains the Irish influence. You'll occasionally detect an Irish accent from the staff, and the comfortable and attractive hotel pub, Biddy Mulligan's, proudly features a bar imported from the Emerald Isle. Claddaghs, the hotel restaurant, serves an American buffet breakfast every morning and American fare with an Irish flair at other meals. To get the best rates, check the website or call the hotel directly.

1500 New Hampshire Ave. NW (across from Dupont Circle), Washington, DC 20036. © 800/42-DOYLE or 202/483-6000. Fax 202/232-1130. www.jurysdoyle.com. 314 units. $145–$235 double; from $600 suite. Extra person $15. Children 17 and under stay free in parents' room. AE, DC, DISC, MC, V. Parking $17. Metro: Dupont Circle. **Amenities:** Restaurant (Irish/American); bar; exercise room; 24-hr. concierge; business center; same-day laundry/dry cleaning; room service (6:30am–midnight); 11 rooms for guests with disabilities, 4 with roll-in showers. *In room:* A/C, TV w/pay movies, 2-line phone w/dataport, minibar, coffeemaker, hair dryer, iron, safe.

Tabard Inn Hotel If you favor the offbeat and the personal over brand names and cookie-cutter chains, this might be the place for you. The Tabard Inn, named for the hostelry in Chaucer's *Canterbury Tales,* is actually three Victorian town houses that were joined in 1914 and have operated as an inn ever since. Situated on a quiet street of similarly old dwellings, the Tabard is a well-worn, funky hotel that's looked after by a chummy, peace-love-and-understanding sort of staff who clearly cherish the place.

The heart of the ground floor is the dark-paneled lounge, with worn furniture, a wood-burning fireplace, the original beamed ceiling, and bookcases. This is a favorite spot for Washingtonians to come for a drink, especially in winter, or to linger before or after dining in the charming **Tabard Inn restaurant** 𝒜 (see p. 147 for a full review).

Moments "There's a Small Hotel"

If you're in Washington on a Sunday night and you're staying at the **Tabard Inn,** be sure to plant yourself in the paneled parlor by 7:30pm. Even if you're not staying at the Tabard, you might want to get yourself there. From 7:30 to 10:30pm each Sunday, bassist Victor Dvoskin, usually accompanied by a guitarist, plays world-class jazz for free. Order a drink from the bar in the next room, then settle into one of the old chairs or sofas to enjoy the show. "There's a Small Hotel" is the name of a CD released by Dvoskin, in honor of Tabard owners Fritzi Cohen and her late husband, Edward, whose private program, the Capitals Citizens' Exchange, first brought Dvoskin to this country from Russia in 1988.

From the lounge, the inn leads you up and down stairs, along dim corridors, and through nooks and crannies to guest rooms. Can you dig chartreuse? (Ask for room 3.) How about aubergine? (Ask for room 11.) Each is different, but those facing N Street are largest and brightest, and some have bay windows. Furnishings are a mix of antiques and flea-market finds. Perhaps the most eccentric room is the top-floor "penthouse," which has skylights, exposed brick walls, its own kitchen, and a deck accessed by climbing out a window. The inn is not easily accessible to guests with disabilities.

1739 N St. NW (between 17th and 18th sts.), Washington, DC 20036. © 202/785-1277. Fax 202/785-6173. www.tabardinn.com. 40 units, 27 with private bathroom (6 with shower only). $100–$120 double with shared bathroom; $125–$190 double with private bathroom. Extra person $15. Rates include continental breakfast. AE, DC, DISC, MC, V. Limited street parking, plus 2 parking garages on N St. Metro: Dupont Circle. Small and confined pets allowed ($20 fee). **Amenities:** Restaurant (regional American) with lounge (free live jazz Sun evenings); free access to nearby YMCA (with extensive facilities that include indoor pool, indoor track, and racquetball/basketball courts); laundry service; fax, iron, hair dryer and safe available at front desk. *In room:* A/C, dataport.

6 Foggy Bottom/West End

VERY EXPENSIVE

Monarch Hotel ＲＲ The Monarch offers one of the best fitness facilities in town, an ever-popular Sunday brunch, and a favorite setting for wedding receptions and business functions (the Colonnade, an elegant, enclosed gazebo with a skylight ceiling and mullioned windows overlooking the hotel's interior garden courtyard). Because of these features, as well as the appealing, greenhouse-like lobby lounge, the Monarch draws locals through its doors as often as hotel guests. (That might be D.C. Mayor Anthony C. Williams himself sweating next to you in the fitness center.) The hotel lies in a tame part of town, but it's a short walk from both Georgetown and Dupont Circle.

Things are quieter upstairs, where rooms overlook the courtyard, 24th Street, or M Street. Ask for a room on the 24th Street side if you want to make sure you're not disturbed by events taking place in the Colonnade and courtyard. Guest rooms, last renovated in 2000, are spacious, and so are the bathrooms, which are tiled in Italian marble. The hotel offers two kinds of suites: one-room studios and those in which the bedroom is separate from the parlor and dining room. The hotel recently furnished each room with a CD player and a scale.

The 17,500-square-foot Fitness Company West End includes an indoor pool and spa facilities, squash and racquetball courts, and every kind of exercise equipment. (This is where Demi Moore learned how to do her one-arm push-up for the movie *GI Jane*.) Guests pay $10 a day to use certain exercise equipment or to take aerobics classes, but may use the pool, the Jacuzzi, the StairMaster, and the treadmill for free.

2401 M St. NW (entrance on 24th St.), Washington, DC 20037. © 877/222-2266 or 202/429-2400. Fax 202/457-5010. www.monarchdc.com. 415 units. Weekdays $255–$400 double, weekends $189–$350 double; $1,100–$3,000 suite. Extra person $30. Children under 18 stay free in parents' room. AE, DC, DISC, MC, V. Valet parking $23. Metro: Foggy Bottom. Small pets accepted ($150 deposit). **Amenities:** Restaurant (contemporary American); bar; extensive health club and spa ($10 fee for classes or use of certain equipment); concierge; 24-hr. technology center (staffed 7am–7pm; guests are charged $30 per half-hour, after hours); 24-hr. room service; same-day laundry/dry cleaning; 9 rooms for guests with disabilities, some with roll-in showers. *In-room:* A/C, TV w/pay movies, 2-line phones w/dataport, minibar, CD player, hair dryer, iron, safe, robes.

Park Hyatt 🏵🏵   This luxury hotel across the street from the Monarch Hotel wrapped up a full renovation in 2000. The large guest rooms now have goose-down duvets on the beds, and new furniture, wall coverings, and fabrics. Specially commissioned artwork hangs throughout the hotel. More than half of the rooms are suites (meaning the parlor and bedroom are separate), and the remaining rooms are deluxe kings. The suites also have dressing rooms with full vanities. Each bathroom has a TV, a radio, and a telephone, along with the usual amenities. The 15-year-old 10-story hotel hosts big names, royal families (who use the Presidential Suite, with its fireplace and grand piano), lobbyists, and tourists. Rooms are handsome and service is superb.

The bright and lovely Melrose dining room offers four-star cuisine with an emphasis on seafood (see p. 151 for a full review); the amiable chef, Brian McBride, pops into the dining room personally from time to time to make sure all is well. Adjoining the Melrose is a bar, where there's swing dancing to live jazz every weekends.

1201 24th St. NW (at M St.), Washington, DC 20037. © 800/778-7477 or 202/789-1234. Fax 202/419-6795. www.parkhyatt.com. 223 units. Weekdays $320–$450 double; weekends $215–$289 double. Extra person $25. Children 18 and under stay free in parents' room. AE, DC, DISC, MC, V. Valet parking $24. Metro: Foggy Bottom or Dupont Circle. Pets allowed. **Amenities:** Restaurant (American); bar/lounge (with live entertainment Fri–Sat); health club (with indoor pool, whirlpool, and sauna and steam rooms); spa with hair and skin salon; concierge; business center; 24-hr. room service; in-room massage; same-day laundry/dry cleaning; 10 rooms for guests with disabilities, 3 with roll-in showers. *In room:* A/C, TV w/pay movies, 2-line phone w/dataport, minibar, hair dryer, iron, safe, robes.

The Ritz-Carlton 🏵🏵🏵   This new Ritz-Carlton, which opened in October 2000, surpasses all other Washington hotels for service and amenities. From the cadre of doormen and valet parking attendants who greet you effusively when you arrive, to the graceful young women in long dresses who swan around you serving cocktails in the bar and lounge, the Ritz staff is always looking after you.

The hotel is built around a multitiered Japanese garden and courtyard with reflecting pools and cascading waterfall; guest rooms on the inside of the complex overlook the waterfall or terraced garden, while guest rooms on the outside perimeter view landmarks and cityscapes. The woman who showed me to my terrace-view room inadvertently, but appropriately, kept referring to the hotel as the "Rich-Carlton." My standard room was very large, and richly furnished with a firm king-size bed covered in both duvet and bedspread, decorative inlaid wooden furniture, a comfy armchair and ottoman, and very pretty artwork. The marble bathroom was immense, with long counter space, separate bathtub and shower stall, and the toilet in its own room behind a louvered door. The clock radio doubles as a CD player and the phone features a button for summoning the "technology butler" (a complimentary, 24/7 service for guests with computer questions). Other nice touches in the rooms include an umbrella, windows that open, and an outlet for recharging laptops. Don't make the same mistake that I did when I passed up the evening turndown—the maid places a warm, freshly baked brownie upon your pillow instead of the usual mint.

Among the different versions of suites available, most are "executives," which include a sitting room and separate bedroom.

Guests enjoy free use of the hotel's fitness center, the two-level, 100,000-square-foot Sports Club/LA, which officially leaves all other hotel health clubs in the dust with its state-of-the-art weight-training equipment and free weights, two regulation-size basketball courts and four squash courts, an indoor heated swimming pool and an aquatics pool with a sun deck, exercise classes, personal trainers, the full-service Splash Spa and Salon, and its own restaurant and cafe.

The Ritz's bar and lounge are also exceptionally inviting, with lots of plush upholstered couches and armchairs, a fire blazing in the fireplace in winter, and a pianist playing every day. Afternoon tea is served in the lounge daily.

The Ritz's restaurant, The Grill, is still getting its feet wet. My guess is that by the time you read this, the restaurant will have ironed out its kinks and be a place worth trying.

1150 22nd St. NW (at M St.), Washington, DC 20037. (℃) **800/241-3333** or 202/835-0500. Fax 202/835-1588. www.ritzcarlton.com. 300 units. $450 double; from $595 suite. No charge for extra person in the room. Ask about discount packages. AE, DC, DISC, MC, V. Valet parking $18, self-parking $15. Metro: Foggy Bottom or Dupont Circle. Pets accepted (no fee). **Amenities:** Restaurant (American); lounge; fabulous health club and spa (the best in the city; see above); 24-hr. concierge; business center (open weekdays); 24-hr.fax and currency-exchange services; salon; 24-hr. room service; in-room massage; babysitting; same-day laundry/dry cleaning; 1-hr. pressing; club level with 5 complimentary food presentations throughout the day (including a chef station each morning to prepare individual requests); 10 rooms for guests with disabilities. *In-room:* A/C, TV w/pay movies, 2-line phone w/high-speed Internet access, minibar/fridge, hair dryer, iron, safe, robes, umbrella.

EXPENSIVE

Hotel Lombardy ℛ From its handsome walnut-paneled lobby with carved Tudor-style ceilings to its old-fashioned manual elevator (fasten your seat belts—it's going to be a bumpy ride), the 11-story Lombardy offers a lot of character and comfort for the price. Originally built in 1929, it's located about 5 blocks west of the White House. George Washington University's campus is just across Pennsylvania Avenue, so this area remains vibrant long after other downtown neighborhoods have rolled up the sidewalks. Peace Corps, World Bank, and corporate guests make up a large part of the clientele, but other visitors will also appreciate the Lombardy's warm, welcoming ambience and the attentive service of the multilingual staff.

The decor in each spacious room has a unique touch. All are entered via pedimented louver doors, and are furnished with original artwork and Chinese and European antiques. All rooms have large desks, precious dressing rooms, and roomy walk-in closets; new drapes, bedspreads, and carpeting were installed in the spring of 2001. Most of the 38 one-bedroom suites have small kitchens with dining areas. Front rooms overlook Pennsylvania Avenue and the small triangular park across the street, named for Pres. James Monroe. Back rooms are quieter; some overlook the garden of the hotel's next-door neighbor, the Arts Club of Washington, where Monroe once lived. Coming in 2003: an on-site fitness center.

2019 Pennsylvania Ave. NW (between 20th and 21st sts.), Washington, DC 20006. ℂ 800/424-5486 or 202/828-2600. Fax 202/872-0503. www.hotellombardy.com. 130 units. Weekdays $149–$199 double, weekends and some off-season weekdays $119–$149 double; weekdays $199–$239 suite for 2, weekends $169–$219 suite for 2. Extra person $20. Children under 16 stay free in parents' room. AE, DC, DISC, MC, V. Self-parking $17. Metro: Farragut West or Foggy Bottom. **Amenities:** Restaurant (American); lounge (shares a menu with the restaurant, as well as offering an appetizer menu); concierge; room service (6:30am–10pm); same-day laundry/dry cleaning. *In room:* A/C, TV w/pay movies, 2-line phone w/dataport, kitchens (in some rooms), minibar, coffeemaker, hair dryer, iron, robes.

MODERATE

George Washington University Inn   Rumor has it that this whitewashed brick inn, another former apartment building, used to be a favorite spot for clandestine trysts for high-society types. These days you're more likely to see Kennedy Center performers and visiting professors. The university purchased the hotel (formerly known as the Inn at Foggy Bottom) in 1994 and renovated it. The most recent refurbishment, in 2001, replaced linens, drapes, and the like in the guest rooms.

Rooms are a little larger and corridors are a tad narrower than those in a typical hotel, and each room includes a roomy dressing chamber. More than one-third of the units are one-bedroom suites. These are especially spacious, with living rooms that hold a sleeper sofa and a TV hidden in an armoire (there's another in the bedroom). The suites, plus the 16 efficiencies, have kitchens. The spaciousness and the kitchen facilities make this a popular choice for families and for long-term guests.

This is a fairly safe and lovely neighborhood, within easy walking distance to Georgetown, the Kennedy Center, and downtown. But keep an eye peeled—you have to pass through wrought-iron gates into a kind of cul-de-sac to find the inn.

Off the lobby is the restaurant (a new one will be in place by the time you read this).

If it's not full, the inn may be willing to offer reduced rates. Mention prices quoted in the inn's *New York Times* ad, if you've seen it; or your affiliation with George Washington University, if you have one.

824 New Hampshire Ave. NW (between H and I sts.), Washington, DC 20037. ℂ 800/426-4455 or 202/337-6620. Fax 202/298-7499. www.gwuinn.com. 95 units. Weekdays $130–$175 double, weekends $99–$135 double; weekdays $140–$185 efficiency, weekends $110–$155 efficiency; weekdays $155–$220 1-bedroom suite, weekends $125–$170 1-bedroom suite. Children under 12 stay free in parents' room. AE, DC, MC, V. Limited parking $18. Metro: Foggy Bottom. **Amenities:** Restaurant (hadn't opened yet, so cuisine still undecided); complimentary passes to nearby fitness center; room service; coin-op washer/dryers; same-day laundry/dry cleaning; 5 rooms for guests with disabilities, one with roll-in showers. *In room:* A/C, TV, 2-line phone w/dataport, fridge, coffeemaker, microwave, hair dryer, iron.

7 Georgetown

VERY EXPENSIVE

Four Seasons 🏵🏵🏵   Although the Four Seasons now has a spectacular rival in the new and nearby Ritz-Carlton (p. 108), the hotel continues to attract the rich and famous, who appreciate the superb service. Staff members are trained to know the names, preferences, and even allergies of guests, and repeat clientele rely on this discreet attention.

The hotel sits at the mouth of Georgetown, backing up against Rock Creek Park and the C&O Canal. Accommodations, many of which overlook the park or canal, are newly renovated and have an upscale, homey feel. Beds are outfitted with down-filled bedding, dust ruffles, and scalloped spreads; and rooms have large desks and plump cushioned armchairs with hassocks. An adjoining building that opened in 1999 holds 25 rooms and 35 suites for clients who want state-of-the-art business amenities (each is soundproof and has an office equipped with a fax machine, at least 3 telephones with 2-line speakers, portable telephones, and headsets for private TV listening). These rooms are also larger than those in the main hotel. Three of the suites have kitchenettes. Original avant-garde artwork from the personal collection of owner William Louis-Dreyfus (yes, Julia's dad) hangs in every room and public space. Transmitters installed throughout the hotel allow you wireless connection to the Internet on your laptop, wherever you go in the hotel. In 2002, the hotel introduced its "Travel Light" service, which allows a guest to leave at the hotel a garment bag of clothing and personal items, which the hotel stores securely until the guest returns for another visit; upon arrival, the guest checks in and finds the garment bag hanging in his/her guest room closet.

2800 Pennsylvania Ave. NW (which becomes M St. a block farther along), Washington, DC 20007. *C* 800/ 332-3442 or 202/342-0444. Fax 202/944-2076. www.fourseasons.com. 260 units. Weekdays $455–$615 double, weekends from $295 double; weekdays $695–$5,150 suite, weekends from $550 suite. Extra person $40. Children under 16 stay free in parents' room. AE, DC, MC, V. Parking $26, plus tax. Metro: Foggy Bottom. Pets allowed, up to 15 lb. **Amenities:** Formal restaurant (seasonal American); lounge (for afternoon tea, and cocktails); extensive state-of-the-art fitness club and spa with personal trainers, lap pool, Vichy shower, hydrotherapy, and synchronized massage (2 people work on you at the same time); bike rentals; children's program (various goodies provided, but no organized activities); 24-hr. concierge; complimentary sedan service weekdays within the District; business center; salon; 24-hr. room service; in-room massage; babysitting; same-day laundry/dry cleaning; 7 rooms for guests with disabilities. *In room:* A/C, TV w/pay movies and Web access, high-speed Internet access, high-tech CD player, minibar, hair dryer, iron, safe, robes.

EXPENSIVE

Georgetown Inn *☞*   Like its sister inn, the Latham (see below), this hotel is in the thick of Georgetown. Most guests are here on business, but come Memorial Day weekend, the hotel is full of the proud parents of graduating Georgetown University students. (The hotel books up 2 years in advance for graduation weekend.)

The Georgetown is smaller than the Latham, but has larger rooms. Furnishings are European-handsome, heavy on the dark woods. Half of the rooms hold two double beds, although a couple of rooms have twin single beds, connecting with suites, helpful to families traveling with children. Ask for an "executive room" if you'd like a sitting area with pullout sofa, and extra conveniences like a reading lamp over the bed. Even better are the 10 one-bedroom suites, in which bedroom and large living room are separate. The bathrooms have only showers (some also have bidets), no tub.

The **Daily Grill** has an outpost here, offering the same generous portions of American food served at its original D.C. location, at 1200 18th St. NW (see p. 137 for a full review).

1310 Wisconsin Ave. NW (between N and O sts.), Washington, DC 20007. *C* 800/368-5922 or 202/333-8900. Fax 202/333-8308. www.georgetowninn.com. 96 units. Weekdays $195–$245 double, weekends $139–$245 double. Suites from $345. Ask about promotional rates. Extra person $20. Children under 12 stay free in parents' room. AE, DC, DISC, MC, V. Valet parking $22. Metro: Foggy Bottom, with a 30-minute walk, or take a cab. **Amenities:** Restaurant (American); bar; outdoor pool (at the Latham; see below); exercise room, plus free access to Monarch Hotel's extensive health club and spa (p. 107); concierge; room service during restaurant hours; same-day laundry/dry cleaning; 4 rooms for guests with disabilities, all with roll-in showers. *In room:* A/C, TV w/pay movies and Nintendo, 2-line phones w/dataport and high-speed Internet access, hair dryer, iron.

Hotel Monticello of Georgetown ✿   This hotel gets a lot of repeat business from both corporate and leisure travelers, who appreciate the intimacy of a small hotel, including personalized service from a staff who greets you by name and protects your privacy. It's also a favorite choice for families celebrating weddings or graduations (both Georgetown and George Washington universities are close by); they sometimes book several suites, or maybe a whole floor. A major renovation in 2000 gutted the whole building and created a more upscale setting (this used to be the Georgetown Dutch Inn). Rooms now bring in much more light, thanks to layout and design changes, better use of windows, and the placement of French doors with frosted glass between rooms. You'll notice that the top sheet on your bed is monogrammed, the sofa in the living room folds out, and those are Hermès bath products in the new marble bathrooms. Next in the works is a total remodeling of the penthouse suites, which may still be going on when you read this.

Accommodations are medium-size one- and two-bedroom apartment-like suites. Six of the suites are studios, in which the living room and bedroom are joined, and nine of them are duplex penthouses with 1½ bathrooms. Every suite has a wet bar with a microwave and refrigerator. The duplex penthouses have full kitchens. In addition to continental breakfast in the morning, fresh fruit, coffee, and herbal tea are available in the lobby all day.

The hotel is in the heart of Georgetown, surrounded by shops and restaurants. The C&O Canal towpath, just down the block, is ideal for jogging and cycling, though you should be wary at night.

1075 Thomas Jefferson St. NW (just below M St.), Washington, DC 20007. ℂ **800/388-2410** or 202/337-0900. Fax 202/333-6526. www.monticellohotel.com. 47 suites. Peak-season weekdays $219–$269, off-peak weekdays $169–$189; peak-season weekends $169–$189, off-peak weekends $149–$169. Call for penthouse suite rates (renovation may affect prices). Extra person $20. Rates include continental breakfast. Children under 14 stay free in parents' room. Promotional rates and discounts may be available. AE, DC, DISC, MC, V. Parking $10. Metro: Foggy Bottom, with a 20-min. walk. Bus: 32, 34, and 36 go to all major Washington tourist attractions. **Amenities:** Free access to Monarch Hotel's extensive health club and spa (p. 107); business center; in-room massage; babysitting; same-day laundry/dry cleaning except Sun; 4 rooms for guests with disabilities, 3 with roll-in showers. *In room:* A/C, TV, 2-line phone w/dataport, kitchenette with microwave, fridge, coffeemaker, hair dryer, iron.

The Latham ✿   The Latham is at the hub of Georgetown's trendy nightlife/restaurant/shopping scene, but since its accommodations are set back from the street, none of the noise of nighttime revelers will reach your room. Charming earth-tone rooms are decorated in a French-country motif, with pine furnishings and multipaned windows; cable TVs are housed in armoires. All rooms have large desks. Some 7th- through 10th-floor rooms offer gorgeous canal views; third-floor accommodations, all two-room suites, have windows facing a hallway designed to replicate a quaint Georgetown street. Most luxurious are the two-story carriage suites with cathedral ceilings, full living rooms, and 1½ bathrooms. Fax machines/printers are in a third of the rooms; CD players with headphones are in third-floor and carriage suites. All of the suites have mini-refrigerators. A renovation completed in 2000 refurbished hallways and replaced linens, carpeting, and furnishings in guest rooms. Most of the rooms are "executive kings," which means their beds are made up with Egyptian cotton sheets, down comforters, duvets, and feather pillows, and added amenities include printer/fax machines and heated towel bars.

Michel Richard's highly acclaimed **Citronelle** ✿✿, one of D.C.'s best restaurants, is on the premises (see p. 153 for a full review). And fronting the hotel is the country-French La Madeleine; another branch is fully described in the Alexandria section of chapter 10.

3000 M St. NW (between 30th and Thomas Jefferson sts.), Washington, DC 20007. © 800/528-4261 or 202/726-5000. Fax 202/337-4250. www.thelatham.com. 143 units. Weekdays $195–$245 double, weekends $139–$245 double; from $345 suite. Call hotel directly for promotional rates. Extra person $20. Children under 12 stay free in parents' room. AE, DC, DISC, MC, V. Valet parking $22. Metro: Foggy Bottom, with a 20-min. walk, or take a cab. **Amenities:** Restaurant (French) with bar; small, unheated, outdoor pool; free access to Monarch Hotel's extensive health club and spa (p. 107); 24-hr. concierge; business center; room service during restaurant hours; same-day laundry/dry cleaning; 2 rooms for guests with disabilities, both with roll-in showers. *In room:* A/C, TV w/pay movies and Nintendo, 2-line phone w/dataport and high-speed Internet access, hair dryer, iron, robes.

MODERATE

Georgetown Suites   This hotel was designed to meet the needs of business travelers making extended visits, but its casual atmosphere and suites with kitchens work well for families, too. It has two locations, within a block of each other.

The main building, which I prefer, is the one on 30th Street, a quiet residential street that's only steps away from Georgetown's action. This building offers a large lobby for hanging out; it almost feels like a student lounge, with the TV going; games, books, magazines, and daily newspapers scattered across table tops in front of love seats and chairs, and a cappuccino machine on the counter. In the morning, an extensive breakfast, featuring everything from waffles to fresh pastries, is laid out here. By contrast, the property on 29th Street (known as the "Harbor Building") is situated right next to the Whitehurst Freeway, is much noisier, and has a very small lobby (although you can linger outside in the brick courtyard where there are flowering plants and Victorian white wooden benches). Continental breakfast is served here, too, in the lobby.

Accommodations at both locations have living rooms, dining areas, and fully equipped kitchens. About half of the units are studios and half are one-bedroom suites. Glass-topped tables, chrome-framed chairs, and pastel-striped fabrics figure prominently in the decor. The biggest and best suites are the three two-level, two-bedroom town houses attached to the main building. Newly renovated, the town houses have brand-new furnishings, sunken Jacuzzi tubs and double sinks in the bathrooms, TVs with VCRs, CD players, and other deluxe features. These town houses have their own doors on 29th Street, through which you may exit only; to enter a town house, you must go through the hotel, as your key will not unlock the 29th Street door. This building also has two penthouse suites, which have their own terraces overlooking the rooftops of Georgetown.

1111 30th St. NW (just below M St.) and 1000 29th St. NW (at K St.), Washington, DC 20007. © 800/348-7203 or 202/298-1600. Fax 202/333-2019. www.georgetownsuites.com. 220 units. Weekdays $155 studio, $215 1-bedroom suite; weekends $155 studio, $185 1-bedroom suite. Penthouse suites from $350, town houses from $425. Rollaways or sleeper sofa $10 extra. Rates include continental breakfast. AE, DC, DISC, MC, V. Limited parking $15. Metro: Foggy Bottom, with a 15-min. walk. **Amenities:** Small exercise room; coin-op laundry; same-day laundry/dry cleaning; 2 rooms for guests with disabilities, both with roll-in showers. *In room:* A/C, TV, 2-line phone w/dataport, full kitchen (with fridge, coffeemaker, microwave, and dishwasher), hair dryer, iron.

8 Woodley Park

VERY EXPENSIVE

Marriott Wardman Park ✦   This is Washington's biggest hotel, resting on 16 acres just down the street from the National Zoo and several good restaurants.

Its size and location (the Woodley Park–Zoo Metro station is literally at its doorstep) make it a good choice for conventions, tour groups, and individual travelers. (*Warning:* you can get lost here, and I have.) Built in 1918, it is also one of Washington's oldest hotels. A massive $100 million renovation completed in 1999 replaced bed and bath linens, carpeting, and wall coverings in all the guest rooms, upgraded the ballroom and meeting rooms, restructured the outdoor pools, revamped the restaurants, and topped the lobby with a soaring four-story dome.

From the outside, the hotel resembles a college campus: There's an old part, whose entrance is draped by stately trees, and a new part, preceded by a great green lawn. The oldest section is the nicest. The 85-year-old redbrick Tower houses 205 guest rooms, each featuring high ceilings, ornate crown moldings, and an assortment of antique French and English furnishings. This was once an apartment building whose residents included presidents Hoover, Eisenhower, and Johnson, as well as actors like Douglas Fairbanks Jr. and authors such as Gore Vidal.

The hotel has 125 suites in all, ranging in size from one to five bedrooms. Best are the 54 suites in the Wardman Tower, many of which have balconies overlooking the gardens. The size of the hotel enables it to accommodate requests for different setups: two double beds, king beds, and so on. All rooms offer high-speed Internet access.

2660 Woodley Rd. NW (at Connecticut Ave. NW), Washington, DC 20008. © 800/325-3535 or 202/328-2000. Fax 202/234-0015. www.marriotthotels.com/wasdt. 1,340 units. Weekdays $289 double, weekends $119–$289 double; $350–$2,500 suite. Children under 18 stay free in parents' room. AE, DC, DISC, MC, V. Valet parking $23, self-parking $19. Metro: Woodley Park–Zoo. Pets under 20 lb. permitted but charges may apply; call for details. **Amenities:** 2 restaurants (American, Mediterranean); pub; deli/pastry shop; lobby bar; Starbucks; 2 outdoor heated pools with sun deck; well-equipped fitness center; concierge; business center; salon; room service; in-room massage; babysitting; coin-op washer/dryers; same-day laundry/dry cleaning; concierge-level rooms; 47 rooms for guests with disabilities. *In room:* A/C, TV w/pay movies, 2-line phone w/dataport and high-speed Internet access, coffeemaker, hair dryer, iron.

EXPENSIVE

Omni Shoreham 🐦 *(Kids* This is Woodley Park's *other* really big hotel, though with 836 rooms, the Omni Shoreham is still 500 short of the behemoth Marriott Wardman Park. And it's all the more appealing for it, since it's not quite so overwhelming as the Marriott. Its design—wide corridors, vaulted ceilings and archways, and arrangements of pretty sofas and armchairs in the lobby and public spaces—endows the Shoreham with the air of a grand hotel. A massive $80 million renovation completed in 2000 installed a new air-conditioning system, restructured the pool, upgraded the already excellent fitness center health spa, and restored a traditional, elegant look to guest rooms and the lobby. The spacious guest rooms remain twice the size of your average hotel room. Most of the 52 suites are junior suites, with the sitting room and bedroom combined. The hotel sits on 11 acres overlooking Rock Creek Park; park-side rooms are a little smaller but offer spectacular views.

With its 22 meeting rooms and 7 ballrooms (some of which open to terraces overlooking the park!), the hotel is popular as a meeting and convention venue. Leisure travelers appreciate the Shoreham for its large outdoor swimming pool, its proximity to the National Zoo and excellent restaurants, and the immediate access to biking, hiking, and jogging paths through Rock Creek Park. The hotel is just down the street from the Woodley Park–Zoo Metro station. You can also walk to the more hip neighborhoods of Adams-Morgan and Dupont Circle from the hotel; the stroll to Dupont Circle, taking you over the bridge that spans Rock Creek Park, is especially nice (and safe at night, too).

Built in 1930, the Shoreham has been the scene of inaugural balls for every president since FDR. Do you believe in ghosts? Ask about Room 870, the haunted suite (available for $3,000 a night).

2500 Calvert St. NW (near Connecticut Ave.), Washington, DC 20008. ℭ 800/843-6664 or 202/234-0700. Fax 202/265-7972. www.omnihotels.com. 836 units. $179–$309 double; from $350–$3,000 suite. Call the hotel directly for best rates. Extra person $20. Children under 18 stay free in parents' room. AE, DC, DISC, MC, V. Valet parking $22; self-parking $19. Metro: Woodley Park–Zoo. **Amenities:** Restaurant (continental; terrace overlooks Rock Creek Park), gourmet carryout; bar/lounge (serves light fare and has live music nightly); fitness center and spa with heated outdoor pool, separate kids' pool, and whirlpool; children's gifts; concierge; travel/sightseeing desk; business center; shops; 24-hr. room service; massage; same-day laundry/dry cleaning; 41 rooms for guests with disabilities, half with roll-in showers. *In room:* A/C, TV w/pay movies and Nintendo, 2-line phone w/dataport, hair dryer, iron, robe.

INEXPENSIVE

You might consider the Woodley Park location of the **Kalorama Guest House,** at 2700 Cathedral Ave. NW (entrance on 27th St.; ℭ **202/328-0860**), which has 19 units, 12 with private bathrooms. Rates are $55 to $75 for a double with a shared bathroom, $75 to $100 for a double with private bathroom, and include continental breakfast. Limited parking is available for $7, and the Woodley Park–Zoo Metro stop is nearby. See p. 102 for the full listing for the main location of the Kalorama Guest House in Adams-Morgan for more information.

6

Where to Dine

Sightseeing works up an appetite, you can count on it. Instead of waiting for hunger to hit and then appeasing your pangs with junk food from the nearest street vendor, why not plan ahead and make restaurant stops part of your itinerary? Sure, you may have come to Washington to visit the Capitol and the Smithsonian museums, but if you leave without dining at least once at one of the city's excellent restaurants, you've missed a delicious and quintessential Washington experience. I've sampled a variety of the city's restaurants, and in this chapter, I've selected some of the best the capital has to offer.

Some tips to keep in mind: Call ahead for **reservations,** especially for a Saturday night, which books up especially fast. A number of restaurants are affiliated with an online reservation service called **www.opentable.com,** so if you've got Internet access, you might reserve your table on the Web.

If you prefer spontaneity, you might wait until the last minute to make a reservation, as long as you don't mind dining really early, say 5:30 or 6pm, or really late (by Washington standards, 9:30pm qualifies as late—this is not a late-night town). Or you can sit at the bar and eat, which can be fun. Better yet, consider a restaurant that doesn't take reservations. This practice seems to be on the upswing and works for places like Johnny's Half-Shell and Lauriol Plaza, where the atmosphere is casual, the wait becomes part of the experience, and the food is worth standing in line for.

Few places require men to wear a jacket and tie; I've made a special note in the listings for those places that do. If you're driving, call ahead to inquire about valet parking, complimentary or otherwise—on Washington's crowded streets, this service can be a true bonus. Finally, if you are meeting chronically late people for dinner, find out if the restaurant has a "full party must be present to be seated" policy, which can really throw a wrench in your plans if you lose a table because someone is late.

I've listed the closest Metro station to each restaurant only when it's within walking distance of a restaurant. If you need bus-routing information, call ✆ **202/637-7000.**

ABOUT THE PRICES

I've selected a range of menus and prices in almost every Washington neighborhood. Restaurants are grouped first by location, then alphabetically by price category. Keep in mind that the price categories refer to dinner prices, but some very expensive restaurants offer affordable lunches, early-bird dinners, tapas, or bar meals. (Or consider something totally different, like high tea in the late afternoon—look for "A Spot of Tea," on p. 160, which lists some swell places to swill tea.) The prices within each review refer to the cost of individual entrees, not the entire meal. I've used the following price categories: **Very Expensive,** main courses at dinner average more than $25; **Expensive,** $16 to $25; **Moderate,** $10 to $15; and **Inexpensive,** $10 and under.

1 Restaurants by Cuisine

AMERICAN

Ben's Chili Bowl (U Street Corridor, $, p. 142)

Butterfield 9 ✿✿ (Downtown East, $$$$, p. 123)

Cashion's Eat Place ✿✿ (Adams-Morgan, $$$, p. 142)

Clyde's of Georgetown (Georgetown, $$, p. 157)

Daily Grill ✿ (Downtown West, Georgetown, $$$, p. 137)

DC Coast ✿ (Downtown East, $$$, p. 129)

Equinox ✿✿ (Downtown West, $$$, p. 137)

Felix Restaurant and Lounge ✿ (Adams-Morgan, $$$, p. 144)

Kinkead's ✿✿✿ (Foggy Bottom, $$$, p. 152)

Melrose ✿✿ (Foggy Bottom, $$$$, p. 151)

Mendocino Grille and Wine Bar ✿ (Georgetown, $$$, p. 154)

The Monocle ✿ (Capitol Hill, $$$, p. 122)

New Heights ✿ (Woodley Park/Cleveland Park, $$$, p. 161)

Nora ✿✿ (Dupont Circle, $$$$, p. 146)

Occidental Grill ✿ (Downtown East, $$$$, p. 127)

Old Ebbitt Grill (Downtown East, $$, p. 133)

Oval Room at Lafayette Square ✿✿ (Downtown West, $$, p. 138)

Red Sage Grill ✿ (Downtown East, $$$$, p. 127)

The Restaurant at the Jefferson ✿ (Downtown West, $$$$, p. 136)

701 ✿ (Downtown East, $$$, p. 131)

1789 ✿✿ (Georgetown, $$$$, p. 154)

Signatures ✿ (Downtown East, $$$$, p. 127)

Tabard Inn ✿ (Dupont Circle, $$$, p. 147)

Tahoga ✿ (Georgetown, $$$, p. 156)

The Willard Room ✿ (Downtown East, $$$$, p. 128)

Vidalia ✿✿ (Downtown West, $$$, p. 139)

ASIAN FUSION

Asia Nora ✿ (Foggy Bottom, $$$, p. 151)

Oodles Noodles (Downtown West, $, p. 141)

Teaism (Downtown East, Downtown West, Dupont Circle, $, p. 149)

TenPenh ✿✿ (Downtown East, $$$, p. 132)

BARBECUE

Old Glory Barbecue (Georgetown, $$, p. 157)

CHINESE

Ching Ching Cha (Georgetown, $, p. 158)

City Lights of China (Dupont Circle, $$, p. 148)

Eat First ✿ (Downtown East, $, p. 133)

Full Kee ✿ (Downtown East, $, p. 134)

ETHIOPIAN

Meskerem (Adams-Morgan, $, p. 145)

Zed's (Georgetown, $, p. 158)

FRENCH

Bistro Bis ✿✿ (Capitol Hill, $$$, p. 121)

Bistrot du Coin ✿ (Dupont Circle, $$, p. 148)

Bistrot Lepic ✿✿ (Georgetown, $$, p. 156)

Gerard's Place ✿✿✿ (Downtown East, $$$$, p. 126)

La Colline ✿ (Capitol Hill, $$$, p. 122)

La Fourchette (Adams-Morgan, $$, p. 144)

Les Halles ✶ (Downtown East, $$$, p. 130)

Marcel's ✶✶ (Foggy Bottom, $$$$, p. 150)

Michel Richard Citronelle ✶✶✶ (Georgetown, $$$$, p. 153)

Montmartre ✶ (Capitol Hill, $$, p. 123)

Palena ✶✶ (Woodley Park/ Cleveland Park, $$$$, p. 160)

Petits Plats ✶ (Woodley Park/ Cleveland Park, $$$, p. 162)

The Willard Room ✶ (Downtown East, $$$$, p. 128)

GERMAN

Café Berlin (Capitol Hill, $$, p. 122)

INDIAN

Aditi (Georgetown, $, p. 158)

Bombay Club ✶ (Downtown West, $$, p. 140)

INTERNATIONAL

New Heights ✶ (Woodley Park/Cleveland Park, $$$, p. 161)

701 ✶ (Downtown East, $$$, p. 131)

ITALIAN

Al Tiramisu ✶✶ (Dupont Circle, $$$, p. 146)

Barolo ✶✶ (Capitol Hill, $$$, p. 120)

Café Milano ✶ (Georgetown, $$$, p. 154)

Coppi's (U Street Corridor, $, p. 142)

Etrusco ✶✶ (Dupont Circle, $$, p. 148)

Famous Luigi's Pizzeria Restaurant (Downtown West, $, p. 141)

Finemondo ✶ (Downtown West, $$$, p. 129)

Galileo ✶✶✶ (Downtown West, $$$$, p. 135)

Il Radicchio (Capitol Hill, $, p. 123)

I Ricchi ✶ (Downtown West, $$$$, p. 136)

Obelisk ✶✶✶ (Dupont Circle, $$$$, p. 146)

Oliveoil Cucina Italiano (Adams-Morgan, $$, p. 144)

Olives ✶ (Downtown West, $$$, p. 138)

Palena ✶✶ (Woodley Park/ Cleveland Park, $$$$, p. 160)

Pasta Mia (Adams-Morgan, $, p. 145)

Pizzeria Paradiso ✶ (Dupont Circle, $, p. 149)

Teatro Goldoni ✶✶ (Downtown West, $$$, p. 139)

Tosca ✶✶ (Downtown East, $$$, p. 132)

JAPANESE

Kaz Sushi Bistro (Foggy Bottom, $$, p. 152)

Sushi-Ko ✶ (Glover Park, $$$, p. 159)

LATIN AMERICAN

Café Atlantico ✶✶ (Downtown East, $$$, p. 129)

Lauriol Plaza ✶ (Adams-Morgan/ Dupont Circle, $$, p. 144)

MEXICAN

Andale ✶ (Downtown East, $$$, p. 128)

Lauriol Plaza ✶ (Adams-Morgan/ Dupont Circle, $$, p. 144)

Mixtec (Adams-Morgan, $, p. 145)

MIDDLE EASTERN

Lebanese Taverna (Woodley Park/Cleveland Park, $$, p. 162)

SEAFOOD

Blackie's ✶ (Foggy Bottom, $$$$, p. 150)

Georgetown Seafood Grill on 19th St. ✶ (Downtown West, $$$, p. 138)

Johnny's Half Shell ✶ (Dupont Circle, $$$, p. 147)

Legal Sea Foods ✶ (Downtown West, $$, p. 140)

Book your air, hotel, and transportation all in one place.

Hotel or hostel? Cruise or canoe? Car? Plane? Camel? Wherever you're going, visit Yahoo! Travel and get total control over your arrangements. Even choose your seat assignment. So. One hump or two? travel.yahoo.com

powered by COMPAQ

YAHOO!
Travel

DO YOU YAHOO!?

Kinkead's ✶✶✶ (Foggy Bottom,
$$$, p. 152)

McCormick & Schmick's
(Downtown West, $$, p. 140)

Morton's of Chicago ✶
(Downtown West, Georgetown,
$$$$, p. 153)

Oceanaire Seafood Room ✶
(Downtown East, $$$, p. 131)

The Prime Rib ✶ (Downtown
West, $$$$, p. 136)

Sea Catch ✶ (Georgetown, $$$,
p. 156)

SOUTHERN/SOUTHWESTERN

Austin Grill (Downtown East,
Glover Park, $, p. 159)

B. Smith's ✶ (Capitol Hill, $$$,
p. 119)

Georgia Brown's ✶ (Downtown
East, $$$, p. 130)

Red Sage Border Café ✶
(Downtown East, $, p. 127)

Vidalia ✶✶ (Downtown West,
$$$, p. 139)

SPANISH

Jaleo ✶ (Downtown East, $$,
p. 133)

Lauriol Plaza ✶ (Adams-Morgan/
Dupont Circle, $$, p. 144)

Taberna del Alabardero ✶✶
(Downtown West, $$$$,
p. 136)

STEAK

Blackie's ✶ (Foggy Bottom, $$$$,
p. 150)

The Caucus Room ✶✶
(Downtown East, $$$$, p. 126)

Les Halles ✶ (Downtown East,
$$$, p. 130)

Morton's of Chicago ✶
(Downtown West, Georgetown,
$$$$, p. 153)

The Palm ✶ (Downtown West,
$$$, p. 139)

The Prime Rib ✶ (Downtown
West, $$$$, p. 136)

Signatures ✶ (Downtown East,
$$$$, p. 127)

THAI

Busara (Glover Park, $$, p. 159)

Haad Thai (Downtown East, $,
p. 135)

Sala Thai (Dupont Circle, $,
p. 149)

VIETNAMESE

Miss Saigon (Georgetown, $$,
p. 157)

2 Capitol Hill

For information on eating at the Capitol and other government buildings, see
the box titled "Dining at Sightseeing Attractions," below.

EXPENSIVE

B. Smith's ✶ *(Finds)* TRADITIONAL SOUTHERN This is one of the few
upscale restaurants on Capitol Hill, and the only one in Union Station, and even
if the restaurant isn't on your route, it's worth coming here—for the food, of
course, but also to admire the restaurant's amazing interior. The dramatic din-
ing room once served as a presidential reception room hall, and now its 30-foot-
high ceilings, white marble floors, and towering Ionic columns make it a fitting
place for lobbyists, senators, and other well-paid Washingtonians to discuss seri-
ous business. On weekends, the ambience lightens up and romantic couples and
families dine here. Background music is always mellow (Nat King Cole, Ray
Charles, Sarah Vaughan). The restaurant features live jazz on Friday and Satur-
day evenings and at Sunday brunch.

The restaurant's Southern cuisine and its quality seldom change. Chef James
Oakley's menu offers such appetizers as jambalaya or red beans and rice studded
with andouille sausage and *tasso* (spicy smoked pork). Standouts among the

Dining at Sightseeing Attractions

With so many great places to eat in Washington, I have a hard time recommending those at sightseeing attractions. Most are overpriced and too crowded, even if they are convenient. But a few places stand out, for their admirable cuisine, noteworthy setting, or both.

Prior to September 11, 2001, three restaurants within the Capitol building itself were open to the public at lunchtime, with certain conditions. As I write this, the Capitol Guide Service tells me that the **House of Representatives Restaurant** (also called the "Members' Dining Room") in Room H118, at the South end of the Capitol (✆ **202/225-6300**), the **Senate Dining Room** (✆ **202/224-2350**), and the **Refectory,** first floor, Room S112, Senate side of the Capitol (✆ **202/224-4870**), remain closed to the public. I mention them here on the chance that they may have reopened by the time you read this; if they have, and you would like to dine at one of them, be sure to call and find out the specific dress code and other requirements.

You are always welcome (after you've gone through security, of course) in the eateries located in the Capitol office buildings across the street from the Capitol. You'll be surrounded by Hill staffers, who head to places like the immense, full-service **Rayburn House Office Building Cafeteria** (✆ **202/225-7109**), which is in the basement of the building, at First Street and Independence Avenue SW. Adjoining the cafeteria is a carryout that sells pizza and sandwiches. At the **Longworth Building Cafeteria,** Independence Avenue and South Capitol Street SE (✆ **202/225-4410**), you can grab a bite from a fairly nice food court. By far the

main dishes are the trout imperial (sautéed Virginia trout piled high with crab meat/vegetable "stuffing" and served over mesclun with rice) and something called "Swamp Thing" (seafood served over greens with a mustard sauce). A basket of minibiscuits, corn and citrus poppy-seed muffins, and sourdough rolls accompanies all dishes. For dessert, try either pecan sweet-potato pie or coconut cake. An almost all-American wine list features many by-the-glass selections.

In Union Station, 50 Massachusetts Ave. NE. ✆ **202/289-6188.** Reservations recommended. Main courses mostly $15–$30. AE, DC, DISC, MC, V. Mon–Sat 11:30am–4pm; Mon–Thurs 5–11pm; Fri–Sat 5–midnight; Sun 11:30am–9pm. Metro: Union Station.

Barolo ✰✰ PIEDMONTESE ITALIAN   This excellent, sophisticated Italian restaurant stands out among the pubs and inexpensive eateries that line this stretch of Pennsylvania Avenue on Capitol Hill. In fact, Barolo lies upstairs from its less costly sister restaurant, Il Radicchio; both are owned by chef/proprietor, Roberto Donna, the dynamo behind Galileo, too. (See review of Il Radicchio on p. 123, and of Galileo on p. 135). The intimate main room is paneled and has wooden floors, a working fireplace, and well-spaced tables. Encircling the upper reaches of the room is a charming, narrow balcony set with tables for two; look out the window and you'll just be able to glimpse the Capitol. You can also expect to stumble across Washington notables, since the private room is a popular fundraising spot at both lunch and dinner.

best deal for visitors is the **Dirksen Senate Office Building South Buffet Room,** First and C streets NE (℃ **202/224-4249**). For just $10.95 per adult, $7.95 per child under 10, you can choose from a buffet that includes a carving station and eight other hot entrees; the price covers a nonalcoholic drink and dessert, too. The dining room is often crowded, but accepts reservations for parties of more than five.

In the same neighborhood, two institutions offering great deals and views (of famous sights or people) at weekday lunch are the **Library of Congress's** Cafeteria and its more formal Montpelier Room (℃ **202/707-8300 or 707-7512** for both), where the lunch options always cost under $10 per person; and the **Supreme Court's** Cafeteria (℃ **202/479-3246**), where you'll likely spy a justice or two enjoying the midday meal.

Among museum restaurants, the ones that shine are the **Corcoran Gallery of Art's** Café des Artistes (℃ **202/639-1786**); the six-story Atrium Cafe in the **National Museum of Natural History** (℃ **202/357-2700**); the **National Gallery of Art's** Sculpture Garden Pavilion Café (℃ **202/289-3360**) and Garden Café (℃ **202/216-2480**); and the **Phillips Collection's** snug Café (℃ **202/387-2151**).

Finally, the **Kennedy Center's** two restaurants, the Roof Terrace Restaurant and the Hors d'Oeuvrerie (℃ **202/416-8555**, for both), offer theater-goers convenient, gourmet dining in glamorous settings. The Roof Terrace and the KC Café are especially dramatic, since immense windows provide panoramic views of the Potomac River and Washington landmarks.

Though the menu changes daily, you can expect Piedmontese cuisine that may include a white endive salad with balsamic vinaigrette and basil dressing; saffron pappardelle with sautéed lobster, asparagus, roasted garlic, and fresh basil; or roasted filet of red snapper over sweet potato, rosemary, black olives, and fresh basil. The pastas are always good. The wine list is entirely Italian, focusing on Piedmont wines, with emphasis on those produced from the Barolo grape.

223 Pennsylvania Ave. SE. ℃ 202/547-5011. Reservations recommended. Lunch main courses $15–$17.50; dinner main courses $15–$23. AE, DC, DISC, MC, V. Mon–Fri 11:30am–2:30pm; Mon–Thurs 5:30–10pm; Fri–Sat 5:30–10:30pm. Metro: Capitol South.

Bistro Bis *ℛℛ* FRENCH BISTRO   The chic Hotel George is the home of this excellent French restaurant, whose owner-chef, Jeff Buben, and his wife, Sallie, also run Vidalia (p. 139). You can sit at tables in the bar area (which always seem loud, even when it's not that crowded), on the balcony overlooking the bar, or at leather banquettes in the main dining room, where you can watch Buben and staff at work in the glass-fronted kitchen. (In warm weather, there's a sidewalk cafe.) The menu covers French classics like bouillabaisse, pistou, steak *frites* (fries), as well as Buben's own take on grilled salmon (with a fricassee of oysters and leeks on brioche), pan-seared red snapper, and seared scallops with tomatoes, garlic, olives, and an eggplant custard. Some items, such as steak au poivre, appear on both the lunch and dinner menus but are considerably cheaper at lunch. The restaurant has been popular from the day it opened, with hungry movers and shakers intermingling with ordinary folk who just love good food. The wine list is mostly French and American.

15 E St. NW. ℂ **202/661-2700.** Reservations recommended. Breakfast $6.75–$12; lunch main courses $15–$22; dinner main courses $18.50–$28.50 AE, DC, DISC, MC, V. Daily 7–10am, 11:30am–2:30pm, and 5:30–10:30pm. Metro: Union Station.

La Colline ⭐ FRENCH   This is the perfect spot for that breakfast fund-raiser. Hill people like La Colline for its convenience to the Senate side of the Capitol, the great bar, the four private rooms, the high-backed leather booths that allow for discreet conversations, and, last but not least, the food. You'll always get a good meal here. The regular menu offers an extensive list of French standards, including salade Niçoise, terrine of foie gras, and fish—poached, grilled, or sautéed. Almost as long is the list of daily specials—the soft-shell crab is superb here in season, and so is the gratin of crayfish. Trout and salmon are smoked in-house—try them. The wine list concentrates on French and California wines; by-the-glass choices change with the season to complement the menu. Don't let the dessert cart roll past you; the apple pie is a winner, as is the restaurant, which has been in business for 21 years.

400 N. Capitol St. NW. ℂ **202/737-0400.** Reservations recommended. Breakfast $5–$8.75; lunch main courses $8–$17; dinner main courses $17–$24. AE, DC, MC, V. Mon–Fri 7–10am and 11:30am–3pm; Mon–Sat 6–10pm. Metro: Union Station.

The Monocle ⭐ *Finds* AMERICAN   A Capitol Hill institution, the Monocle has been around since 1960. This is a men-in-suits place, where the litter of briefcases resting against the too-close-together tables can make for treacherous navigating. But you might want to take a look at whose briefcase it is you're stumbling over, for its proximity to both the Supreme Court and the Capitol guarantees that the Monocle is the haunt of Supreme Court justices and members of Congress. At lunch you'll want to order either the hamburger, which is excellent, the tasty federal salad (field greens and tomatoes tossed with balsamic vinaigrette), the penne pasta with tomato-basil sauce and olives, or the white-bean soup, whenever it's on the menu. At dinner, consider the baked oysters or the pork-rib chop with pommery mustard sauce. Don't bother with the crab cakes. Service is old-style, all-male.

107 D St. NE. ℂ **202/546-4488.** Reservations recommended. Lunch main courses $7.50–$17.95; dinner main courses $13.75–$28.50. AE, DC, MC, V. Mon–Fri 11:30am–midnight. Closed 2 weeks preceding Labor Day. Metro: Union Station.

MODERATE

Café Berlin *Value* GERMAN   You have to walk past the dessert display on your way to your table at Café Berlin, so forget your diet. These delicious home-made confections are the best reason to come here. The vast spread might include a dense pear cheesecake, raspberry Linzer torte, sour-cherry crumb cake, or vanilla-custard cake. Look for items like the *rahm schnitzel,* which is a center cut of veal topped with a light cream and mushroom sauce, or a *wurstplatte* of mixed sausages, among the entrees. Seasonal items highlight asparagus in spring, game in the fall, and so on. Lunch is a great deal: a simple chicken-salad-on-whole wheat sandwich (laced with tasty bits of mandarin orange), the soup of the day, and German potato salad, all for $6.75. The owners and chef are German; co-owner Peggy Reed emphasizes that their dishes are "on the light side—except for the beer and desserts." This 16-year-old restaurant occupies two prettily decorated dining rooms on the bottom level of a Capitol Hill town house, whose front terrace serves as an outdoor cafe in warm weather.

322 Massachusetts Ave. NE. ℭ 202/543-7656. Reservations recommended. Main courses $14.95–$18.95; soups, sandwiches, and salads $6.95–$10.95 at lunch. AE, DC, DISC, MC, V. Mon–Thurs 11:30am–10pm; Fri–Sat 11:30am–11pm; Sun 4–10pm. Metro: Union Station.

Montmartre ℱ FRENCH   I liked the restaurant (Bluestone Café) that used to occupy this space, but I also like its successor. Montmartre has kept the pale yellow-orange walls, exposed wood ceiling, cozy bar, and old wooden tables, which means a warm ambience prevails as before. The new owners are French and Montmartre is their little French restaurant offering big French pleasures: chicory salad tossed with crisped bacon and duck-gizzard confit, pistou, seared tuna with chopped red pepper and olives, hangar steak served over fingerling potatoes and topped with sautéed shallots and demi-glace sauce, and calves liver sautéed with smothered onions, bok choy, potato puree, and a balsamic vinegar sauce. Desserts, like the Alsatian apple tart, don't disappoint.

327 Seventh St. SE. ℭ 202/544-1244. Reservations recommended. Lunch main courses $8–$15, dinner main courses $10–$25. AE, DC, DISC, MC, V. Tues–Sun 11:30am–2:30pm and 5:30am–10pm. Metro: Eastern Market.

INEXPENSIVE

Il Radicchio ⟨Value⟩ ITALIAN   What a great idea: Order a replenishable bowl of spaghetti for the table at a set price of $6.50, and each of you chooses your own sauce from a long list, at prices that range from $1.50 to $4. Most are standards, like the puttanesca with black olives, capers, garlic, anchovies, and tomato. My favorite is the radicchio, sausage, red wine, and tomato sauce. It's a great deal.

The kitchen prepares daily specials, like a sautéed fresh trout with sautéed green beans, and garlic and tomato sauce, as well as sandwiches, and an assortment of 14 wood-baked pizzas, with a choice of 26 toppings.

Ingredients are fresh and flavorful, the service quick and solicitous. The restaurant gets a lot of overworked and underpaid Hill staffers, who appreciate Il Radicchio's heartening food, and its low prices. See review of Barolo, above, if you are more interested in fine Italian dining.

223 Pennsylvania Ave. SE. ℭ 202/547-5114. Reservations not accepted. Main courses $5.50–$15.95. AE, DC, DISC, MC, V. Mon–Thurs 11:30am–10pm; Fri–Sat 11:30am–11pm; Sun 5–10pm. Metro: Capitol South.

3 Downtown, East of 16th Street NW

VERY EXPENSIVE

Butterfield 9 ℱℱ NEW AMERICAN   In spring 2001, less than a year after opening, Butterfield 9 was chosen by *Condé Nast Traveler* magazine as one of the top 100 new restaurants *in the world*. It continues to win kudos. My husband and I have been pleased with our meals. Specifically, we like an appetizer called the "foie gras pancake," which is warmed goose liver within a pastry; as well as fried calamari, which is not the deep-fried ringlets you might expect, but a breaded slice of squid that has been stuffed with chorizo; and entrees, such as the pan-seared filet mignon, the horseradish-crusted Chilean sea bass with leek puree, and a pan-roasted rockfish served with lump crabmeat hash. Executive chef Martin Saylor changes his menu four times a year.

The highlight of Butterfield 9's classy decor is a series of large, stylized black-and-white prints of handsome men and women dressed in 1930s, '40s, and '50s

Capitol Hill, Downtown & Foggy Bottom Dining

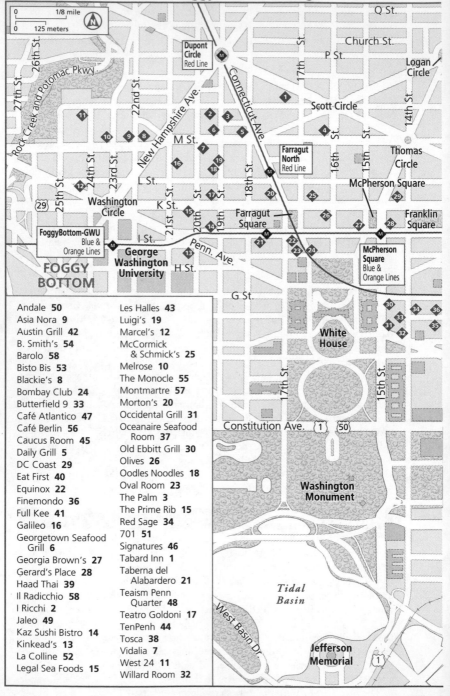

Andale **50**
Asia Nora **9**
Austin Grill **42**
B. Smith's **54**
Barolo **58**
Bisto Bis **53**
Blackie's **8**
Bombay Club **24**
Butterfield 9 **33**
Café Atlantico **47**
Café Berlin **56**
Caucus Room **45**
Daily Grill **5**
DC Coast **29**
Eat First **40**
Equinox **22**
Finemondo **36**
Full Kee **41**
Galileo **16**
Georgetown Seafood
  Grill **6**
Georgia Brown's **27**
Gerard's Place **28**
Haad Thai **39**
Il Radicchio **58**
I Ricchi **2**
Jaleo **49**
Kaz Sushi Bistro **14**
Kinkead's **13**
La Colline **52**
Legal Sea Foods **15**

Les Halles **43**
Luigi's **19**
Marcel's **12**
McCormick
  & Schmick's **25**
Melrose **10**
The Monocle **55**
Montmartre **57**
Morton's **20**
Occidental Grill **31**
Oceanaire Seafood
  Room **37**
Old Ebbitt Grill **30**
Olives **26**
Oodles Noodles **18**
Oval Room **23**
The Palm **3**
The Prime Rib **15**
Red Sage **34**
701 **51**
Signatures **46**
Tabard Inn **1**
Taberna del
  Alabardero **21**
Teaism Penn
  Quarter **48**
Teatro Goldoni **17**
TenPenh **44**
Tosca **38**
Vidalia **7**
West 24 **11**
Willard Room **32**

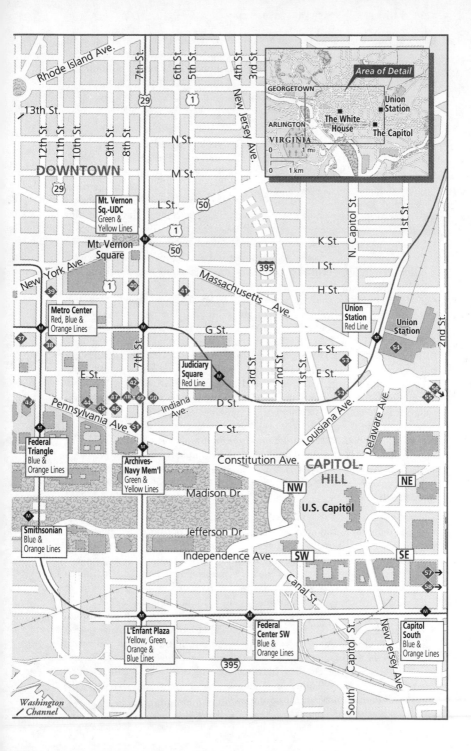

Area of Detail

GEORGETOWN

ARLINGTON
VIRGINIA

The White House

Union Station

The Capitol

0   1 mi
0   1 km

Rhode Island Ave.

13th St.

DOWNTOWN

12th St.
11th St.
10th St.
9th St.
8th St.
7th St.
6th St.
5th St.
4th St.
3rd St.

New Jersey Ave.

N. Capitol St.

1st St.

2nd St.

29

1

29

N St.

M St.

L St.

K St.

I St.

H St.

50

50

1

50

Massachusetts Ave.

395

New York Ave.

Mt. Vernon Sq.-UDC
Green & Yellow Lines

Mt. Vernon Square

39

1

40

41

Metro Center
Red, Blue & Orange Lines

37

38

Union Station
Red Line

Union Station

54

G St.

F St.

E St.

53

Judiciary Square
Red Line

3rd St.
2nd St.
1st St.

Louisiana Ave.

Delaware Ave.

52

56

55

E St.

7th St.

42

43

Pennsylvania Ave.

44

45

46

47

48

49

50

Indiana Ave.

D St.

Federal Triangle
Blue & Orange Lines

51

C St.

Archives-Navy Mem'l
Green & Yellow Lines

Constitution Ave.

CAPITOL-HILL

NW

NE

Madison Dr.

U.S. Capitol

Smithsonian
Blue & Orange Lines

Jefferson Dr

Independence Ave.

SW

SE

57

58

Canal St.

L'Enfant Plaza
Yellow, Green, Orange & Blue Lines

Federal Center SW
Blue & Orange Lines

Capitol South
Blue & Orange Lines

Capitol St.

South

New Jersey Ave.

395

Washington Channel

fashions. Butterfield 9 is the latest venture of restaurateur Amarjeet (Umbi) Singh, owner of New Heights (p. 161). A bar menu of about nine items priced from $8 to $13 is available all day, featuring items like the soup of the day, a cheese plate with fresh fruit, and a sliced bison sandwich, crab cake, and gnocchi.

600 14th St. NW. ⟨ 202/BU9-8810. Reservations recommended. Lunch main courses $18–$22; dinner main courses $18–$33. AE, DC, DISC, MC, V. Mon–Fri 11:30am–2:30pm; Sun–Thurs 5:30–10pm; Fri–Sat 5:30–11pm. Metro: Metro Center.

The Caucus Room 𝄞𝄞 STEAK Washington's powerful people like steakhouses, and that's a fact. Since the Caucus Room is owned by a bipartisan bunch of heavy-hitting politicos and entrepreneurs (Democratic fundraiser and Clinton bud Terry McAuliffe and former Republican National Committee chairman Haley Barbour, to name but 2 of the 70 investors), the Caucus Room was almost a guaranteed success even before it opened in August 2000. At lunch and dinner, it's a true Washington scene, with all that that entails: a sprinkling of congressmen and -women, television newscasters, and corporate VIPs throughout the main dining room; lots of backslapping and shaking of hands; and private meetings taking place behind closed doors (the restaurant has a number of private dining rooms).

· But I'm here to tell you, the food is good. Haley's chopped salad of diced bell peppers, blue cheese, and mustard vinaigrette is a hit. The porterhouse steak is juicy, and the rack of lamb, which bears a crust of goat cheese and fresh basil, is thoroughly delicious. The restaurant also is known for certain nonmeat entrees, such as the crab cakes (the pass/fail test for a D.C. restaurant) and the timbale of lobster and crab, which layers romaine, diced yellow tomato and avocado, and corn, with lobster and crab meat placed on top, drizzled with a tequila-lime vinaigrette. Even side dishes, like the creamed spinach and the horseradish-spiked mashed potatoes, are winners.

When you've finished all that, you can lean back against the leather banquettes and discreetly search for famous faces while you enjoy dessert. I polished off a big slice of coconut cake, but I hear the pecan pie is pretty good, too.

401 9th St. NW (at D St.). ⟨ 202/393-0777. Reservations recommended. Lunch items $10–$25; dinner main courses $24–$59. AE, DISC, MC, V. Mon–Fri 11:30am–2:30pm; Mon–Sat 5:30–10:30pm. Metro: Navy/Archives or Gallery Place.

Gerard's Place 𝄞𝄞𝄞 FRENCH Gerard Pangaud is the only Michelin two-star chef working in this country. His restaurant has been here for quite some time now and his popularity shows no signs of abating. Though Pangaud changes his menu every 2 weeks, he can be counted on to combine exquisite taste sensations, like Jerusalem artichokes with foie gras and truffles, or Chilean sea bass served over leeks stewed with black truffles, or fricassee of monkfish in a red wine sauce. Every once in a while you'll see his famous lobster with ginger, lime, and sauterne on the menu, and if you do, order it, for it's justly famous. The dining room itself is small, seating only 50 at a time, and is rather underwhelming in design. And this is a quiet restaurant, not a place to get rowdy. You're here for the food, and quiet conversation. And though Gerard's Place is also very expensive, the restaurant bows to your budget in offering a three-course fixed-price lunch for $29.50 ($34.50 with a glass of wine), and by waiving the corkage fee (usually $25) on Monday nights.

915 15th St. NW. ⟨ 202/737-4445. Reservations recommended. Lunch and dinner main courses $21–$41.50; fixed-price menu $78. AE, MC, V. Mon–Fri 11:30am–2:30pm; Mon–Thurs 5:30–10pm; Fri–Sat 5:30–10:30pm. Metro: McPherson Square.

Occidental Grill ⚑ NEW AMERICAN   The Occidental has always been a place to go for atmosphere as much as food. Dark-wood paneling, a classic bar, and walls lined with booths give the place a clubby feel, making it a favorite spot for business lunches and dinners. (Its proximity to National Theatre also makes it convenient for theater-goers.) On the walls hang more than 2,000 auto-graphed photographs of famous customers, from Buffalo Bill Cody (the original restaurant opened in 1906, closed in 1972, then reopened in 1986), to recent celebs like Oprah Winfrey and Madeleine Albright. In pleasant weather, you can sit at the outdoor patio on Pennsylvania Avenue, where you have a grand view of the Capitol. The upstairs dining room is more formal, with larger booths, a smaller bar, and no photos.

For a while there, food was secondary to atmosphere, but chef Patrick Bazin has rescued the menu, updating the traditional meat-and-potatoes fare with ele-gant sauces and sophisticated accents. So now, look for a heavenly lobster salad; a soft-shell crab sandwich with scallion aioli; the ubiquitous Chilean sea bass, here nicely roasted and served with fennel confit, garlic-roasted croutons, and bouillabaisse emulsion; and a beef stew whose meat is tender and moist in its reduced red-wine sauce. One thing hasn't changed, though: The potato dishes are always good.

1475 Pennsylvania Ave. NW. © 202/783-1475. Reservations recommended. Lunch items $6–$22; dinner main courses $20–$30. AE, DC, MC, V. Mon–Thurs 11:30am–10:30pm; Fri–Sat 11:30am–11:30pm; Sun 11am–9:30pm (brunch 11am–4pm). Metro: Metro Center or Federal Triangle.

Red Sage Grill/Red Sage Border Café ⚑ AMERICAN/SOUTHWEST-ERN   There's Red Sage, the Grill, which is downstairs, and Red Sage, the Bor-der Café, upstairs: two different chefs and two menus, but the same decor, which conjures up a whimsical Wild West fantasy. Downstairs, the main dining room is a warren of cozy, candlelit alcoves under a curved ponderosa-log-beamed ceiling. The menu dares you to try something different, with offerings of grilled Atlantic salmon served with black sticky rice and rhubarb sauce, and grilled ostrich filet with sugar-cane poblano chicken sausage–stuffed quail. You should like things spicy, for Red Sage is famous for entrees like the roasted red chile pecan-crusted chicken. I prefer and highly recommend the more casual Border Café and its inexpensive light fare, especially the sweetish State of the Union chili, which features red beans and bits of bacon; the salmon tacos, for which the salmon has been marinated and grilled; and the hickory-grilled chicken que-sadillas. The margaritas are superb.

605 14th St. NW (at F St.). © 202/638-4444. Reservations recommended for main dining room, not accepted for Border Café. Lunch main courses $12–$16; dinner main courses $20–$38; Border Café main courses $5–$13. AE, DISC, MC, V. Restaurant Mon–Thurs 11:30am–2pm and 5–10pm; Fri 11:30am–2pm and 5:30–10:30pm; Sat–Sun 5:30–10:30pm. Border Café Mon–Thurs 11:30am–11:30pm; Fri–Sat 11:30am–12:30am; Sun 4:30–11pm. Metro: Metro Center.

Signatures ⚑ AMERICAN/STEAK   If you're one for gimmicks, dress to impress and bring a lot of money and an appetite to Signatures. The restaurant, which opened about a year ago, serves up large portions of delicious American fare—lavender-scented rack of lamb, a 10-ounce slab of Kobe steak, and shrimp and grits—as it displays for your appraisal 50 or more artifacts throughout the dining room. Diners are encouraged to walk around for a good look at, say, Pres. John F. Kennedy's rocker, or an original letter by Pres. Franklin Delano Roo-sevelt, or a handwritten poem by Vincent Van Gogh. Prices range from $1,000 to $500,000—for the artifacts, that is. Even if the concept is not to your taste, the food may well be. In addition to its regular menu, Signatures has a sushi bar, with a wide range of rather reasonably priced sushi, and a bar-bar, where you can order drinks with names like "The FBI," "The Lobbyist," and "The Journalist." The restaurant, which overlooks the Navy Memorial fountain, attracts some of the types for which the drinks are named. (Don't think you'll catch any FBI agents in here, though.)

801 Pennsylvania Ave. NW (at 9th St.). © 202/628-5900. Reservations recommended. Jacket recommended for men at dinner. Breakfast main courses $5–$18; lunch main courses $12–$25; dinner main courses $23–$33 (Kobe steak goes for $74); sushi items $3–$28. AE, DISC, MC, V. Mon–Fri 7:30–9:30am and 11:30am–3pm; Sat noon–4pm; Mon–Thurs 5:30–10pm; Fri–Sat 5:30–10:30pm. Metro: Navy Memorial/Archives.

The Willard Room *&* AMERICAN/FRENCH   The Willard Room is something to see. Like the rest of the hotel (see chapter 5), the dining room has been restored to its original turn-of-the-20th-century splendor, with gorgeous carved-oak paneling, towering scagliola columns, brass and bronze torchiers and chandeliers, and a faux-bois beamed ceiling. Scattered among the statesmen and diplomats dining here are local couples seeking romance; the Willard has been the setting for more than one betrothal. The room has also been used in many movies.

Chef de cuisine Gerard Madani changes the lunch menu daily (which reads like a dinner menu; for simple sandwiches go elsewhere), the dinner menu seasonally, and has a light touch at all times. I've actually found it too light: a gazpacho that was blindingly red, but regrettably thin (I prefer my gazpacho with texture); steamed lobster unaccompanied even by butter. Dishes with a little more heft to them include steamed Dover sole with a mustard crust and a mustard-seed sauce, and beef tenderloin with red-wine and bone-marrow sauce. Two of the most popular desserts are the double-vanilla crème brûlée and the chocolate tears, which combines dark chocolate and white chocolate in a tear-shaped, mousselike confection. The wine list offers more than 250 fine selections.

In the Willard Inter-Continental hotel, 1401 Pennsylvania Ave. NW. © 202/637-7440. Reservations recommended. Jacket and tie for men preferred. Breakfast $7–$15; lunch main courses $21–$35; dinner main courses $32–$42. AE, DC, DISC, MC, V. Mon–Fri 7:30–10am and 11:30am–2pm; Mon–Sat 6–10pm. Metro: Metro Center.

EXPENSIVE

Andale *&* MEXICAN   During a visit to the Yucatan peninsula in 2001, chef Allison Swope was so taken with the cuisine of Oaxaca, Mexico, that upon her return to Washington she set about transforming her "robust American" restaurant, The Mark, into the inventive Mexican Andale (*andale* means "let's go!"). The menu features dishes that combine authentic regional Mexican cuisine with fresh and often non-traditional ingredients: sushi grade tuna marinated with achiote, garlic, Mexican oregano, and sour orange juice; *pato al mole Negro oaxaqueno,* which is roasted duck served over Mexican red rice with a nut-based sauce that includes dried chiles, garlic, tomatillos, chocolate, and cinnamon. The slow-roasted leg of lamb, which has been rubbed with a paste of red chiles, garlic, and oregano, is a standout. Not to miss: the smoky, spicy salsa picante appetizer and the Mexican-style doughnuts with dipping chocolate for dessert. The bar offers 35 brands of tequila and concocts an excellent margarita.

Avoid being shown to the windowless back room, opting instead for seating in either the storefront window for optimum people-watching (Andale is in the middle of downtown), or in the main dining room, where Mexican artwork now hangs. Great deal: Every Monday after 5pm, you can order a bottle of wine or champagne for half price with the order of an entree.

401 7th St. NW. © 202/783-3133. Reservations recommended. Lunch main courses $8–$14; dinner main courses $14–$22. AE, DC, DISC, MC, V. Mon–Sat 11:30am–3pm; Mon 5–9pm; Tues–Thurs 5–10pm; Fri–Sat 5–11pm; Mon–Fri bar stays open but no food is served, 3–5pm. Metro: Gallery Place or Archives/Navy Memorial.

Café Atlantico *Finds* LATIN AMERICAN This place rocks all week long, but especially on weekend nights, it's a favorite hot spot in Washington's still-burgeoning downtown. The colorful three-tiered restaurant throbs with Latin, calypso, and reggae music, and everyone is having a fiesta—including, it seems, the waiters. If the place is packed, try to snag a seat at the second-level bar, where you can watch the genial bartender mix the potent drinks for which Café Atlantico is famous: the *caipirinha*, made of limes, sugar, and *cachacha* (sugar-cane liqueur); the *mojito*, a rum and crushed mint cocktail; or the passion-fruit cocktail, a concoction of passion-fruit juice, ginger, and jalapeño mixed with mandarin orange-flavored vodka. But take a gander at the remarkable, award-winning wine list, too, whose 150 selections are mostly from South America, with many bottles priced under $30.

Seated at the bar or table, you'll watch as your waiter makes fresh guacamole right before your eyes. As for the main dishes, you can't get a more elaborate meal for the price. The ceviche, duck confit quesadilla with roasted red onions, Ecuadorian seared scallops, and Argentine rib eye are standouts (though the menu may change, you'll almost always find these on the menu), and tropical side dishes and pungent sauces produce a burst of color on the plate. Feel free to ask your friendly waiter for guidance.

405 8th St. NW. © 202/393-0812. Reservations recommended. Lunch main courses $9–$13; dinner main courses $18–$24; pretheater menu $22 (5–6:30pm); Latino dim sum $19.95 all you can eat (Sat 11:30am–1:30pm). AE, DC, DISC, MC, V. Mon–Fri 11:30am–2:30pm; Sun brunch 11:30am–3pm; Sun–Thurs 5–10pm; Fri–Sat 5–11pm. The bar stays open late on weekends. Metro: Archives–Navy Memorial and Gallery Place/MCI Center.

DC Coast AMERICAN The dining room is sensational: two stories high, with glass-walled balcony, immense oval mirrors hanging over the bar, and a full-bodied stone mermaid poised to greet you at the entrance. Gather at the bar first to feel a part of the loud and trendy scene; while you're there, why not nosh on something from the bar menu, perhaps the Chinese lacquered duck and scallions or maybe a luscious lobster spring roll? This continues as one of the city's most popular restaurants, so call way ahead to book a reservation. Chef Jeff Tunks returned in 1998 from stints in Texas, California, and New Orleans, and some of the dishes Washingtonians remember from his years at the River Club have returned with him. His Chinese-style smoked lobster with crispy fried spinach is the most famous, and deservedly so—it's still tasty. Other entrees to recommend include the pan-seared sea scallops with gnocchi, crabmeat, Smithfield ham, and truffled veal jus, and the fish filet encrusted with portobello paste and served with truffled potatoes and porcini broth. Seafood is a big part of the menu, but there are a handful of meat dishes, too.

1401 K St. NW. © 202/216-5988. Reservations recommended. Lunch main courses $12–$18; dinner main courses $16–$29; light fare $6–$11. AE, DC, DISC, MC, V. Mon–Fri 11:30am–2:30pm; Mon–Thurs 5:30–10:30pm; Fri–Sat 5:30–11pm (light fare weekdays 2:30–5:30pm). Metro: McPherson Square.

Finemondo CLASSIC ITALIAN This "Italian Country Kitchen," as the restaurant call itself, is another welcome Italian addition to this part of downtown, and less formal than its neighbor, Tosca (p. 132), just down the street. Finemondo is especially attractive in warm weather, when its entire glass front opens to the sidewalk, giving the place an airy and inviting ambience. A center divider separates the more casual and livelier bar/dining room from a quieter area at the back. Come here for whole roasted fish, beef tenderloin, roasted guinea hen with caramelized cauliflower, and exotically Italian desserts, like the grappa pear mousse cake. But plan on a leisurely meal, since service can be slow and waiters have been known to confuse the orders.

1319 F St. NW (between 13th and 14th sts.). ℂ 202/737-3100. Reservations recommended. Lunch main courses $10–$22; dinner main courses $12–$25. AE, DISC, MC, V. Mon–Fri 11:30am–2:30pm; Mon–Thurs 5:30–10pm; Fri–Sat 5:30–11pm. Metro: Metro Center.

Georgia Brown's 𝕲 SOUTHERN   In Washington restaurants, seldom do you find such a racially diverse crowd. The harmony may stem from the waiters, whose obvious rapport results in gracious service, and certainly extends from the open kitchen, where the chef directs his multicultural staff. But in this large, handsome room, whose arched windows overlook McPherson Square, the food may capture all of your attention. A plate of corn bread and biscuits arrives, to be slathered with butter that's been whipped with diced peaches and honey. The menu is heavily Southern, with the emphasis on the Low Country cooking of South Carolina and Savannah: collards, grits, and lots of seafood, especially shrimp dishes. The Charleston *perlau* is a stewlike mix of duck, spicy sausage, jumbo shrimp, and rice, topped with toasted crumbs and scallions. It has bite but isn't terribly spicy. For something totally decadent, try the buttermilk batter-fried chicken. Georgia Brown's is famous for its Sunday brunch, lively with the sounds of jazz and conversation, and luscious with the tastes of country sausage, omelets made to order, creamy grits, and many other dishes.

950 15th St. NW. ℂ 202/393-4499. Reservations recommended. Lunch main courses $7–$20; dinner main courses $12–$23; Sun jazz brunch $22.95. AE, DC, DISC, MC, V. Mon–Thurs 11:30am–10:30pm; Fri 11:30am–11:30pm; Sat 5:30–11:30pm; Sun 11:30am–4:30pm (brunch 10:30am–2:30pm) and 5:30–10:30pm. Metro: McPherson Square.

Les Halles 𝕲 FRENCH/STEAK   We took our French exchange student here, and guess what she ordered: steak *frites.* I did the same. In fact, everyone in the restaurant was devouring the *onglet* (a boneless French cut hangar steak hard to find outside France), steak au poivre, steak tartare, New York sirloin, and other cuts, all of which come with *frites,* which are a must. (Actually, 2 diners at our table ordered ravioli and a chicken salad, and boy were they sorry.) The menu isn't all beef, but it is classic French, featuring cassoulet, *confit de canard,* escargots, onion soup, *choucroutte garni,* and an irresistible *frisée aux lardons* (a savory salad of chicory studded with hunks of bacon and toast, smeared thickly with Roquefort). Should you spy something on the menu that's not Gallic, ignore it.

Les Halles is big and charmingly French, with French-speaking waiters providing breezy, flirtatious service. The banquettes, pressed-tin ceiling, mirrors, wooden floor, and side bar capture the feel of a brasserie. A vast window front overlooks Pennsylvania Avenue and the awning-covered sidewalk cafe, which is enclosed in cold weather and a superb spot to dine year-round. Every July 14, this is the place to be for the annual Bastille Day race, which Les Halles hosts. (See the "Calendar of Events," in chapter 2 for details.) Les Halles is a favorite hangout for cigar smokers, but the smoking area is well ventilated.

1201 Pennsylvania Ave. NW. ℂ 202/347-6848. Reservations recommended. Lunch main courses $11.75–$20; dinner main courses $13.25–$22.50. AE, DC, DISC, MC, V. Sun–Thurs 11:30am–midnight; Fri–Sat 11:30am–2am. Metro: Metro Center or Federal Triangle.

ⓘ Vegetarian Times

You know when a restaurant called The Prime Rib starts to list a "vegetable plate entree" on its dinner menu that vegetarianism has officially entered the mainstream of American eating habits. And it's clear that restaurants are ready to accommodate non-meat-eaters, recognizing that vegetarians like to dine out as much as carnivores. In addition to The Prime Rib's entree (which, by the way, is a spread of fresh asparagus, broccoli, spinach, whole tomato gratiné, and baked potato), here are some other restaurants whose menus cater to vegetarians. See individual listings within this chapter for full descriptions of each establishment.

On the upscale end of the spectrum are **Nora** (p. 146) and **Equinox** (p. 137). At Nora, restaurateur Nora Pouillon's passion for organic ingredients means that her menus always include at least one fresh vegetarian entree, like the wild-mushroom and asparagus risotto described on a recent menu. Equinox owner and chef Todd Gray, whose wife is a vegetarian, is expert at creating wonderful accompaniments to entrees, like parsnip fritters or leek fondue, but also offers at least one veggie entree on the menu, such as the egg noodles with spring asparagus, baby carrots, and roasted garlic cream and Parmesan.

Indian restaurants are always a good bet for vegetarians. The **Bombay Club** (p. 140) offers a full page of nine vegetarian entrees, everything from a mixed-vegetable curry spinach to lentil dumplings simmered in a yogurt and herb sauce. Other ethnic restaurants worth checking out are the inexpensive Italian cafe **Pasta Mia** (p. 145), Ethiopian restaurant **Meskerem** (p. 145), and the **Lebanese Taverna** (p. 162), great options all.

Oceanaire Seafood Room ⚑ SEAFOOD   The Oceanaire is a good spot for a lively party, with its red-leather booths, Art Deco-ish decor, long bar, and festive atmosphere. It would be hard to get romantic or serious about business here—there's just too much to distract you, like the sight of mile-high desserts en route to another table. Oceanaire serves big portions of everything (including cocktails, another reason to bring a bunch of friends here). Two of the best items on the menu are the crab cakes, which are almost all lump crab meat, and the fisherman's platter, a fresh, fried selection of oysters, scallops, shrimp, and other seafood, with hot matchstick fries alongside it all. The dozen varieties of oysters are fresh and plump, but if you want to start with a salad, consider the Caesar. The desserts turn out to look more enticing than they taste; the cherry brown Betty is probably the best of the bunch.

1201 F St. NW. ⓒ 202/347-2277. Reservations recommended. Lunch main courses $16–$25; dinner main courses $18–$35. AE, DISC, MC, V. Mon–Thurs 11:30am–10pm; Fri 11:30am–11pm; Sat 5–11pm; Sun 5–9pm. Metro: Metro Center.

701 ⚑ AMERICAN/INTERNATIONAL   701 has gained renown for its extensive caviar and vodka selections. But don't disregard the main menu, which features sophisticated American fare and always includes a few vegetarian items. For starters, try the five-onion soup with roasted potatoes and blue cheese.

Other recommendable dishes are the double rack pork chop with littleneck clams, fingerling potatoes and roasted root vegetables; and the grilled yellowfin tuna, which is served with balsamic Vidalia onions-and-avocado salad. I can vouch for the double chocolate and lime tart with berry compote. Artful presentation makes the food all the more enticing. Portions are generous and service is marvelous.

This restaurant is literally steps away from the Archives–Navy Memorial Metro stop and a short walk from several theaters. Its plate-glass windows allow you to watch commuters, theatergoers, and tourists scurrying along Pennsylvania Avenue. Walls, glass partitions, and columns in the dining room create pockets of privacy throughout. Live jazz plays nightly.

701 Pennsylvania Ave. NW. (© 202/393-0701. Reservations recommended. Lunch main courses $12.50–$20; dinner main courses $15–$26.50; pretheater dinner $24.95. AE, DC, MC, V. Mon–Fri 11:30am–3pm; Mon–Thurs 5:30–10:30pm; Fri–Sat 5:30–11:30pm; Sun 5–9:30pm. Metro: Archives–Navy Memorial.

TenPenh 🟊🟊 ASIAN FUSION   We'd heard that the service was excellent here, and this proved to be true: Our waiter actually split a glass of wine for me and my friend, when we both wanted a little more, but not an entire additional glass. And then our waiter checked out someone we thought was Rob Lowe in the bar, reporting back to us, alas, that it was not he. Anyway, what should bring you here is not just great service, but a warm atmosphere and stellar food. This is one of those restaurants that has a separate, loungy, hard-to-leave bar, but the dining room itself is inviting, with soft lighting, comfortable booths, and an open kitchen. In this, his second restaurant (DC Coast is his other), Jeff Tunks presents translations of dishes he's discovered in travels throughout Asia: smoked salmon and crisp wonton napoleon (which actually had too much salmon); halibut dusted with ground macadamia nuts and Japanese bread crumbs; whole deep-fried flounder; wok-seared calamari; and dumplings filled with chopped shrimp and water chestnuts. We finished with a trio of crème brûlée, the best of which was the coffee-crème.

1001 Pennsylvania Ave. NW (at 10th St.). (© 202/393-4500. Reservations recommended. Lunch main courses $11.95–$16.95; dinner main courses $13.95–$23.95. AE, DISC, MC, V. Mon–Fri 11:30am–2:30pm; Mon–Thurs 5:30–10:30pm; Fri–Sat 5:30–11pm. Metro: Archives–Navy Memorial.

Tosca 🟊🟊 NORTHERN ITALIAN   Washington probably has more Italian restaurants than any other kind of ethnic eatery, yet this central part of downtown has almost no Italian fare. In fact, when it opened in spring 2001, Tosca's was the only fine *ristorante italiano* between Capitol Hill and the western edge of downtown, a range of at least 20 blocks. (Since then, the new, less formal, Finemondo joined the neighborhood, p. 129.) Tosca's interior design of pale pastels in the thick carpeting and heavy drapes creates a hushed atmosphere, a suitable foil to the rich food.

The menu, meanwhile, emphasizes the cooking of chef Cesare Lanfranconi's native Lake Como region of Italy. A good example of a traditional pasta dish is the "scapinasch," a ravioli of aged ricotta and raisins (or sometimes it's made with amaretto cookies) with butter and sage sauce. Lanfranconi's take on a veal filet is to marinate and grill the meat, serving it with braised cabbage and veal roasted-porcini mushroom sauce. Tosca has something for everyone, including simply grilled fish accompanied by organic vegetables for the health conscious, tiramisu and apple fritters for those with a sweet tooth. No wonder the restaurant is always full. Remarkably, even when there's a crowd, Tosca doesn't get too noisy—the restaurant's designers kept the acoustics in mind.

1112 F St. NW. ℂ 202/367-1990. Reservations recommended. Lunch main courses $12–$18; dinner main courses $15–$26. AE, DC, MC, V. Mon–Fri 11:30am–2:30pm; Sun–Thurs 5:30–10:30pm; Fri–Sat 5:30–11pm. Metro: Metro Center.

MODERATE

Jaleo ℛ *(Finds)* SPANISH   In theater season, Jaleo's dining room fills and empties each evening according to the performance schedule of the Shakespeare Theater, right next door. Lunchtime always draws a crowd from nearby office buildings and the Hill. This restaurant, which opened in 1993, may be credited with initiating the tapas craze in Washington. The menu lists about 55 tapas, including a very simple but not-to-be-missed grilled bread layered with a paste of fresh tomatoes and topped with anchovies; savory warm goat cheese served with toast points; a skewer of grilled chorizo sausage atop garlic mashed potatoes; and a delicious mushroom tart served with roasted red-pepper sauce. Paella is among the few heartier entrees (it feeds 4). Spanish wines, sangrias, and sherries are available by the glass. Finish with a rum-and-butter–soaked apple charlotte in bread pastry or a plate of Spanish cheeses. The casual-chic interior focuses on a large mural of a flamenco dancer inspired by John Singer Sargent's painting *Jaleo*. On Wednesday at 8 and 9pm, flamenco dancers perform.

Jaleo recently opened a second and very pretty restaurant in the suburbs, at 7271 Woodmont Ave., Bethesda, Maryland (ℂ 301/913-0003). Though this new branch is within walking distance of my house, I prefer the ambience of the original D.C. location.

480 7th St. NW (at E St.). ℂ 202/628-7949. Reservations accepted until 6:30pm. Lunch main courses $7.50–$10.75; dinner main courses $10.50–$28; tapas $3.95–$7.95. AE, DC, DISC, MC, V. Sun–Mon 11:30am–10pm; Tues–Thurs 11:30am–11:30pm; Fri–Sat 11:30pm–midnight. Metro: Archives or Gallery Place.

Old Ebbitt Grill AMERICAN   You won't find this place listed among the city's best culinary establishments, but you can bet it's included in every tour book. It's an institution. Located 2 blocks from the White House, this is the city's oldest saloon, founded in 1856. Among its artifacts are animal trophies bagged by Teddy Roosevelt, and Alexander Hamilton's wooden bears—one with a secret compartment in which it's said he hid whiskey bottles from his wife. The Old Ebbitt is attractive, with Persian rugs strewn on beautiful oak and marble floors, beveled mirrors, flickering gaslights, etched-glass panels, and paintings of Washington scenes. The long, dark mahogany Old Bar area emphasizes the men's saloon ambience.

Tourists and office people fill the Ebbitt during the day, flirting singles take it over at night. You'll always have to wait for a table if you don't reserve ahead. The waiters are friendly and professional in a programmed sort of way; service could be faster. Menus change daily but always include certain favorites: burgers, trout Parmesan (Virginia trout dipped in egg batter and Parmesan cheese, deep-fried), crab cakes, and oysters (there's an oyster bar). The tastiest dishes are usually the seasonal ones, whose fresh ingredients make the difference.

675 15th St. NW (between F and G sts.). ℂ 202/347-4801. Reservations recommended. Breakfast $6.95–$9.95; brunch $5.95–$13.95; lunch main courses $6.95–$13.95 (as much as $24.95 when crab cakes are on the menu); dinner main courses $13.95–$20.95 (again, up to $24.95 for crab cakes); burgers and sandwiches $6.95–$10.95; raw bar $8.95–$18.50. AE, DC, DISC, MC, V. Mon–Thurs 7:30am–2am; Fri 7:30am–3am; Sat 8:30am–3am; Sun 9:30am–2am (kitchen closes at 1am nightly). Raw bar open until midnight daily. Metro: McPherson Square or Metro Center.

INEXPENSIVE

Eat First ℛ CHINESE   The dining room is cramped and rather plain, but the food, the friendly service, and the sight of the goings-on in the open kitchen are

Kids Family-Friendly Restaurants

Austin Grill (p. 159)   Another easygoing, good-service joint, with great background music. Kids will probably want to order from their own menu here, and their drinks arrive in unspillable plastic cups with tops and straws.

Legal Sea Foods (p. 140)   Believe it or not, this seafood restaurant has won awards for its kids' menu. It features the usual macaroni and cheese and hot dogs, but also kids' portions of steamed lobster; fried popcorn shrimp; a small fisherman's platter of shrimp, scallops, and clams; and other items, each of which comes with fresh fruit and a choice of baked potato, mashed potatoes, or french fries. Prices range from $3.95 for the hot dog to $15.95 for the 1-pound lobster.

Luigi's (p. 141)   Introduce your kids to pre-Domino's pizza. Luigi's, which has been around since 1943, serves the real thing: big, thick, ungreasy pizza, with fresh toppings. The restaurant also offers a full slate of pastas, sized and priced for children, everything from a $4.25 spaghetti and tomato sauce to a $4.95 lasagna. You sit at tables covered in red-checked cloths that have probably withstood countless spilled drinks and splotches of tomato sauce in their time. The restaurant gets noisy, so chances are that any loud ones in your party will blend right in.

Old Glory Barbecue (p. 157)   A loud, laid-back place where the waiters are friendly without being patronizing. Go early, since the restaurant becomes more of a bar as the evening progresses. There is a children's menu, but you may not need it—the barbecue, burgers, muffins, fries, and desserts are so good that everyone can order from the main menu.

all reasons enough to come here. When choosing from the menu, you'll want to look especially at the page of seasonal specials, where the baked soft shell crab with ginger and scallions, and the shrimp cake with Chinese broccoli are recommended in spring and summer. This restaurant also is known for its Cantonese roast duck, soy sauce chow mein, and barbeque pork—sometimes these items appear only on the takeout menu, even though they may be available for eat-in meals.

609 H St. NW. ✆ 202/289-1703. Reservations accepted. Main courses at lunch and dinner $3.95–$14.95 (seasonal specials may be slightly more). AE, DC, MC, V. Sun–Thurs 11am–2am; Fri–Sat 11am–3am. Metro: Gallery Place–Chinatown.

Full Kee ⨍ CHINESE   Washington's Chinatown restaurants tend to look a little sketchy and Full Kee is no exception. Full Kee's two rooms are brightly lit and crammed with Chinese-speaking customers sitting on metal-legged chairs at plain rectangular tables. There's no such thing as a no-smoking section. A cook works in the small open kitchen at the front of the room, hanging roasted pig's parts on hooks and wrapping dumplings. Still, it has the best food in Chinatown.

Chefs from some of Washington's best restaurants sometimes congregate here after hours, and here's their advice: Ask the waitress for translations of the seasonal specials written (in Chinese) on the wall. If you don't hear them mentioned, be sure to ask about two selections I can personally vouch for: the jumbo breaded oyster casserole with ginger and scallions, and the whole steamed fish. If you love dumplings, you must order the Hong Kong–style shrimp dumpling broth: You get either eight shrimp dumplings or four if you order the broth with noodles. Bring your own wine or beer if you'd like to have a drink, since Full Kee does not serve any alcohol.

509 H St. NW. (C) 202/371-2233. Reservations accepted. Lunch main courses $4.25–$9; dinner main courses $6.95–$17. No credit cards. Sun–Thurs 11am–1am; Fri–Sat 11am–3am. Metro: Gallery Place/Chinatown.

Haad Thai THAI   The Washington area has lots of Thai restaurants, but not many are downtown. Fewer still offer such good food in such pretty quarters. Haad Thai is a short walk from the Convention Center, the MCI Center, and surrounding hotels. Plants and a pink and black mural of a Thai beach decorate the dining room. The standards are the best, including *pad thai, panang gai* (chicken sautéed with fresh basil leaves in curry, with peanut sauce), and satays. All dishes are flavorful and only mildly spicy; speak up if you want your food spicier.

1100 New York Ave. NW (entrance on 11th St. NW). (C) 202/682-1111. Reservations recommended. Lunch main courses $5–$8.50; dinner main courses $7.95–$16.95. AE, DC, MC, V. Mon–Fri 11:30am–2:30pm and 5–10:30pm; Sat–Sun 5–10pm. Metro: Metro Center.

4 Downtown, 16th Street NW & West
VERY EXPENSIVE

Galileo ✹✹✹ PIEDMONTESE ITALIAN   Food critics mention Galileo as one of the best Italian restaurants in the country and Roberto Donna as one of the nation's best chefs. The likable Donna opened the white-walled grottolike Galileo in 1984; since then, he has opened several other restaurants in the area, including Il Radicchio (p. 123) and Barolo (p. 120), both on Capitol Hill. He's also written a cookbook, and has established himself as an integral part of Washington culture.

Donna cures his own ham for salami and prosciutto, and his sausages, pastas, mozzarella, marmalades, and breads are all made in-house. Galileo features the cuisine of Donna's native Piedmont region, an area in northern Italy influenced by neighboring France and Switzerland—think truffles, hazelnuts, porcini mushrooms, and veal. The atmosphere is relaxed; some diners are dressed in jeans, others in suits. Waiters can be supercilious, though.

You have many options. You can order a la carte, or choose either of two different fixed-price menus, at $60 or $80. Typical entrees include a risotto with black truffles, whole roasted baby pig stuffed with sausage and porcini mushrooms, a house-made saffron pasta with ragout of veal, or a roasted black sea bass served with sesame sauce. Finish with a traditional tiramisu, or, better yet, the milk chocolate passion fruit torte with a crème brûlée center. The cellar boasts more than 900 vintages of Italian wine (40% Piedmontese).

But wait—there's more. For the ultimate dining experience, book a seat at the table in Donna's **Laboratorio del Galileo** ✹✹✹, a private dining area and kitchen enclosed by glass, where Donna prepares the 10- to 12-course tasting menu ($98 weekdays, $110 weekends) and entertains you and 29 other lucky diners. There is also a terrace for warm-weather dining.

1110 21st St. NW. (C) 202/293-7191. Reservations recommended. Lunch main courses $12–$19; dinner main courses $24–$35. AE, DC, DISC, MC, V. Mon–Fri 11:30am–2pm and 5:30–10pm; Sat 5:30–10:30pm; Sun 5:30–10pm. Metro: Foggy Bottom.

I Ricchi 🍴 TUSCAN ITALIAN   Now in its 14th year, I Ricchi remains a popular and convivial place to enjoy Italian food a la Tuscany. An open kitchen with a blazing wood-burning grill creates a warming bustle in the large room. The daily specials are great, especially if you're into fish. Those of hearty appetite will be happy with minestrone; the quill pasta with Tuscan meat sauce; and the rolled medallions of pork loin, turkey breast, and veal, each medallion stuffed with spinach and prosciutto. Start with grilled radicchio.

1220 19th St. NW. ℂ 202/835-0459. Reservations recommended. Lunch main courses $20–$25; dinner main courses $28–$35. AE, DC, MC, V. Mon–Fri 11:30am–2pm; Mon–Sat 5:30–10pm. Metro: Dupont Circle.

The Prime Rib 🍴 STEAK/SEAFOOD   The Prime Rib has plenty of competition now, but it makes no difference. Beef lovers still consider this The Place. It's got a definite men's club feel about it, with brass-trimmed black walls, leopard-skin carpeting, and comfortable black-leather chairs and banquettes. Waiters are in black tie, and a pianist at the baby grand plays show tunes and Irving Berlin classics.

The meat is from the best grain-fed steers and has been aged for 4 to 5 weeks. Steaks and cuts of roast beef are thick, tender, and juicy. In case you had any doubt, The Prime Rib's prime rib is the best item on the menu, juicy and thick, top-quality meat. For less carnivorous diners, there are about a dozen seafood entrees, including an excellent crab imperial. Mashed potatoes are done right, as are the fried potato skins, but I recommend the hot cottage fries.

2020 K St. NW. ℂ 202/466-8811. Reservations recommended. Jacket and tie required for men. Lunch main courses $11–$20; dinner main courses $20–$35. AE, DC, MC, V. Mon–Thurs 11:30am–3pm and 5–11pm; Fri 11:30am–3pm and 5–11:30pm; Sat 5–11:30pm. Metro: Farragut West.

The Restaurant at the Jefferson 🍴 AMERICAN   Cozy rather than intimidatingly plush, the Jefferson Hotel's restaurant is actually pretty romantic—ask to be seated in "the snug" (tables 39 or 40). The emphasis on privacy and the solicitous but not imposing service also make it a good place to do business.

Chef Thomas Russell changes his menus seasonally, but you can count on them being elegant versions of traditional American fare. The Jefferson crab cake is almost always on the menu as a starter; here it is served with tomato, tarragon coulis and avocado vinaigrette, and radish sprouts. Entrees include pan-roasted duck breast with confit risotto, glazed figs, and orange ginger sauce, and seared halibut with crispy spaetzle, English peas, and smoked veal bacon. You'll usually see one pasta dish listed, such as a spinach linguini with steamed mussels, clams, and leeks, in a lemongrass-garlic broth. An extensive wine list includes many by-the-glass selections.

1200 16th St. NW (at M St.). ℂ 202/833-6206. Reservations recommended. Breakfast $10–$14; $20, lunch main courses $18–$28; dinner main courses $25–$35; Sun brunch $34; tea $25. AE, DC, DISC, MC, V. Daily 6:30–11am, 11:30am–2:30pm, and 5:30–10:30pm; tea daily 3–5pm. Metro: Farragut North.

Taberna del Alabardero 🍴🍴 *Finds* SPANISH   Dress up to visit this truly elegant restaurant, where you receive royal treatment from the Spanish staff, which is quite used to attending to the real thing (Spain's King Juan Carlos and Queen Sofia and their children regularly dine here when in Washington). In 1999, the Spanish ministry of agriculture named Taberna the best Spanish restaurant in the United States.

Newly refurbished, the dining room remains ornate, with green leather covering booths and stools, satin stretched across chairs, and gilded cherubs placed at ceiling corners. Order a plate of tapas to start: lightly fried calamari, shrimp in garlic and olive oil, thin smoky ham, and marinated mushrooms. Although the a la carte menu changes with the seasons, four paellas (the menu says each feeds 2, but you can ask for a single serving) are always available. The lobster and seafood paella served on saffron rice is rich and flavorful. (Ask to have the lobster shelled; otherwise, you do the cracking.) Another signature dish is the stuffed squid sauced in its own ink. The wine list features 250 Spanish wines.

This is the only Taberna del Alabardero outside of Spain, where there are seven locations. All are owned and operated by Father Luis de Lezama, who opened his first tavern outside the palace gates in Madrid in 1974, as a place to train delinquent boys for employment.

1776 I St. NW (entrance on 18th St. NW). ℭ 202/429-2200. Reservations recommended. Jacket and tie for men suggested. Lunch main courses $17.25–$20.75; dinner main courses $19–$32; tapas $7.75–$12. AE, DC, DISC, MC, V. Mon–Fri 11:30am–2:30pm and 5:30–10:30pm; Sat 5:30–11pm. Metro: Farragut West.

EXPENSIVE

Daily Grill ℛ AMERICAN   Talk about retro. In the case of the Daily Grill, retro means revisiting the food favorites of decades past (though the restaurant itself is only a few years old). Step right in and get your Cobb salad, your chicken potpie, your fresh fruit cobbler, your meat and potatoes, made with high quality ingredients (of high caloric value).

It's a big space, with a nice bar at the front and windows on three sides. The winding bar offers an extensive selection: good wines, lots of single malts, tequilas, and small-batch bourbons. The Daily Grill is a favorite lunchtime spot—where else can you order eggs Benedict at noon on a weekday?

Like its chain siblings, the Daily Grill is gaining a reputation for good service and large portions of grilled meats and fish. (The lunch menu boasts a BLT made with "half a pound of bacon.") You might find it hard to choose from the more than 40 menu items, but favorite orders are the short ribs and the "Grill Combo" of tiny onion rings over skinny fries—a must for table-sharing.

Another Daily Grill is located in the Georgetown Inn, 1310 Wisconsin Ave. NW (ℭ 202/337-4900).

1200 18th St. NW. ℭ 202/822-5282. Reservations recommended. Lunch main courses $8.95–$15; dinner main courses $12.95–$23.95. AE, DC, DISC, MC, V. Mon–Thurs 11:30am–11pm; Fri–Sat 11:30am–midnight; Sun 10am–3pm (brunch) and 4–10pm. Metro: Farragut North or Dupont Circle.

Equinox ℛℛ NEW AMERICAN   Everyone seems to love Equinox. It's not splashy in any way, just a pretty, comfortable restaurant that serves creatively delicious American food. Even if you aren't vegetarian, you'll eat all your vegetables here, because as much care is taken with these garnishes as with the entree itself. And every entree comes with a garnish or two, like the leek fondue or the forest mushrooms with applewood bacon, or the cherry tomatoes with Indian corn sauce. You can order additional side dishes; consider the macaroni and cheese: Vermont cheddar, Parmesan, and black truffle reduction. The home runs, of course, are the entrees: the crab cakes, which are made with lump crab mixed with capers, brioche bread crumbs, mayonnaise, and lemon-butter sauce; or perhaps the pork chop with Calvados sauce and braised kale. For love of vegetables, Equinox always offers a vegetable entree, such as the wide spinach noodles with caramelized salsify, baby carrots, and roasted garlic cream. Equinox has two tasting menus, a $60 five-course dinner available most nights, and the $35 three-course tasting menu served only on Sunday evenings.

818 Connecticut Ave. NW. ℭ 202/331-8118. Reservations recommended. Lunch main courses $15–$24; dinner main courses $19–$29. AE, DC, DISC, MC, V. Mon–Fri 11:30am–2pm, Mon–Thurs 5:30–10pm; Fri–Sat 5:30–10:30pm; Sun 5–9pm. Metro: Farragut West.

Georgetown Seafood Grill on 19th St. ℛ SEAFOOD   In the heart of downtown is this hint of the seashore. Two big tanks of lobsters greet you as you enter, and the decor is nautical throughout: aquariums set in walls, canoes fastened to the ceiling, models of tall ships placed here and there. Meanwhile, jazz music from another era wafts in the background. It's enough to make you forget what city you're in.

A bar and tables sit at the front of the restaurant, an open kitchen is in the middle, and tall wooden booths on platforms occupy the rear. If you like lobster and are here at lunchtime, order the "Golden Triangle Club," which is chunks of lobster served on brioche with applewood smoked bacon and mayo, for $14.95. Otherwise, as is the rule in many seafood restaurants, your best bets are the most simply prepared items. You can choose the lobster or from a list of at least eight "simply grilled" fish entrees. Raw bar selections list oysters from six different locations daily, including Canada, Virginia, and Oregon, and these may be the freshest in town. Service is excellent. Also check out happy hour here, when small plates of seafood dishes and burgers, as well as drinks, are available at reduced prices.

1200 19th St. NW. ℂ 202/530-4430. Reservations recommended. Lunch main courses $14.95–$22; dinner main courses $14.95–$24.95; salads and sandwiches $8.95–$14.95. AE, DC, DISC, MC, V. Mon–Thurs 11:30am–10pm; Fri 11:30am–11pm; Sat 5:30–11pm; Sun 6–10pm. Metro: Dupont Circle.

Olives ℛ ITALIAN   No sooner had Olives opened than Washington Redskins owner Dan Snyder reserved the entire restaurant for a private party. Then he did it again a year later. It's that kind of place—a restaurant that comes with its own buzz and keeps it going.

Big and loud, Olives lives up to its hype. Its dining rooms, on three floors, attempt a Tuscan ambience, with stone walls, earth tones, wood-burning oven, and lots of greenery. The menu is Italian by way of Boston, where chef-owner Todd English's original Olives continues to flourish. Leave your diet at home, for these dishes are decadent, like the five-clam chowder with bacon, truffled ricotta ravioli, asparagus tart with fontina cheese, and slow-cooked lamb shank with green olive and fennel salad—all scrumptious. (**Note:** Downstairs is not nearly as much fun, upstairs, or on the patio in pleasant weather, is where all the action is.)

1600 K St. NW. ℂ 202/452-1866. Reservations required. Lunch main courses $10–$16.50; dinner main courses $15.50–$27; pretheater dinner Mon–Fri until 7pm $35. AE, DC, MC, V. Mon–Fri 11:30am–2:30pm; Mon–Sat 5:30–10pm. Metro: Farragut North.

Oval Room at Lafayette Square ℛℛ NEW AMERICAN   The Oval Room is a local favorite, another winner for owner Ashok Bajaj, who also owns the Bombay Club (p. 140), across the street, and several other restaurants around town. Everyone talks about how nicely the renovation turned out, but since I never saw the original look, all I can tell you is that the Oval Room's new decor and layout do make for a congenial atmosphere. It is a handsome restaurant, with contemporary art hanging on its lettuce-colored walls. But it isn't stuffy, no doubt because the bar area separating the restaurant into two distinct rooms sends cheerful sounds in either direction. The quality of the food has always been top-notch: I've liked the napoleon of jumbo lump crab with cracked spices, and the roasted New York strip steak with oven roasted potatoes, grilled asparagus, and béarnaise sauce. In case you haven't figured it out, the Oval Room is a short walk from the White House.

800 Connecticut Ave. NW, at Lafayette Square. ℂ 202/463-8700. Reservations recommended. Lunch main courses $12–$18; dinner main courses $17.50–$25.50. AE, DISC, MC, V. Mon–Fri 11:30am–3pm; Mon–Thurs 5:30–10pm; Fri–Sat 5:30–10:30pm. Metro: Farragut West.

The Palm ✿ *(Finds* STEAK The Palm is one in a chain of 28 locations that started nearly 80 years ago in New York—but here in D.C., it feels like an original. The Washington Palm is 31 years old; its walls, like those in all Palms, are covered with the caricatures of regulars, famous and not-so. (Look for my friend Bob Harris.) If you think you see Tim Russert or Larry King at a table, you're probably right. You can't go wrong with steak, whether it's the 36-ounce dry-aged New York strip, or sliced in a steak salad. Oversize lobsters are a specialty, and certain side dishes are a must: creamed spinach, onion rings, Palm fries (something akin to deep-fried potato chips), and hash browns. The restaurant allows you to order half-portions of these, so you have no excuse but to order at least one. Several of the longtime waiters like to kid with you a bit, but the service is always fast.

1225 19th St. NW. ✆ 202/293-9091. Reservations recommended. Lunch main courses $16–$30; dinner main courses $21–$35. AE, DC, MC, V. Mon–Fri 11:45am–10:30pm; Sat 5:30–10:30pm; Sun 5:30–9:30pm. Metro: Dupont Circle.

Teatro Goldoni ✿✿ VENETIAN ITALIAN In the beginning, around 1997, there was a restaurant named Goldoni, which, when it moved nearby a couple of years later, assumed the new name, Osteria Goldoni, which soon gave birth to a sister restaurant, Teatro Goldoni. Now, the Osteria has closed, leaving Teatro to carry on the Goldoni traditions of festive ambience and superb Venetian Italian cuisine. Teatro's dining room is dramatic, displaying Venetian masks, immense murals, and harlequin colored glass panels. Chef/owner Fabrizio Aielli is on view, performing as if on stage, inside his elevated glass-enclosed kitchen. ("Teatro" is the Italian word for theater and Goldoni was an 18th-century Venetian playwright and gastronome.) As dramatic as the decor is the food, which is served with a flourish. Try the lobster risotto, the flounder filet with braised fennel and fried oysters, or the ravioli stuffed with truffle-oil flavored potatoes and leeks. Sorbets are a specialty, as is the beautiful tiramisu. Bring a party of people; in true Goldoni tradition, the Teatro is a good spot for a celebration.

1909 K St. NW. ✆ 202/955-9494. Reservations recommended. Lunch main courses $10–$15; dinner main courses $18–$29.50. AE, DC, DISC, MC, V. Mon–Fri 11:30am–2pm; Mon–Thurs 5:30–10pm; Fri–Sat 5–11pm. Metro: Farragut North or Farragut West.

Vidalia ✿✿ REGIONAL AMERICAN/SOUTHERN If you're hesitant to dine at a restaurant that's down a flight of steps from the street, your doubts will vanish as soon as you enter Vidalia's tiered dining room. There's a party going on down here. In fact, Vidalia is so popular, you may have to wait a short time in the narrow bar, even if you arrive on time for your reservation. But the bar is fun, too, and gives you a jump start on getting into the mood of the place.

Executive chef Peter Smith adds Asian and French accents to owner/chef Jeff Buben's regional Southern cuisine. The menu changes frequently, but recommended constants include crisp East Coast lump crab cakes and a fried grits cake with taso ham. Venture from the regular items and you may delight in a timbale of roasted onion and foie gras, sautéed sea scallops with udon cake, or monkfish on a creamy saffron risotto. A signature entree is the scrumptious sautéed shrimp on a mound of creamed grits and caramelized onions in a thyme-and-shrimp cream sauce. Corn bread and biscuits with apple butter are served at every meal. Vidalia is known for its lemon chess pie, which tastes like pure sugar; I prefer the pecan pie. A carefully chosen wine list highlights American vintages.

1990 M St. NW. ✆ 202/659-1990. Reservations recommended. Lunch main courses $6.75–$18.75; dinner main courses $19–$29. AE, DC, DISC, MC, V. Mon–Fri 11:30am–2:30pm; Mon–Thurs 5:30–10pm; Fri–Sat 5:30–10:30pm; Sun 5–9pm (closed Sun July 4–Labor Day). Metro: Dupont Circle.

MODERATE

Bombay Club ☆ *Finds* INDIAN   This used to be a favorite stop for the Clintons, but perhaps the menu is too exotic for the current president—no word yet of Bush sightings here. (The White House is just across Lafayette Park.) But I would encourage the Bushes to come by, especially since the Bombay Club dishes present an easy introduction to Indian food for the uninitiated, and are sensitive to varying tolerances for spiciness.

The Indian menu ranges from fiery green chile chicken ("not for the fainthearted," the menu warns) to the delicately prepared lobster malabar, a personal favorite. Tandoori dishes, like the chicken marinated in a yogurt, ginger, and garlic dressing, are specialties, as is the vegetarian fare—try the black lentils cooked overnight on a slow fire. Patrons are as fond of the service as the cuisine: Waiters seem straight out of *Jewel in the Crown*, attending to your every whim. This is one place where you can linger over a meal as long as you like. The Bombay Club is known for its vegetarian offerings (at least 9 items are on the menu) and for its Sunday champagne brunch, which offers a buffet of fresh juices, fresh baked breads, and assorted Indian dishes. Slow-moving ceiling fans and wicker furniture accentuate the colonial British ambience.

815 Connecticut Ave. NW. ℂ 202/659-3727. Reservations recommended. Main courses $7.50–$18.95; Sun brunch $18.50. AE, DC, MC, V. Mon–Fri and Sun brunch 11:30am–2:30pm; Mon–Thurs 6–10:30pm; Fri–Sat 6–11pm; Sun 5:30–9pm. Metro: Farragut West.

Legal Sea Foods ☆ *Kids* SEAFOOD   This famous family run Boston-based seafood empire, whose motto is "If it's not fresh, it's not Legal," made its Washington debut in 1995. The softly lit dining room is plush, with terrazzo marble floors and rich cherry-wood paneling. Sporting events, especially Boston games, are aired on a TV over the handsome marble bar/raw bar, and you can usually pick up a copy of the *Boston Globe* near the entrance. As for the food, not only is everything fresh, but it's all from certified-safe waters.

Legal's buttery-rich clam chowder is a classic. Other worthy appetizers include garlicky golden-brown farm-raised mussels au gratin and fluffy pan-fried Maryland lump crab cakes served with a green salad and apple slices. You can have one of eight or so varieties of fresh fish grilled or opt for one of Legal's specialty dishes, like the Portuguese fisherman's stew, in which cod, mussels, clams, and chorizo are prepared in a saffron-tomato broth. Top it off with a slice of Boston cream pie. Wine lovers will be happy to know that Legal's wine list has received recognition from *Wine Spectator* magazine; parents will be glad that Legal's award-winning kid's menu offers not just macaroni and cheese, but steamed lobster, popcorn shrimp, and other items, each of which comes with fresh fruit and a choice of baked potato, mashed potatoes, or french fries. At lunch, oyster po' boys and the lobster roll are real treats.

You'll find another Legal Sea Foods in the new terminal at National Airport (ℂ 703/413-9810); a third location is at 704 Seventh St. NW (ℂ 202/347-0007), across from the MCI Center.

2020 K St. NW. ℂ 202/496-1111. Reservations recommended, especially at lunch. Lunch main courses $8–$15; sandwiches $9–$17; dinner main courses $12–$30. AE, DC, DISC, MC, V. Mon–Thurs 11am–10pm; Fri 11am–10:30pm; Sat 4–10:30pm. Metro: Farragut North or Farragut West.

McCormick & Schmick's *Value* SEAFOOD   In this branch of a Pacific Northwest–based restaurant, stained glass in the chandeliers and ceiling evince a patriotic theme. This huge place seats its patrons in booths, at a 65-foot bar, and at linen-laid tables. The vast, fresh daily menu of more than 30 items offers selections of fresh fish from both nearby and Pacific waters—the more simply prepared, the better. Oyster lovers will choose happily from the half-dozen kinds stocked daily. For good value, look at the list of light entrees, ranging from oyster stew to chicken piccata, and costing $6.50 to $11.65. Or head to the bar to enjoy a giant burger, fried calamari, quesadillas, fish tacos, and more, for only $1.95, Monday through Friday from 3:30 to 6:30pm, Monday through Thursday from 10:30pm to midnight, and Friday and Saturday from 10pm to midnight. Friendly bartenders make you feel at home as they concoct "handmade from scratch" mixed drinks with freshly squeezed juices.

A surf-and-turf version of McCormick & Schmick's, the **M&S Grill** is located near the MCI Center, at 13th and F streets NW (℗ 202/347-1500).

1652 K St. NW (at the corner of 17th St. NW). ℗ **202/861-2233.** Reservations recommended. Main courses $6.60–$23.95. AE, DC, DISC, MC, V. Mon–Thurs 11am–11pm; Fri 11am–midnight; Sat 5pm–midnight; Sun 5–10pm. Bar opens at 4pm Sat and Sun. Metro: Farragut North and Farragut West.

INEXPENSIVE

Famous Luigi's Pizzeria Restaurant *(Kids* ITALIAN Before there was Domino's or Pizza Hut or Papa John's, there was Luigi's. Make that *way* before— Luigi's opened in 1943. People who grew up in Washington consider Luigi's an essential part of their childhood. So I took my daughters here one weekday several summers ago, and sure enough, it's remained a favorite place ever since. (They often ask to be taken here on their birthdays.) Whether you go at lunch or dinner, you can expect to be among a sea of office folks. At night, the restaurant's atmosphere changes a little, as office workers come in groups to unwind, have a drink, or get a bite; but this isn't a bar, so it doesn't get rowdy. The menu is long, listing all kinds of pastas, sandwiches, grilled dishes, and pizzas. Come here for a little local color, and to please everyone in the family. Luigi's children's menu is really children's portions of Luigi specialties: spaghetti with tomato sauce, cheese ravioli, lasagna, penne with cream sauce, plain cheese pizza, and cheese manicotti, for less than $5 each.

1132 19th St. NW (between L and M sts.). ℗ **202/331-7574.** Main courses $4.25–$14.95. AE, DC, DISC, MC, V. Mon–Sat 11am–midnight; Sun noon–midnight. Metro: Dupont Circle or Farragut North.

Oodles Noodles *(Value* ASIAN FUSION Asian waiters, Asian background music, and calligraphy figures drawn on the walls put you in the right frame of mind for Pan-Asian noodle dishes. This is a good choice for bargain hunters, since there are plenty of cheap one-dish meals that can satisfy. You can order dumplings, Szechwan *dan dan* noodles (egg noodles), Vietnamese vermicelli, and Thai drunken noodles, among others. Many of the items come in a soup, such as the Shanghai roast pork noodles soup and the Siam noodles soup, which is a spicy sweet-and-sour broth with shrimp, minced chicken, and squid.

But not everything is a noodle. Appetizers include satays, spring onion cakes, and vegetable spring rolls. Curries, teriyaki, and other spicy non-noodle fare round out the menu. Though Washington food critics give Oodles Noodles high marks, I find it hit or miss.

1120 19th St. NW. ℗ **202/293-3138.** Reservations recommended for 5 or more at dinner. Main courses $7–$10. AE, DC, MC, V. Mon–Fri 11:30am–3pm; Mon–Thurs 5–10pm; Fri–Sat 5–10:30pm. Metro: Dupont Circle or Farragut North.

5 U Street Corridor

INEXPENSIVE

Ben's Chili Bowl *Finds* AMERICAN   Ben's is a veritable institution, a mom-and-pop place, where everything looks, tastes, and probably even costs the same as when the restaurant opened in 1958. The most expensive item on the menu is the turkey sub, for $6.10. Formica counters, red bar stools, and a jukebox that plays Motown and reggae tunes—that's Ben's. Ben's continues as a gathering place for black Washington and visitors like Bill Cosby, who's a longtime customer (a chili dog is named after him). Everyone's welcome, though, even the late-nighters who come streaming out of nearby nightclubs at 2 or 3 in the morning on the weekend. Of course, the chili, cheese fries, and half-smokes are great, but so are breakfast items. Try the salmon cakes, grits, scrapple, or blueberry pancakes.

1213 U St. NW. © 202/667-0909. Reservations not accepted. Main courses $2.48–$6.11. No credit cards. Mon–Thurs 6am–2am; Fri–Sat 6am–4am; Sun noon–8pm. Metro: U St.–Cardozo.

Coppi's *Value* ITALIAN   Crowded with neighborhood patrons and hungry club-goers headed for one of the nearby music houses, Coppi's is a narrow room decorated with wooden booths and bicycle memorabilia from Italian bike races. The wood-burning oven turns out a mean pizza, a stiff competitor to that of top-dog Pizzeria Paradiso (p. 149). The crust is chewy, and your choice of toppings includes quality ham, pancetta, cheeses, and vegetables. Coppi's also makes all its pastas and ice cream in-house. At lunch, you can order from the a la carte menu or choose the $10.95 fixed-price meal, which allows you an appetizer or salad and an entree. You can count on finding an extensive Italian wine list. Service is friendly but can be spotty; if it seems like your waiter has forgotten you, there's a chance that he has, so speak up before too much time passes.

1414 U St. NW. © 202/319-7773. Reservations accepted. Main courses $10.50–$16.95. AE, DC, DISC, MC, V. Mon–Fri noon–3pm; Sun–Thurs 6–11pm; Fri–Sat 5pm–midnight. Metro: U St.–Cardozo.

6 Adams-Morgan

EXPENSIVE

Cashion's Eat Place *Finds* AMERICAN   Cashion's has all the pleasures of a neighborhood restaurant—easy, warm, comfortable—combined with cuisine that is out of this world. Owner/chef Ann Cashion continues to rack up culinary awards as easily as she pleases her patrons. Her menu changes daily, always featuring about eight entrees, split between seafood and meat: fritto misto of whole jumbo shrimp and black sea bass filet, served with onion rings and house-made tartar sauce, or fried sweetbreads on a bed of sautéed spinach, and so on. The side dishes that accompany each entree, such as lemon cannelloni bean purée or radish and sprout salad, are worth as much attention. Chocolate cinnamon mousse, lime tartalette, and other desserts are worth saving room for. Sunday brunch is popular, too; you can choose from breakfast fare (challah French toast, spinach and Gruyère omelets) or heartier items (grilled rainbow trout, croque monsieurs).

The charming dining room curves around a slightly raised bar. In warm weather, the glass-fronted Cashion's opens invitingly to the sidewalk, where you can also dine. Tables at the back offer a view of the small kitchen, where Cashion and her staff work away. In winter, ask for a table away from the front door, which lets in a blast of cold air with each new arrival.

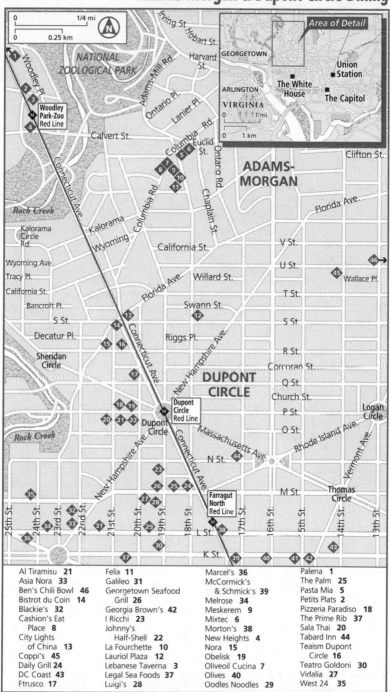

Al Tiramisu **21**	Felix **11**	Marcel's **36**	Palena **1**
Asia Nora **33**	Galileo **31**	McCormick's	The Palm **25**
Ben's Chili Bowl **46**	Georgetown Seafood	& Schmick's **39**	Pasta Mia **5**
Bistrot du Coin **14**	Grill **26**	Melrose **34**	Petits Plats **2**
Blackie's **32**	Georgia Brown's **42**	Meskerem **9**	Pizzeria Paradiso **18**
Cashion's Eat	I Ricchi **23**	Mixtec **6**	The Prime Rib **37**
Place **8**	Johnny's	Morton's **38**	Sala Thai **20**
City Lights	Half-Shell **22**	New Heights **4**	Tabard Inn **44**
of China **13**	La Fourchette **10**	Nora **15**	Teaism Dupont
Coppi's **45**	Lauriol Plaza **12**	Obelisk **19**	Circle **16**
Daily Grill **24**	Lebanese Taverna **3**	Oliveoil Cucina **7**	Teatro Goldoni **30**
DC Coast **43**	Legal Sea Foods **37**	Olives **40**	Vidalia **27**
Etrusco **17**	Luigi's **28**	Oodles Noodles **29**	West 24 **35**

1819 Columbia Rd. NW (between 18th St. and Mintwood Place). © **202/797-1819.** Reservations recommended. Brunch $7–$17; dinner main courses $17–$26. MC, V. Tues 5:30–10pm; Wed–Sat 5:30–11pm; Sun 11:30am–2:30pm and 5:30–10pm.

Felix Restaurant and Lounge ☆ *Moments* AMERICAN   Fans of Sarah Jessica Parker, martinis, good food, and live music will all be happy at Felix's. Sunday nights mean viewings of *Sex and the City;* the rest of the week, there's a different live music group every night (jazz Mon and Tues, Sinatra standards Wed, rhythm and soul Thurs, funk rock Fri and Sat). And every night presents a menu of martinis and delicious dinner options: herb-crusted sea bass with French lentils and raspberry coulis, pan-roasted rib-eye steak, or fresh yellowfin tuna pan-seared and served with sticky rice, snow peas, and wasabi cream sauce. Felix is famous for its Bananas Foster, which is always available; caramelized bananas are topped with vanilla-bean gelato, hot fudge, chopped walnuts, and whipped cream. Also see chapter 9 for a description of Felix's offspring, the Spy Lounge, which shares its entrance with Felix.

2406 18th St. NW. © **202/483-3549.** Reservations recommended. Main courses $17–$27. AE DC DISC MC V. Nightly 5:30pm–3am.

MODERATE

La Fourchette FRENCH   The nonsmoking section is upstairs, but even if you don't smoke, you'll want to be downstairs, among the French-speaking clientele and Adams-Morgan regulars. The waiters are suitably crusty and the ambience is as Parisian as you'll get this side of the Atlantic—as is the food. The menu lists escargots, onion soup, bouillabaisse, and mussels Provençal, along with specials like the grilled salmon on spinach mousse and the shrimp Niçoise, ever-so-slightly crusted and sautéed in tomato sauce touched with anchovy. Saturday and Sunday brunch offers French toast, omelets, and the like. A colorful mural covers the high walls; wooden tables and benches push up against bare brick walls. In warm weather, you can sit outside at tables set up on the sidewalk.

2429 18th St. NW. © **202/332-3077.** Reservations recommended on weekends. Main courses $13.95–$23.95. AE, DC, MC, V. Mon–Thurs 11:30am–10:30pm; Fri 11:30am–11pm; Sat 10am–11pm; Sun 10am–10pm.

Lauriol Plaza ☆ MEXICAN/SPANISH/LATIN AMERICAN   This place is gigantic—it seats 330—but it's immensely popular, so you may still have to wait for a table. Lauriol Plaza looks like a factory from the outside, but inside it's stunning. You have a choice of sitting at sidewalk tables, on the rooftop deck, or in the two-tiered dining room with its large mural of a Spanish fiesta on one wall and windows covering another. We had good, though warm, margaritas, the standout carne asada fajitas, and tasty *camarones diablo* (6 broiled jumbo shrimp seasoned with spices). Anything mesquite grilled is sure to please. Servings are as large as the restaurant. Sunday brunch, also recommended, is served all day. With so many people dining here, Lauriol Plaza is a good place to people-watch.

1835 18th St. NW. © **202/387-0035.** Reservations not accepted. Main courses $8–$16. AE, DC, DISC, MC, V. Sun 11am–11pm; Mon–Thurs 11:30am–11pm; Fri–Sat 11:30am–midnight. Metro: Dupont Circle.

Oliveoil Cucina Italiano ITALIAN   Oliveoil offers moderate prices, excellent trattoria food, and lively atmosphere, as befits a restaurant in the wild and crazy Adams-Morgan neighborhood. Tables are set a little too tightly together, but this probably adds to the party atmosphere. The Italian owner travels to Italy several times a year and returns with ideas for dishes, changing the menu twice a year to serve osso buco and hearty pastas in fall and winter, and lighter entrees such as risotto with asparagus tips and Parmesan and simply grilled fresh fish in spring and summer. The owner changed the name of the restaurant in 2002 from "I Matti," but kept the same staff and the same offerings of authentic Italian cuisine. The restaurant has acquired a new look, though: The first floor features the dining room and bar area, while the second floor is now a lounge, where you can sip a drink and enjoy bar fare.

2436 18th St. NW. ℂ 202/462-8844. Reservations recommended, especially on weekends. Lunch main courses $6–$11; dinner main courses $9–$14. AE, DC, MC, V. Sat–Sun noon–2pm; daily 5:30–10:30pm.

INEXPENSIVE

Meskerem ETHIOPIAN   Washington has a number of Ethiopian restaurants, but this is probably the best. It's certainly the most attractive; the three-level high-ceilinged dining room (sunny by day, candlelit at night) has an oval skylight girded by a painted sunburst and walls hung with African art and musical instruments. On the mezzanine level, you sit at *messobs* (basket tables) on low, carved Ethiopian chairs or upholstered leather poufs. Ethiopian music enhances the ambience.

Diners share large platters of food, which they scoop up with a sourdough crepelike pancake called *injera* (no silverware here). Items listed as *watt* are hot and spicy; *alitchas* are milder and more delicately flavored. You might also share an entree—perhaps *yegeb kay watt* (succulent lamb in thick, hot *berbere* sauce)—along with a platter of five vegetarian dishes served with tomato and potato salads. Some combination platters comprise an array of beef, chicken, lamb, and vegetables. There's a full bar; the wine list includes Ethiopian wine and beer.

2434 18th St. NW (between Columbia and Belmont rds.). ℂ 202/462-4100. Reservations recommended. Lunch main courses $7.95–$9.95; dinner main courses $9.95–$11.95. AE, DC, MC, V. Daily noon–midnight

Mixtec *Value* REGIONAL MEXICAN   This cheerful Adams-Morgan spot attracts a clientele of neighborhood folks, D.C. chefs, and Hispanics from all over, all of whom appreciate the delicious authenticity of the regional Mexican cuisine. The kitchen is open, the dining room colorfully decorated, and the Mexican music lively.

Two items are served here that you can't find at any of the many other Southwestern eateries in the capital: the authentic *menudo,* a stew of tripe and calf's feet (granted, not for everyone); and *tortas,* which are a kind of Mexican sub, layered with grilled pork, chiles, guacamole, and salsa. You will also find delicious small dishes called *antojitos* ("little whims"), in the $2.50 to $4.95 range, which include *queso fundido* (a bubbling hot dish of broiled Chihuahua cheese topped with shredded spicy chorizo sausage flavored with jalapeños and cilantro); and the *enrollados mexicanos,* large flour tortillas wrapped around a variety of fillings, including grilled chicken, beef, vegetables, and salmon. The freshly prepared guacamole is excellent. Choose from 30 kinds of tequila, tequila-mixed drinks, Mexican beers, and fresh fruit juices.

1792 Columbia Rd. (just off 18th St.). ℂ 202/332-1011. Main courses $3.95–$11.95. MC, V. Sun–Thurs 8:30am–10pm, Fri–Sat 8:30am–11pm.

Pasta Mia *Value* ITALIAN   Right next door to Mixtec (see above) is another excellent and inexpensive choice that stays busy all night. You might have to wait for a table, too, especially on a Friday or Saturday night, since the restaurant doesn't take reservations. But you'll agree it's worth it, after you dive into a plate heaped with one of the nearly 25 pasta dishes on the menu. Eight have meat sauces, three have seafood, and the remainder are vegetarian. I recommend the green fettuccine with creamy porcini-mushroom sauce. Bread is made in-house, and appetizers, like the Caesar salad or fresh mozzarella and tomatoes, are all flavorful. This place is as low-key as Washington gets, with a simple, brightly lit interior of red-checked covered tables packed together, and dishes served to a table as they are ready.

1790 Columbia Rd. NW. ⓒ **202/328-9114.** Reservations not accepted. Main courses $9–$10. MC, V. Mon–Sat 6:30–10pm.

7 Dupont Circle

VERY EXPENSIVE

Nora 🎭🎭 ORGANIC AMERICAN   Owner-chef Nora Pouillon brings haute panache to politically correct organic cookery in this charming restaurant. The cozy paneled bar is an inviting place to wait for your table; up a short flight of stairs lies the main dining room. This converted stable, part of which is skylit, has a weathered-looking beamed pine ceiling, tables lit by shaded paraffin lamps, and a display of Amish and Mennonite patchwork crib quilts on the walls. The atmosphere is relaxed and cozy, and the dress code is anything goes. It's always a full house.

Don't expect brown rice and beans. Instead you'll find chemical-free, organically grown, free-range fare, all extremely healthful. Nightly menus vary with the seasons and everything tastes very fresh. Recent popular dishes included sautéed Maine diver scallops served with truffle mashed potatoes, garlicky spinach, and snow peas; Italian veal and crimini mushroom ragout with butternut goat cheese ravioli; and crispy Amish duck breast with caramelized apple relish and creamy polenta. A vegetarian entree, like green olive risotto, is always an option. Many desserts use fruits and nuts—for instance, banana cheesecake with caramel sauce. An extensive wine list includes, but is not limited to, selections made with organically grown grapes.

2132 Florida Ave. NW (at R St.). ⓒ **202/462-5143.** Reservations recommended. Main courses $25–$30. AE, MC, V. Mon–Thurs 5:30–10pm; Fri–Sat 5:30–10:30pm. Closed 2 weeks at end of Aug/beginning of Sept. Metro: Dupont Circle.

Obelisk 🎭🎭🎭 ITALIAN   Obelisk is the most consistently excellent restaurant in the city. Service and food are simply the best. In this pleasantly spare room that seats only 36, the walls are decorated with 19th-century French botanical prints and Italian lithographs. Here, owner/chef Peter Pastan presents his small fixed-price menus of sophisticated Italian cuisine, using the freshest possible ingredients. Each night diners are offered two or three choices for each of five courses. Dinner might begin with mushroom crostini, followed by Tuscan bean soup, and then an artfully arranged dish of pan-cooked cod with fried asparagus and green sauce, or soft-shell crab upon a bed of white beans, or beef filet topped with anchovy paste. Dessert is a choice of cheese or baked specialties, like pear spice cake. Breads and desserts are all baked in-house and are divine. Pastan's carefully crafted wine list represents varied regions of Italy, as well as California vintages. The fixed-price menu is a deal, but the cost of wine and coffees can easily double the price per person.

2029 P St. NW. (near 21st St.) ⓒ **202/872-1180.** Reservations recommended. Fixed-price 5-course dinner $55 Tues–Thurs, $58 Fri–Sat. DC, MC, V. Tues–Sat 6–10pm. Metro: Dupont Circle.

EXPENSIVE

Al Tiramisu 🎭🎭 (Finds) ITALIAN   I called last minute for a reservation and the staff was kind enough to squeeze in four of us (*squeeze* being the operative word, as the tables are a little snug in this narrow but intimate restaurant). But the charming servers have time to chat a little without keeping you waiting. It was refreshing to have our waiter, without any discussion, hand the wine list to me, rather than to one of the men at the table. Make sure you give the menu due consideration; this is one place where the mainstays are just as good (and certainly cheaper) than the daily specials. Al Tiramisu is known for its grilled fish and for its black and white truffles, a favorite item of certain Kennedy clan members. Also exceptional are the grilled squid, house-made spinach-ricotta ravioli with butter and sage sauce, and the osso buco. This is a place to come if you need cheering up. Ebullient chef/owner Luigi Diotaiuti makes his presence known sometimes. In 2002, Luigi directed a staff of 15 Italian chefs serving food to the Italian athletes, media, and dignitaries at the Salt Lake City Winter Olympics.

2014 P St. NW. © 202/467-4466. Reservations required. Lunch main courses $6–$17; dinner main courses $14–$20. AE, DC, MC, V. Mon–Fri noon–2:30pm; Mon–Sat 5:30–10:30pm; Sun 5–9:30pm. Metro: Dupont Circle.

Johnny's Half Shell ✦ *(Finds* SEAFOOD Whenever a friend visits from out of town and I haven't gotten around to making a restaurant reservation, we usually end up at Johnny's. It's easy, fun, and comfortable; it's open continuously from lunch through the afternoon to closing, and it takes no reservations, so you can usually walk right in and get something fresh from the sea (though weekend nights after 8:30pm, you'll probably have at least a 20-min. wait); and it feels like a hometown restaurant, a rare thing in a city whose residents tend to originate from many other hometowns. Johnny's owners, Ann Cashion and John Fulchino, own another very popular restaurant, Cashion's Eat Place (p. 142) in Adams-Morgan. The restaurant is small, with a decor that features an aquarium behind the long bar, booths along one paneled wall, a tile floor, and a partly open kitchen. The professional yet friendly waiters seem to be enjoying themselves.

Everything on the menu looks good, from the farm-raised chicken with old-fashioned Eastern Shore slippery dumplings, garden peas, and button mushrooms, to the crab meat imperial with a salad of *haricots verts* (young green beans), tomatoes, and shallots. I recently opted for the delicious fried oyster po'boy sandwich, while my friend Sue went for the Maryland crab cakes with coleslaw and french fries; we both devoured every morsel. If the sautéed soft-shell crabs with Old Bay and basil beurre blanc and corn pudding are on the menu, get them. My daughter Cait likes the barbecued shrimp appetizer with Asiago cheese grits. Oysters and Wellfleet clams on the half shell are always available, of course. The short wine list includes a few selections by the glass; there are four beers on tap. Desserts are simple but perfect, including homemade ice cream, a choice of hazelnut, almond, pecan or chocolate tart, and chocolate angel food cake with caramel sauce.

2002 P St. NW. © 202/296-2021. Reservations not accepted. Lunch main courses $5.95–$19.95; dinner main courses $11.95–$21.95. AE, MC, V. Mon–Thurs 11:30am–10:30pm; Fri–Sat 11:30am–11pm. Metro: Dupont Circle.

Tabard Inn ✦ AMERICAN The restaurant here is only a shade more conventional than the inn in which it resides (see chapter 5). From the cozy though tattered lounge, where you can enjoy a drink in front of a crackling fire, you enter a narrow room, where hanging plants dangle from skylights and a mural of a ponytailed waiter points the way to the kitchen. A small bar hugs one side of the passage, a series of small tables the other, and both lead to the main space.

Or you can head up a set of stairs to another dining room and its adjoining courtyard. The restaurant staff, like the inn staff, is disarmingly solicitous.

The food is fresh and seasonal, making use of the inn's own homegrown and organically grown vegetables and herbs. Chef Andrew Saba came on board in late 2001, having worked most recently as executive chef at Marcel's (p. 150). Sample dishes from Saba's seasonally changing menus include grilled rabbit loin with fava beans, salsify and fried shallots, or a seafood and green herb stew of spring vegetables, pistou and crostini. Sunday brunch is an a la carte feast of both breakfast and supper choices, from hazelnut praline brioche French toast, to grilled salmon with black trumpet mushrooms. The Tabard is a favorite spot for Washingtonians.

1739 N St. NW. ✆ **202/833-2668.** Reservations recommended. Breakfast $2.50–$7.50, brunch $9–$12; lunch main courses $10–$16; dinner main courses $19–$27. AE, DC, MC, V. Mon–Fri 7–10am and 11:30am–2:30pm; Sat 8–10am and 11am–2:30pm; Sun 8–9:30am and 10:30am–2:30pm; Sun 6–9pm; Mon–Thurs 6–10pm; Fri–Sat 6–10:30pm. Metro: Dupont Circle.

MODERATE

Bistrot du Coin ★ FRENCH When Michel Richard, acclaimed chef of Michel Richard Citronelle (p. 153), is homesick, he visits this restaurant, because he thinks it feels like France. I think so, too. The wooden facade that draws your attention from the street, the way the whole glass front of the dining room opens right to the sidewalk, the zinc bar, the moody waiters—everything speaks of a Paris cafe, most of all the food.

I keep hearing that the mussels are the thing to order, either curried and creamed, or hiding in a thick gratin of leeks, but so far I have chosen other dishes and been pleased. The cassoulet is delicious, and not too hearty; the *tartine baltique* turned out to be an open-faced sandwich with smoked salmon, tamara onions, capers, and olive oil, and I slurped down every bite. The steak *frites* are just what you'd hope for, tasty and comforting. The menu presents a very limited number of wines, along with a list of 16 aperitifs. I chose the licorice-flavored Ricard, which is similar to pastis.

1738 Connecticut Ave. NW (near Florida Ave.). ✆ **202/234-6969.** Main courses $12.75–$26.50. AE, DISC, MC, V. Sun 11am–11pm; Mon–Wed 11:30am–11pm; Thurs–Sat 11:30am–1am. Metro: Dupont Circle.

City Lights of China CHINESE One of Washington's best Chinese restaurants outside of Chinatown, City Lights is a favorite of White House workaholics, whatever administration, who frequently order takeout from here. If you are staying at a nearby hotel, you might consider ordering food to go, as well; takeout prices are cheaper for some items. Some of the most popular dishes include crisp fried Cornish hen prepared in a cinnamon-soy marinade and served with a tasty dipping sauce, Chinese eggplant in garlic sauce, stir-fried spinach, crisp fried shredded beef, and Peking duck. The setting, a three-tiered dining room with much of the seating in comfortable leather booths and banquettes, is unpretentious. Neat white-linen tablecloths, cloth flower arrangements in lighted niches, and green neon track lighting complete the picture. There's a full bar.

1731 Connecticut Ave. NW (between R and S sts.). ✆ **202/265-6688.** Reservations recommended. Lunch main courses $6.95–$23.95 (most are about $8.95); dinner main courses $9.95–$25.95 (most are about $12.95). AE, DC, DISC, MC, V. Mon–Fri 11:30am–11pm; Sat noon–11pm; Sun noon–10:30pm; dinner from 3pm daily. Metro: Dupont Circle.

Etrusco ★★ ITALIAN Etrusco is just the sort of place you'd hope to stumble upon as a stranger in town. It's pretty, with a sophisticated but relaxed atmosphere, and the food is excellent. Lately, diners have been complaining about indifferent service, though, and I hope that by the time you read this, the wait staff will have regained its former professionalism. From the slate terrace at street level with umbrella tables, you descend a short flight of steps to the exquisite dining room, which resembles a trattoria with ochre and burnt-sienna walls, arched skylight, and tile floor.

On the menu you'll find warm baby octopus salad, *ribollita* (minestrone thickened with bread and Parmesan cheese), pappardelle with shredded duck, crumb-coated grilled tuna, and the more traditional veal scaloppini and osso buco. It's all very, very good. End with "Grandfather's cake," a light chocolate pie.

1606 20th St. NW. © 202/667-0047. Reservations recommended. Main courses $10–$17. AE, DC, MC. V. Mon–Sat 5:30–10:30pm. Metro: Dupont Circle.

INEXPENSIVE

Pizzeria Paradiso ✿ ITALIAN   Peter Pastan, master chef/owner of Obelisk (located right next door and reviewed just above), owns this classy, often crowded, 16-table pizzeria. An oak-burning oven at one end of the charming room produces exceptionally doughy but light pizza crusts. As you wait, you can munch on mixed olives and gaze up at the ceiling painted to suggest blue sky peeking through ancient stone walls. Pizzas range from the plain Paradiso, which offers chunks of tomatoes covered in melted mozzarella, to the robust Siciliano, a blend of nine ingredients including eggplant and red onion. Or you can choose your own toppings from a list of 29. As popular as the pizzas are the *panini* (sandwiches) of homemade focaccia stuffed with marinated roasted lamb and vegetables and other fillings, and the salads, such as tuna and white bean. Good desserts, but a limited wine list.

2029 P St. NW. © 202/223-1245. Reservations not accepted. Pizzas $7.95–$16.25; sandwiches and salads $3.95–$6.95. DC, MC, V. Mon–Thurs 11:30am–11pm; Fri–Sat 11:30am–midnight; Sun noon–10pm. Metro: Dupont Circle.

Sala Thai THAI   At lunch, you'll see a lot of diners sitting alone and reading newspapers, happy to escape the office. At dinner, the restaurant is filled with groups and couples, plus the occasional family. Among the 53 items to recommend on the menu are no. 41, *nua kra ting tone,* which is spicy beef with onion, garlic, and parsley sauce ("not found at any other Thai restaurant in Washington," said my Thai waitress, sporting multicolored streaks in her hair), and, no. 26, *ka prow,* which is an even spicier dish of either beef, chicken, or pork sautéed with basil leaves and chile. The restaurant lies downstairs from the street; with no windows to watch what's happening on P Street, you're really here for the food, which is excellent and cheap. Even conventional pad thai doesn't disappoint. Pay attention if your waiter cautions you about the level of spiciness of a dish you order—for some dishes (like no. 38, stir-fried sliced pork in red curry sauce with peppers), you'll need an asbestos tongue.

2016 P St. NW. © 202/872-1144. Reservations accepted for 5 or more. Lunch main courses $6.25–$9; dinner main courses $7.25–$13. AE, DC, DISC, MC, V. Mon–Fri 11:30am–3pm; Mon 4–10:30pm; Tues–Thurs 4–11pm; Fri 4–11:30pm; Sat noon–11:30pm; Sun noon–10:30pm. Metro: Dupont Circle.

Teaism Dupont Circle *(Finds* ASIAN FUSION   Occupying a turn-of-the-20th-century neoclassic building on a tree-lined street, Teaism has a lovely rustic interior such as you might find in the Chinese countryside. A display kitchen and tandoor oven dominate the sunny downstairs room, which offers counter seating along a wall of French windows, open in warm weather. Upstairs seating is on banquettes and small Asian stools at handcrafted mahogany tables.

The impressive tea list comprises close to 50 aromatic blends, most of them from India, China, and Japan. Many have exotic names: golden water turtle, jasmine pearl. On the menu is light Asian fare served on stainless-steel plates or in lacquer lunch boxes (Japanese "bento boxes," which hold a delicious meal of, for example, teriyaki salmon, cucumber-ginger salad, a scoop of rice with seasoning, and fresh fruit—all $8). Dishes include salmon cured in lapsang souchong (a smoky Chinese tea) with chopped bok choy, tandoor-baked lamb kebabs, and stir-fried chicken with coconut. Baked goods, coconut ice cream, and lime shortbread cookies are among desserts. At breakfast, you might try ginger scones or cilantro eggs and sausage with fresh tandoor-baked onion nan bread. Everything's available for takeout. Teapots, cups, and other gift items are for sale.

Note: Teaism has two other locations, both convenient for sightseeing. **Teaism Lafayette Square,** 800 Connecticut Ave. NW (© 202/835-2233), is across from the White House; it's open weekdays from 7:30am to 5:30pm and serves afternoon tea. **Teaism Penn Quarter** ✸, 400 Eighth St. NW (© 202/638-6010), which is near the MCI Center, the FBI Building, the National Gallery, and nightspots, is the only branch that serves beer, wine, and cocktails. Teaism Penn Quarter is open daily, serving all three meals and afternoon tea, and brunch on Saturday and Sunday; its happy hour on Thursday and Friday, from 5:30 to 7:30pm, features free hors d'oeuvres (with purchased drink) like curries and Asian noodle salads.

2009 R St. NW (between Connecticut and 21st sts.). © **202/667-3827.** All menu items 90¢–$8. AE, MC, V. Mon–Thurs 8am–10pm; Fri 8am–11pm; Sat 9am–11pm; Sun 9am–10pm. Metro: Dupont Circle.

8 Foggy Bottom/West End

VERY EXPENSIVE

Blackie's ✸ STEAK/SEAFOOD   The best bouillabaisse I ever had was at Blackie's House of Beef. That's because Blackie's (it doesn't really go by "house of beef" anymore) has a fine French chef in the kitchen. In addition to turning out house specialties of filet mignon, prime rib, strip steak, and porterhouse, Claude Rodier produces outstanding lobster fricassee, pan-seared Chilean sea bass with braised leeks, and made-to-order soufflés.

Blackie's is an institution in Washington, having opened in 1946. A $5 million renovation completed in 2001 has brought the kitchen and the building up to date, while holding on to some of the classic touches, like its stained-glass windows and the emphasis on beef, that locals associate with the old Blackie's. This is a large restaurant, with several rooms and lots of history, so you wander around while you're here.

1217 22nd St. NW (at M St.). © **202/333-1100.** Reservations recommended. Lunch main courses $10–$35, dinner main courses $23.95–$38. AE, DC, MC, V. Mon–Fri 11:30am–2pm; daily 5:30–10pm. Metro: Foggy Bottom or Dupont Circle.

Marcel's ✸✸ FRENCH   When you walk through the front door, look straight ahead into the exhibition kitchen—chances are you'll be staring directly into the eyes of owner/chef Robert Wiedmaier. He is firmly at the helm here, creating French dishes that include nods to his Belgian training: pan-seared halibut with a ragout of spinach and potatoes in a Ghent mustard essence; boneless quail stuffed with duck confit, with cherry-thyme sauce; and, for dessert, seasonal tarts such as spring pear tart with raspberry coulis. The French sommelier is expert.

Marcel's, named after Wiedmaier's young son, occupies the space that once was home to the restaurant Provence, and Wiedmaier has kept that restaurant's country French decor, including panels of rough-hewn stone framed by rustic shutters and antique hutches displaying Provençal pottery. Stone walls and floors don't do much to buffer all the bustle, however, so you can expect to have a very noisy time of it. To the right of the exhibition kitchen is a spacious bar area. Marcel's offers seating on the patio, right on Pennsylvania Avenue, in warm weather, and live jazz nightly year-round.

2401 Pennsylvania Ave. NW. ℭ 202/296-1166. Reservations recommended. Dinner main courses $26–$39; pretheater dinner 5:30–7pm (including round-trip limo to/from Kennedy Center) $42. AE, MC, V. Mon–Thurs 5:30–10:30pm; Fri–Sat 5:30–11pm; Sun 5–10pm. Metro: Foggy Bottom.

Melrose ✿✿ AMERICAN   Situated in an upscale hotel, this pretty restaurant offers fine cuisine presented with friendly flourishes. In nice weather, dine outdoors on the beautifully landscaped, sunken terrace whose greenery and towering fountain protect you from traffic noises. The glass-walled dining room overlooks the terrace and is decorated in accents of marble and brass, with more greenery and grand bouquets of fresh flowers.

Brian McBride is the beguiling executive chef who sometimes emerges from the kitchen to find out how you like the angel-hair pasta with mascarpone and lobster, or his sautéed Dover sole with garlic and salsify, or his pan-seared veal chop with herb butter and black truffle sauce. McBride is known for his use of seafood, which makes up at least half of the entrees and nearly all of the appetizers. Specialties of the house include shrimp ravioli with sweet corn, black pepper, tomato, and lemongrass beurre blanc, and Melrose crab cakes with grilled vegetables in a rémoulade sauce. Desserts, like the raspberry crème brûlée or the chocolate bread pudding with chocolate sorbet, are excellent. The wine list offers 30 wines by the glass. Sunday night, the restaurant dispenses with corkage fees; feel free to bring your own bottle. Friday and Saturday nights from 7 to 11pm, a quartet plays jazz, swing, and big-band tunes; lots of people get up and dance.

In the Park Hyatt Hotel, 1201 24th St. NW (at M St.). ℭ 202/419-6755. Reservations recommended. Breakfast $9–$18.50; lunch main courses $17–$32; dinner main courses $24–$36; pretheater dinner $35; Sun brunch $50 ($53 with champagne); light fare daily 2:30–5:30pm. AE, DC, DISC, MC, V. Mon–Fri 6:30–10am; Sat–Sun 7–10am; daily 11am–2:30pm and 5:30–10:30pm. Metro: Foggy Bottom.

EXPENSIVE

Asia Nora ✿ ASIAN FUSION   This is Nora's Asian offshoot (see the review of Nora on p. 146) and it's just as organic as the original, but with an Asian bent. Literally. Everything's set at a slant here: the tables, the bar, the banquette at the back on the first floor, and the triangular cutaway balcony on the second. Museum-quality artifacts from Asia—batik carvings, Japanese helmets, and Chinese puppets—decorate the gold-flecked jade walls. It's intimate and exotic, a charged combination. Try sitting at the bar first, on the most comfortable bar stools in town. If you like good bourbons and single-malt scotches, you're in luck.

Waiters dressed in black-satin pajamas serve Asian fusion cuisine, all prepared with organic ingredients, including a salad of baby Asian greens with clementine-sesame vinaigrette, a starter of shu mai dumplings with tender beef short ribs, and a main dish of crispy wild rockfish with rice noodles, prawns, and basil. The menu changes monthly. As at Nora, the desserts here are not to be missed; try the warm chocolate five spice cake with coconut sorbet.

2213 M St. NW. ℭ 202/797-4860. Reservations recommended. Main courses $20–$28. AE, DISC, MC, V. Mon–Thurs 5:30–10pm; Fri–Sat 5:30–10:30pm. Closed at end of Aug/beginning of Sept. Metro: Dupont Circle or Foggy Bottom.

Value Pretheater Dinners = Great Deals

Some of Washington's finest restaurants make you an offer you shouldn't refuse: a three-course dinner for just a little bit more than the cost of a typical entree. It's the pretheater dinner, available in early evening on certain nights at certain restaurants; and while your choices may be limited, your meal will undoubtedly be delicious.

At one end of the spectrum is **Marcel's** ☆☆ (p. 150), whose $42 fixed-price includes a starter, an entree (like pan-seared Norwegian salmon), and a dessert of either crème brûlée or chocolate terrine. Marcel's offers this menu Monday through Saturday from 5:30 to 7pm, and throws in complimentary limo service if you're headed to the Kennedy Center.

Café Atlantico's ☆☆ (p. 129) pretheater tasting menu allows you three courses for $26 with a glass of wine, $22 without; sample dishes are salmon ceviche as a first course, soft-shell crab with a Veracruz sauce for the main course, and rice-pudding mousse to finish.

Other restaurants in this chapter that offer a pretheater menu are **The Caucus Room** ☆☆ (p. 126), **1789** ☆☆ (p. 154), **Melrose** ☆☆ (p. 151), and **701** ☆ (p. 131).

Kinkead's ☆☆☆ AMERICAN/SEAFOOD   When a restaurant has been as roundly praised as Kinkead's, you start to think no place can be *that* good—but Kinkead's really is. An appetizer like grilled squid with creamy polenta and tomato fondue leaves you with a permanent longing for squid. The signature dish, pepita-crusted salmon with shrimp, crab, and chiles, provides a nice hot crunch before melting in your mouth. Vegetables you may normally disdain—sweet potatoes, for instance—taste delicious here.

Award-winning chef/owner Bob Kinkead is the star at this three-tier, 220-seat restaurant. He wears a headset and orchestrates his kitchen staff in full view of the upstairs dining room, where booths and tables neatly fill the nooks and alcoves of the town house. At street level is a scattering of tables overlooking the restaurant's lower level, the more casual bar and cafe, where a jazz group or pianist performs every evening. *Beware:* If the waiter tries to seat you in the "atrium," you'll be stuck at a table mall-side just outside the doors of the restaurant—yuck.

Kinkead's menu (which changes daily for lunch and again for dinner) features primarily seafood, but always includes at least one meat and one poultry entree. The wine list comprises more than 300 selections. You can't go wrong with the desserts either, like the chocolate dacquoise with cappuccino sauce. If you're hungry but not ravenous in the late afternoon, stop in for some delicious light fare: fish and chips, lobster roll, soups, and salads.

2000 Pennsylvania Ave. NW. © 202/296-7700. Reservations recommended. Lunch main courses $13–$21; dinner main courses $21–$29; light fare daily 2:30–5:30pm $5–$22. AE, DC, DISC, MC, V. Daily 11:30am–10:30pm. Metro: Foggy Bottom.

MODERATE

Kaz Sushi Bistro JAPANESE   Amiable chef/owner Kazuhiro ("Kaz") Okochi opened his own place after having worked at Sushi-Ko (p. 159) for many years. This is said to be the best place for sushi in the Washington area, and aficionados vie for one of the six chairs at the bar to watch Kaz and his staff do their thing, preparing salmon roe, sea urchin, tuna, and many other fish for sushi.

Besides sushi, Kaz is known for his napoleon of sea trout and wonton skins, his broiled scallops, and for his bento boxes, offering exquisite tastings of pan-seared salmon, spicy broiled mussels, and the like. This is also the place to come for premium sakes.

1915 I St. NW. ⓒ 202/530-5500. Reservations recommended. Sushi a la carte $3.25–$6; lunch main courses $9.25–$16.50; dinner main courses $12.95–$22.50. AE, DC, DISC, MC, V. Mon–Fri 11:30am–2pm; Mon–Sat 6–10pm. Metro: Farragut West.

9 Georgetown
VERY EXPENSIVE

Michel Richard Citronelle 🌟🌟🌟 INNOVATIVE FRENCH   If Citronelle's ebullient chef/owner Michel Richard is in the kitchen (and you know when he is, since the dining room views the open kitchen), diners in the know decline the menu and ask simply for whatever it is Richard wants to make. Whether you go that route, or choose from the fixed-price or tasting menus, you're in for a (very expensive) treat. Emerging from the bustling kitchen are appetizers like the fricassee of escargots, sweetbreads, porcinis, and crunchy pistachios, and entrees like the crispy lentil-coated salmon or venison with mushrooms, butternut squash, and celery sauce. But each presentation is a work of art, with swirls of colorful sauce surrounding the main event.

Citronelle's decor is also breathtaking and includes a wall that changes colors, a state-of-the-art wine cellar (a glass-enclosed room that encircles the dining room, displaying its 8,000 bottles and a collection of 18th- and 19th-century corkscrews), and a Provençal color scheme of mellow yellow and raspberry red.

The dessert of choice: Michel Richard's richly layered chocolate "bar" with sauce noisette. Citronelle's extensive wine list offers 20 premium by-the-glass selections, but with all those bottles staring out at you from the wine cellar, you may want to spring for one.

In the Latham Hotel, 3000 M St. NW. ⓒ 202/625-2150. Reservations required. Jacket required, tie optional for men at dinner. Breakfast $4–$14; lunch main courses $16–$25; fixed-price dinner $70 or $82; tasting menus $95 or $115. AE, DC, MC, V. Daily 6:30–10:30am; Mon–Fri noon–2pm; Sun–Thurs 6:30–9:30pm; Fri 6:30–10pm; Sat 6–10:30pm.

Morton's of Chicago 🌟 STEAK/SEAFOOD   Maybe when the first Morton's opened in 1978, a customer looked at the prices and shouted, "Show me the beef!" and a waiter complied by wheeling out a cart full of slabs of uncooked meat for inspection, thus starting a tradition. So our meal began, with this kitschy display of raw meat and vegetable props, and so will yours, too, at this and any other Morton's (the D.C. area has 5 locations in all). It will not be cheap, though—our entrees were each $33, though portions were so large that my children had my leftovers for dinner the next day.

Although the city is full of steakhouses, this is the only one in Georgetown. Its ambience is less relentlessly masculine than the others, probably because of its varied clientele (couples, businessmen, parents treating their college kid to dinner), and because of a glow emanating from the open kitchen. On a weeknight in winter, the restaurant was not totally full, and we were able to sit in our leather-cushioned booth and talk quietly, pausing only to swallow bites of tender filet mignon, porterhouse steak (both cooked perfectly), oysters on the half-shell, sautéed mushrooms, and asparagus (a tad tough) with hollandaise sauce. End with Godiva chocolate cake, a round derby of chocolate casing, which, when cut, releases a thick stream of melty hot chocolate—heavenly!

Other Morton's locations are downtown, at 1050 Connecticut Ave. NW, at L Street NW (✆ 202/955-5997), and in Tysons Corner, Virginia, at 8075 Leesburg Pike (✆ 703/883-0800). A Morton's in Arlington, Virginia opened in 2002.

3251 Prospect St. NW (between Wisconsin Ave. and Potomac St. NW). ✆ **202/342-6258.** Reservations recommended. Main courses $29–$35. AE, DC, MC, V. Mon–Sat 5:30–11pm; Sun 5–10pm. (Other locations open for lunch weekdays.)

1789 🖈🖈 AMERICAN In my brown corduroy skirt and tan wool sweater, I felt I'd dressed too casually, when I dined here recently. The staff never made me feel uncomfortable, it was a quick look around the room that did it, for fellow female diners (of all ages) were dressed in lacey tops, short flouncy dresses, and fancy long skirts.

So put on your best duds for the 1789. The formal but cozy restaurant is housed in a Federal town house near Georgetown University. The best of the five intimate dining rooms is the John Carroll Room, where the walls are hung with Currier and Ives prints and old city maps, a log fire blazes in the hearth, and a gorgeous flower arrangement tops a hunting-themed oak sideboard. Throughout, silk-shaded brass oil lamps provide romantic lighting.

Noted chef Ris Lacoste varies her menus seasonally. Appetizers might include macadamia-crusted grilled shrimp or grilled quail with barley and mushrooms. Typical entrees range from osso buco with risotto Milanese, to Nantucket Bay scallops in a creamy broth of ginger-lime coconut milk with mushrooms and curried mango rice, to roast rack of Colorado lamb with creamy feta potatoes au gratin in red-pepper-purée–infused Merlot sauce. Finish with the decadent hot fudge sundae.

The pretheater menu offered nightly through 6:45pm includes appetizer, entree, dessert, and coffee for $29.

1226 36th St. NW (at Prospect St.). ✆ **202/965-1789.** Reservations recommended. Jacket required for men. Main courses $18–$36; fixed-price pretheater menu $29. AE, DC, DISC, MC, V. Mon–Thurs 6–10pm; Fri 6–11pm; Sat 5:30–11pm; Sun 5:30–10pm.

EXPENSIVE

Café Milano 🖈 ITALIAN The beautiful people factor rises exponentially here as the night wears on. Café Milano has long been a magnet for Washington's famous and attractive, and their visitors. But this restaurant/nightclub/bar also serves very good food. Salads are big, pasta servings are small, and fish and meat entrees are just the right size. We had the endive, radicchio, and arugula salad topped with thin sheets of Parmesan cheese; a panzanella salad of tomatoes, potatoes, red onion, celery, and cucumber basking in basil and olive oil; cappellacci pockets of spinach and ricotta in cream sauce; sautéed sea bass on a bed of vegetables with lemon chive sauce; and the Santa Babila pizza, which has tomatoes, fresh mozzarella, oregano, and basil on a light pizza crust. All were delicious. At Café Milano, it's the nonsmokers who are relegated to the back room, while the smoking section takes over the main part of the restaurant and bar, which opens through the glass front to the sidewalk cafe. A bevy of good-humored waiters takes care of you.

3251 Prospect St. NW (between Wisconsin Ave. and Potomac St.). ✆ **202/333-6183.** Reservations recommended. Lunch main courses $9.50–$19; dinner main courses $14.50–$39. Sun–Wed 11:30am–11pm (bar menu served until midnight); Thurs–Sat 11:30am–midnight (bar menu served until 1am).

Mendocino Grille and Wine Bar 🖈 AMERICAN As its name suggests, you should come here to enjoy West Coast wine, along with contemporary

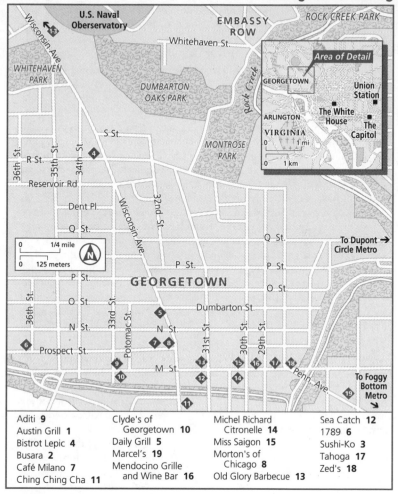

U.S. Naval
Oberservatory

EMBASSY
ROW

ROCK CREEK PARK

Whitehaven St.

WHITEHAVEN
PARK

DUMBARTON
OAKS PARK

Rock Creek

Area of Detail

GEORGETOWN

Union
Station

ARLINGTON

The White
House

The
Capitol

VIRGINIA

0   1 mi

0   1 km

S St.

MONTROSE
PARK

R St.

Reservoir Rd

Dent Pl.

Q St.

Wisconsin Ave.

32nd St.

Q St.

To Dupont →
Circle Metro

0   1/4 mile

0   125 meters

N

P St.

P St.

P St.

GEORGETOWN

O St.

Dumbarton St.

O St.

Potomac St.

N St.

N St.

31st St.

30th St.

29th St.

Prospect St.

M St.

Penn. Ave.

To Foggy
Bottom
Metro

Aditi **9**	Clyde's of Georgetown **10**	Michel Richard Citronelle **14**	Sea Catch **12**
Austin Grill **1**	Daily Grill **5**	Miss Saigon **15**	1789 **6**
Bistrot Lepic **4**	Marcel's **19**	Morton's of Chicago **8**	Sushi-Ko **3**
Busara **2**	Mendocino Grille and Wine Bar **16**	Old Glory Barbecue **13**	Tahoga **17**
Café Milano **7**			Zed's **18**
Ching Ching Cha **11**			

American cuisine and a California-causal ambience. Of the 150-or-so bottles on the wine list, all are highly rated West Coast selections, 95% of them from California. Waiters are knowledgeable about these, so don't hesitate to ask questions. California-casual doesn't mean cheap, though: Bottles range from $20 to $600, although most are about $50. The restaurant offers 23 wines by the glass, in different sizes, the better for tastings.

The menu highlights grilled seafood, with offerings like mustard spiced yellowfin tuna presented on orzo with English peas and artichokes, and nori-seared Chilean sea bass with potato-ginger pot stickers. Nonseafood choices include free-range chicken served with scallion mashed potatoes and grilled vegetables, and grilled tenderloin of beef.

Rough-textured slate walls alternate with painted patches of Big Sur sky to suggest a West Coast winery in California's wine-growing region. The wall sconces resemble rectangles of sea glass and the dangling light fixtures look like turned-over wineglasses. It's a very pleasant place.

2917 M St. NW. ℂ 202/333-2912. Reservations recommended. Lunch main courses $6.75–$18.75; dinner main courses $17–$29; prix fixe: lunch $20, dinner $33. AE, DC, DISC, MC, V. Mon–Sat 11:30am–3pm; Sun–Thurs 5:30–10pm; Fri–Sat 5:30–11pm.

Sea Catch ℛ *Finds* SEAFOOD   If you're walking around Georgetown and the crowds are starting to get to you, duck into the brick passageway that lies to the right of a little coffee bar and Mr. Smith's bar on M Street (at 31st St.) and follow it back to the little plaza, where you will find the entrance to the Sea Catch, a true refuge. (Or else you can walk south on 31st St. from M St., and turn right, into the plaza.) Since 1988, the Sea Catch has perched on the bank of the C&O Canal, with an awning-covered wooden deck where you can watch ducks, punters, and mule-drawn barges glide by while you dine. The innlike main dining room has a working fireplace and rough-hewn fieldstone walls from Georgetown quarries. There's also a handsome white Carrara-marble raw bar and a deluxe brasserie. Classic jazz tapes play in the background.

For openers, plump farm-raised oysters, clams, house-smoked fish, and other raw-bar offerings merit consideration. Daily fresh fish and seafood specials may include big, fluffy jumbo lump crab cakes served with crunchy Oriental-style Napa cabbage slaw or grilled marinated squid with fennel and basil aioli. The kitchen willingly prepares dishes to your specifications, including live lobster from the tanks. An extensive wine list highlights French, Italian, and American selections. Fresh-baked desserts usually include excellent Key lime pie.

1054 31st St. NW (just below M St.). ℂ 202/337-8855. Reservations recommended. Lunch main courses $7.50–$25; dinner main courses $15–$28. AE, DC, DISC, MC, V. Mon–Sat noon–3pm; Mon–Thurs 5:30–10pm; Fri–Sat 5:30–10:30pm.

Tahoga ℛ AMERICAN   Even if the food and the sparkling atmosphere don't lure you into Tahoga, two other unique features might: its hidden, brick-walled garden patio reached through French doors and its lunchtime offering of every wine, by the bottle or glass, at half price. The modern American dishes are always evolving and the menu tends to change every 2 weeks. Consider apricot-roasted duck, citrus-spiced shrimp, lamb skewers, and simple herb-roasted chicken. What do you serve for brunch? The curving bar beyond the main dining room is a comfortable spot for even a woman alone to have a drink.

2815 M St. NW. ℂ 202/338-5380. Reservations recommended. Lunch main courses $9–$13; dinner main courses $19–$26. AE, DC, MC, V. Mon–Fri 11:30am–2:30pm; Sun–Wed 5:30–10pm; Thurs–Sat 5:30–11pm; Sun brunch 11am–3pm.

MODERATE

Bistrot Lepic ℛℛ FRENCH   Tiny Bistrot Lepic is the real thing—a charming French restaurant that seems plucked right off a Parisian side street. The atmosphere is bustling and cheery, and you hear a lot of French spoken—not just by the waiters, but also by customers. The Bistrot is a neighborhood place, and you'll often see diners waving hellos across the room to each other, or even leaving their table to visit with those at another. In its 8 years, the restaurant has made some changes to accommodate its popularity, most recently turning the upstairs into a tapas bar and lounge; this means that if you arrive early for your reservation, you now have a place to wait (in the past, one had to hover hungry-eyed at the door).

This is traditional French cooking, updated. The seasonal menu offers such entrees as grilled rainbow trout with carrot sauce, beef medallions with polenta and shiitake mushroom sauce, and sautéed sea scallops with ginger broccoli mousse. We opted for specials: rare tuna served on fennel with citrus vinaigrette, and grouper with a mildly spicy lobster sauce upon a bed of spinach.

The modest French wine list offers a fairly good range. The house red wine, Le Pic Saint Loup, is a nice complement to most menu choices and is less than $20 a bottle.

1736 Wisconsin Ave. NW (near S St.). ℂ 202/333-0111. Reservations recommended. Lunch main courses $9–$14.95; dinner main courses $14–$19. AE, DC, DISC, MC, V. Tues–Sun 11:30am–2:30pm and 5:30–10:30pm.

Clyde's of Georgetown AMERICAN   Clyde's has been a favorite watering hole for an eclectic mix of Washingtonians since 1963. You'll see university students, Capitol Hill types, affluent professionals, Washington Redskins, romantic duos, and well-heeled ladies who lunch. A 1996 renovation transformed Clyde's from a saloon to a theme park, whose dining areas include a cherry-paneled front room with oil paintings of sport scenes, and an atrium with vintage model planes dangling from the glass ceiling and a 16th-century French limestone chimney piece in the large fireplace.

Clyde's is known for its burgers, chili, and crab-cake sandwiches. Appetizers are a safe bet, and Clyde's take on the classic Niçoise (chilled grilled salmon with greens, oven-roasted roma tomatoes, green beans, and grilled new potatoes in a tasty vinaigrette) is also recommended. Sunday brunch is a tradition, and some brunch items are available on Saturday, too. The menu is reassuringly familiar—steak and eggs, omelets, waffles—with variations thrown in for good measure. Among bar selections are about 10 draft beers.

Note: You can park in the underground Georgetown Park garage for $1 per hour for first 2 hours (a deal in Georgetown!). Just show your meal receipt and ask the mall concierge to validate your parking ticket.

3236 M St. NW. ℂ 202/333-9180. Reservations recommended. Lunch/brunch $7.95–$14.95; dinner main courses $10.95–$23.95 (most under $12); burgers and sandwiches (except for crab-cake sandwich) under $10 all day. AE, DC, DISC, MC, V. Mon–Thurs 11:30am–2am; Fri 11:30am–3am; Sat 10am–3am; Sun 9:30am–9pm; Sun brunch 9am–4pm.

Miss Saigon VIETNAMESE   This is a charming restaurant, with tables scattered amid a "forest" of tropical foliage, and twinkly lights strewn upon the fronds of the potted palms and ferns.

The food here is delicious and authentic, though the service can be a trifle slow when the restaurant is busy. To begin, there is the crispy calamari, or the shrimp and pork-stuffed garden rolls. House specialties include steamed flounder, caramel salmon, and "shaking beef" (cubes of tender Vietnamese steak, marinated in wine, garlic, butter, and soy sauce, then sautéed with onions and potatoes and served with rice and salad). There's a full bar. Desserts range from bananas *flambé au rhum* to ice cream with Godiva liqueur. Not to be missed is drip-pot coffee, brewed table side and served iced over sweetened condensed milk.

3057 M St. NW. ℂ 202/333-5545. Reservations recommended, especially weekend nights. Lunch main courses $4.50–$8.95; dinner main courses $8.95–$22.95. AE, DC, MC, V. Mon–Fri 11:30am–10:30pm (lunch menu served until 3pm); Sat–Sun noon–11pm (dinner menu served all day).

Old Glory Barbecue *(Kids* BARBECUE   Raised wooden booths flank one side of the restaurant; an imposing, old-fashioned dark-wood bar with saddle-seat stools extends down the other. Taped swing music during the day, more mainstream music into the night, plays in the background. Old Glory boasts the city's "largest selection of single-barrel and boutique bourbons" and a new rooftop deck with outdoor seating and views of Georgetown.

After 9pm or so, the two-story restaurant becomes packed with the hard-drinkin' young and restless. In early evening, though, Old Glory is prime for anyone—singles, families, or an older crowd—although it's almost always noisy. Come for the messy, tangy, delicious spare ribs; hickory-smoked chicken; tender, smoked beef brisket; or marinated, wood-fired shrimp. Six sauces are on the table, the spiciest being the vinegar-based East Carolina and Lexington. My Southern-raised husband favored the Savannah version, which reminded him of that city's famous Johnny Harris barbecue sauce. The complimentary corn muffins and biscuits; side dishes of collard greens, succotash, and potato salad; and desserts like apple crisp and coconut cherry cobbler all hit the spot.

3139 M St. NW. (C) 202/337-3406. Reservations accepted for 6 or more Sun–Thurs, reservations not accepted Fri–Sat. Main courses $7.95–$21.95; Sun brunch buffet $13.95, $5.95 for children 11 and under. AE, DC, DISC, MC, V. Sun 11am–2am; Mon–Thurs 11:30am–2am; Fri–Sat 11:30am–3am; Sun brunch 11am–3pm.

INEXPENSIVE

Aditi INDIAN   This charming two-level restaurant provides a serene setting in which to enjoy first-rate Indian cooking to the tune of Indian music. A must here is the platter of assorted appetizers, which features *bhajia* (a deep-fried vegetable fritter), deep-fried cheese-and-shrimp pakoras, and crispy vegetable samosas stuffed with spiced potatoes and peas. Favorite entrees include lamb biryani, which is basmati rice pilaf tossed with savory pieces of lamb, cilantro, raisins, and almonds; and the skewered jumbo tandoori prawns, chicken, lamb, or beef—all fresh and fork tender—barbecued in the tandoor. Sauces are on the mild side, so if you like your food fiery, inform your waiter. A kachumber salad, topped with yogurt and spices, is a refreshing accompaniment to entrees. For dessert, try *kheer*, a cooling rice pudding garnished with chopped nuts. There's a full bar.

3299 M St. NW. (C) 202/625-6825. Reservations recommended. Lunch main courses $6.60–$13; dinner main courses $8–$15. AE, DC, DISC, MC, V. Daily 11:30am–2:30pm; Sun–Thurs 5:30–10pm; Fri–Sat 5:30–10:30pm.

Ching Ching Cha *(Finds* CHINESE   Located just below M Street, this skylit Chinese tearoom offers a pleasant respite from the crowds. You can sit on pillows at low tables or on chairs set at rosewood tables. Choices are simple: individual items like a tea-and-spice boiled egg, puff pastry stuffed with lotus-seed paste, or five-spice peanuts; or the tea meal, which consists of miso soup, three marinated cold vegetables, rice, a salad, and tastings of soy-ginger chicken, salmon with mustard-miso sauce, or steamed teriyaki-sauced tofu. Tea choices include several different green, black, medicinal, and oolong teas, plus a Fujian white tea and a ginseng brew.

1063 Wisconsin Ave. NW. (C) 202/333-8288. Reservations not accepted. Tea meal $11; appetizers $1.50–$4.50. AE, DISC, MC, V. Tues–Sat 11:30am–9pm; Sun 11:30am–6pm.

Zed's ETHIOPIAN   Though Ethiopian cuisine has long been popular in Washington, few restaurants can match Zed's truly authentic, high-quality fare. Zed's is a charming little place with indigenous paintings, posters, and artifacts adorning pine-paneled walls. Tables are set with fresh flowers, and Ethiopian music enhances the ambience.

Diners eschew silverware in favor of using a sourdough crepelike pancake called *injera* to scoop up food. Highly recommended are the *doro watt* (chicken stewed in a tangy, hot red chile-pepper sauce), the *infillay* (strips of tender chicken breast flavored with seasoned butter and honey wine served with a delicious chopped spinach and rice side dish), flavorful lamb dishes, and the deep-fried whole fish. Vegetables have never been tastier. Consider ordering more of the garlicky chopped collard greens, red lentil purée in spicy red-pepper sauce, or a chilled purée of roasted yellow split peas mixed with onions, peppers, and garlic. There's a full bar, and, should you have the inclination, there are Italian pastries for dessert.

1201 28th St. NW (at M St.). *(*) 202/333-4710. Reservations accepted for 6 or more. Lunch main courses $6.50–$12.50; dinner main courses $7.50–$15.50. AE, DC, DISC, MC, V. Sun–Thurs 11am–10pm; Fri–Sat 11am–11pm.

10 Glover Park

Buses (the no. 30 series) travel to Glover Park, which is just north of Georgetown, but the easiest thing to do is take a taxi.

EXPENSIVE

Sushi-Ko *✿* JAPANESE   Sushi-Ko was Washington's first sushi bar when it opened 27 years ago and it remains popular. The sushi chefs are fun to watch— try to sit at the sushi bar. You can expect superb sushi and sashimi standards, but the best items are daily specials, like a sea trout napoleon (diced sea trout layered between rice crackers), and the "small dishes," like the grilled baby octopus with mango, or asparagus with smoked salmon and mustard dashi sauce. The tempuras and teriyakis are also excellent. And there's a long list of sakes, as well as burgundy wines and Japanese beer.

2309 Wisconsin Ave. NW. *(*) 202/333-4187. Reservations recommended. Main courses $12–$25. AE, MC, V. Tues–Fri noon–2:30pm; Mon–Thurs 6–10:30pm; Fri 6–11pm; Sat 5:30–11pm; Sun 5:30–10pm.

MODERATE

Busara THAI   Like many Thai restaurants, Busara gives you big portions for a pretty good price. The pad thai is excellent—less sweet than most—the satays are well marinated, and an appetizer called "shrimp bikini" serves up not-at-all-greasy deep-fried shrimp in a thin spring-roll covering.

Busara's dining room is large, with a picture window overlooking Wisconsin Avenue, modern art on the neon-blue walls, and dimly set track lighting angled this way and that. Service is solicitous, but not pushy. If the dining room is full, you can eat at the bar (at dinner only), which is in a separate, rather inviting room. In warm weather, Busara also serves diners in its Oriental garden.

2340 Wisconsin Ave. NW. *(*) 202/337-2340. Reservations recommended. Lunch main courses $7–$9; dinner main courses $10–$17. AE, DISC, MC, V. Mon–Fri 11:30am–3pm; Sat–Sun 11:30am–3:45pm; Sun–Thurs 5–10:30pm; Fri–Sat 5–11:30pm.

INEXPENSIVE

Austin Grill *Kids* SOUTHERN/SOUTHWESTERN   Rob Wilder opened his grill in 1988 to replicate the easygoing lifestyle, Tex-Mex cuisine, and music he loved when he lived in Austin. The good food and festive atmosphere make this a great place for the kids, a date, or a group of friends. Austin Grill is loud; as the night progresses, conversation eventually drowns out the sound of the taped music (everything from Ry Cooder to Natalie Merchant).

Fresh ingredients are used to create outstanding crab-meat quesadillas, "Lake Travis" nachos (tostadas slathered with red onion, refried beans, and cheese), a daily fish special (like rockfish fajitas), Key lime pie, and excellent versions of standard fare (chicken enchiladas, guacamole, pico de gallo, and so on). The margaritas are awesome.

✐ A Spot of Tea

When you think about it, afternoon tea might well have been designed with tourists in mind. At 3 in the afternoon, you may find yourself longing for a break from all the sightseeing, but not wanting to return to your hotel room. The following are some of my favorite teatime stops:

A popular tea is served in the Garden Terrace of the **Four Seasons Hotel,** M Street NW (✆ **202/342-0444**), where one wall of windows overlooks the C&O Canal. The Garden Terrace serves drinks and light fare, as well as tea, so expect a mix of businesspeople, couples, and families. This is one place where a children's tea is offered (a choice of tea, milkshake, or soda, with a brownie, peanut-butter-and-jelly sandwich, chocolate-chip cookie, and strawberries dipped in chocolate). Adults get one scone with double Devon cream and both raspberry and blueberry jam, and a variety of finger sandwiches, tartlets, tea cakes, and cookies that change daily. Among the 16 teas are some herbal and decaffeinated brews; champagne and sherries are available at a surcharge. A pianist plays during afternoon tea, Friday through Sunday. Tea is served Monday through Friday from 3 to 4:30pm, Saturday and Sunday from 2 to 5pm. The price is $25 per adult and $12 per child; reservations suggested. Dress presentably casual.

At the **Jefferson Hotel,** 1200 16th St. NW (at M St.; ✆ **202/833-6206**), scones are baked while you wait—they take about 15 minutes—so they come to you hot and fragrant, served with Devon cream and jam. Afternoon tea is served in the cozy bar/lounge, where original letters and other documents written by Thomas Jefferson hang on the paneled walls. Sink into a red-leather chair and relax as you nibble on those

Austin Grill's upstairs overlooks the abbreviated bar area below. An upbeat decor includes walls washed in shades of teal and clay and adorned with whimsical coyotes, cowboys, Indians, and cacti. Arrive by 6pm weekends if you don't want to wait; weekdays are less crowded.

This is the original Austin Grill; another District Austin Grill is located near the MCI Center at 750 E St. NW (✆ 202/393-3776). Suburban locations are in Old Town Alexandria (see chapter 10) and West Springfield, Virginia, and Bethesda, Maryland.

2404 Wisconsin Ave. NW. ✆ 202/337-8080. Reservations not accepted. Main courses $8–$15. AE, DC, DISC, MC, V. Mon 11:30am–10:30pm; Tues–Thurs 11:30am–11pm; Fri 11:30am–midnight; Sat 11am–midnight; Sun 11am–10:30pm.

11 Woodley Park & Cleveland Park

VERY EXPENSIVE

Palena 🍴🍴 ITALIAN/FRENCH   One Metro stop past the Woodley Park–Zoo station takes you to the residential neighborhood of Cleveland Park, which is exploding with good restaurants. Palena is the latest, and it's worth that extra bit of travel.

Palena is the creation of two former White House chefs, executive chef Frank Ruta and pastry chef Ann Amernick, who worked together at the White House scones; tea sandwiches filled with cucumber and cheese, duck paté, or smoked salmon; and homemade cookies and miniature fruit tarts. You may choose from a selection of 10 to 16 teas. Afternoon tea is served daily from 3 to 5pm for $25 per person. Dress neatly.

Teaism, 400 Eighth St. NW (*C* **202/638-6010**), offers a choice of two very different kinds of afternoon teas: the more traditional menu of tea sandwiches, ginger scone, cookies, lime curd tartlets, Swiss chocolates, and a pot of tea; or the Asian menu, which offers you rice balls with pickle and sesame, tea-cured salmon and nori, tofu with ginger, green tea ice cream, mochi, plum truffle, and a pot of tea. Both are delicious, and are served daily from 2:30 to 5:30pm, for $15 each. *Note:* The Lafayette Square branch of Teaism also offers afternoon tea.

The tea at **Washington National Cathedral,** Massachusetts and Wisconsin avenues NW (*C* **202/537-8993**), begins with a tour of the world's sixth-largest cathedral (see chapter 7), or, in May and September, a choice of either a garden or cathedral tour, winding up on the seventh floor of the West tower, whose arched windows take in a stunning view of the city and beyond to the Sugarloaf Mountains in Maryland. Tea consists of scones and jam; sandwich triangles of egg salad or smoked salmon, or maybe pastry cups of tarragon chicken salad; tiny pastries; and brewed tea. During the school year, you can descend from the tower in time to enjoy evensong services performed at 4:30pm by the Youth Choir. Tea is served every Tuesday and Wednesday at 3pm following a 1:30pm tour, for $18 per person. Reserve as far in advance as possible (the cathedral accepts reservations up to 6 months ahead).

in the 1980s. As partners in Palena, the two turn out French- and Italian-inspired dishes, such as Portuguese sardines in puff pastry, boudin blanc, Dover sole filet stuffed with porcini and pan roasted with artichokes and endive, a veal chop that *Washington Post* restaurant critic Tom Sietsema calls "the best in the city," and so on. Amernick's contributions range from complimentary caramels at dinner's conclusion, to the fresh sorbets, cheesecake, bread pudding, and other offerings on the dessert menu. This is an elegant restaurant, with an old-world feel (even though it's only about 2 years old). Because of its immediate and sustained success, it's hard to get a reservation, but worth trying for.

3529 Connecticut Ave. NW (near Porter St.). *C* 202/537-9250. Reservations recommended. Main courses $28. AE, DC, DISC, MC, V. Mon–Sat 5:30–10pm. Metro: Cleveland Park.

EXPENSIVE

New Heights *C* AMERICAN/INTERNATIONAL   This attractive second-floor dining room has a bank of windows looking out over Rock Creek Park, and walls hung with the colorful works of local artists. New Heights attracts a casually upscale clientele, which fills the room every night. An Indian influence will always be found in at least one or two items on the menu, to please the palate of owner Amarjeet (Umbi) Singh, as well as those of his patrons. My husband and I have dined at New Heights a lot over the years, our constancy outlasting a number of fine chefs, who seem to come and go here rather quickly.

Once again, New Heights has a new chef in the kitchen, and I hope Arthur Rivaldo stays. Our recent dinner here was our best ever: seared diver scallops with creamer potatoes, spinach, and puttanesca sauce for me, and a half-seared coriander ahi tuna with sushi rice, langoustine, seaweed salad, and wasabi-tobiko aioli for Jim. Our appetizers were decadent, too: a rich lobster soup and a duckling foie gras on apple galette. In the past, I've found New Heights's innovative cuisine too adventurous, but these dishes I can handle. Sunday brunch is heavenly, too: brioche French toast, soup of puréed chestnut with foie gras, and the like.

2317 Calvert St. NW (near Connecticut Ave.). ℂ 202/234-4110. Reservations recommended. Brunch $8.95–$17.50; dinner main courses $17.50–$28. AE, DC, DISC, MC, V. Sun–Thurs 5:30–10pm; Fri–Sat 5:30–11pm; Sun brunch 11am–2:30pm. Metro: Woodley Park–Zoo.

Petits Plats ✿ FRENCH   Petits Plats is another French bistro, and a very pretty one, ensconced in a town house that's situated directly across from the Woodley Park Metro entrance and the Marriott Wardman Park Hotel. You can sit at the sidewalk cafe, on the porch above, or in the front room, back room, or upstairs rooms of the town house. Watching the passersby on busy Connecticut Avenue is a major amusement. Bistro fare includes shrimp bisque with crab meat; five different mussels dishes, like the mussels in a mustard, cream, and white wine sauce (each comes with french fries); Provençal-styled shrimp on an artichoke-bottom dish; Belgian endive salad with apples, walnuts, and Roquefort; and roasted rack of lamb with potatoes au gratin. The reasonably priced Petits Plats becomes even more so Tuesday through Friday at lunch, when a two-course set menu is available for $13.95; daily at early dinner, 5:30 to 7pm, when a three-course set menu is available for $18.95; and at Saturday and Sunday brunch, when $15.95 gets you a choice of entree (from eggs Benedict to steak *frites*), a house salad, and all the champagne you like. Since it opened in spring 2000, Petits Plats has gained a loyal following.

2653 Connecticut Ave. NW. ℂ 202/518-0018. Reservations recommended. Lunch main courses $10.95–$14.95; dinner main courses $14.95–$21.95. AE, MC, V. Tues–Sun 11:30am–2:30pm and 5:30–10 or 10:30pm. Metro: Woodley Park–Zoo.

MODERATE

Lebanese Taverna MIDDLE EASTERN   This family owned restaurant gives you a taste of Lebanese culture—its cuisine, decor, and music. It's very popular on weekends, so expect to stand in line (reservations are accepted for seating before 6:30pm only). Diners, once seated in the courtyardlike dining room, where music plays and prayer rugs hang on the walls, hate to leave. The wood-burning oven in the back bakes the pita breads and several appetizers. Order a *demi mezze*, with pita for dipping, and you get 10 sampling dishes, including hummus, tabbouleh, baba ghanoush, and pastry-wrapped spinach pies (*fatayer bi sabanikh*), enough for dinner for two or hors d'oeuvres for four. The wealth of meatless dishes will delight vegetarians, while rotisserie items, especially the chicken and the chargrilled kebabs of chicken and shrimp, will please all others.

There are Lebanese Tavernas in Arlington, Virginia, at 5900 Washington Blvd. (ℂ 703/241-8681); and in Rockville, Maryland, at Congressional Plaza, 1605 Rockville Pike (ℂ 301/468-9086).

2641 Connecticut Ave. NW. ℂ 202/265-8681. Reservations accepted before 6:30pm. Lunch main courses $10–$14; dinner main courses $11–$19. AE, DC, DISC, MC, V. Mon–Fri 11:30am–2:30pm; Sat 11:30am–3pm; Mon–Thurs 5:30–10:30pm; Fri–Sat 5:30–11pm; Sun 5–10pm. Metro: Woodley Park–Zoo.

7

Exploring Washington, D.C.

Crammed within Washington's compact 67 square miles are hundreds, yes, hundreds of attractions. You are not going to be able to explore all of them. So, you need a strategy.

Although this chapter organizes attractions by theme ("the three houses of government," "the Smithsonian museums," and so on) rather than by neighborhood, you're probably going to want to tour the city by covering one area at a time, visiting your first-choice attractions in a particular neighborhood and checking out whatever other sights are nearby. So start off by consulting the "Washington, D.C., Attractions" map below.

Right away, you'll notice that most of Washington's attractions fall nicely into geographic clusters—seven major clusters, to be exact. These are: **Memorials** (the Lincoln, Jefferson, FDR, George Mason, Korean War Veterans, and Vietnam War Veterans Memorials, the Washington Monument, and Arlington National Cemetery); the **National Mall** (all the Smithsonian museums, plus the National Archives, the National Gallery of Art, the U.S. Holocaust Memorial Museum, and the Bureau of Engraving & Printing); **Capitol Hill** (the Capitol, the Library of Congress, the Supreme Court, the Folger Shakespeare Library, Union Station, and the National Postal Museum); the **White House** (the White House and Visitor Center, the Corcoran Gallery of Art, the Renwick Gallery, Decatur House,

and the Kennedy Center); **Dupont Circle** (the Phillips Gallery, the Textile Museum, Woodrow Wilson House, Anderson House, and the National Geographic Society); **Downtown** (the FBI, Ford's Theatre and Petersen House, the International Spy Museum, the National Museum of Women in the Arts, and the Navy Memorial); and **Georgetown** (Tudor House, Dumbarton House, Dumbarton Oaks, and the C&O Canal).

Six of the seven sections are doable in a day. The National Mall cluster is the only one that is not (in fact, you could spend a week and still not get to all of its 13 museums). Naturally, the National Mall is the cluster with the capital's most popular attractions, so chances are that you're going to want to see at least some of its museums, and chances are, you don't have a week to do it.

So here's what you do: Read this chapter, then pick the cluster that holds most of your top choices, and decide which of these you want to visit. Look at neighboring clusters, like the National Mall and Memorials, or the Downtown and the National Mall, and see whether there aren't other sites near your top choices where you might like to go. (You can use the suggested itineraries that follow as a guideline for ways to mix and match things to see around the city.) Think about how much time you have and what you can fit into the allotted time. My descriptions within this chapter

Washington, D.C., Attractions

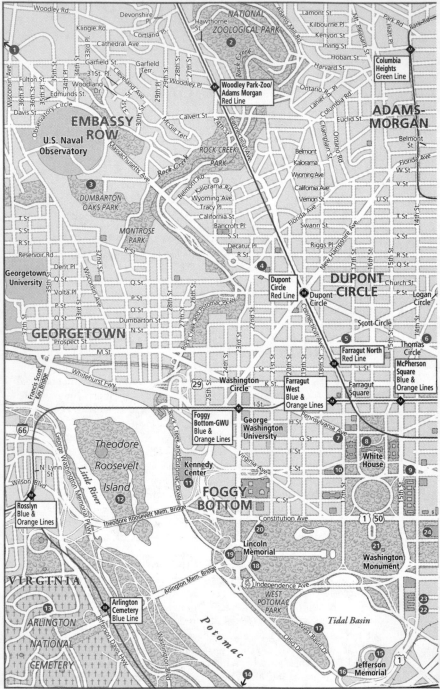

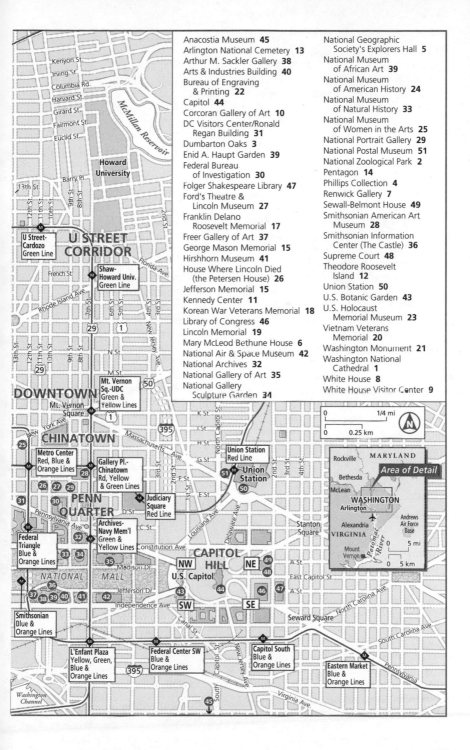

Anacostia Museum **45**
Arlington National Cemetery **13**
Arthur M. Sackler Gallery **38**
Arts & Industries Building **40**
Bureau of Engraving
 & Printing **22**
Capitol **44**
Corcoran Gallery of Art **10**
DC Visitors Center/Ronald
 Regan Building **31**
Dumbarton Oaks **3**
Enid A. Haupt Garden **39**
Federal Bureau
 of Investigation **30**
Folger Shakespeare Library **47**
Ford's Theatre &
 Lincoln Museum **27**
Franklin Delano
 Roosevelt Memorial **17**
Freer Gallery of Art **37**
George Mason Memorial **15**
Hirshhorn Museum **41**
House Where Lincoln Died
 (the Petersen House) **26**
Jefferson Memorial **15**
Kennedy Center **11**
Korean War Veterans Memorial **18**
Library of Congress **46**
Lincoln Memorial **19**
Mary McLeod Bethune House **6**
National Air & Space Museum **42**
National Archives **32**
National Gallery of Art **35**
National Gallery
 Sculpture Garden **34**

National Geographic
 Society's Explorers Hall **5**
National Museum
 of African Art **39**
National Museum
 of American History **24**
National Museum
 of Natural History **33**
National Museum
 of Women in the Arts **25**
National Portrait Gallery **29**
National Postal Museum **51**
National Zoological Park **2**
Pentagon **14**
Phillips Collection **4**
Renwick Gallery **7**
Sewall-Belmont House **49**
Smithsonian American Art
 Museum **28**
Smithsonian Information
 Center (The Castle) **36**
Supreme Court **48**
Theodore Roosevelt
 Island **12**
Union Station **50**
U.S. Botanic Garden **43**
U.S. Holocaust
 Memorial Museum **23**
Vietnam Veterans
 Memorial **20**
Washington Monument **21**
Washington National
 Cathedral **1**
White House **8**
White House Visitor Center **9**

✐ Call Ahead

If there were only one piece of advice I could give to a visitor, it would be to call ahead to the places you plan to tour, to make sure they're open. I don't mean in advance of your trip (although that can't hurt)—I mean on each day of touring, before you set out. Many of Washington's government buildings, museums, memorials, and monuments are open to the general public nearly all the time—except when they are not.

Because buildings like the Capitol, the Supreme Court, and the White House are "offices" as well as tourist destinations, the business of the day always poses the potential for closing one of those sites, or at least sections, to sightseers. (The White House is probably most vulnerable to this situation.) This caveat is even more important in the wake of the terrorist attack on the Pentagon; there may be changes in touring procedures and what's open to the public. At this writing, neither the Pentagon nor the White House had reopened to the general public, but staff at both sites hoped that their pre–September 11 touring schedules would eventually resume. At these and other government buildings, you can expect to see increased security as well.

The steady stream of visitors to Washington's attractions necessitates ongoing maintenance and, sometimes, new construction, which may require closing an entire landmark, or part of it, to the public, or put in place new hours of operation or procedures for visiting. (Construction of the Capitol's Visitor Center is one such example; see information within the Capitol's description, later in this chapter.)

Finally, Washington's famous museums, grand halls, and public gardens double as settings for press conferences, galas, special exhibits, festivals, and other special events, so you might arrive at, say, the National Air and Space Museum on a Sunday afternoon, as I did not long ago, only to find some of its galleries off limits because caterers were setting up for an event.

Want to avoid frustration and disappointment? Call ahead.

---

roughly estimate the amount of time you should allow for touring each place. Now write it down. Voilà—you've got your strategy.

Except for one or two little things. A handful of sights, like the Pentagon, the Washington National Cathedral, Hillwood Museum, the National Zoo, and the Vatican Center, don't fit nicely into an attraction-filled neighborhood, but are certainly worth a trip. So be sure to consider those.

And then, maybe you have a special interest, like American portraiture in the late 17th century, which, when the time comes, keeps you in the National Gallery when, according to your schedule, you're supposed to be across Pennsylvania Avenue taking an FBI tour. Maybe you get terribly hungry or thirsty while standing in line for a trip to the top of the Washington Monument, and you absolutely must wander up 15th Street for a bite to eat *right now*, even though it means relinquishing your spot. Or maybe you had not pictured your family becoming quite so fascinated by the insects at the National Museum of Natural History, which means that a tour of the Capitol (where you had envisioned your children would be enthralled, asking lots of astute questions about U.S. history) is off, at least for the day.

When these things happen, there's only one thing to do: Relax. Because isn't this really what you came for? To become fascinated? To be caught up in the experience? To take in new territory? In the end, a plan is just a way to get started, and spontaneity is more important than adhering to a rigid schedule.

Just remember: Have fun.

SUGGESTED ITINERARIES
If You Have 1 Day

Make the Mall your destination, visiting whichever museums appeal to you the most. Then take a breather: If you have young kids, take them for a ride on the carousel across from the Smithsonian's Arts & Industries Building. With or without kids, stroll across the Mall to the National Gallery Sculpture Garden, where you can get a bite to eat in the cafe or relax by the reflecting pool. Rest up, dine in Dupont Circle, stroll Connecticut Avenue, then take a cab to visit the Lincoln Memorial at night.

If You Have 2 Days

On your first day, take a narrated tour of the city (see the list of tours at end of this chapter) for an overview of the city's attractions, stopping at the Jefferson, FDR, Lincoln, and Vietnam War Veterans memorials, and at the Washington Monument. Use the tour to determine which Mall museums you'll want to visit. After taking in the Washington Monument, walk up 15th Street to F Street, turn right, and walk to Red Sage at 14th and F for some Southwestern fare in the restaurant's open-all-day Border Café (which doesn't take reservations).

Following lunch, visit your top-pick museums on the Mall.

Start your second day by visiting the Capitol, followed by a tour of the Supreme Court. Walk to Massachusetts Avenue for lunch at Café Berlin, then spend the afternoon visiting the Library of Congress, the Folger Shakespeare Library, and, if you have time, Union Station and the National Postal Museum. Have dinner in Georgetown and browse the shops.

If You Have 3 Days

Spend your first 2 days as described above.

On the morning of your third day, tour the White House, then visit the Corcoran Gallery of Art, and, if you have time, the Renwick Gallery, both of which are a stone's throw from the White House. In the afternoon, ride the bus (an N bus from Dupont Circle, or a 30-series bus from Georgetown) to visit the Washington National Cathedral, or take in some of the non-Mall art museums (say, the National Museum of Women in the Arts). Enjoy a pretheater dinner at one of the many restaurants that offer these good deals (1789 in Georgetown and the Bombay Club near the White House are two fine choices, and they're described along with others in chapter 6). Then head to the Kennedy Center for a performance.

If You Have 4 Days or More

Spend your first 3 days as suggested above.

On the fourth day, get an early start on the FBI tour, then walk back to Ford's Theatre, on 10th Street, where Lincoln was shot, and the Petersen House, across from Ford's, where he died. Have lunch at one of the many good restaurants in this area, such as the Caucus Room (where you need to be well dressed), Café Atlantico, or Teaism (see chapter 6 for addresses and other suggestions). Spend the rest of the afternoon outdoors—go to the zoo or take a hike along the C&O Canal. Alternatively, you might visit the U.S. Holocaust Memorial Museum (not recommended for children under 12); this will require most of your day. Have dinner in Adams-Morgan, followed by club-hopping up and down 18th Street. (Or take in a salsa lesson at Habana Village, on Columbia Rd. in Adams Morgan; see chapter 9 for other suggestions for places to boogie.)

If you have a fifth day, consider a day trip to Alexandria, Virginia. Or board a boat for Mount Vernon and spend most of the morning touring the estate (see chapter 10 for details), with the afternoon set aside for seeing sights you've missed. Have dinner in downtown Washington at one of the Seventh Street–district restaurants, then see Shakespeare performed at the Shakespeare Theatre, or head to the Blue Bar at the Henley Park Hotel to sip a nightcap as you listen to live jazz.

1 The Three Houses of Government

Three of the most visited sights in Washington have always been the buildings housing the executive, legislative, and judicial branches of the U.S. government. All three, the Capitol, the White House, and the Supreme Court, are stunning and offer fascinating lessons in American history and government. Nevertheless, it's possible in the wake of the terrorist acts of September 11, 2001, that you will not be able to tour one or more of these sites while you are here, or that touring restrictions may prevent you from seeing all that you'd like. I'm thinking positive, though, and hoping that during your visit to the capital, general public tours are operating normally at the Capitol, White House, and Supreme Court. And if they are, here is some information that will help you as you go.

The Capitol 𝘈𝘈𝘈 The Capitol is as majestic up close at it is from afar. For 135 years it sheltered not only both houses of Congress, but also the Supreme Court and, for 97 years, the Library of Congress as well. When you tour the Capitol, you'll learn about America's history as you admire the place in which it unfolded. Classical architecture, interior embellishments, and hundreds of paintings, sculptures, and other artworks are integral elements of the Capitol.

On the massive bronze doors leading to the **Rotunda** are portrayals of events in the life of Columbus. The Rotunda—a huge 96-foot-wide circular hall capped by a 180-foot-high dome—is the hub of the Capitol. The dome was completed, at Lincoln's direction, while the Civil War was being fought. Nine presidents have lain in state here; when Kennedy's casket was displayed, the line of mourners stretched 40 blocks. On the circular walls are eight immense oil paintings of events in American history, such as the presentation of the Declaration of Independence and the surrender of Cornwallis at Yorktown. In the dome is an allegorical fresco masterpiece by Constantino Brumidi, *Apotheosis of Washington,* a symbolic portrayal of George Washington surrounded by Roman gods and goddesses watching over the progress of the nation. Brumidi was known as the "Michelangelo of the Capitol" for the many works he created throughout the building. (Take another look at the dome and find the woman directly below Washington; the triumphant *Armed Freedom* figure is said to be modeled after Lola Germon, a beautiful young actress with whom the 60-year-old Brumidi had a child.) Beneath the dome is a trompe-l'oeil frieze depicting

Capitol Hill

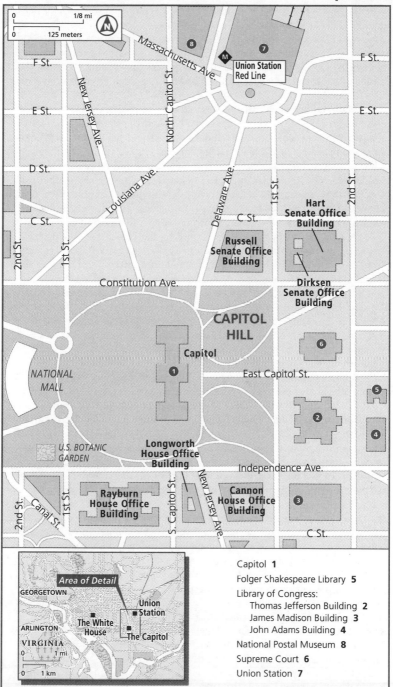

0   1/8 mi
0   125 meters

F St.

New Jersey Ave.

Massachusetts Ave.

North Capitol St.

E St.

D St.

Louisiana Ave.

C St.

2nd St.

1st St.

Constitution Ave.

NATIONAL
MALL

U.S. BOTANIC
GARDEN

2nd St.

Canal St.

1st St.

Rayburn
House Office
Building

S. Capitol St.

Longworth
House Office
Building

New Jersey Ave.

Cannon
House Office
Building

Independence Ave.

C St.

Delaware Ave.

Union Station
Red Line

F St.

E St.

1st St.

2nd St.

Hart
Senate Office
Building

Russell
Senate Office
Building

Dirksen
Senate Office
Building

CAPITOL
HILL

Capitol ❶

East Capitol St.

❻

❷

❸

❺

❹

Capitol **1**
Folger Shakespeare Library **5**
Library of Congress:
   Thomas Jefferson Building **2**
   James Madison Building **3**
   John Adams Building **4**
National Postal Museum **8**
Supreme Court **6**
Union Station **7**

Area of Detail

GEORGETOWN

Union
Station

ARLINGTON

The White
House

The Capitol

VIRGINIA

0   1 mi
0   1 km

events in American history, from the arrival of Columbus through the Wright brothers' flight at Kitty Hawk.

Newly added to the Rotunda is the sculpture of suffragists Elizabeth Cady Stanton, Susan B. Anthony, and Lucretia Mott. Until recently, the ponderous monument had been relegated to the Crypt, one level directly below the Rotunda. Women's groups successfully lobbied for its more prominent position in the Rotunda.

The **National Statuary Hall** was originally the chamber of the House of Representatives. In 1864, it became Statuary Hall, and the states were invited to send two statues each of native sons and daughters to the hall. There are 97 statues in all, since three states, Nevada, New Mexico, and North Dakota, have sent only one. As the room filled up, statues spilled over into the Hall of Columns, corridors, and any space that might accommodate the bronze and marble artifacts. Many of the statues honor individuals who played important roles in American history, such as Henry Clay, Ethan Allen, Daniel Webster, and six women, including Jeannette Rankin, the first woman to serve in Congress.

The **south and north wings** are occupied by the House and Senate chambers, respectively. The House of Representatives chamber is the largest legislative chamber in the world, and the setting for the president's annual State of the Union addresses. (See information further along about watching Senate and House activity when the bodies are in session.) The Capitol also houses the **Old Supreme Court Chamber,** which has been restored to its mid-19th-century appearance. The Old Supreme Court Chamber is where Chief Justice John Marshall established the foundations of American constitutional law. Keep your eyes peeled for senators and representatives as you walk around because you're likely to see several.

Allow at least an hour for touring here, longer if you plan to attend a session of Congress. Remember to allow time for waiting in line, too.

Very Important Note: In mid-2002, construction started on a comprehensive, underground Capitol Visitor Center, with completion scheduled for 2005. Since the Capitol Visitor Center is being created directly beneath the plaza where people traditionally line up for tours on the east side of the Capitol, touring procedures have changed. The best thing to do is to call ahead (© 202/ 225-6827) to find out the new procedures in place for the time you are visiting, and whether the construction work will temporarily close parts of the building you wish to visit.

At this time, I can tell you that self-guided tours and "VIP" tours (tours reserved in advance by individuals through their congressional offices) have been suspended, for the foreseeable future. The only way now to tour the Capitol Building is in groups of 40. The tours are free and last about 30 minutes.

You have two options: If you are part of an organized bunch, say a school class on a field trip, you may arrange a tour in advance, putting together groups of no more than 40 each, by contacting your congressional office at least one month ahead, and following the procedures that office outlines for you. If you are on your own, or with family or friends, you will want to get to the Capitol early, by 7:30am, to stand in line for one of only 540 timed tickets the Capitol distributes daily, starting at 8:15am. It's a first-come, first-served system, with only one ticket given to each person, and each person, including children of any age, must have a ticket. The good news is that once you receive your ticket, you are free to go somewhere nearby to get a bite to eat, or to sightsee, while you wait for your turn to tour the Capitol. The bad news is that all of you, even 1-year-old baby

Louie, have to rise early and get to the Capitol by about 7:30am and then stand in line for another hour or more to be sure of touring the Capitol that day. Still, I think this is an improvement over the old touring procedure, which required all of you to stay in the queue until you entered the Capitol—if you left the line, you lost your place. Again, I emphasize that you must call the **recorded information line** (✆ **202/225-6827**) on the morning of your planned visit to find out exactly where you should go and what you should do to obtain your ticket.

Now, if you wish to visit either or both the House and Senate galleries, you follow a different procedure. These galleries are always open to visitors, when the galleries are **in session** ☆☆☆, but you must have a pass to visit each gallery on weekdays until 6pm. (Families, take note that children under 6 are not allowed in the Senate gallery.) After 6pm weekdays and on Saturday and Sunday, however, you may enter either gallery without a pass and watch the session to its conclusion. Once obtained, the passes are good through the remainder of the Congress. To obtain visitor passes in advance, contact your representative for a House gallery pass, or your senator for a Senate gallery pass; District of Columbia and Puerto Rico residents should contact their delegate to Congress. If you don't receive visitor passes in the mail (not every senator or representative sends them), they're obtainable at your senator's office on the Constitution Avenue side of the building or your representative's or delegate's office on the Independence Avenue side. (Visitors who are not citizens can obtain a gallery pass by presenting a passport at the Senate or House appointments desk, located on the first floor of the Capitol.) Call the **Capitol switchboard** at ✆ **202/224-3121** to contact the office of your senator or congressperson. Your congressional office will issue you a pass and direct you to the House or Senate Gallery line outside the Capitol, for entry into the Capitol. If you're there after 6pm weekdays, or on a Saturday or Sunday, when a gallery is in session, simply ask a Capitol Guide or police officer to direct you to the right entrance.

You'll know the House and/or the Senate is in session if you see flags flying over their respective wings of the Capitol (House: south side, Senate: north side), or you can check the weekday "Today in Congress" column in the *Washington Post* for details on times of the House and Senate sessions and committee hearings. This column also tells you which sessions are open to the public, allowing you to pick one that interests you.

At the east end of the Mall, entrance on E. Capitol St. and 1st St. NW. ✆ 202/225-6827. www.aoc.gov, www.house.gov, www.senate.gov. Free admission. Year-round 9am–4:30pm Mon–Sat, with first tour starting at 9:30am and last tour starting at 3:30pm. Closed for tours Sun and Jan 1, Thanksgiving, and Dec 25. Parking at Union Station or on neighborhood streets. Metro: Union Station or Capitol South.

The Supreme Court of the United States ☆☆   The highest tribunal in the nation, the Supreme Court is charged with deciding whether actions of Congress, the president, the states, and lower courts are in accord with the Constitution, and with applying the Constitution's enduring principles to novel situations and a changing country. The Supreme Court's chief justice and eight associate justices have the power of judicial review—that is, authority to invalidate legislation or executive action that conflicts with the Constitution. Out of the 7,000 or so cases submitted to it each year, the Supreme Court hears only about 100 cases, many of which deal with issues vital to the nation. The Court's rulings are final, reversible only by another Supreme Court decision, or in some cases, an Act of Congress or a constitutional amendment.

Until 1935, the Supreme Court met in the Capitol. Architect Cass Gilbert designed the stately Corinthian marble palace that houses the Court today. The building was considered rather grandiose by early residents: One justice remarked that he and his colleagues ought to enter such pompous precincts on elephants.

If you're in town when the Court is in session, try to **see a case being argued** 🐘🐘🐘 (call 📞 **202/479-3211** for details). The Court meets Monday through Wednesday from 10am to noon, and, on occasion, from 1 to 2pm, starting the first Monday in October through late April, alternating in approximately 2-week intervals between "sittings" to hear cases and deliver opinions and "recesses" for consideration of Court business and writing opinions. From mid-May to late June, you can attend brief sessions (about 15 min.) at 10am on Monday, when the justices release orders and opinions. You can find out what cases are on the docket by checking the *Washington Post*'s "Supreme Court Calendar." Arrive at least an hour early—even earlier for highly publicized cases—to line up for seats, about 150 of which are allotted to the general public.

There are many rituals here. At 10am, the entrance of the justices is announced by the marshal, and all present rise and remain standing while the justices are seated following the chant: "The Honorable, the Chief Justice and Associate Justices of the Supreme Court of the United States. Oyez! Oyez! Oyez! All persons having business before the Honorable, the Supreme Court of the United States, are admonished to draw near and give their attention, for the Court is now sitting. God save the United States and this Honorable Court!" Unseen by the gallery is the "conference handshake"; following a 19th-century tradition symbolizing a "harmony of aims if not views," each justice shakes hands with each of the other eight when they assemble to go to the bench. The Court has a record before it of prior proceedings and relevant briefs, so each side is allowed only a 30-minute argument.

Call the Supreme Court information line to find out days and times that court arguments will take place. You may view these on a first-come, first-served basis, choosing between the 3-minute line, which ushers visitors in and out of the court every 3 minutes, starting at 10am in the morning and at 1pm in the afternoon; or the "regular" line, which admits visitors who wish to stay for the entire argument, starting at 9:30am and 12:30pm (you should try to arrive about 90 min. ahead of time to snag a spot).

The Supreme Court is cloaked in mystery, purposefully. You can't take cameras or recording devices into the courtroom, and you're not allowed to take notes, either. The justices seldom give speeches and never give press conferences.

When the Court is not in session, you can tour the building and attend a **free lecture** in the courtroom about Court procedure and the building's architecture. Lectures are given every hour on the half-hour from 9:30am to 3:30pm. After the talk, explore the Great Hall and go down a flight of steps to see the **24-minute film** on the workings of the Court. On the same floor is an exhibit highlighting the "History of High Courts Around the World," on display indefinitely. If you tour the building on your own, you should allow about an hour. You might also consider contacting your senator or congressperson—at least 2 months in advance—to arrange for a 40-minute guided tour of the building led by a Supreme Court staff member, who will take you places you won't be able to go on your own.

There's also a gift shop and a cafeteria that's open to the public and serves good food.

One 1st St. NE (between E. Capitol St. and Maryland Ave. NE). 📞 **202/479-3000**. www.supremecourtus.gov. Free admission. Mon–Fri 9am–4:30pm. Closed all federal holidays. Metro: Capitol South or Union Station.

The White House ★★   It's amazing when you think about it: This house has served as a residence, office, reception site, and world embassy for every U.S. president since John Adams. The White House is the only private residence of a head of state that has opened its doors to the public for tours, free of charge. It was Thomas Jefferson who started this practice, which is stopped only during wartime; the administration considers that we are currently fighting a war on terrorism, and, therefore, the White House, at this writing, remains closed for public tours. The White House is open for tours by certain groups, however: school groups (students in grades 4–12, who are enrolled in the same school or school district) and organized veterans groups. **If you are hoping to arrange a White House tour for your student or veterans group, you must submit a request to your senator or congressperson's office.** For those who have arranged such tours, and in the hope that general public tours have resumed by the time you read this, I provide the following information. To find out the latest White House tour information, call ☎ **202/456-7041.**

An Act of Congress in 1790 established the city, now known as Washington, District of Columbia, as the seat of the federal government. George Washington and city planner Pierre L'Enfant chose the site for the White House (or "President's House," as it was called before whitewashing brought the name "White House" into use) and staged a contest to find a builder. Although Washington picked the winner—Irishman James Hoban—he was the only president never to live in the White House. The structure took 8 years to build, starting in 1792, when its cornerstone was laid, and its facade is made of the same stone as that used to construct the Capitol. In 1814, during the War of 1812, the British set fire to the White House, gutting the interior; the exterior managed to endure only because a rainstorm extinguished the fire. What you see today is Hoban's basic creation: a building modeled after an Irish country house (in fact, Hoban had in mind the house of the duke of Leinster in Dublin).

Alterations over the years have incorporated the South Portico in 1824, the North Portico in 1829, and electricity in 1891, during Benjamin Harrison's presidency. In 1902, repairs and refurnishings of the White House cost nearly $500,000. No other great change took place until Harry Truman's presidency, when the interior was completely renovated, after the leg of Margaret Truman's piano cut through the dining room ceiling. The Trumans lived at Blair House across the street for nearly 4 years while the White House interior was shored up with steel girders and concrete. It's as solid as Gibraltar now.

In 1961, Jacqueline Kennedy formed a Fine Arts Committee to help restore the famous rooms to their original grandeur, ensuring treatment of the White House as a museum of American history and decorative arts. "It just seemed to me such a shame when we came here to find hardly anything of the past in the house, hardly anything before 1902," Mrs. Kennedy observed. Presidents and their families through the years have put their own stamp on the White House, the most recent example being President Bush's addition of the T-ball field to the South Lawn.

Highlights of the tour include the **Gold-and-White East Room,** the scene of presidential receptions, weddings (Lynda Bird Johnson, for one), and other dazzling events. This is where the president entertains visiting heads of state and the place where seven of the eight presidents who died in office (all but Garfield) laid in state. It was also where Nixon resigned. The room's early-18th-century style was adopted during the Theodore Roosevelt renovation of 1902; it has parquet Fontainebleau oak floors and white-painted wood walls with fluted pilasters and classical relief inserts. Note the famous Gilbert Stuart portrait of George Washington that Dolley Madison saved from the British torch during the War of 1812. The portrait is the only object to have remained continuously in the White House since 1800 (except during times of reconstruction).

You'll visit the **Green Room,** which was Thomas Jefferson's dining room but today is used as a sitting room. Mrs. Kennedy chose the green watered-silk-fabric wallcovering. In the **Oval Blue Room,** decorated in the French Empire style chosen by James Monroe in 1817, presidents and first ladies have officially received guests since the Jefferson administration. It was, however, Van Buren's decor that began the "blue room" tradition. The walls, on which hang portraits of five presidents (including Rembrandt Peale's portrait of Thomas Jefferson and G. P. A. Healy's of Tyler), are covered in reproductions of early-19th-century French and American wallpaper. Grover Cleveland, the only president to wed in the White House, was married in the Blue Room. This room was also where the Reagans greeted the 52 Americans liberated after being held hostage in Iran for 444 days, and every year it's the setting for the White House Christmas tree.

The **Red Room,** whose satin-covered walls and Empire furnishings are red, is used as a reception room, usually for afternoon teas. Several portraits of past presidents and a Gilbert Stuart portrait of Dolley Madison, hang here. Dolley Madison used the Red Room for her famous Wednesday-night receptions.

From the Red Room, you enter the **State Dining Room.** Modeled after late-18th-century neoclassical English houses, this room is a superb setting for state dinners and luncheons. Below G. P. A. Healy's portrait of Lincoln is an inscription written by John Adams on his second night in the White House (FDR had it carved into the mantel): "I Pray Heaven to Bestow The Best of Blessings on THIS HOUSE and on All that shall here-after Inhabit it. May none but Honest and Wise Men ever rule under this Roof."

White House tours take place mornings only, Tuesday through Saturday. There are no public restrooms or telephones in the White House, and picture-taking and videotaping are prohibited.

Note: Even if you have successfully reserved a White House tour for your group, you should still call ⓒ **202/456-7041** before setting out in the morning; in case the White House is closed on short notice because of unforeseen events. If this should happen to you, you should make a point of walking by the White House anyway, since its exterior is still pretty awesome. Stroll past it on Pennsylvania Avenue, down 17th Street, and along the backside and South Lawn, on E Street.

1600 Pennsylvania Ave. NW (visitor entrance gate at E St. and E. Executive Ave.). ⓒ 202/456-7041 or 202/208-1631. www.whitehouse.gov. Free admission. Tours only for school and veterans groups, which have arrange the tour through their congressional offices. Metro: McPherson Square.

The White House Visitor Center 🐾 Even—especially—if you are not able to tour the White House, you should stop here. The Visitor Center opened in 1995 to provide extensive interpretive data about the White House (as well as other Washington tourist attractions) and to serve as a ticket-distribution center (though that function is suspended indefinitely). It is run under the auspices of the National Park Service and the staff is particularly well informed. Try to catch the 30-minute video about the White House, *Within These Walls,* which provides interior views of the presidential precincts (it runs continuously throughout the day). Before you leave the Visitor Center, pick up a copy of the National Park Service's brochure on the White House, which tells you a little about what

The White House Area

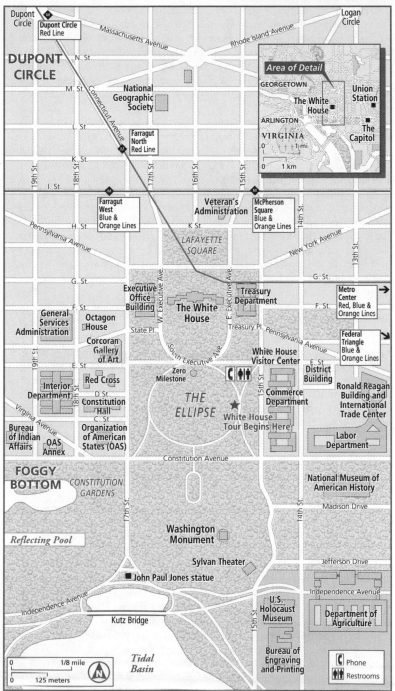

Dupont Circle

Logan Circle

Massachusetts Avenue

Rhode Island Avenue

DUPONT CIRCLE

Dupont Circle Red Line

N. St.

M. St.

Connecticut Avenue

National Geographic Society

L. St.

Farragut North Red Line

K. St.

I. St.

19th St.

18th St.

17th St.

16th St.

15th St.

Area of Detail

GEORGETOWN

The White House

Union Station

ARLINGTON

VIRGINIA

The Capitol

0   1 mi.

0   1 km

Pennsylvania Avenue

H. St.

Farragut West Blue & Orange Lines

K St.

Veteran's Administration

McPherson Square Blue & Orange Lines

14th St.

New York Avenue

13th St.

LAFAYETTE SQUARE

G. St.

Executive Office Building

W. Executive Ave.

The White House

E. Executive Ave.

Treasury Department

F. St.

G. St.

Metro Center Red, Blue & Orange Lines →

General Services Administration

Octagon House

Corcoran Gallery of Art

State Pl.

Treasury Pl.

Pennsylvania Avenue

White House Visitor Center

Federal Triangle Blue & Orange Lines →

19th St.

E. St.

Interior Department

Red Cross

D St.

Constitution Hall

C. St.

Zero Milestone

South Executive Ave.

THE ELLIPSE

15th St.

Commerce Department

E. St.

District Building

Ronald Reagan Building and International Trade Center

Virginia Avenue

Bureau of Indian Affairs

OAS Annex

Organization of American States (OAS)

★ White House Tour Begins Here

C 🚻

Labor Department

Constitution Avenue

FOGGY BOTTOM

CONSTITUTION GARDENS

17th St.

14th St.

National Museum of American History

Madison Drive

Reflecting Pool

Washington Monument

Sylvan Theater

■ John Paul Jones statue

Jefferson Drive

Independence Avenue

Independence Avenue

Kutz Bridge

15th St.

U.S. Holocaust Museum

Department of Agriculture

Tidal Basin

0   1/8 mile

0   125 meters

Ⓝ

Bureau of Engraving and Printing

C Phone

🚻 Restrooms

you'll see in the eight or so rooms you tour and a bit about the history of the White House. The White House Historic Association runs a small shop here.

The association operates an informative website, **www.whitehousehistory. org**, although much of it seems designed to make you order something.

Before you leave the Visitor Center, take a look at the exhibits, which include:

Architectural History of the White House, including the grounds and extensive renovations to its structure and interior that have taken place since its cornerstone was laid in 1792.

Symbol and Image, showing how the White House has been portrayed by photographers, artists, journalists, political cartoonists, and others.

First Families, with displays about the people who have lived here (such as prankster Tad Lincoln, who once stood in a window above his father and waved a Confederate flag at a military review).

The Working White House, focusing on the vast staff of servants, chefs, gardeners, Secret Service people, and others who maintain this institution.

Ceremony and Celebration, depicting notable White House events, from a Wright Brothers' aviation demonstration in 1911 to a ballet performance by Baryshnikov during the Carter administration.

White House Interiors, Past and Present, including photographs of the ever-changing Oval Office as decorated by administrations from Taft through Clinton.

1450 Pennsylvania Ave. NW (in the Dept. of Commerce Building, between 14th and 15th sts.). © 202/ 208-1631, or 202/456-7041 for recorded information. Free admission. Daily 7:30am–4pm. Closed Jan 1, Thanksgiving, and Dec 25. Metro: Federal Triangle.

2 The Major Memorials

The capital's major memorials honor esteemed presidents, war veterans, and, most recently, George Mason, the patriot and author of the Virginia Declaration of Rights, the prototype for our Bill of Rights. In the offing are memorials to veterans of World War II and to Dr. Martin Luther King Jr. All of these memorials are located in picturesque **West Potomac Park** (See p. 215 for full details on the park and its famous **cherry blossoms**), which lies at the western end of the National Mall, where it borders the Potomac River and encircles the Tidal Basin. Unfortunately, none of the memorials lie directly on a Metro line, so you can expect a bit of a walk from the specified station.

The easiest thing to do, if you're up to it, is to walk from one monument or memorial to the next. You'll want to dress for the weather: light clothing, shades, and sunscreen in summer; a hat, gloves, and warm jacket in winter—these monuments are set in wide open spaces, providing no or little protection from the elements. But when the weather is lovely, so is the experience of sauntering around West Potomac Park.

Or, you can go by **Tourmobile** (p. 221), which continually picks up and discharges passengers at each of these sites throughout the day. The National Park Service manages all of these properties and maintains information about each of them, including upcoming events, at **www.nps.gov** (click on the "Select a Park" function to find the one you want).

Some believe the best time to visit the memorials is at night, when they're illuminated in all their imposing white-stone glory and all the crowds are gone. Try it—all of the memorials are safe to visit after dark, with park rangers on hand until 11:45pm year-round, except for the Washington Monument, which closes at 5pm now. You may view the exteriors any time.

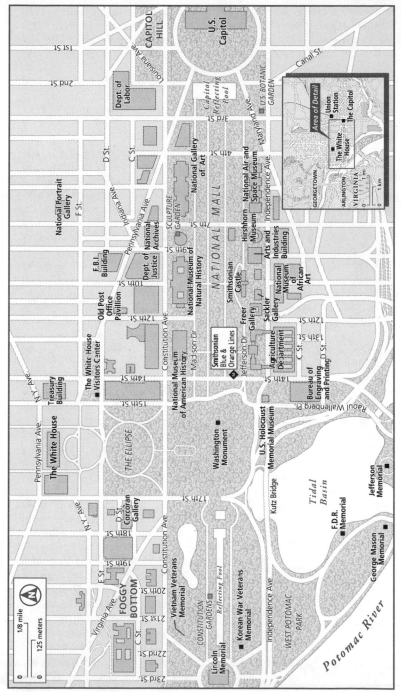

The Mall

U.S. Capitol

CAPITOL HILL

1st St.

2nd St.

Louisiana Ave.

D St.

Dept. of Labor.

C St.

Canal St.

Capitol Reflecting Pool

3rd St.

U.S. BOTANIC GARDEN

Maryland Ave.

National Portrait Gallery

F St.

Pennsylvania Ave.

Indiana Ave.

4th St.

National Gallery of Art

SCULPTURE GARDEN

7th St.

National Air and Space Museum

Independence Ave.

N A T I O N A L   M A L L

Hirshhorn Museum

Arts and Industries Building

F.B.I. Building

Dept. of National Justice Archives

9th St.

National Museum of Natural History

10th St.

Smithsonian Castle

National Museum of African Art

Old Post Office Pavillion

Freer Gallery

Sackler Gallery

12th St.

Constitution Ave.

Madison Dr.

Agriculture Department

C St.

13th St.

D St.

The White House Visitors Center

Smithsonian Blue & Orange Lines

Jefferson Dr.

14th St.

N.Y. Ave.

Treasury Building

National Museum of American History

15th St.

Bureau of Engraving and Printing

Raoul Wallenberg Pl.

Pennsylvania Ave.

The White House

THE ELLIPSE

Washington Monument

U.S. Holocaust Memorial Museum

Tidal Basin

Jefferson Memorial

N.Y. Ave.

D St.

Corcoran Gallery

18th St.

Constitution Ave.

Kutz Bridge

F.D.R. Memorial

17th St.

George Mason Memorial

E St.

19th St.

FOGGY BOTTOM

Vietnam Veterans Memorial

Constitution Ave.

CONSTITUTION GARDENS

Reflecting Pool

Independence Ave.

WEST POTOMAC PARK

Virginia Ave.

20th St.

21st St.

C St.

Korean War Veterans Memorial

22nd St.

23rd St.

Lincoln Memorial

Potomac River

N

1/8 mile

125 meters

Area of Detail

Union Station

The Capitol

Georgetown

The White House

VIRGINIA

ARLINGTON

1 mi

1 km

Washington Monument 🌟🌟🌟 *Kids*　The idea of a tribute to George Washington first arose 16 years before his death, at the Continental Congress of 1783. But the new nation had more pressing problems and funds were not readily available. It wasn't until the early 1830s, with the 100th anniversary of Washington's birth approaching, that any action was taken.

Then there were several fiascoes. A mausoleum was provided for Washington's remains under the Capitol Rotunda, but a grand-nephew, citing Washington's will, refused to allow the body to be moved from Mount Vernon. In 1830, Horatio Greenough was commissioned to create a memorial statue for the Rotunda. He came up with a bare-chested Washington, draped in classical Greek garb; a shocked public claimed he looked as if he were "entering or leaving a bath," and so the statue was relegated to the Smithsonian. Finally, in 1833, prominent citizens organized the Washington National Monument Society. Treasury Building architect Robert Mills's design (originally with a circular colonnaded Greek temple base, which was later discarded for lack of funds) was accepted.

The cornerstone was laid on July 4, 1848, and for the next 37 years, watching the monument grow, or not grow, was a local pastime. Declining contributions and the Civil War brought construction to a halt at an awkward 150 feet (you can still see a change in the color of the stone about halfway up). The unsightly stump remained until 1876, when President Grant approved federal monies to complete the project. Dedicated in 1885, it was opened to the public in 1888.

A major 2-year restoration completed in 2000 repaired the monument's exterior masonry and mortar, refurbished its elevator, installed a new climate-control system, scrubbed the 897 interior steps, and polished the 193 carved commemorative stones.

Visiting the Washington Monument: The Washington Monument is the world's tallest freestanding work of masonry. It stands at the very center of Washington, D.C., landmarks, and the 360° views from the top are spectacular. Due east are the Capitol and Smithsonian buildings; due north is the White House; due west is the Lincoln Memorial (with Arlington National Cemetery beyond); and due south is the Jefferson Memorial, overlooking the Tidal Basin and the Potomac River. It's like being at the center of a compass, and it provides a marvelous orientation to the city.

Climbing the 897 steps is not allowed, but the large elevator whisks visitors to the top in just 70 seconds. If you're dying to see more of the interior, **"Walk Down" tours** are given, every Saturday at 10am and 2pm. To be sure of a spot on this tour, you need to call the National Park Reservation Service (📞 **800/967-2283**) and reserve a ticket for the "Walk Down" tour; the tour itself is free, but you'll pay $1.50 per ticket plus a 50¢ service charge per transaction. For details, call before you go or ask a ranger on duty. On this tour you'll learn more about the building of the monument and get to see the 193 carved stones inserted into the interior walls. The stones are gifts from foreign countries, all 50 states, organizations, and individuals. The most expensive stone was given by the state of Alaska in 1982—it's pure jade and worth millions. There are stones from Siam (now Thailand), the Cherokee Nation, and the Sons of Temperance. Allow half an hour here, plus time spent waiting in line.

Impressions

May the spirit which animated the great founder of this city descend to future generations.
—John Adams

Light snacks are sold at a snack bar on the grounds, where you'll also find a few picnic tables. There's limited but free 2-hour **parking** at the 16th Street Oval.

Ticket Information: Although admission to the Washington Monument is free, you'll still have to get a ticket. The ticket booth is located at the bottom of the hill from the monument, on 15th Street NW between Independence and Constitution avenues. It's open daily from 8am to 4:30pm. Tickets are usually gone by 9:30am, so plan to get there by 7:30 or 8am, especially in peak season, if you really want to ascend to the top of the monument. The tickets grant admission at half-hour intervals between the stated hours, on the same day you visit. If you want to save yourself the trouble and get them in advance, call the National Park Reservation Service (© **800/967-2283**) or go online at http://reservations.nps.gov; you'll pay $1.50 per ticket plus a 50¢ service charge per transaction.

Directly south of the White House (at 15th St. and Constitution Ave. NW). © 202/426-6841. Free admission. Daily 9am–5pm. Last elevators depart 15 min. before closing (arrive earlier). Closed Dec 25, open until noon July 4. Metro: Smithsonian, then a 10-min. walk.

Lincoln Memorial ✯✯✯ *Kids*   This beautiful and moving testament to the nation's greatest president attracts millions of visitors annually. Like its fellow presidential memorials, this one was a long time in the making. Although it was planned as early as 1867—2 years after Lincoln's death—it was not until 1912 that Henry Bacon's design was completed, and the memorial itself was dedicated in 1922.

The neoclassical templelike structure, similar in architectural design to the Parthenon in Greece, has 36 fluted Doric columns representing the states of the Union at the time of Lincoln's death, plus two at the entrance. On the attic parapet are 48 festoons symbolizing the number of states in 1922, when the monument was erected. Hawaii and Alaska are noted in an inscription on the terrace. Due east is the Reflecting Pool, lined with American elms and stretching 2,000 feet toward the Washington Monument and the Capitol beyond.

The memorial chamber has limestone walls inscribed with the Gettysburg Address and Lincoln's Second Inaugural Address. Two 60-foot-high murals by Jules Guerin on the north and south walls depict, allegorically, Lincoln's principles and achievements. On the south wall, an Angel of Truth freeing a slave is flanked by groups of figures representing Justice and Immortality. The north-wall mural depicts the unity of North and South and is flanked by groups of figures symbolizing Fraternity and Charity. Most powerful, however, is Daniel Chester French's 19-foot-high seated statue of Lincoln, which disappears from your sightline as you get close to the base of the memorial, then emerges slowly into view as you ascend the stairs.

Lincoln's legacy has made his memorial the site of numerous demonstrations by those seeking justice. Most notable was a peaceful demonstration of 200,000 people on August 28, 1963, at which the Rev. Dr. Martin Luther King Jr. proclaimed, "I have a dream."

An information booth, a small museum, and a bookstore are on the premises. Rangers present 20- to 30-minute programs as time permits throughout the day Limited free **parking** is available along Constitution Avenue and south along Ohio Drive. Twenty to thirty minutes is sufficient time for viewing this memorial.

Directly west of the Mall in Potomac Park (at 23rd St. NW, between Constitution and Independence aves.). © 202/426-6842. Free admission. Daily 8am–11:45pm. Closed Dec 25. Metro: Foggy Bottom, then a 30-min. walk.

Korean War Veterans Memorial *⚔* This privately funded memorial, founded in 1995, honors those who served in Korea, a 3-year conflict (1950–53) that produced almost as many casualties as Vietnam. It consists of a circular "Pool of Remembrance" in a grove of trees and a triangular "Field of Service," highlighted by lifelike statues of 19 infantrymen, who appear to be trudging across fields. In addition, a 164-foot-long black-granite wall depicts the array of combat and support troops that served in Korea (nurses, chaplains, airmen, gunners, mechanics, cooks, and others); a raised granite curb lists the 22 nations that contributed to the U.N.'s effort there; and a commemorative area honors KIAs, MIAs, and POWs. Allow 15 minutes for viewing. Limited parking is available along Ohio Drive.

Tip: If you don't mind a walk, try to snag a **parking** spot along West Basin Drive near the FDR Memorial; the Korean War and the Vietnam War Veterans memorials, as well as the Lincoln Memorial, are then all within reach.

Just across from the Lincoln Memorial (east of French Dr., between 21st and 23rd sts. NW). *©* 202/ 426-6841. Free admission. Rangers on duty daily 8am–11:45pm except Dec 25. Ranger-led interpretive programs are given throughout the day. Metro: Foggy Bottom.

Vietnam Veterans Memorial *⚔⚔* The Vietnam Veterans Memorial is possibly the most poignant sight in Washington: two long, black-granite walls in the shape of a V, each inscribed with the names of the men and women who gave their lives, or remain missing, in the longest war in American history. Even if no one close to you died in Vietnam, it's wrenching to watch visitors grimly studying the directories to find out where their loved ones are listed, or rubbing pencil on paper held against a name etched into the wall. The walls list close to 60,000 people, many of whom died very young.

Because of the raging conflict over U.S. involvement in the war, Vietnam veterans had received almost no recognition of their service before the memorial was conceived by Vietnam veteran Jan Scruggs. The nonprofit Vietnam Veterans Memorial Fund raised $7 million and secured a 2-acre site in tranquil Constitution Gardens to erect a memorial that would make no political statement about the war and would harmonize with neighboring memorials. By separating the issue of the wartime service of individuals from the issue of U.S. policy in Vietnam, the VVMF hoped to begin a process of national reconciliation.

Yale senior Maya Lin's design was chosen in a national competition open to all citizens over 18 years of age. The two walls are angled at 125° to point to the Washington Monument and the Lincoln Memorial. The wall's mirrorlike surface reflects surrounding trees, lawns, and monuments. The names are inscribed in chronological order, documenting an epoch in American history as a series of individual sacrifices from the date of the first casualty in 1959 to the last death in 1975.

The wall was erected in 1982. In 1984, a life-size sculpture of three Vietnam soldiers by Frederick Hart was installed at the entrance plaza. Near the statue, a flag flies from a 60-foot staff. Another sculpture, the *Vietnam Veterans Women's Memorial,* which depicts three servicewomen tending a wounded soldier, was installed on Veterans Day 1993. You should allow about 20 minutes here.

The park rangers at the Vietnam Veterans Memorial are very knowledgeable and are usually milling about—be sure to seek them out if you have any questions. Limited **parking** is available along Constitution Avenue.

Just across from the Lincoln Memorial (east of Henry Bacon Dr. between 21st and 22nd sts. NW). *©* 202/ 426-6841. Free admission. Rangers on duty daily 8am–11:45pm except Dec 25. Ranger-led programs are given throughout the day. Metro: Foggy Bottom.

Franklin Delano Roosevelt Memorial 𝕽𝕽𝕽 The FDR Memorial has proven to be one of the most popular of the presidential memorials since it opened on May 2, 1997. Its popularity has to do as much with its design as the man it honors. This is a 7½-acre outdoor memorial that lies beneath a wide-open sky. It stretches out, rather than rising up, across the stone-paved floor. Granite walls define the four "galleries," each representing a different term in FDR's presidency from 1933 to 1945. Architect Lawrence Halprin's design includes waterfalls, sculptures (by Leonard Baskin, John Benson, Neil Estern, Robert Graham, Thomas Hardy, and George Segal), and Roosevelt's own words carved into the stone.

One drawback of the FDR Memorial is the noise. Planes on their way to or from nearby Reagan National Airport zoom overhead, and the many displays of cascading water can sound thunderous. When the memorial first opened, adults and children alike arrived in bathing suits and splashed around on warm days (the memorial is unsheltered and unshaded). Park rangers don't allow that anymore, but they do allow you to dip your feet in the various pools. A favorite time to visit is at night, when dramatic lighting reveals the waterfalls and statues against the dark parkland.

Conceived in 1946, the FDR Memorial had been in the works for 50 years. Part of the delay in its construction can be attributed to the president himself. FDR had told his friend Supreme Court Justice Felix Frankfurter, "If they are to put up any memorial to me, I should like it to be placed in the center of that green plot in front of the Archives Building. I should like it to consist of a block about the size [of this desk]." In fact, such a plaque sits in front of the National Archives Building. Friends and relatives struggled to honor Roosevelt's request to leave it at that, but Congress and national sentiment overrode them.

As with other presidential memorials, this one opened to some controversy. Advocates for people with disabilities were incensed that the memorial sculptures did not show the president in a wheelchair, which he used from the age of 39 after he contracted polio. President Clinton asked Congress to allocate funding for an additional statue portraying a wheelchair-bound FDR. You will now see a small statue of FDR in a wheelchair, placed at the very front of the memorial, to the right. Step inside the gift shop to view a replica of Roosevelt's wheelchair, as well as one of the rare photographs of the president sitting in a wheelchair. The memorial is probably the most accessible tourist attraction in the city; as at most of the National Park Service locations, wheelchairs are available for free use on-site.

If you don't see a posting of tour times, look for a ranger and request a tour; the rangers are happy to oblige. Thirty minutes is sufficient time to allot here.

In West Potomac Park, about midway between the Lincoln and Jefferson memorials, on the west shore of the Tidal Basin. ℂ 202/426-6841. Free admission. Ranger staff on duty daily 8am–11:45pm. Closed Dec 25. Free parking along W. Basin and Ohio drs. Metro: Smithsonian, with a 30-min. walk; or take the Tourmobile.

George Mason Memorial 𝕽 This most recent addition to the National Mall honors George Mason, author of the Virginia Declaration of Rights, which had much to do with the establishment of our national Bill of Rights. Dedicated on April 9, 2002, the memorial consists of a bronze statue of Mason, set back in a landscaped grove of trees and flower beds (lots and lots of pansies), arranged in concentric circles around a pool and fountain. Mason appears in 18th-century garb, from buckled shoes to tricorn hat, seated on a marble bench, but leaning backward on one arm and gazing off in the general direction of the Washington Monument. Two stone slabs are inscribed with some of Mason's words, like these, referring to Mason's rejection of slavery, "that slow Poisin, which is daily contaminating the Minds & Morals of our People." Wooden benches placed within the circles of flowers present a pleasant opportunity to learn about Mason, and take a break, before moving on.

In West Potomac Park, on Ohio Drive at the Tidal Basin, between the Jefferson and FDR memorials. © 202/ 426-6841. Free admission. Ranger staff on duty 8am–midnight. Closed Dec 25. Free parking along W. Basin and Ohio drs. Metro: Smithsonian, with a 2- to 3-min. walk, or take the Tourmobile.

Jefferson Memorial 🏛🏛   President John F. Kennedy, at a 1962 dinner honoring 29 Nobel Prize winners, told his guests they were "the most extraordinary collection of talent, of human knowledge, that has ever been gathered together at the White House, with the possible exception of when Thomas Jefferson dined alone." Jefferson penned the Declaration of Independence and served as George Washington's secretary of state, John Adams's vice president, and America's third president. He spoke out against slavery, although, like many of his countrymen, he kept slaves himself. In addition, he established the University of Virginia and pursued wide-ranging interests, including architecture, astronomy, anthropology, music, and farming.

The site for the Jefferson Memorial was of extraordinary importance. The Capitol, the White House, and the Mall were already located in accordance with architect Pierre L'Enfant's master plan for the city, but there was no spot for such a project that would maintain L'Enfant's symmetry. So the memorial was built on land reclaimed from the Potomac River, now known as the Tidal Basin. Franklin Delano Roosevelt, who laid the cornerstone in 1939, had all the trees between the Jefferson Memorial and the White House cut down so that he could see the memorial every morning.

The memorial is a columned rotunda in the style of the Pantheon in Rome, whose classical architecture Jefferson himself introduced to this country (he designed his home, Monticello, and the earliest University of Virginia buildings in Charlottesville). On the Tidal Basin side, the sculptural group above the entrance depicts Jefferson with Benjamin Franklin, John Adams, Roger Sherman, and Robert Livingston, all of whom worked on drafting the Declaration of Independence. The domed interior of the memorial contains the 19-foot bronze statue of Jefferson standing on a 6-foot pedestal of black Minnesota granite. The sculpture is the work of Rudolph Evans, who was chosen from more than 100 artists in a nationwide competition. Jefferson is depicted wearing a fur-collared coat given to him by his close friend, the Polish general Tadeusz Kosciuszko.

Rangers present 20- to 30-minute programs throughout the day as time permits. Twenty to thirty minutes is sufficient time to spend here.

ⓘ Tips Parking Near the Mall

First of all: Don't drive. Use the Metro.

But if you're hell-bent on driving on a weekday, set out early to nab one of the Independence or Constitution avenues spots that become legal at 9:30am, when rush hour ends. Arrive about 9:15am and just sit in your car until 9:30am (to avoid getting a ticket), then hop out and stoke the meter. So many people do this that if you arrive at 9:30am or later, you'll find most of the street parking spots gone.

Spring through fall, a refreshment kiosk at the Tourmobile stop offers snacks. A gift shop, a small museum, and a bookstore are located on the bottom floor of the memorial. There's free 1-hour **parking.**

South of the Washington Monument on Ohio Dr. SW (at the south shore of the Tidal Basin). ℂ **202/426-6841.** Free admission. Daily 8am–11:45pm. Closed Dec 25. Metro: Smithsonian, with a 20- to 30-min. walk; or take the Tourmobile.

3 The Smithsonian Museums

Wealthy English scientist James Smithson (1765–1829), the illegitimate son of the duke of Northumberland, never explained why he willed his vast fortune to the United States, a country he had never visited. Speculation is that he felt a new nation, lacking established cultural institutions, most needed his bequest. Smithson died in Genoa, Italy, in 1829. Congress accepted his gift in 1836; 2 years later, half a million dollars' worth of gold sovereigns (a considerable sum in the 19th century) arrived at the U.S. Mint in Philadelphia. For the next 8 years, Congress debated the best possible use for these funds. Finally, in 1846, James Polk signed an act into law establishing the Smithsonian Institution and authorizing a board to receive "all objects of art and of foreign and curious research, and all objects of natural history, plants, and geological and mineralogical specimens . . . for research and museum purposes."

Since then, private donations have swelled Smithson's original legacy many times over. Although the Smithsonian acquires approximately 70% of its yearly budget from congressional allocations, the institution depends quite heavily on these monies from private donors. Lately, the Smithsonian's pursuit of contributions has been criticized by people both within (some longtime Smithsonian curators and directors have resigned) and without the organization, who fear that donors are given too much say in curatorial matters, that important research is underfunded, and that the institution itself is being crassly commercialized as its new wings and exhibits open bearing the names of the companies and individuals who have paid for them. Stay tuned.

The Smithsonian's collection of nearly 141 million objects spans the entire world and all of its history, its peoples and animals (past and present), and our attempts to probe into the future. The sprawling institution comprises 14 museums (the opening of the National Museum of the American Indian in 2004 will bring that number to 15, with 10 of them on the Mall; see "The Mall," on p. 177), as well as the National Zoological Park in Washington, D.C. (there are 2 additional museums in New York City). Still, the Smithsonian's collection is so vast that its museums display only about 1% or 2% of the collection's holdings at any given time. Its holdings, in every area of human interest, range from a 3.5-billion-year-old fossil to part of a 1902 Horn and Hardart Automat. Thousands of scientific expeditions sponsored by the Smithsonian have pushed into remote frontiers in the deserts, mountains, polar regions, and jungles.

In 1987, the Sackler Gallery (Asian and Near Eastern art) and the National Museum of African Art were added to the Smithsonian's Mall attractions. The National Postal Museum opened in 1993. The National Museum of the American Indian is scheduled to open on the Mall in 2004.

To find out information about any of the Smithsonian museums, you call the same number: ℂ **202/357-2700** or TTY 202/357-1729. The information specialists who answer are very professional and always helpful. The Smithsonian museums also share the same website, **www.si.edu**, which will help get you to their individual home pages.

Smithsonian Information Center (the "Castle")   Make this your first stop. Built in 1855, this Norman-style red-sandstone building, popularly known as the "Castle," is the oldest building on the Mall, yet it holds the impressively high-tech and comprehensive Smithsonian Information Center.

The main information area here is the Great Hall, where a 24-minute video overview of the institution runs throughout the day in two theaters. There are two large schematic models of the Mall (as well as a 3rd in Braille), and two large electronic maps of Washington allow visitors to locate nearly 100 popular attractions and Metro and Tourmobile stops. Interactive videos, some at children's heights, offer extensive information about the Smithsonian and other capital attractions and transportation (the menus seem infinite).

The entire facility is accessible to persons with disabilities and information is available in a number of foreign languages. Daily Smithsonian events appear on monitors; in addition, the information desk's volunteer staff can answer questions and help you plan a Smithsonian sightseeing itinerary. Most of the museums are within easy walking distance of the facility.

While you're here, notice the charming vestibule, which has been restored to its turn-of-the-20th-century appearance. It was originally designed to display exhibits at a child's eye level. The gold-trimmed ceiling is decorated to represent a grape arbor with brightly plumed birds and blue sky peeking through the trellis.

The **Castle Commons Room** is open to the public Monday through Saturday, 11am to 2pm, for lunch (entrees $7.95–$14.95), and is the location of a sumptuous Sunday brunch from 10:30am to 3:30pm. The price is $29.95 for adults, $10.95 for children (ages 12 and under), and you must make reservations by calling Ⓒ **202/357-2957.**

1000 Jefferson Dr. SW. Ⓒ **202/357-2700** or TTY 202/357-1729. Daily 9am–5:30pm, info desk 9am–4pm. Closed Dec 25. Metro: Smithsonian.

Anacostia Museum and Center for African-American History and Culture   This museum is inconveniently located, but that's because it was initially created in 1967 as a neighborhood museum (which makes it unique among the Smithsonian branches). It's devoted to the African-American experience, focusing on Washington, D.C., and the Upper South. The permanent collection includes about 7,000 items, ranging from videotapes of African-American church services to art, sheet music, historic documents, textiles, glassware, and anthropological objects. In addition, the Anacostia produces a number of shows each year and offers a comprehensive schedule of free educational programs and activities in conjunction with exhibit themes. Allow about an hour here.

1901 Fort Place SE (off Martin Luther King Jr. Ave.). Ⓒ **202/357-2700.** www.si.edu/anacostia. Free admission. Daily 10am–5pm. Closed Dec 25. Metro: Anacostia, head to the exit marked "Local," then take a W2 or W3 bus directly to the museum.

⌒Tips Information, Please

If you want to know what's happening at any of the Smithsonian museums, just get on the phone. **Dial-a-Museum** (Ⓒ **202/357-2020,** or 202/633-9126 for Spanish), a recorded information line, lists daily activities and special events. For other information, call Ⓒ 202/357-2700.

Arthur M. Sackler Gallery ℛ   Asian art is the focus of this museum and the neighboring Freer (together, they form the National Museum of Asian Art in the United States). The Sackler opened in 1987, thanks to a gift from Arthur M. Sackler of 1,000 priceless works. Since then, the museum has received 11th- to 19th-century Persian and Indian paintings, manuscripts, calligraphies, miniatures, and bookbindings from the collection of Henri Vever.

The Sackler's permanent collection displays Khmer ceramics; ancient Chinese jades, bronzes, paintings, and lacquerware; 20th-century Japanese ceramics and works on paper; ancient Near Eastern works in silver, gold, bronze, and clay; and stone and bronze sculptures from South and Southeast Asia. Supplementing the permanent collection are traveling exhibitions from major cultural institutions in Asia, Europe, and the United States. In the past, these have included such wide-ranging areas as 15th-century Persian art and culture, contemporary Japanese woodblock prints and ceramics, photographs of Asia, and art highlighting personal devotion in India. A visit here is an education in Asian decorative arts, but also in antiquities.

To learn more, arrive in time for a highlights tour, offered daily, except Wednesday, at 11:30am. Also enlightening, and more fun, are the public programs that both the Sackler and the Freer Gallery frequently stage, such as performances of contemporary Asian music, tea ceremony demonstrations, and Iranian film screenings. All are free, but you might need tickets; for details, call the main information number or check out the website. Allow at least an hour to tour the Sackler.

The Sackler is part of a museum complex that also houses the National Museum of African Art. And it shares its staff and research facilities with the adjacent Freer Gallery, to which it is connected via an underground exhibition space.

1050 Independence Ave. SW. ℂ 202/357-2700. www.asia.si.edu. Free admission. Daily 10am–5:30pm; in summer, museum often stays open Thurs until 8pm, but call to confirm. Closed Dec 25. Metro: Smithsonian.

Arts & Industries Building *Kids*   Completed in 1881 as the first U.S. National Museum, this redbrick and sandstone structure was the scene of President Garfield's Inaugural Ball. (It looks quite similar to the Castle, so don't be confused; from the Mall, the Arts & Industries Building is the one on the left.) From 1976 through the mid-1990s, it housed exhibits from the 1876 U.S. International Exposition in Philadelphia—a celebration of America's centennial that featured the latest advances in technology. Some of these Victorian tools, products, art, and other objects are on permanent display. The building displays rotating exhibits, such as one offered in 2002: "Corridos sin Fronteras: A New World Ballad Tradition," which used photographs, recordings, and other memorabilia to explore the history of the ballad in North and South America since 1980.

Singers, dancers, puppeteers, and mimes perform in the **Discovery Theater** (open all year except Aug, with performances weekdays and on selected Sat). Call ℂ **202/357-1500** for show times and ticket information; admission of about $5 is charged.

Don't miss the charming Victorian-motif shop on the first floor. Weather permitting, a 19th-century **carousel** operates across the street, on the Mall.

900 Jefferson Dr. SW (on the south side of the Mall). ℂ 202/357-2700. www.si.edu/ai. Free admission. Daily 10am–5:30pm. Closed Dec 25. Metro: Smithsonian.

Freer Gallery of Art ℛ   Charles Lang Freer, a collector of Asian and American art from the 19th and early 20th centuries, gave the nation 9,000 of these works for his namesake gallery's opening in 1923. Freer's original interest was American art, but his good friend James McNeill Whistler encouraged him to collect Asian works as well. Eventually the latter became predominant. Freer's gift included funds to construct a museum and an endowment to add to the Asian collection only, which now numbers more than 28,000 objects. It includes Chinese and Japanese sculpture, lacquer, metalwork, and ceramics; early Christian illuminated manuscripts; Iranian manuscripts, metalwork, and miniatures; ancient Near Eastern metalware; and South Asian sculpture and paintings.

The Freer is mostly about Asian art, but it also displays some of the more than 1,200 American works (the world's largest collection) by **Whistler.** In 2003, the Freer marks the centenary of Whistler's death by staging two exhibits back to back. On view January 19 to June 15, 2003, are 18 pastels of Venetian scenes, executed by Whistler between September 1879 to November 1880. From June 15 to November 3, the museum re-creates a show that Whistler himself designed for a London art gallery in 1884, displaying at least 50 of his paintings. Most remarkable and always on view is the famous **Peacock Room.** Originally a dining room designed for the London mansion of F. R. Leyland, the Peacock Room displayed a Whistler painting called *The Princess from the Land of Porcelain.* But after his painting was installed, Whistler was dissatisfied with the room as a setting for his work. When Leyland was away from home, Whistler painted over the very expensive leather interior and embellished it with paintings of golden peacock feathers. Not surprisingly, a rift ensued between Whistler and Leyland. After Leyland's death, Freer purchased the room, painting and all, and had it shipped to his home in Detroit. It is now permanently installed here. Other American painters represented in the collections are Thomas Wilmer Dewing, Dwight William Tryon, Abbott Henderson Thayer, John Singer Sargent, and Childe Hassam. All in all, you could spend a happy 1 to 2 hours here.

Freeze Frame

About 90% of the American works in the Freer are in their original frames, many of them designed by architect Stanford White or painter James McNeill Whistler.

Housed in a grand granite-and-marble building that evokes the Italian Renaissance, the pristine Freer has lovely skylit galleries. The main exhibit floor centers on an open-roof garden court. An underground exhibit space connects the Freer to the neighboring Sackler Gallery, and both museums share the **Meyer Auditorium,** which is used for free chamber-music concerts, dance performances, Asian feature films, and other programs. Inquire about these, as well as children's activities and free tours given daily, at the information desk.

On the south side of the Mall (at Jefferson Dr. and 12th St. SW). © 202/357-2700. www.asia.si.edu. Free admission. Daily 10am–5:30pm; in summer, gallery often stays open Thurs until 8pm, but call to confirm. Closed Dec 25. Metro: Smithsonian (Mall or Independence Ave. exit).

Hirshhorn Museum & Sculpture Garden ⚐

This museum of modern and contemporary art is named after Latvian-born Joseph H. Hirshhorn, who, in 1966, donated his vast art collection—more than 4,000 drawings and paintings and some 2,000 pieces of sculpture—to the United States "as a small repayment for what this nation has done for me and others like me who arrived here as immigrants." At his death in 1981, Hirshhorn bequeathed an additional 5,500 artworks to the museum, and numerous other donors have greatly expanded his legacy.

Constructed 14 feet above ground on sculptured supports, the doughnut-shaped concrete-and-granite building shelters a verdant plaza courtyard where sculpture is displayed. The light and airy interior follows a simple circular route that makes it easy to see every exhibit without getting lost in a honeycomb of galleries. Natural light from floor-to-ceiling windows makes the inner galleries the perfect venue for viewing sculpture—second only, perhaps, to the beautiful tree-shaded sunken **Sculpture Garden** 𝆕 across the street (don't miss it). Paintings and drawings are installed in the outer galleries, along with intermittent sculpture groupings.

A rotating show of about 600 pieces is on view at all times. The collection features just about every well-known 20th-century artist and touches on most of the major trends in Western art since the late 19th century, with particular emphasis on our contemporary period. Among the best-known pieces are Rodin's *The Burghers of Calais* (in the Sculpture Garden), Hopper's *First Row Orchestra,* de Kooning's *Two Women in the Country,* and Warhol's *Marilyn Monroe's Lips.*

Pick up a free calendar when you enter to find out about free films, lectures, concerts, and temporary exhibits. An outdoor cafe is open during the summer. Free tours of the collection and the Sculpture Garden are given daily; call about them.

On the south side of the Mall (at Independence Ave. and 7th St. SW). 𝄞 **202/357-2700.** http://hirshhorn.si.edu. Free admission. Museum daily 10am–5:30pm; in summer museum often stays open Thurs until 8pm, but call to confirm. Sculpture Garden daily 7:30am–dusk. Closed Dec 25. Metro: L'Enfant Plaza (Smithsonian Museums/Maryland Ave. exit).

National Air and Space Museum 𝆕𝆕 *Kids* This museum chronicles the story of the mastery of flight, from Kitty Hawk to outer space. It holds the largest collection of historic aircraft and spacecraft in the world—so many, in fact, that the museum is able to display only about 20% of its artifacts at any one time. To supplement its space, the National Air and Space Museum is opening an extension facility, the Steven F. Udvar-Hazy Center, at Dulles Airport, to display many more. The center, which is scheduled to open in late 2003, will also serve as the Air & Space Museum's primary restoration facility. In the meantime, you should plan to spend several hours at the main Air & Space museum on the Mall.

During the tourist season and on holidays, arrive before 10am to make a beeline for the film ticket line when the doors open. The not-to-be-missed **IMAX films** 𝆕 shown here are immensely popular, and tickets to most shows sell out quickly. You can purchase tickets up to 2 weeks in advance, but they are available only at the Lockheed Martin IMAX Theater box office on the first floor. Two or more films play each day, most with aeronautical or space-exploration themes; *To Fly* and *Space Station 3D* are two that should continue into 2003. Tickets cost $7.50 for adults, $6 for ages 2 to 12 and 55 or older; they're free for children under 2. You can also see IMAX films most evenings after the museum's closing; call for details (𝄞 **202/357-1686**).

You'll also need tickets to attend a show at the **Albert Einstein Planetarium** 𝆕, which creates "an astronomical adventure" as projectors display blended space imagery upon a 70-foot diameter dome, making you feel as if you're traveling in 3-D dimension through the cosmos. The planetarium's main feature, called "Infinity Express, A 20-Minute Tour of the Universe," gives you the sensation that you are zooming through the solar system, as it explores such questions as "how big is the universe?" and "where does it end?" Tickets are $7.50

Museum Exhibits Scheduled for 2003

The following listing, though hardly comprehensive, is enough to give you an idea about upcoming or current exhibits at major Washington museums. Because schedules sometimes change, it's always a good idea to call ahead. See individual entries in this chapter for phone numbers and addresses.

Arthur M. Sackler Gallery "A Way Into India: Photographs by Raghubir Singh" (Mar 9–Aug 10, 2003) is an exhibit of 50 photographs of street and rural scenes in India, as viewed from, framed by, or reflected in mirrors of the Indian ambassador's car.

Corcoran Gallery of Art "Robert Frank: Places" (late Mar–June 2003) presents 80 photographs and a new video by one who has been called "the most important and influential photographer since World War II." The photographs were shot between 1947 and 2001, and include scenes in London and Wales.

Folger Shakespeare Library "Elizabeth I, Then and Now" (Mar 19–late July 2003) is an in-depth examination of the reign of Elizabeth I, exactly 400 years after her death. On display are 85 treasures, including letters to and from the Virgin Queen.

Freer Gallery "Whistler in Venice: The Pastels" (Jan 19–June 15, 2003) showcases 18 of the more than 100 pastels of Venice that Whistler created between September 1879 and November 1880. These paintings have been rarely exhibited. The show includes related etchings by Whistler.

Hirshhorn Museum and Sculpture Garden "Gerhard Richter: Forty Years of Painting" (Feb–May 2003) was organized by the Museum of Modern Art, in New York. The 40-year survey presents landscapes, portraits, and other photo-based paintings, as well as gestural abstractions by a German artist who is credited with invigorating contemporary painting.

for adults, $6 for ages 2 to 12 and 55 or older; you can buy an IMAX film and planetarium combo ticket for $12 per adult, $9 per child.

How Things Fly, a gallery that opened in 1996 to celebrate the museum's 20th anniversary, includes wind and smoke tunnels, a boardable Cessna 150 airplane, and dozens of interactive exhibits that demonstrate principles of flight, aerodynamics, and propulsion. All the aircraft, by the way, are originals.

Kids love the walk-through **Skylab orbital workshop** on the first floor. Other galleries here highlight the solar system, U.S. manned space flights, sea-air operations, and aviation during both world wars. An important exhibit is **Beyond the Limits: Flight Enters the Computer Age,** illustrating the primary applications of computer technology to aerospace. A wonderful exhibit that opened in September 2001 is **Explore the Universe,** which presents the major discoveries that have shaped the current scientific view of the universe; it illustrates how the universe is taking shape, and probes the mysteries that remain. In 2002, the museum added a set of six, two-seat **Flight Simulators** to its first floor

National Gallery of Art "Edouard Vuillard" (Jan 19–Apr 20, 2003) displays 200 works revealing both the public and the private sides of this "quintessentially Parisian" artist. Later in the year, the Gallery offers "The Art of Romare Bearden, 1911–1988" (Sept 14, 2003–Jan 4, 2004), which is the first complete retrospective of the artist's work in more than a decade, and includes collages, photographs, montages, and watercolors, depicting scenes of the rural South, northern cities, Harlem, the Caribbean, and subjects ranging from jazz clubs to the religious.

National Museum of Women in the Arts "An Imperial Collection: Women Artists from the State Hermitage Museum" (Feb 14–June 8, 2003) features 49 sculptures and paintings that show how women as both painters and patrons contributed to Russian imperialism and social and cultural history. The women artists were all trained in the European tradition.

National Museum of American History "West Point in the Making of America, 1802–1918" (Oct 19, 2002–Jan 2004) marks the bicentennial of the U.S. Military Academy at West Point by focusing on the graduates of West Point and their contributions to this country, and highlighting the achievements of West Point leaders and their families, from Ulysses S. Grant to John F. Pershing.

Phillips Collection "Marsden Hartley: American Modernist" (June 7–Sept 7, 2003). This retrospective of works by "the painter of Maine," as he called himself, is the first in 20 years and features 90 paintings and 12 drawings that cover Hartley's Maine, American Southwest, France and the Alps, and Mexico periods.

Renwick Gallery "Light Screens: The Leaded Glass of Frank Lloyd Wright" (Mar 4–July 20, 2003) shows 50 decorative glass windows, 30 drawings, 60 photographs, and more, tracing Wright's evolving designs of "light screens" between 1886 and 1923.

galleries (the Udvar-Hazy Center has another 9), allowing visitors to climb aboard and use a joystick to pilot an aircraft. For 3 minutes you truly feel as if you are in the cockpit and airborne, maneuvering your craft up, down, and upside-down on a wild adventure, thanks to virtual reality images and high-tech sounds. You must pay $6.50 to enjoy the ride and measure at least 48 inches to go it alone; children under 48 inches must measure at least 42 inches and be accompanied by an adult.

The museum's cafeteria, The Wright Place, offers food from three popular American chains: McDonald's, Boston Chicken, and Donato's Pizza. Best of all, the cafeteria serves up a great view of the Capitol.

On the south side of the Mall (between 4th and 7th sts. SW), with entrances on Jefferson Dr. or Independence Ave. ℂ 202/357-2700, or 202/357-1686 for IMAX ticket information. www.nasm.edu. Free admission. Daily 10am–5:30pm. The museum often opens at 9am in summer, but call to confirm. Free 1½-hr. highlight tours daily at 10:15am and 1pm. Closed Dec 25. Metro: L'Enfant Plaza (Smithsonian Museums/Maryland Ave. exit) or Smithsonian.

National Museum of African Art 🌿 Founded in 1964, and part of the Smithsonian since 1979, the National Museum of African Art moved to the Mall in 1987 to share a subterranean space with the Sackler Gallery (see above) and the Ripley Center. Its aboveground domed pavilions reflect the arch motif of the neighboring Freer.

The museum collects and exhibits ancient and contemporary art from the entire African continent, but its permanent collection of more than 7,000 objects (shown in rotating exhibits) highlights the traditional arts of the vast sub-Saharan region. Most of the collection dates from the 19th and 20th centuries. Also among the museum's holdings are the *Eliot Elisofon Photographic Archives,* comprising 300,000 photographic prints and transparencies and 120,000 feet of film on African arts and culture. Permanent exhibits include *The Ancient West African City of Benin,* A.D. *1300–1897; The Ancient Nubian City of Kerma, 2500–1500* B.C. (ceramics, jewelry, and ivory animals); *The Art of the Personal Object* (everyday items such as chairs, headrests, snuff-boxes, bowls, and baskets); and *Images of Power and Identity.*

Inquire at the desk about special exhibits, workshops (including excellent children's programs), storytelling, lectures, docent-led tours, films, and demonstrations. A comprehensive events schedule provides a unique opportunity to learn about the diverse cultures and visual traditions of Africa. Plan on spending a minimum of 30 minutes here.

950 Independence Ave. SW. ℭ **202/357-4600.** www.si.edu/nmafa. Free admission. Daily 10am–5:30pm. Closed Dec 25. Metro: Smithsonian.

National Museum of American History 🌿🌿🌿 *(Kids)* Well, you could spend days in here (OK, well, just plan on a few hours). This museum and its neighbor, the National Museum of Natural History, are the behemoths of the Smithsonian, each filled to the gills with artifacts American History deals with "everyday life in the American past" and the external forces that have helped to shape our national character. Its massive contents range from General Washington's Revolutionary War tent to Archie Bunker's chair. It's all very interesting, but since you do have a life to lead, consider this approach to touring.

Start at the top, that is, the third floor, where **The American Presidency** exhibit explores the power and meaning of the presidency by studying those who have held the position. (There's a gift shop just for this exhibit on this floor.) Also on this floor, don't miss the first American flag to be called Old Glory (1824).

If you have an interest in ship models, uniforms, weapons, and other military artifacts; the experiences of GIs in World War II (and the postwar world); the wartime internment of Japanese Americans; money, medals, textiles, printing and graphic arts, or ceramics, check out third-floor exhibits on those subjects. Otherwise, head downstairs to the second floor.

Here, don't miss the intriguing opportunity to see the huge **original Star-Spangled Banner** 🌿🌿🌿, whose 30-by-34-foot expanse has just been painstakingly conserved by expert textile conservators. This is the very flag that inspired Francis Scott Key to write the poem that became the U.S. national anthem in 1814. Though its 3-year conservation was completed in 2002, the flag remains on view and outstretched, flat, behind glass, in its specially designed conservation lab.

One of the most popular exhibits on the second floor is **First Ladies: Political Role and Public Image,** which displays the first ladies' gowns (look for that of our current first lady, Laura Welch Bush, in the American Presidency exhibit), and tells you a bit about each of these women. Infinitely more interesting, I think, is the neighboring exhibit, **From Parlor to Politics: Women and Reform in America, 1890–1925,** which chronicles the changing roles of women as they've moved from domestic to political and professional pursuits. Following that, find the exhibit called **Within These Walls . . . ,** which interprets the rich history of America by tracing the lives of the people who lived in this 200-year-old house, transplanted from Ipswich, MA. If this personal approach to history appeals to you, continue on to **Field to Factory,** which tells the story of African-American migration from the South between 1915 and 1940.

Finally, you're ready to hit the first floor, where some exhibits explore the development of farm machinery, power machinery, timekeeping, phonographs, and typewriters. A temporary exhibit that opened in August 2002 may still be here when you visit and is worth touring: **Bon Appetit: Julia Child's Kitchen at the Smithsonian,** which is a presentation of the famous chef's actual kitchen from her home in Cambridge, Massachusetts. When she moved to California in late 2001, Child donated her kitchen and all that it contained (1,200 items in all) to the museum. Most of these are on display, vegetable peeler to kitchen sink. An exhibit scheduled to open in November 2003 on this level is **America on the Move,** which details the story of transportation in America since 1876.

Longtime exhibits continue: **Material World** displays artifacts from the 1700s to the 1980s, everything from a spinning wheel to a jukebox. You can have your mail stamped "Smithsonian Station" at a post office that had been located in Headsville, West Virginia, from 1861 to 1971, when it was brought, lock, stock, and barrel, to the museum. Best of all is the **Palm Court Ice Cream Parlor,** where you can stop and have an ice cream; the Palm Court includes the interior of Georgetown's Stohlman's Confectionery Shop as it appeared around 1900, and part of an actual 1902 Horn and Hardart Automat.

Many changes are afoot at the American History museum. It's possible that by the time you read this, part, or even all, of the museum will be closed for renovations. For the most up-to-date information, call © **202/357-2700** or check out the museum's website, www.americanhistory.si.edu.

The museum holds many other major exhibits. Inquire at the information desk about highlight tours, films, lectures, concerts, and hands-on activities for children and adults. The museum has four gift shops, and its main one is vast—it's the second-largest of the Smithsonian shops (the largest is the one at the National Air and Space Museum).

On the north side of the Mall (between 12th and 14th sts. NW), with entrances on Constitution Ave. and Madison Dr. © **202/357-2700.** www.americanhistory.si.edu. Free admission. Daily 10am–5:30pm. Closed Dec 25. Metro: Smithsonian or Federal Triangle.

National Museum of Natural History 🌟🌟 *Kids*   Before you step inside the museum, stop outside first, on the Ninth Street side of the building, to visit the new **butterfly garden.** Four habitats—wetland, meadow, wood's edge, and urban garden—are on view, designed to beckon butterflies and visitors alike. The garden is at its best in warm weather, but it's open year-round.

Now go inside. Children refer to this Smithsonian showcase as "the dinosaur museum," since there's a dinosaur hall, or sometimes "the elephant museum," since a huge African bush elephant is the first amazing thing you see if you enter the museum from the Mall. Whatever you call it, the National Museum of Natural History is the largest of its kind in the world, and one of the most visited museums in Washington. It contains more than 124 million artifacts and specimens, everything from Ice Age mammoths to the legendary Hope Diamond.

The same warning applies here as at the National Museum of American History: You're going to suffer artifact overload, so take a reasoned approach to sight-seeing.

If you have children in your crew, you might want to make your first stop the first-floor **Discovery Room,** which is filled with creative hands-on exhibits "for children of all ages." Call ahead or inquire at the information desk about hours. Also popular among little kids is the second floor's **O. Orkin Insect Zoo** ⚘, where they enjoy looking at tarantulas, centipedes, and the like, and crawling through a model of an African termite mound. The Natural History, like its sister Smithsonian museums, is struggling to overhaul and modernize its exhibits, some of which are quite dated in appearance, if not in the facts presented. So a renovation of the gems and minerals hall has made the **Janet Annenberg Hooker Hall of Geology, Gems, and Minerals** ⚘⚘ worth a stop. You can learn all you want about earth science, from volcanology to the importance of mining in our daily lives. Interactive computers, animated graphics, and a multimedia presentation of the "big picture" story of the earth are some of the things that have moved the exhibit and the museum a bit further into the 21st century.

Scheduled to open on the first floor (the Rotunda floor) in fall 2003 is the Kenneth E. Behring Hall of Mammals, where visitors can operate interactive dioramas that explain how mammals evolved and adapted to changes in habitat and climate over the course of millions of years. In the meantime, don't miss **African Voices Hall,** which presents the people, cultures, and lives of Africa, through photos, videos, and more than 400 objects.

Other Rotunda-level displays include the **fossil collection,** which traces evolution back billions of years and includes a 3.5-billion-year-old stromatolite (blue-green algae clump) fossil—one of the earliest signs of life on Earth—and a 70-million-year-old dinosaur egg. **Life in the Ancient Seas** features a 100-foot-long mural depicting primitive whales, a life-size walk-around diorama of a 230-million-year-old coral reef, and more than 2,000 fossils that chronicle the evolution of marine life. The **Dinosaur Hall** displays giant skeletons of creatures that dominated the earth for 140 million years before their extinction about 65 million years ago. Suspended from the ceiling over Dinosaur Hall are replicas of ancient birds, including a life-size model of the pterosaur, which had a 40-foot wingspan. Also residing above this hall is the jaw of an ancient shark, the *Carcharodon megalodon,* which lived in the oceans 5 million years ago. A monstrous 40-foot-long predator, with teeth 5 to 6 inches long, it could have consumed a Volkswagen Bug in one gulp! In an effort to update this exhibit, the museum in 2001 did mount a digital triceratops (that is, a computerized rendering of that dinosaur); you can manipulate the image to learn more about it.

Don't miss the **Discovery Center,** funded by the Discovery Channel, featuring the Johnson **IMAX theater** with a six-story-high screen for 2-D and 3-D movies (*T-Rex: Back to the Cretaceous* and *Galapagos* were among those shown in 2002), a six-story Atrium Cafe with a food court, and expanded museum shops. In spring 2002, the museum opened the small **Fossil Café,** located within the dinosaur exhibit on the first floor. In this 50-seat cafe, the tables' clear plastic tops are actually fossil cases that present fossilized plants and insects for your inspection as you munch away on smoked turkey sandwiches, goat cheese quiche, and the like.

The theater box office is on the first floor of the museum; purchase tickets as early as possible, or at least 30 minutes before the screening. The box office is open daily from 9:45am through the last show. Films are shown continuously throughout the day. Ticket prices are $7.50 for adults and $6 for children (2–12) and seniors 55 or older. On Friday nights from 6 to 10pm, the theater stages live jazz nights, starring excellent local musicians

On the north side of the Mall (at 10th St. and Constitution Ave. NW), with entrances on Madison Dr. and Constitution Ave. © 202/357-2700, or 202/633-7400 for information about IMAX films. www.mnh.si.edu. Free admission. Daily 10am–5:30pm. In summer the museum often stays open until 8pm, but call to confirm. Closed Dec 25. Free highlight tours Mon–Thurs 10:30am and 1:30pm, Fri 10:30am. Metro: Smithsonian or Federal Triangle.

National Postal Museum *☆*   This museum is, somewhat surprisingly, a hit, a pleasant hour spent for the whole family. Bring your address book and you can send postcards to the folks back home through an interactive exhibit that issues a cool postcard and stamps it. That's just one feature that makes this museum visitor-friendly. Many of its exhibits involve easy-to-understand activities, like postal-themed video games.

The museum documents America's postal history from 1673 (about 170 years before the advent of stamps, envelopes, and mailboxes) to the present. (Did you know that a dog sled was used to carry mail in Alaska until 1963, when it was replaced by an airplane?) In the central gallery, titled **Moving the Mail,** three planes that carried mail in the early decades of the 20th century are suspended from a 90-foot atrium ceiling. Here, too, are a railway mail car, an 1851 mail/passenger coach, a Ford Model-A mail truck, and a replica of an airmail beacon tower. In **Binding the Nation,** historic correspondence illustrates how mail kept families together in the developing nation. Several exhibits deal with the famed Pony Express, a service that lasted less than 2 years but was romanticized to legendary proportions by Buffalo Bill and others. In the Civil War section you'll learn about Henry "Box" Brown, a slave who had himself "mailed" from Richmond to a Pennsylvania abolitionist in 1856.

The Art of Cards and Letters gallery displays rotating exhibits of personal (sometimes wrenching, always interesting) correspondence taken from different periods in history, as well as greeting cards and postcards. And an 800-square-foot gallery, called **Artistic License: The Duck Stamp Story,** focuses on federal duck stamps (first issued in 1934 to license waterfowl hunters), with displays on the hobby of duck hunting and the ecology of American water birds. In addition, the museum houses a vast research library for philatelic researchers and scholars, a stamp store, and a museum shop. Inquire about free walk-in tours at the information desk.

Opened in 1993, this most recent addition to the Smithsonian complex occupies the lower level of the palatial beaux arts quarters of the City Post Office Building, which was designed by architect Daniel Burnham and is situated next to Union Station.

2 Massachusetts Ave. NE (at 1st St.). © 202/633-9360. www.si.edu/postal. Free admission. Daily 10am–5:30pm. Closed Dec 25. Metro: Union Station.

National Zoological Park *☆☆* *(Kids)*   The big news here, in case you missed it, is that the National Zoo now has **giant pandas** again. Say hello to Mei Xiang and Tian Tian.

Established in 1889, the National Zoo is home to some 500 species, many of them rare and/or endangered. A leader in the care, breeding, and exhibition of animals, it occupies 163 beautifully landscaped and wooded acres and is one of the country's most delightful zoos. You'll see cheetahs, zebras, camels, elephants, tapirs, antelopes, brown pelicans, kangaroos, hippos, rhinos, giraffes, apes, and, of course, lions, tigers, and bears (oh my).

Consider calling ahead (allow at least 4 weeks and call during weekday business hours) for a **free 90-minute highlights tour** (© 202/673-4956), though it's not recommended for kids under age 4. The tour guide will tell you how to look at the animals; where, why, and when to look; and will fill your visit with lots of surprises.

Pointers: Enter the zoo at the Connecticut Avenue entrance; you'll be right by the Education Building, where you can pick up a map and find out about feeding times and any special activities. Note that from this main entrance, you're headed downhill; the return uphill walk can prove trying if you have young children and/or it's a hot day. But the zoo rents strollers, and snack bars and ice-cream kiosks are scattered throughout the park.

The zoo animals live in large, open enclosures—simulations of their natural habitats—along two easy-to-follow numbered paths: **Olmsted Walk** and the **Valley Trail.** You can't get lost and it's hard to miss a thing. Be sure to catch **Amazonia,** where you can hang out for an hour peering up into the trees and still not spy the sloth (do yourself a favor and ask the attendant where it is).

Zoo facilities include stroller-rental stations, a number of gift shops, a bookstore, and several paid-parking lots. The lots fill up quickly, especially on weekends, so arrive early or take the Metro.

Adjacent to Rock Creek Park, main entrance in the 3000 block of Connecticut Ave. NW. © 202/673-4800 (recording), or 202/673-4717. www.si.edu/natzoo. Free admission. Daily May to mid-Sept (weather permitting): grounds 6am–8pm, animal buildings 10am–6pm. Daily mid-Sept to May: grounds 6am–6pm, animal buildings 10am–4:30pm. Closed Dec 25. Metro: Woodley Park–Zoo or Cleveland Park.

Renwick Gallery of the Smithsonian American Art Museum ⊛ (Finds)   A
department of the Smithsonian American Art Museum (though located nowhere near it), the Renwick is a showcase for American creativity in crafts, housed in a historic mid-1800s landmark building of the French Second Empire style. The original home of the Corcoran Gallery, it was saved from demolition by First Lady Jacqueline Kennedy in 1963, when she recommended that it be renovated as part of the Lafayette Square restoration. In 1965, it became part of the Smithsonian and was renamed for its architect, James W. Renwick, who also designed the Smithsonian Castle.

Although the setting—especially the magnificent Victorian Grand Salon with its wainscoted plum walls and 38-foot skylight ceiling—evokes another era, the museum's contents are mostly contemporary. On view on the first floor are temporary exhibits of American crafts and decorative arts. On the second floor, the museum's rich and diverse displays boast changing crafts exhibits and contemporary works from the museum's permanent collection, such as Larry Fuente's *Game Fish,* or Wendell Castle's *Ghost Clock.* The **Grand Salon** on the second floor, styled in 19th-century opulence, is newly refurbished and currently displays 170 paintings and sculptures from the American Art Museum, which is closed for renovation. The great thing about this room, besides its fine art and grand design, is its cushiony, velvety banquettes, perfect resting stops for the weary sightseer. Tour the gallery for about an hour, rest for a minute, then go on to your next destination.

The Renwick offers a comprehensive schedule of crafts demonstrations, lectures, and films. Inquire at the information desk. And check out the museum shop near the entrance for books on crafts, design, and decorative arts, as well as craft items, many of them for children. *Note:* It is the main branch of the Smithsonian American Art Museum that is closed for renovation, not this offshoot.

Pennsylvania Ave. and 17th St. NW. © 202/357-2700. www.nmaa.si.edu. Free admission. Daily 10am–5:30pm. Closed Dec 25. Metro: Farragut West or Farragut North.

4 Elsewhere on the Mall

National Archives   The Rotunda of the National Archives closed for renovation on July 5, 2001, and will reopen in the summer or fall of 2003. Until then, you won't be able to look at the nation's three most important documents—the Declaration of Independence, the Constitution of the United States, and the Bill of Rights—as well as the 1297 version of the Magna Carta. You will, however, be able to use the National Archives center for genealogical research—this is where Alex Haley began his work on *Roots.*

This federal institution is charged with sifting through the accumulated papers of a nation's official life—billions of pieces a year—and determining what to save and what to destroy. The Archives' vast accumulation of census figures, military records, naturalization papers, immigrant passenger lists, federal documents, passport applications, ship manifests, maps, charts, photographs, and motion picture film (and that's not the half of it) spans 2 centuries. And it's all available for the perusal of anyone age 16 or over (call for details). If you're interested, visit the building, entering on Pennsylvania Avenue, and head to the fourth floor, where a staff member can advise you about the time and effort that will be involved, and, if you decide to pursue it, exactly how to proceed.

The National Archives building itself is worth an admiring glance. The neoclassical structure, designed by John Russell Pope (also the architect of the National Gallery of Art and the Jefferson Memorial) in the 1930s, is an impressive example of the beaux arts style. Seventy-two columns create a Corinthian colonnade on each of the four facades. Great bronze doors mark the Constitution Avenue entrance, and allegorical sculpture centered on *The Recorder of the Archives* adorns the pediment. On either side of the steps are male and female figures symbolizing guardianship and heritage, respectively. *Guardians of the Portals* at the Pennsylvania Avenue entrance represent the past and the future, and the theme of the pediment is destiny.

Constitution Ave. NW (between 7th and 9th sts.; enter on Pennsylvania Ave.). ℂ **202/501-5000** for general information, or 202/501-5400 for research information. www.nara.gov. Free admission. Call for research hours. Closed Dec 25. Metro: Archives–Navy Memorial.

National Gallery of Art 🏛🏛🏛   Most people don't realize it, but the National Gallery of Art is not part of the Smithsonian complex. Housing one of the world's foremost collections of Western painting, sculpture, and graphic arts, spanning from the Middle Ages through the 20th century, the National Gallery has a dual personality. The original West Building, designed by John Russell Pope (architect of the Jefferson Memorial and the National Archives), is a neoclassic marble masterpiece with a domed rotunda over a colonnaded fountain and high-ceilinged corridors leading to delightful garden courts. It was a gift to the nation from Andrew W. Mellon, who also contributed the nucleus of the collection, including 21 masterpieces from the Hermitage, two Raphaels among them. The ultramodern East Building, designed by I. M. Pei and opened in 1978, is composed of two adjoining triangles with glass walls and lofty tetrahedron skylights. The pink Tennessee marble from which both buildings were

---

Tips **Avoiding the Crowds at the National Gallery of Art**

The best time to visit the National Gallery is Monday morning; the worst is Sunday afternoon.

constructed was taken from the same quarry; it forms an architectural link between the two structures.

The West Building: On the main floor of the West Building, about 1,000 paintings are always on display. To the left (as you enter off the Mall) is the **Art Information Room,** housing the **Micro Gallery,** where those so inclined can design their own tours of the permanent collection and enhance their knowledge of art via user-friendly computers.

Continuing to the left of the rotunda are galleries of 13th- through 18th-century Italian paintings and sculpture, including what is generally considered the finest **Renaissance collection** outside Italy; here you'll see the only painting by Leonardo da Vinci housed outside Europe: *Ginevra de'Benci.* Paintings by El Greco, Ribera, and Velázquez highlight the Spanish galleries; Grünewald, Dürer, Holbein, and Cranach can be seen in the German; Van Eyck, Bosch, and Rubens in the Flemish; and Vermeer, Steen, and Rembrandt in the Dutch. To the right of the rotunda, galleries display 18th- and 19th-century French paintings (including one of the world's greatest **Impressionist collections**), paintings by Goya, works of late 18th- and 19th-century Americans—such as Cole, Stuart, Copley, Homer, Whistler, and Sargent—and of somewhat earlier British artists, such as Constable, Turner, and Gainsborough. Room decor reflects the period and country of the art shown: Travertine marble adorns the Italian gallery, and somber oak panels define the Dutch galleries.

Down a flight of stairs are prints and drawings, 15th- through 20th-century sculpture (with many pieces by Daumier, Degas, and Rodin), American naive 18th- and 19th-century paintings, Chinese porcelains, small Renaissance bronzes, 16th-century Flemish tapestries, and 18th-century decorative arts.

The **National Gallery Sculpture Garden** ⟨⟨, just across Seventh Street from the West Wing, opened to the public in May 1999. The park takes up 2 city blocks and features open lawns; a central pool with a spouting fountain (the pool turns into an ice rink in winter); an exquisite glassed-in pavilion housing a cafe; 17 sculptures by renowned artists like Roy Lichtenstein and Ellsworth Kelly (and Scott Burton, whose *Six-Part Seating* you're welcome to sit upon); and informally landscaped shrubs, trees, and plants. It continues to be a hit, especially in warm weather, when people sit on the wide rim of the pool and dangle their feet in the water while they eat their lunch. Friday evenings in summer, the gallery stages live jazz performances here.

The East Building: Hard to miss outside the building is Frank Stella's giant sculpture, newly installed at the corner of Third Street and Pennsylvania Avenue. Called "Prince of Homburg," the aluminum and fiberglass creation is more than 30 feet high, weighs 10 tons, and moves with the wind.

Inside this wing is a showcase for the museum's collection of 20th-century art, including works by Picasso, Miró, Matisse, Pollock, and Rothko; this is also the home of the art history research center. Always on display are the massive aluminum Calder mobile dangling under a seven-story skylight and an exhibit called **Small French Paintings,** which I love.

Altogether, you should allow a leisurely 2 hours to see everything here.

Pick up a floor plan and calendar of events at an information desk to find out about National Gallery exhibits, films, tours, lectures, and concerts. Highly recommended are the free highlight tours (call for exact times) and audio tours. The gift shop is a favorite. The gallery offers several good dining options, among them the concourse-level Cascade Café, which has seven food stations; the Garden Café, on the ground floor of the West Building, which sometimes tailors its menu to complement a particular exhibit; and the sculpture garden's Pavilion Café.

4th St. and Constitution Ave. NW, on the north side of the Mall (between 3rd and 7th sts. NW). © 202/ 737-4215. www.nga.gov. Free admission. Mon–Sat 10am–5pm; Sun 11am–6pm. Closed Jan 1 and Dec 25. Metro: Archives, Judiciary Square, or Smithsonian.

United States Holocaust Memorial Museum 🌟🌟   This museum remains a top draw, as it has been since it opened in 1993. If you arrive without a reserved ticket specifying an admission time, you'll have to join the line of folks seeking to get one of the 1,575 day-of-sale tickets the museum makes available each day (see the note titled "Holocaust Museum Touring Tips," below). The museum opens its doors at 10am and the tickets are usually gone by 10:30am. Get in line early in the morning (around 8am).

The noise and bustle of so many visitors can be disconcerting, and it's certainly at odds with the experience that follows. But things settle down as you begin your tour. When you enter, you will be issued an identity card of an actual victim of the Holocaust. By 1945, 66% of those whose lives are documented on these cards were dead.

The tour begins on the fourth floor, where exhibits portray the events of 1933 to 1939, the years of the Nazi rise to power. On the third floor (documenting 1940–44), exhibits illustrate the narrowing choices of people caught up in the Nazi machine. You board a Polish freight car of the type used to transport Jews from the Warsaw ghetto to Treblinka and hear recordings of survivors telling what life in the camps was like. This part of the museum documents the details of the Nazis' "Final Solution" for the Jews.

The second floor recounts a more heartening story: It depicts how non-Jews throughout Europe, by exercising individual action and responsibility, saved Jews at great personal risk. Denmark—led by a king who swore that if any of his subjects wore a yellow star, so would he—managed to hide and save 90% of its Jews. Exhibits follow on the liberation of the camps, life in Displaced Persons camps, emigration to Israel and America, and the Nuremberg trials. A highlight at the end of the permanent exhibition is a 30-minute film called *Testimony,* in which Holocaust survivors tell their personal stories. The tour concludes in the hexagonal Hall of Remembrance, where you can meditate on what you've experienced and light a candle for the victims. The museum notes that most people take 2 to 3 hours on their first visit; many people take longer.

In addition to its permanent and temporary exhibitions, the museum has a Resource Center for educators, which provides materials and services to Holocaust educators and students; an interactive computer learning center; and a registry of Holocaust survivors, a library, and archives, which researchers may use to retrieve historic documents, photographs, oral histories, films, and videos.

The museum recommends not bringing children under 11; for older children, it's advisable to prepare them for what they'll see. There's a cafeteria and museum shop on the premises.

You can see some parts of the museum without tickets. These include two special areas on the first floor and concourse: **Daniel's Story: Remember the Children** and the **Wall of Remembrance** (Children's Tile Wall), which commemorates the 1.5 million children killed in the Holocaust, and the **Wexner Learning Center.**

100 Raoul Wallenberg Place SW (formerly 15th St. SW; near Independence Ave., just off the Mall). © 202/ 488-0400. www.ushmm.org. Free admission. Daily 10am–5:30pm, staying open until 8pm Tues and Thurs mid-Apr to mid-June. Closed Yom Kippur and Dec 25. Metro: Smithsonian.

Tips **Holocaust Museum Touring Tips**

Because so many people want to visit the museum (it has hosted as many as 10,000 visitors in a single day), tickets specifying a visit time (in 15-min. intervals) are required. Reserve as many as 10 tickets in advance via Tickets. com (© **800/400-9373;** www.tickets.com) for a small service charge. If you order well in advance, you can have tickets mailed to you at home. If you didn't plan ahead, you can also get same-day tickets at the museum beginning at 10am daily (lines form earlier, usually around 8am). Note that same-day tickets are limited, and one person may obtain a maximum of four.

5 Other Government Agencies

Bureau of Engraving & Printing *Kids*   This is where they will literally show you the money. A staff of 2,600 works around the clock churning it out at the rate of about $700 million a day. Everyone's eyes pop as they walk past rooms overflowing with new greenbacks. But although the money draws everyone in, it's not the whole story. The bureau prints many other products, including 25 billion postage stamps a year, presidential portraits, and White House invitations.

Many people line up each day to get a peek at all that moola, so arriving early, especially during the peak tourist season, is essential. Consider securing VIP tickets from your senator or congressperson; VIP tours are offered Monday through Friday at 8:15 and 8:45am, with additional 4, 4:15, 4:30 and 5pm tours added in summer, and last about 45 minutes. Write at least 3 months in advance for tickets.

Tickets for general public tours are required every day, and every person taking the tour must have a ticket. To obtain a ticket, go to the ticket booth on Raoul Wallenberg Place and show a valid photo ID. You will receive a ticket specifying a tour time for that same day, and be directed to the 14th Street entrance of the bureau. Booth hours are from 8am to 2pm all year long, and reopening in summer from 3:30 to 7pm.

The 40-minute guided tour begins with a short introductory film. Then you'll see, through large windows, the processes that go into the making of paper money: the inking, stacking of bills, cutting, and examination for defects. Most printing here is done from engraved steel plates in a process known as *intaglio*, the hardest to counterfeit, because the slightest alteration will cause a noticeable change in the portrait in use. Additional exhibits include bills no longer in use, counterfeit money, and a $100,000 bill designed for official transactions (since 1969, the largest denomination printed for the general public is $100).

After you finish the tour, allow time to explore the **Visitor Center,** open from 8:30am to 3:30pm (until 8pm in summer), where exhibits include informative videos, money-related electronic games, and a display of $1 million. Here, too, you can buy gifts ranging from bags of shredded money—no, you can't tape it back together—to copies of documents such as the Gettysburg Address.

14th and C sts. SW. © **800/874-3188** or 202/874-2330. www.bep.treas.gov. Free admission. Mon–Fri 9am–2pm (last tour begins at 1:40pm); in summer, extended hours 5–6:40pm. Closed Dec 25–Jan 1 and federal holidays. Metro: Smithsonian (Independence Ave. exit).

Federal Bureau of Investigation *(Kids)* More than half a million visitors (many of them kids) come here annually to learn why crime doesn't pay. Tours begin with a short videotape presentation about the priorities of the bureau. You'll see some of the weapons used by big-time gangsters such as Al Capone, John Dillinger, Bonnie and Clyde, and "Pretty Boy" Floyd; and an exhibit on counterintelligence operations. There are photographs of the 10 most-wanted fugitives (2 were recognized at this exhibit by people on the tour, and 10 have been located via the FBI-assisted TV show *America's Most Wanted*). Other exhibits deal with white-collar crime, organized crime, terrorism, drugs, and agent training. On display are more than 5,000 weapons, most of them confiscated from criminals.

You'll also visit the **Firearms Unit** (where agents determine whether a bullet was fired from a given weapon); the **Material Analysis Unit** (where the FBI can deduce the approximate make and model of a car from a tiny piece of paint); the unit where hairs and fibers are examined; and a **Forfeiture and Seizure Exhibit,** a display of jewelry, furs, and other proceeds from illegal narcotics operations. The tour ends with a bang, lots of them in fact, when an agent gives a sharpshooting demonstration and discusses the FBI's firearm policy and gun safety.

If you're coming between April and August, try to arrange for tickets ahead of time. At the height of this season, you could get in line at 8am and still not get in. Even if you call for advance tickets, the tour office might tell you that they won't confirm your tickets until a week before your visit. You can expect to pass through a metal detector to enter the FBI Building.

J. Edgar Hoover FBI Building, E St. NW (between 9th and 10th sts.). (C) 202/324-3447. www.fbi.gov. Free admission. Mon–Fri 8:45am–4:15pm. Closed Jan 1, Dec 25, and other federal holidays. Metro: Metro Center or Federal Triangle.

Library of Congress *(Ax)* The question most frequently asked by visitors to the Library of Congress is: Where are the books? The answer is: on the 532 miles of shelves located throughout the library's three buildings: the **Thomas Jefferson, James Madison Memorial,** and **John Adams** buildings. Established in 1800, "for the purchase of such books as may be necessary for the use of Congress," the library today serves the nation, with holdings for the visually impaired (for whom books are recorded on cassette and/or translated into Braille), research scholars, and college students—and tourists. Its first collection of books was destroyed in 1814 when the British burned the Capitol (where the library was then housed) during the War of 1812. Thomas Jefferson then sold

---

⟨Tips⟩ FBI Touring Tips

To beat the crowds, arrive before 8:45am or write to a senator or congressperson for a scheduled reservation as far in advance as possible. Guided congressional tours take place at 9:45 and 11:45am, and 1:45 and 3:15pm, with an additional 2:45pm tour added in summer. Contact your senator or representative at least 3 months ahead to schedule an appointment for constituent groups of six or fewer. Tours last 1 hour and are conducted every 20 to 30 minutes, depending upon staff availability. The building closes at 4:15pm, so you must arrive at least 1 hour before closing if you want to make the last tour (arrive even earlier in high season). Once inside, you'll undergo a security check.

the institution his personal library of 6,487 books as a replacement, and this became the foundation of what would grow to become the world's largest library. Today, the collection contains a mind-boggling 121 million items. Its buildings house more than 18 million catalogued books, 54 million manuscripts, 12 million prints and photographs, 2.5 million audio holdings (discs, tapes, talking books, and so on), more than 700,000 movies and videotapes, musical instruments from the 1700s, and the letters and papers of everyone from George Washington to Groucho Marx. The library offers a year-round program of free concerts, lectures, and poetry readings, and houses the Copyright Office.

Just as impressive as the scope of the library's holdings is its architecture. Most magnificent is the ornate Italian Renaissance–style **Thomas Jefferson Building,** which was erected between 1888 and 1897 to hold the burgeoning collection and establish America as a cultured nation with magnificent institutions equal to anything in Europe. Fifty-two painters and sculptors worked for 8 years on its interior. There are floor mosaics of Italian marble, allegorical paintings on the overhead vaults, more than 100 murals, and numerous ornamental cornucopias, ribbons, vines, and garlands within. The building's exterior has 42 granite sculptures and yards of bas-reliefs. Especially impressive are the exquisite marble **Great Hall** and the **Main Reading Room,** the latter under a 160-foot dome. Originally intended to hold the fruits of at least 150 years of collecting, the Jefferson Building was, in fact, filled up in a mere 13 years. It is now supplemented by the James Madison Memorial Building and the John Adams Building.

On permanent display in the Jefferson Building's Great Hall are several exhibits: The **American Treasures of the Library of Congress** rotates a selection of more than 200 of the rarest and most interesting items from the library's collection—like Thomas Jefferson's rough draft of the Declaration of Independence with notations by Benjamin Franklin and John Adams in the margins, and the contents of Lincoln's pockets when he was assassinated. Across the Great Hall from the American Treasures exhibit is one that showcases the **World Treasures of the Library of Congress.** Its multimedia display of books, maps, videos, and illustrations invites visitors to examine artifacts from the library's vast international collections. Tucked away in a corner of the Jefferson Building is another permanent exhibit, the **Bob Hope Gallery of American Entertainment,** which presents on a rotating basis, film clips, memorabilia, and manuscript pages from a collection that the comedian donated to the library in 2000.

If you are waiting for your tour to start (see schedule below), take in the 12-minute orientation film in the Jefferson's visitors' theater or browse in its gift shop. Pick up a calendar of events when you visit. Concerts take place in the Jefferson Building's elegant **Coolidge Auditorium.** The concerts are free but require tickets, which you can obtain through Ticketmaster (© **800/551-7328** or 202/432-7328).

The **Madison Building,** across Independence Avenue from the Jefferson Building, at 10 Independence Ave. SE, offers interesting exhibits and features classic, rare, and unusual films in its **Mary Pickford Theater.** Find out more about the library's free film series by accessing the LOC website (www.loc.gov), clicking on "The Library Today," then scrolling down to find the postings for the free concert series and the free film series. The Madison Building also houses a cafeteria and the more formal Montpelier Room restaurant, both of which are open for lunch weekdays.

Anyone over high school age may use the library's collections, but first you must obtain a user card with your photo on it. Go to Reader Registration in

Room LM 140 (street level of the Madison Bldg.) and present a driver's license or passport. Then head to the Information Desk in either the Jefferson or Madison buildings to find out about the research resources available to you and how to use them. Most likely, you will be directed to the Main Reading Room. All books must be used on-site.

1st St. SE (between Independence Ave. and E. Capitol St.). (C) 202/707-8000. www.loc.gov. Free admission. Madison Bldg. Mon–Fri 8:30am–9:30pm; Sat 8:30am–6pm. Jefferson Bldg. Mon–Sat 10am–5pm. Closed federal holidays. Stop at the information desk inside the Jefferson Building's west entrance on 1st St. to obtain same-day free tickets to tour the Library. Tours of the Great Hall: Mon–Fri 10:30 and 11:30am, and 1:30, 2:30, and 3:30pm; Sat 10:30 and 11:30am, and 1:30 and 2:30pm. Metro: Capitol South.

6 More Museums

Corcoran Gallery of Art 🦆🦆   This elegant art museum, a stone's throw from the White House, is a favorite party site in the city, hosting everything from inaugural balls to wedding receptions.

The first art museum in Washington, the Corcoran Gallery was housed from 1869 to 1896 in the redbrick and brownstone building that is now the Renwick. The collection outgrew its quarters and was transferred in 1897 to its present beaux arts building, designed by Ernest Flagg.

The collection, shown in rotating exhibits, focuses chiefly on American art. A prominent Washington banker, William Wilson Corcoran was among the first wealthy American collectors to realize the importance of encouraging and supporting this country's artists. Enhanced by further gifts and bequests, the collection comprehensively spans American art from 18th-century portraiture to 20th-century moderns like Nevelson, Warhol, and Rothko. Nineteenth-century works include Bierstadt's and Remington's imagery of the American West; Hudson River School artists; expatriates like Whistler, Sargent, and Mary Cassatt; and two giants of the late 19th century, Homer and Eakins.

The Corcoran is not exclusively an American art museum. On the first floor is the collection from the estate of Sen. William Andrews Clark, an eclectic grouping of Dutch and Flemish masters; European painters; French Impressionists; Barbizon landscapes; Delft porcelains; a Louis XVI *salon dore* transported in toto from Paris; and more. Clark's will stated that his diverse collection, which any curator would undoubtedly want to disperse among various museum departments, must be shown as a unit. He left money for a wing to house it and the new building opened in 1928. Don't miss the small walnut-paneled room known as "Clark Landing," which showcases 19th-century French Impressionist and American art; a room of exquisite Corot landscapes; another of medieval Renaissance tapestries; and numerous Daumier lithographs donated by Dr. Armand Hammer. Allow an hour for touring the collection.

Pick up a schedule of events—temporary exhibits, gallery talks, concerts, art auctions, and more. Families should inquire about the Corcoran's series of Saturday Family Days and Sunday Traditions. (Family Days are especially fun and always feature great live music.) Both programs are free, but you need to reserve a slot for the Sunday events. There is some street parking.

The charming Café des Artistes is open for lunch Wednesday through Monday from 11am to 3pm, for dinner on Thursday, and for Sunday brunch from 10:30am to 2pm (reservations accepted for parties of 8 or more), which costs $21.95 per adult, $10.95 per child (12 and under), and includes live gospel music singers; call (C) 202/639-1786 for more information. The Corcoran has a nice gift shop.

(*Fun Fact* **The Height of Her Powers**

Displayed on the second floor of the Corcoran is the white-marble female nude, *The Greek Slave,* by Hiram Powers, considered so daring in its day that it was shown on alternate days to men and women.

---

500 17th St. NW (between E St. and New York Ave.). (202/639-1700. www.corcoran.org. $5 adults, $3 seniors, $1 students 13–18, $8 families, children under 12 free; admission is free all day Mon, and Thurs after 5pm. Open Wed–Mon 10am–5pm, with extended hours Thurs until 9pm. Free walk-in tours daily (except Tues) at noon, as well as at 7:30pm Thurs and at 2:30pm Sat and Sun. Closed Jan 1 and Dec 25. Metro: Farragut West or Farragut North.

Dumbarton Oaks *Finds* Many people associate Dumbarton Oaks, a 19th-century Georgetown mansion named for a Scottish castle, with the 1944 international conference that led to the formation of the United Nations. Today the 16-acre estate is a research center for studies in Byzantine and pre-Columbian art and history, as well as landscape architecture. Its yards, which wind gently down to Rock Creek Ravine, are magical, modeled after European gardens. The pre-Columbian museum, designed by Philip Johnson, is a small gem, and the Byzantine collection is a rich one.

This unusual collection originated with Robert Woods Bliss and his wife, Mildred. In 1940, they turned over their estate, their extensive Byzantine collection, a library of works on Byzantine civilization, and 16 acres (including 10 acres of exquisite formal gardens) to Mr. Bliss's alma mater, Harvard, and provided endowment funds for continuing research in Byzantine studies. In the early 1960s, they also donated their pre-Columbian collection and financed the building of a wing to house it, as well as a second wing for Mrs. Bliss's collection of rare books on landscape gardening. The Byzantine collection includes illuminated manuscripts, a 13th-century icon of St. Peter, mosaics, ivory carvings, a 4th-century sarcophagus, jewelry, and more. The pre-Columbian works feature Olmec jade and serpentine figures, Mayan relief panels, and sculptures of Aztec gods and goddesses.

The historic music room, furnished in European antiques, was the setting for the 1944 Dumbarton Oaks Conversations about the United Nations. It has a painted 16th-century French-style ceiling and an immense 16th-century stone fireplace. Among its notable artworks is El Greco's *The Visitation.*

Pick up a self-guiding brochure to tour the staggeringly beautiful **formal gardens,** which include an Orangery, a Rose Garden, wisteria-covered arbors, groves of cherry trees, and magnolias. Unless you're a fan of Byzantine or pre-Columbian art, you're likely to spend more time in the garden, as much as an hour when everything is in bloom. Exit at R Street, turn left, cross an honest-to-goodness Lovers' Lane, and proceed next door to Montrose Park, where you can picnic. There is parking on the street.

1703 32nd St. NW (entrance to the collections on 32nd St., between R and S sts.; garden entrance at 31st and R sts.). (202/339-6401. www.doaks.org. Collections: suggested donation $1 year-round. Garden Apr–Oct $5 adults, $3 children under 12 and senior citizens; Nov–Mar 15 free admission. Garden Mar 15–Oct daily 2–6pm; Nov–Mar 2–5pm, weather permitting. Collections year-round Tues–Sun 2–5pm. Gardens and collections are closed national holidays and Dec 24.

Folger Shakespeare Library *Finds* "Shakespeare taught us that the little world of the heart is vaster, deeper, and richer than the spaces of astronomy," wrote Ralph Waldo Emerson in 1864. A decade later, Amherst student Henry

Clay Folger was profoundly affected by a lecture Emerson gave similarly extolling the bard. Folger purchased an inexpensive set of Shakespeare's plays and went on to amass the world's largest (by far) collection of the bard's works, today housed in the Folger Shakespeare Library. By 1930, when Folger and his wife, Emily, laid the cornerstone of a building to house the collection, it comprised 93,000 books, 50,000 prints and engravings, and thousands of manuscripts. The Folgers gave it all as a gift to the American people.

The building itself has a marble facade decorated with nine bas-relief scenes from Shakespeare's plays; it is a striking example of Art Deco classicism. A statue of Puck stands in the west garden. An **Elizabethan garden** on the east side of the building is planted with flowers and herbs of the period. Inquire about guided tours scheduled on certain Saturdays from April to October. The garden is also a quiet place to have a picnic.

The facility, which houses some 250,000 books, 100,000 of which are rare, is an important research center not only for Shakespearean scholars, but also for those studying any aspect of the English and continental Renaissance. A multimedia computer exhibition called *The Shakespeare Gallery* offers users a close-up look at some of the Folger's treasures, as well as Shakespeare's life and works. And the oak-paneled **Great Hall,** reminiscent of a Tudor long gallery, is a popular attraction for the general public. On display are rotating exhibits from the permanent collection: books, paintings, playbills, Renaissance musical instruments, and more. Plan on spending at least 30 minutes here.

At the end of the Great Hall is a theater designed to suggest an Elizabethan inn-yard where plays, concerts, readings, and Shakespeare-related events take place (see chapter 9 for details).

201 E. Capitol St. SE. ⓒ 202/544-7077. www.folger.edu. Free admission. Mon–Sat 10am–4pm. Free walk-in tours daily at 11am, with an extra tour added Sat at 1pm. Closed federal holidays. Metro: Capitol South or Union Station.

Ford's Theatre & Lincoln Museum *(Kids*   On April 14, 1865, Pres. Abraham Lincoln was in the audience at Ford's Theatre, one of the most popular playhouses in Washington. Everyone was laughing at a funny line from Tom Taylor's celebrated comedy, *Our American Cousin,* when John Wilkes Booth crept into the president's box, shot the president, and leapt to the stage, shouting *"Sic semper tyrannis!"* ("Thus ever to tyrants!") With his left leg broken from the vault, Booth mounted his horse in the alley and galloped off. Doctors carried Lincoln across the street to the house of William Petersen, where the president died the next morning.

The theater was closed after Lincoln's assassination and used as an office by the War Department. In 1893, 22 clerks were killed when three floors of the building collapsed. It remained in disuse until the 1960s, when it was remodeled and restored to its appearance on the night of the tragedy. Except when rehearsals or matinees are in progress (call before you go), visitors can see the theater and trace Booth's movements on that fateful night. Free 15-minute talks on the history of the theater and the story of the assassination are given throughout the day. Be sure to visit the Lincoln Museum in the basement, where exhibits—including the Derringer pistol used by Booth and a diary in which he outlines his rationalization for the deed—focus on events surrounding Lincoln's assassination and the trial of the conspirators. Thirty minutes is plenty of time to spend here.

The theater stages productions most of the year (see chapter 9 for information).

ⓒ Museums of Special Interest

In addition to the many superb museums described within this chapter, there are many wonderful lesser-known ones around the city, usually focusing on very specific interests. They don't appeal to everyone, but if you're a buff of some kind, you might find one of them fascinating. Don't try to drop in without calling, because most of these museums are not open daily and some require appointments.

Anderson House, 2118 Massachusetts Ave. NW (ⓒ **202/785-2040**): A century-old, 50-room mansion of amazing design and impressive art and furnishings. The mansion is headquarters for the Society of the Cincinnati, which was founded in 1783 by Continental officers (including George Washington) who had served in the American Revolution. Metro: Dupont Circle.

Art Museum of the Americas, 201 18th St. NW, within the Organization of American States (ⓒ **202/458-6016**): Permanent collection of 20th-century Latin American art. Metro: Farragut West, then walk south about 6 blocks.

Capital Children's Museum, 800 3rd St. NE (ⓒ **202/675-4120**): Hands-on educational complex. Metro: Union Station.

Daughters of the American Revolution (DAR) Museum, 1776 D St. NW (ⓒ **202/879-3254**): Early American furnishings and decorative arts. Metro: Farragut West, then walk south about 5 blocks.

Decatur House ⓡ, 748 Jackson Place (ⓒ **202/842-0920**): Historic house museum with permanent collection of Federalist and Victorian furnishings. Metro: Farragut West or McPherson Square.

Dumbarton House, 2715 Q St. NW (ⓒ **202/337-2288**): Another historic house museum, with a permanent collection of 18th- and 19th-century English and American furniture and decorative arts. Metro: Dupont Circle, with a 20-minute walk along Q Street.

Frederick Douglass National Historic Site, 1411 W St. SE (ⓒ **202/426-5961**): Last residence of the famous African-American 19th-century abolitionist. Metro: Anacostia, then catch bus no. B2, which stops right in front of the house.

Hillwood Museum and Gardens, 4155 Linnean Ave. NW (ⓒ **202/686-8500**): Newly renovated estate of Marjorie Merriweather Post, who collected art and artifacts of 18th-century France and Imperial Russia. Formal gardens, grand rooms, high tea. Metro: Van Ness or Cleveland Park.

Interior Department Museum, 1849 C St. NW (ⓒ **202/208-4743**): Permanent exhibits relating to American historical events and locales, including murals by prominent Native American artists, newly on view on the ninth floor. Metro: Farragut West, then walk about 6 blocks south.

Mary McLeod Bethune Council House National Historic Site, 1318 Vermont Ave. NW (ⓒ **202/673-2402**): Last residence of African-American activist/educator Bethune, who was a leading champion of black and women's rights during FDR's administration. Metro: McPherson Square.

National Building Museum, 401 F St. NW (℃ 202/272-2448): Housed within a historic building of mammoth proportions is this fine museum devoted to architecture, building, and historic preservation. Metro: Judiciary Square.

Octagon 🏛, 1799 New York Ave. NW (℃ 202/638-3105): Another historic house museum, it also features exhibits on architecture (its neighbor is the American Institute of Architects headquarters). Metro: Farragut West.

Old Stone House, 3051 M St. NW (℃ 202/426-6851): 1765 structure said to be the oldest in D.C. still standing on its original foundations. Colonial appearance, English garden. Metro: Foggy Bottom, with a 15-minute walk.

Pope John Paul II Cultural Center, 3900 Harewood Rd. NE (℃ 202/635-5400): A large multimedia facility that uses interactive presentations to engage visitors of all denominations in exploring issues of religion, world culture, and spirituality in the new millennium. Metro: Brookland–Catholic University; the center runs a free shuttle every 30 minutes on the half-hour between the Metro stop and the center.

Sewall-Belmont House, 144 Constitution Ave. NE (℃ 202/546-3989): A must for those interested in women's history, the historic house displays memorabilia of the women's suffrage movement, which got its start here. Metro: Union Station.

Textile Museum, 2320 S St. NW (℃ 202/667-0441): Historic and contemporary handmade textile arts, housed in historic John Russell Pope mansion. Metro: Dupont Circle, Q Street exit, then walk a couple of blocks up Massachusetts Avenue until you see S Street.

Treasury Department, 15th Street and Pennsylvania Avenue NW (℃ 202/622-0896): An immense building with marvelous architecture and fascinating history. Metro: Metro Center or Federal Triangle.

Tudor Place, 1644 31st St. NW (℃ 202/965-0400): An 1816 mansion with gardens, home to Martha Washington's descendants until 1984. Metro: Dupont Circle, with a 25-minute walk along Q Street.

United States Navy Memorial and Naval Heritage Center, 701 Pennsylvania Ave. NW (℃ 202/737-2300): Outside plaza honors men and women of the U.S. Navy; museum features interactive video kiosks used to learn about Navy ships, aircraft, and history. Metro: Archives–Navy Memorial.

Woodrow Wilson House, 2340 S St. NW (℃ 202/387-4062): The intriguing former home of this president, preserved the way it was when he lived here. Metro: Dupont Circle, then walk a couple of blocks up Massachusetts Avenue until you reach S Street.

517 10th St. NW (between E and F sts.). ☎ 202/426-6925. www.nps.gov/foth. Free admission. Daily 9am–5pm. Closed Dec 25. Metro: Metro Center.

The House Where Lincoln Died (the Petersen House) *Kids* After he was mortally wounded at Ford's Theatre, the doctors attending Lincoln had him carried out into the street, where boarder Henry Safford, standing in the open doorway of his rooming house, gestured for them to bring the president inside. So Lincoln died in the home of William Petersen, a German-born tailor. Now furnished with period pieces, the dark, narrow town house looks much as it did on that fateful April night. It takes about 5 minutes to troop through the building. You'll see the front parlor where an anguished Mary Todd Lincoln spent the night with her son, Robert. In the back parlor, Secretary of War Edwin M. Stanton held a cabinet meeting and questioned witnesses. From this room, Stanton announced at 7:22am on April 15, 1865, "Now he belongs to the ages." Lincoln died, lying diagonally because he was so tall, on a bed the size of the one you see here. (The Chicago Historical Society owns the actual bed and other items from the room.) In 1896, the government bought the house for $30,000 and it is now maintained by the National Park Service.

516 10th St. NW. ☎ 202/426-6924. Free admission. Daily 9am–5pm. Closed Dec 25. Metro: Metro Center.

International Spy Museum ✫ Though this museum had not opened in time for me to review it, I include a description here, because advance information makes it sound intriguing (at least to this lover of thriller novels and movies). The museum will feature the largest collection of international espionage artifacts ever put on public display. Among the items are: Enigma, the legendary WWII German cipher machine, found within the museum's section on code making and breaking operations; a shoe transmitter, used by Soviets as a listening device, within the museum's section on eavesdropping tools; and escape boots worn by British pilots in World War II, part of an exhibit on escape and evasion techniques in wartime. Interactive exhibits with state-of-the-art audiovisual effects, film, and hands-on components cover the history of spying, famous spies, Cold War spies, every aspect of spying. The museum has a new restaurant, a spy-theme cafe, and a museum store.

800 F St. NW (at 8th St. NW). ☎ 202/393-7798. www.spymuseum.org. Admission $10 adults, $7 children ages 6–11. Daily 10am–8pm. Closed Dec 25. Metro: Gallery Place/Chinatown or National Archive/Navy Memorial.

National Geographic Society's Explorers Hall This museum's exhibit area has been halved, with the startup of the society's National Geographic Channel broadcasts from the section of the hall that once housed **Geographica** and **Earth Station One.** The north side of the hall serves now as the television studio. Meanwhile, the south side of Explorer's Hall rotates exhibits related to exploration, adventure, and earth sciences. Recent exhibits have included *Icons of the Sea: The Artistry of Ship Models,* and *Portraits of America: 40 Years of Photographing Americans,* which presented compelling photos by William Albert Allard. Most exhibits consume about an hour of touring time.

17th and M sts. NW. ☎ 202/857-7588. www.nationalgeographic.com. Free admission. Mon–Sat and holidays 9am–5pm; Sun 10am–5pm. Closed Dec 25. Metro: Farragut North (Connecticut Ave. and L St. exit).

National Museum of Women in the Arts Sixteen years after it opened, this museum remains the only one in the world dedicated to celebrating "the contribution of women to the history of art." Founders Wilhelmina and Wallace Holladay, who donated the core of the permanent collection—more than

200 works by women from the 16th through the 20th century—became interested in women's art in the 1960s. After discovering that no women were included in H. W. Janson's *History of Art*, a standard text (which, by the way, did not address this oversight until 1986!), the Holladays began collecting art by women, and the concept of a women's art museum soon evolved.

Since its opening, the collection has grown to more than 2,700 works by more than 800 artists, including Rosa Bonheur, Frida Kahlo, Helen Frankenthaler, Barbara Hepworth, Georgia O'Keeffe, Camille Claudel, Lila Cabot Perry, Mary Cassatt, Elaine de Kooning, Käthe Kollwitz, and many other lesser-known artists from earlier centuries. You will discover here, for instance, that the famed Peale family of 19th-century portrait painters included a very talented sister, Sarah Miriam Peale. The collection is complemented by an ongoing series of changing exhibits. You should allow an hour here.

The museum is housed in a magnificent Renaissance Revival landmark building designed in 1907 as a Masonic temple by noted architect Waddy Wood. Its sweeping marble staircase and splendid interior make it a popular choice for wedding receptions.

1250 New York Ave. NW (at 13th St.). © 202/783-5000. www.nmwa.org. $5 adults, $3 students over 18 with ID and seniors; youth 18 and under free. Mon–Sat 10am–5pm; Sun noon–5pm. Closed Jan 1, Thanksgiving, and Dec 25. Metro: Metro Center (13th St. exit).

Phillips Collection 🅰🅰 Conceived as "a museum of modern art and its sources," this intimate establishment, occupying an elegant 1890s Georgian Revival mansion and a more youthful wing, houses the exquisite collection of Duncan and Marjorie Phillips, avid collectors and proselytizers of modernism. Carpeted rooms with leaded- and stained-glass windows, oak paneling, plush chairs and sofas, and fireplaces establish a comfortable, homelike setting. Today the collection includes more than 2,500 works. Among the highlights: superb Daumier, Dove, and Bonnard paintings; some splendid small Vuillards; five van Goghs; Renoir's *Luncheon of the Boating Party;* seven Cézannes; and six works by Georgia O'Keeffe. Ingres, Delacroix, Manet, El Greco, Goya, Corot, Constable, Courbet, Giorgione, and Chardin are among the "sources" or forerunners of modernism represented. Modern notables include Rothko, Hopper, Kandinsky, Matisse, Klee, Degas, Rouault, Picasso, and many others. It's a collection you'll enjoy viewing for an hour or so.

A full schedule of events includes temporary shows with loans from other museums and private collections, gallery talks, lectures, and free concerts in the ornate music room. (Concerts take place Sept–May on Sun at 5pm; arrive early. Although the concert is free, admission to the museum on weekends costs $7.50.) On Thursday, the museum stays open until 8:30pm for **Artful Evenings** with music, gallery talks, and a cash bar; admission is $5.

On the lower level, a charming little restaurant serves light fare, right next to the gift shop, which holds clever collectibles tied to the art of the museum.

1600 21st St. NW (at Q St.). © 202/387-2151. www.phillipscollection.org. Admission Sat–Sun $7.50 adults, $4 students and seniors, free for children 18 and under; contribution suggested Tues–Fri. Special exhibits may require an additional fee. Tues–Sat 10am–5pm year-round (Thurs until 8:30pm); Sun noon–7pm. Free tours Wed and Sat 2pm. Closed Jan 1, July 4, Thanksgiving, and Dec 25. Metro: Dupont Circle (Q St. exit).

7 Other Attractions

John F. Kennedy Center for the Performing Arts 🅰 Opened in 1971, the Kennedy Center is both the national performing arts center and a memorial to John F. Kennedy. Set on 17 acres overlooking the Potomac, the striking facility, designed by noted architect Edward Durell Stone, encompasses an opera house, a concert hall, two stage theaters, a theater lab, and a film theater. The best way to see the Kennedy Center is to take a free 50-minute guided tour (which takes you through some restricted areas). You can beat the crowds by writing in advance to a senator or congressperson for passes for a free VIP tour, given year-round Monday through Friday at 9:30am and 4:30pm, and at 9:30am only on Saturday. Call © **202/416-8341** for details.

The tour begins in the **Hall of Nations,** which displays the flags of all nations diplomatically recognized by the United States. Throughout the center you'll see gifts from more than 40 nations, including all the marble used in the building (3,700 tons), which Italy donated. First stop is the **Grand Foyer,** scene of many free concerts and programs and the reception area for all three theaters on the main level; the 18 crystal chandeliers are a gift from Sweden. You'll also visit the **Israeli Lounge** (where 40 painted and gilded panels depict scenes from the Old Testament); the **Concert Hall,** home of the National Symphony Orchestra; the **Opera House** (which may be closed for renovations during your visit); the **African Room** (decorated with beautiful tapestries from African nations); the **Eisenhower Theater;** the **Hall of States,** where flags of the 50 states and four territories are hung in the order they joined the Union; the **Performing Arts Library;** and the **Terrace Theater,** a bicentennial gift from Japan. If there's a rehearsal going on, the tour skips the visits to the theaters.

If you'd like to attend performances during your visit, check out the website or call the toll-free number above and request the current issue of *Kennedy Center News Magazine,* a free publication that describes all Kennedy Center happenings and prices. See chapter 9 for specifics on theater, concert, and film offerings.

Add another 15 minutes after the tour to walk around the building's terrace for a panoramic view of Washington. There is limited **parking** below the Kennedy Center. Construction is underway to improve access and parking at the center, but until it is completed, you should avoid driving here. If you do, you can expect to pre-pay a flat rate of $12 when you enter the garage after 1pm weekdays and all day on weekends, and $8 when you enter and leave the garage between 10am and 7pm weekdays.

New Hampshire Ave. NW (at Rock Creek Pkwy.). © **800/444-1324,** or 202/416-8341 for information or tickets. www.kennedy-center.org. Free admission. Daily 10am–midnight. Free guided tours Mon–Fri 10am–5pm; Sat–Sun 10am–1pm. Metro: Foggy Bottom (there's a free shuttle service between the station and the center, running every 15 min. from 9:45am–midnight weekdays, 10am–midnight Sat, and noon–midnight Sun). Bus: no. 80 from Metro Center.

Union Station ✦   In Washington, D.C., even the very train station where you arrive is an attraction. Union Station, built between 1903 and 1907 in the great age of rail travel, was painstakingly restored in the 1980s at a cost of $160 million. The station was designed by noted architect Daniel H. Burnham, who modeled it after the Baths of Diocletian and Arch of Constantine in Rome.

When it opened in 1907, this was the largest train station in the world. The Ionic colonnades outside were fashioned from white granite. The facade contains 100 eagles. In the front of the building, a replica of the Liberty Bell and a monumental statue of Columbus hold sway. Six carved fixtures over the entranceway represent Fire, Electricity, Freedom, Imagination, Agriculture, and Mechanics. You enter the station through graceful 50-foot Constantine arches and walk across an expanse of white-marble flooring. The **Main Hall** is a massive rectangular room with a 96-foot barrel-vaulted ceiling and a balcony adorned with 36 Augustus Saint-Gaudens sculptures of Roman legionnaires. Off the Main Hall is the **East Hall,** shimmering with scagliola marble walls and columns, a gorgeous hand-stenciled skylight ceiling, and stunning murals of classical scenes inspired by ancient Pompeiian art. Today it's the station's nicest shopping venue.

In its heyday, this "temple of transport" witnessed many important events. President Wilson welcomed General Pershing here in 1918 on his return from France. South Pole explorer Rear Admiral Richard Byrd was also feted at Union Station on his homecoming. And Franklin D. Roosevelt's funeral train, bearing his casket, was met here in 1945 by thousands of mourners.

But after the 1960s, with the decline of rail travel, the station fell on hard times. Rain caused parts of the roof to cave in, and the entire building—with floors buckling, rats running about, and mushrooms sprouting in damp rooms—was sealed in 1981. That same year, Congress enacted legislation to preserve and restore this national treasure.

Today, Union Station is once again a vibrant entity patronized by locals and visitors alike. Every square inch of the facility has been cleaned, repaired, and/or replaced according to the original design. About 120 retail and food shops on three levels offer a wide array of merchandise. And you'll be happy to find that most of the offerings in the Food Court are not fast-food joints but an eclectic mix of restaurants. The skylit **Main Concourse,** which extends the entire length of the station, is the primary shopping area as well as a ticketing and baggage facility. A nine-screen **cinema complex** lies on the lower level, across from the Food Court. The remarkable restoration, which involved hundreds of European and American artisans using historical research, bygone craft techniques, and modern technology, is meticulous in every detail. You could spend half a day here shopping, or about 20 minutes touring.

Stop by the visitor kiosk in the Main Hall. See chapter 6 for information on Union Station **restaurants** and chapter 8 for information about **shops.**

50 Massachusetts Ave. NE. © 202/371-9441. www.unionstationdc.com. Free admission. Daily 24 hr. Shops Mon–Sat 10am–9pm; Sun 10am–6pm. Parking: $1 for 2 hr. with store or restaurant's stamped validation; for 2–3 hr., you pay $6 with validated ticket. Without validation, parking rates start at $5 for the 1st hr., and go up from there. Metro: Union Station.

Washington National Cathedral ⓖ

Pierre L'Enfant's 1791 plan for the capital city included "a great church for national purposes," but possibly because of early America's fear of mingling church and state, more than a century elapsed before the foundation for Washington National Cathedral was laid. Its actual name is the Cathedral Church of St. Peter and St. Paul. The church is Episcopal, but it has no local congregation and seeks to serve the entire nation as a house of prayer for all people. It has been the setting for every kind of religious observance, from Jewish to Serbian Orthodox.

A church of this magnitude—it's the sixth largest cathedral in the world, and the second largest in the U.S.—took a long time to build. Its principal (but not original) architect, Philip Hubert Frohman, worked on the project from 1921 until his death in 1972. The foundation stone was laid in 1907 using the mallet with which George Washington set the Capitol cornerstone. Construction was interrupted by both world wars and by periods of financial difficulty. The cathedral was completed with the placement of the final stone atop a pinnacle on the west front towers on September 29, 1990, 83 years (to the day) after it was begun.

English Gothic in style (with several distinctly 20th-century innovations, such as a stained-glass window commemorating the flight of *Apollo 11* and containing a piece of moon rock), the cathedral is built in the shape of a cross, complete with flying buttresses and 110 gargoyles. It is, along with the Capitol and the Washington Monument, one of the dominant structures on the Washington skyline. Its 57-acre landscaped grounds have two lovely gardens (the lawn is ideal for picnicking), four schools, a greenhouse, and two gift shops.

Over the years the cathedral has seen much history. Services to celebrate the end of world wars I and II were held here. It was the scene of President Wilson's funeral (he and his wife are buried here), as well as President Eisenhower's. Helen Keller and her companion, Anne Sullivan, were buried in the cathedral at her request. And during the Iranian crisis, a round-the-clock prayer vigil was held in the Holy Spirit Chapel throughout the hostages' captivity. When they were released, the hostages came to a service here.

The best way to explore the cathedral is to take a 30- to 45-minute **guided tour;** they leave continually from the west end of the nave. You can also walk through on your own, using a self-guiding brochure available in several languages. Call about group and special-interest tours, both of which require reservations and fees (© **202/537-5700**). Allow additional time to tour the grounds or "close" and to visit the **Observation Gallery** 🐕, where 70 windows provide panoramic views. Tuesday and Wednesday afternoon tours are followed by a high tea in the Observation Gallery for $18 per person; reservations required. Call © **202/537-8993.**

The cathedral hosts numerous events: organ recitals; choir performances; an annual flower mart; calligraphy workshops; jazz, folk, and classical concerts; and the playing of the 53-bell carillon. Check the cathedral's website for schedules.

P.S. for fans of *The West Wing:* That really was the nave of the Washington National Cathedral, up and down whose center aisle Pres. Jed Bartlet paced as he railed at God during the final episode of the 2001 season.

Massachusetts and Wisconsin aves. NW (entrance on Wisconsin Ave.). © **202/537-6200**. www. cathedral.org/cathedral. Donation $3 adults, $2 seniors, $1 children. Cathedral daily 10am–4:30pm; May 1 to Labor Day, the nave level stays open Mon–Fri until 9pm. Gardens daily until dusk. Regular tours Mon–Sat 10–11:30am and 12:45–3:15pm; Sun 12:45–2:30pm. No tours on Palm Sunday, Easter, Thanksgiving, Dec 25, or during services. Worship services vary throughout the year, but you can count on a weekday Evensong service at 4:30pm, a weekday noon service, and an 11am service every Sun; call for other service times. Metro: Tenleytown, with a 20-min. walk. Bus: Any N bus up Massachusetts Ave. from Dupont Circle or any 30-series bus along Wisconsin Ave. This is a stop on the Old Town Trolley Tour.

8 Just Across the Potomac: Arlington

The land that today comprises Arlington County was originally carved out of Virginia as part of the nation's new capital district. In 1847, the land was returned to the state of Virginia, although it was known as Alexandria County until 1920, when the name was changed to avoid confusion with the city of Alexandria.

The county was named to honor Arlington House, built by George Washington Parke Custis, a descendant of Martha Washington whose daughter married Robert E. Lee. The Lees lived in Arlington House on and off until the onset of the Civil War in 1861. After the first Battle of Bull Run, at Manassas, several Union soldiers were buried here; the beginnings of Arlington National Cemetery date from that time. The Arlington Memorial Bridge leads directly from the Lincoln Memorial to the Robert E. Lee Memorial at Arlington House, symbolically joining these two figures into one Union after the Civil War.

Arlington has long been a residential community, with most people commuting into Washington to work and play. In recent years, however, the suburb has come into its own, booming with business, restaurants, and nightlife, giving residents reasons to stay put and tourists more of an inducement to visit (see the box, "Arlington Row," in chapter 9). Here are a couple of sites worth seeing:

Arlington National Cemetery 𝕣𝕣 Upon arrival, head over to the **Visitor Center,** where you can view exhibits, pick up a detailed map, use the restrooms (there are no others until you get to Arlington House), and purchase a **Tourmobile ticket** ($5.25 per adult, $2.50 for children 3–11), which allows you to stop at all major sites in the cemetery and then reboard whenever you like. Service is continuous and the narrated commentary is informative; this is the only guided tour of the cemetery offered. If you've got plenty of stamina, consider doing part or all of the tour on foot. Remember as you go that this is a memorial frequented not just by tourists but also by those attending burial services or visiting the graves of beloved relatives and friends who are buried here.

This shrine occupies approximately 612 acres on the high hills overlooking the capital from the west side of the Memorial Bridge. It honors many national heroes and more than 260,000 war dead, veterans, and dependents. Many graves of the famous at Arlington bear nothing more than simple markers. Five-star Gen. John J. Pershing's is one of those. Secretary of State John Foster Dulles is buried here. So are Pres. William Howard Taft and Supreme Court Justice Thurgood Marshall. Cemetery highlights include:

The Tomb of the Unknowns, containing the unidentified remains of service members from both world wars, the Korean War, and, until 1997, the Vietnam War. In 1997, the remains of the unknown soldier from Vietnam were identified as those of Air Force 1st Lt. Michael Blassie, whose A-37 was shot down in South Vietnam in 1962. Blassie's family, who had reason to believe that the body was their son's, had beseeched the Pentagon to exhume the soldier's remains and conduct DNA testing to determine if what the family suspected was true. Upon confirmation, the Blassies buried Michael in his hometown of St. Louis. The crypt honoring the dead but unidentified Vietnam War soldiers remains empty for the time being. The entire tomb is an unembellished, massive white-marble block, moving in its simplicity. A 24-hour honor guard watches over the tomb, with the changing of the guard taking place every half-hour April to September, every hour on the hour October to March, and every hour at night.

Within a 20-minute walk, all uphill, from the Visitor Center is **Arlington House** (© 703/557-0613). From 1831 to 1861, this was the legal residence of Robert E. Lee, where he and his family lived off and on until the Civil War. Lee married the great-granddaughter of Martha Washington, Mary Anna Randolph Custis, who inherited the estate. It was here that Lee resigned his commission in the U.S. Army when his native Virginia seceded from the Union. During the Civil War, the estate was taken over by Union forces and troops were buried here. A year before the defeat of the Confederate forces at Gettysburg, the U.S. government bought the estate. A fine melding of the styles of the Greek Revival and the grand plantation houses of the early 1800s, the house has been administered by the National Park Service since 1933. Unfortunately, the house is sadly in need of repair.

You tour the house on your own; park rangers are on-site to answer your questions. About 30% of the furnishings are original. Slave quarters and a small museum adjoin. Admission is free. It's open daily from 9:30am to 4:30pm (closed Jan 1 and Dec 25).

Arlington National Cemetery

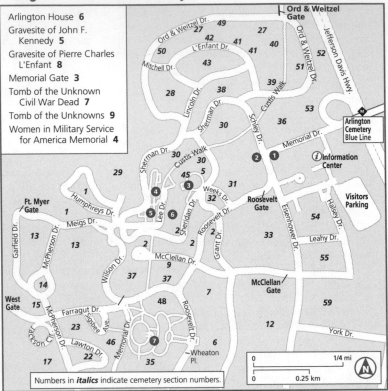

Arlington House **6**

Gravesite of John F. Kennedy **5**

Gravesite of Pierre Charles L'Enfant **8**

Memorial Gate **3**

Tomb of the Unknown Civil War Dead **7**

Tomb of the Unknowns **9**

Women in Military Service for America Memorial **4**

Numbers in *italics* indicate cemetery section numbers.

Pierre Charles L'Enfant's grave was placed near Arlington House at a spot that is believed to offer the best view of Washington, the city he designed.

Below Arlington House, an 8-minute walk from the Visitor Center, is the **Gravesite of John Fitzgerald Kennedy.** John Carl Warnecke designed a low crescent wall embracing a marble terrace, inscribed with the 35th president's most famous utterance: "And so my fellow Americans, ask not what your country can do for you, ask what you can do for your country." Jacqueline Kennedy Onassis rests next to her husband, and Robert Kennedy is buried close by. The Kennedy graves attract streams of visitors. Arrive close to 8am to contemplate the site quietly; otherwise, it's mobbed. Looking north, there's a spectacular view of Washington.

In 1997, the **Women in Military Service for America Memorial (© 800/ 222-2294** or 703/533-1155; www.womensmemorial.org) was added to Arlington Cemetery to honor the more than 1.8 million women who have served in the armed forces from the American Revolution to the present. The impressive new memorial lies just beyond the gated entrance to the cemetery, a 3-minute walk from the Visitor Center. As you approach the memorial, you see a large, circular reflecting pool, perfectly placed within the curve of the granite wall rising behind it. Arched passages within the 226-foot-long wall lead to an upper terrace and dramatic views of Arlington National Cemetery and the monuments of Washington; an arc of large glass panels (which form the roof of the memorial hall) contains etched quotations from servicewomen (and a couple from men). Behind the wall and completely underground is the **Education Center,** housing a **Hall of Honor,** a gallery of exhibits tracing the history of women in the military, a theater, and a computer register of servicewomen, which visitors may access for information about individual military women, past and present. Hours are 8am to 5pm (until 7pm Apr–Sept). Stop at the reception desk for a brochure that details a self-guided tour through the memorial. The memorial is open every day but Christmas.

Plan to spend half a day at Arlington Cemetery and the Women in Military Service Memorial.

Just across the Memorial Bridge from the base of the Lincoln Memorial. ⓒ **703/607-8052.** www.arlington cemetery.org or www.mdw.army.mil/cemetery.htm. Free admission. Apr–Sept daily 8am–7pm; Oct–Mar daily 8am–5pm. Metro: Arlington National Cemetery. If you come by car, parking is $1.25 an hr. for the 1st 3 hr., $2 an hr. thereafter. The cemetery is also accessible via Tourmobile.

Newseum & Freedom Park ⟨ᖳ ⟨Kids⟩ The Newseum opened in 1997 as the world's first museum dedicated exclusively to news, it's been such a hit that it's already outgrown its location. This location is closed, and a new, larger, and higher-profile headquarters is under construction at Sixth Street and Pennsylvania Avenue NW, just off the Mall, though it won't open until 2006. You can visit Freedom Park and the Freedom Forum Journalists Memorial, however.

Adjoining the museum, **Freedom Park,** which opened in the summer of 1996 and sits atop a never-used elevated highway, celebrates the spirit of freedom and the struggle to preserve it. Here, too, are many intriguing exhibits: segments of the Berlin Wall (the largest display of the wall outside of Germany), stones from the Warsaw Ghetto, a bronze casting of a South African ballot box, a headless statue of Lenin (one of many that were pushed over and beheaded when the Soviet Union collapsed in 1991), and a bronze casting of Martin Luther King Jr.'s Birmingham jail-cell door. The glass and steel Freedom Forum Journalists Memorial (honoring more than 900 journalists killed while on assignment) rises above the Potomac, offering views of the Washington Monument, the Lincoln and Jefferson memorials, and the National Cathedral.

1101 Wilson Blvd. (at N. Kent St.). ⓒ **888-NEWSEUM** or 703/284-3544. www.newseum.org. Newseum Tues–Sun 10am–5pm. Freedom Park daily dawn–dusk. Limited parking is available in the building. Metro: Rosslyn.

The Pentagon Damaged in the shocking September 11, 2001, terrorist attack in which a hijacked commercial jet crashed into the building, killing 125 people working at the Pentagon, and 64 more people aboard the plane, the Pentagon building has been restored, but at this writing, it remains closed for public tours. Tour officers hope that tours will soon resume, however, so I include a description here of what your tour might include. Be sure to call ahead or check the website to find out whether tours are on again.

The Pentagon is the headquarters of the American military establishment. This immense five-sided structure was built during the early years of World War II. It's one of the world's largest office buildings, housing approximately 23,000 employees. For their convenience, it contains a complete indoor shopping mall, including two banks, a post office, an Amtrak ticket office, a beauty salon, a dry cleaner, and more. It's a self-contained world. There are many mind-boggling statistics to underscore the vastness of the Pentagon—for example, the building contains enough phone cable to circle the globe three times.

If your tour follows the pattern of past tours, staff will take you on a free 75- to 90-minute walk along certain corridors, covering the distance of a mile. It will begin with an explanation of the Department of Defense hierarchy and a short introductory film about the development of the Pentagon. Then a military guide will take you around. You'll visit the following:

- **The Air Force Art Collection,** which commemorates historic events involving the U.S. Air Force, including cartoons drawn by Walt Disney when he was an ambulance driver during World War I.
- **The Air Force Executive Corridor,** where, as you might have guessed, air force executives have their offices.
- **The POW Alcove,** hung with artists' conceptions of life in POW camps such as the "Hanoi Hilton."
- **The Marine Corps Corridor,** with a small display, because the marines are actually headquartered in the Navy Annex a quarter of a mile away.
- **The Navy Executive Corridor,** lined with portraits of former secretaries and undersecretaries of the navy. Glass cases display models of ships and submarines in the navy's current fleet, and the solid oak doors in this corridor are modeled after old ships captains' doors.
- **The Army Executive Corridor,** or Marshall Corridor, named for Gen. George C. Marshall, the first military man to receive a Nobel Peace Prize (for the Marshall Plan that helped Europe recover after World War II). Displayed here are army command and divisional flags and 172 army campaign streamers dating from 1775 through the Gulf War.
- **The Time-Life Art Collection Corridor.** During World War II Time-Life hired civilian artists to paint battle scenes at the front line. Most affecting is *Two-Thousand-Yard Stare,* showing a soldier suffering from battle fatigue.
- **The MacArthur Corridor** honors Gen. Douglas MacArthur. His career spanned 52 years, during which he served in three wars under nine presidents.
- **The Hall of Heroes** is where Medal of Honor recipients (over 3,400 of them, and counting) are commemorated. The medal is given out only during wartime and usually posthumously.
- **The Military Women's Corridor** documents the role of women throughout U.S. armed services history.
- **The Navajo Code Talkers Corridor** tells the story of the code language developed for military communications after the Japanese bombed Pearl Harbor during World War II. The U.S. military recruited the help of 400 Navajos, all marines, to create an indecipherable means of communication from the Navajo language.
- **The Flag Corridor** displays state and territorial flags, from the first Union Jack to the 50-star flag of today. This is where the tour should conclude.

Note: The best way to get to the Pentagon is via Metro's Blue or Yellow lines. If you must drive, call for directions.

Off I-395. ⓒ **703/695-1776.** www.defenselink.mil/pubs/pentagon. Free admission. Call to find out whether tours are being offered. Metro: Pentagon.

9 Parks & Gardens

Washington is extensively endowed with vast natural areas, all centrally located within the District. Included in all this greenery are thousands of parkland acres, two rivers, the mouth of a 185-mile-long tree-lined canal-side trail, an untamed wilderness area, and a few thousand cherry trees. And there's much more just a stone's throw away.

GARDENS

Enid A. Haupt Garden   Named for its donor, a noted supporter of horticultural projects, this stunning garden presents elaborate flower beds and borders, plant-filled turn-of-the-20th-century urns, 1870s cast-iron furnishings, and lush baskets hung from reproduction 19th-century lampposts. Although on ground level, the garden is actually a 4-acre rooftop garden above the subterranean Sackler and African Art museums. An **"Island Garden"** near the Sackler Gallery, entered via a 9-foot moon gate, has benches backed by English boxwoods under the shade of weeping cherry trees.

A **"Fountain Garden"** outside the African Art Museum provides granite seating walls shaded by hawthorn trees. Three small terraces, shaded by black sourgum trees, are located near the Arts & Industries Building. And five majestic linden trees shade a seating area around the Downing Urn, a memorial to American landscapist Andrew Jackson Downing. Elaborate cast-iron carriage gates made according to a 19th-century design by James Renwick, flanked by four red sandstone pillars, have been installed at the Independence Avenue entrance to the garden.

10th St. and Independence Ave. SW. © 202/357-2700. Free admission. Late May–Aug daily 7am–8pm; Sept to mid-May daily 7am–5:45pm. Closed Dec 25. Metro: Smithsonian.

United States Botanic Garden ⚘   The Botanic Garden re-opened in late 2001 after a major, 5-year renovation. In its new incarnation, the grand conservatory devotes half of its space to exhibits that focus on the importance of plants to people, and half to exhibits that focus on ecology and the evolutionary biology of plants. A 93-foot-high Palm House encloses a jungle of palms, ferns, and vines, the Orchid Room holds 12,000 varieties of orchids, and the new National Garden outside the conservatory includes a First Ladies Water Garden, a formal rose garden, and a lawn terrace. You'll also find a Meditation Garden and gardens created especially with children in mind.

Also visit the garden annex across the street, **Bartholdi Park.** The park is about the size of a city block, with a stunning cast-iron classical fountain created by Frédéric Auguste Bartholdi, designer of the Statue of Liberty. Charming flower gardens bloom amid tall ornamental grasses, benches are sheltered by vine-covered bowers, and a touch and fragrance garden contains such herbs as pineapple-scented sage.

100 Maryland Ave. (at 1st St. SW at the east end of the Mall). © 202/225-8333. www.usbg.gov. Free admission. Daily 10am–5pm. Metro: Federal Center SW.

PARKS
POTOMAC PARK

West and East Potomac parks, their 720 riverside acres divided by the Tidal Basin, are most famous for their spring display of **cherry blossoms** and all the hoopla that goes with it. So much attention is lavished on Washington's cherry blossoms that the National Park Service devotes a home page to the subject: **www.nps.gov/nacc/cherry**. You can access this site to find out forecasts for the blooms and assorted other details. You can also call the National Park Service (© 202/485-9880) for information. In all, there are more than 3,700 cherry trees planted along the Tidal Basin in West Potomac Park, East Potomac Park, the Washington Monument grounds, and in other pockets of the city.

To get to the Tidal Basin by car (*not* recommended in cherry-blossom season), you want to get on Independence Avenue and follow the signs posted near the Lincoln Memorial that show you where to turn to find parking and the FDR Memorial. If you're walking, you'll want to cross Independence Avenue where it intersects with West Basin Drive (there's a stoplight and crosswalk), and follow the path to the Tidal Basin. There is no convenient Metro stop near here.

West Potomac Park encompasses Constitution Gardens; the Vietnam, Korean, Lincoln, Jefferson, and FDR memorials; a small island where ducks live; and the Reflecting Pool (see "The Major Memorials," earlier in this chapter for full listings of the memorials). It has 1,628 trees bordering the Tidal Basin, some of them Akebonos with delicate pink blossoms, but most Yoshinos with white, cloudlike flower clusters. The blossoming of the cherry trees is the focal point of a 2-week-long celebration, including the lighting of the 300-year-old Japanese Stone Lantern near Kutz Bridge, presented to the city by the governor of Tokyo in 1954. (This year's Cherry Blossom Festival is scheduled to run Mar 22–Apr 7, 2003.) The trees bloom for a little less than 2 weeks beginning sometime between March 20 and April 17; April 5 is the average date. Planning your trip around the blooming of the cherry blossoms is an iffy proposition, and I wouldn't advise it. All it takes is one good rain and those cherry blossoms are gone. The cherry blossoms are not illuminated at night. See "Calendar of Events," in chapter 2 for further details on cherry-blossom events.

East Potomac Park has 1,681 cherry trees in 11 varieties. The park also has picnic grounds, tennis courts, three golf courses, a large swimming pool, and biking and hiking paths by the water.

ROCK CREEK PARK

Created in 1890, **Rock Creek Park** 🎔 (www.nps.gov/rocr) was purchased by Congress for its "pleasant valleys and ravines, primeval forests and open fields, its running waters, its rocks clothed with rich ferns and mosses, its repose and tranquillity, its light and shade, its ever-varying shrubbery, its beautiful and extensive views." A 1,750-acre valley within the District of Columbia, extending 12 miles from the Potomac River to the Maryland border, it's one of the biggest and finest city parks in the nation. Parts of it are still wild; it's not unusual to see a deer scurrying through the woods in more remote sections.

The park's offerings include the Old Stone House, Carter Barron Amphitheater (see chapter 9), playgrounds, an extensive system of beautiful hiking and biking trails, sports facilities, remains of Civil War fortifications, and acres and acres of wooded parklands. See also p. 202 for a description of the formal gardens at **Dumbarton Oaks,** which border Rock Creek Park in upper Georgetown.

For full information on the wide range of park programs and activities, visit the **Rock Creek Nature Center and Planetarium,** 5200 Glover Rd. NW (© 202/895-6070), Wednesday through Sunday from 9am to 5pm; or Park Headquarters, 3545 Williamsburg Lane NW (© 202/895-6015), Monday through Friday from 7:45am to 4:15pm. To get to the Nature Center by public transportation, take the Metro to Friendship Heights and transfer to bus no. E2 or E3 to Military Road and Oregon Avenue/Glover Road.

The Nature Center and Planetarium itself is the scene of numerous activities, including weekend planetarium shows for kids (minimum age 4) and adults; nature films; crafts demonstrations; live animal demonstrations; guided nature walks; plus a daily mix of lectures, films, and other events. A calendar is available

Rock Creek Park Area

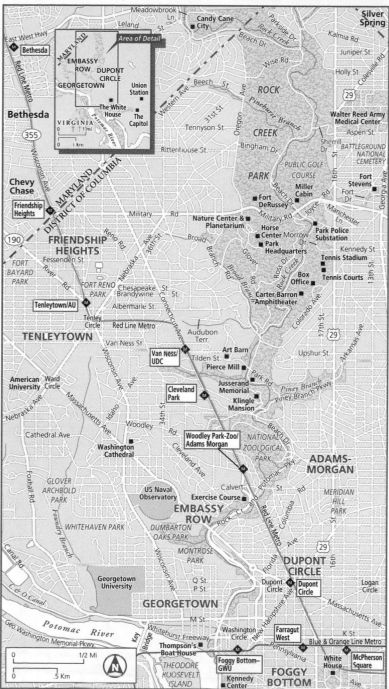

on request. Self-guided nature trails begin here. All activities are free, but for planetarium shows you need to pick up tickets a half-hour in advance. There are also nature exhibits on the premises. The Nature Center is closed on federal holidays.

Not far from the Nature Center is **Fort DeRussey,** one of 68 fortifications erected to defend the city of Washington during the Civil War. From the intersection of Military Road and Oregon Avenue, you walk a short trail through the woods to reach the fort, whose remains include high earth mounds with openings where guns were mounted, surrounded by a deep ditch/moat.

At Tilden Street and Beach Drive, you can see a water-powered 19th-century gristmill grinding corn and wheat into flour (℗ **202/426-6908**). It's called **Peirce Mill** (a man named Isaac Peirce built it), and it's open to visitors Wednesday through Sunday from noon to 4pm. Peirce's old carriage house is now the **Rock Creek Gallery** (℗ **202/244-2482**), where works of local artists are shown; it's open Thursday through Sunday from noon to 6pm (closed federal holidays and 1 month in summer, either July or Aug).

Call ℗ **202/895-6070** to request a brochure that provides details on picnic locations.

Poetry readings and workshops are held during the summer at **Miller's Cabin,** the one-time residence of High Sierra poet Joaquin Miller, Beach Drive north of Military Road. Call ℗ **202/895-6070** for information.

There's convenient free **parking** throughout the park.

THEODORE ROOSEVELT ISLAND PARK 🐾🐾

A serene 91-acre wilderness preserve, Theodore Roosevelt Island is a memorial to the nation's 26th president, in recognition of his contributions to conservation. During his administration, Roosevelt, an outdoor enthusiast and expert field naturalist, set aside a total of 234 million acres of public lands for forests, national parks, wildlife and bird refuges, and monuments.

Native American tribes were here first, inhabiting the island for centuries, until the arrival of English explorers in the 1600s. Over the years, the island passed through many owners before becoming what it is today: an island preserve of swamp, marsh, and upland forest that's a haven for rabbits, chipmunks, great owls, fox, muskrat, turtles, and groundhogs. It's a complex ecosystem in which cattails, arrow arum, and pickerelweed grow in the marshes, and willow, ash, and maple trees root on the mud flats. You can observe these flora and fauna in their natural environs on 2½ miles of foot trails.

In the northern center of the island, overlooking an oval terrace encircled by a water-filled moat, stands a 17-foot bronze statue of Roosevelt. From the terrace rise four 21-foot granite tablets inscribed with tenets of his conservation philosophy.

To drive to the island, take the George Washington Memorial Parkway exit north from the Theodore Roosevelt Bridge. The parking area is accessible only from the northbound lane; park there and cross the pedestrian bridge that connects the lot to the island. You can also rent a canoe at Thompson's Boat Center (p. 225) and paddle over, or take the pedestrian bridge at Rosslyn Circle, 2 blocks from the Rosslyn Metro station. You can picnic on the grounds near the memorial; if you do, allow about an hour or two here.

In the Potomac River, between Washington and Rosslyn, VA. See access information above. ℗ **703/289-2500.** www.nps.gov/gwmp. Free admission. Daily dawn–dusk. Metro: Rosslyn, then walk 2 blocks to Rosslyn Circle and cross the pedestrian bridge to the island.

ACTIVITIES ON THE C&O CANAL

One of the great joys of living in Washington is the **C&O Canal** (**www. nps.gov/choh**) and its unspoiled 184½-mile towpath. You leave urban cares and stresses behind while hiking, strolling, jogging, cycling, or boating in this lush, natural setting of ancient oaks and red maples, giant sycamores, willows, and wildflowers. But the canal wasn't always just a leisure spot for city people. It was built in the 1800s, when water routes were considered vital to transportation. Even before it was completed, the canal was being rendered obsolete by the B&O Railroad, which was constructed at about the same time and along the same route. Today, its role as an oasis from unrelenting urbanity is even more important.

Headquarters for canal activities is the Office of the Superintendent, C&O Canal National Historical Park (📞 **301/739-4200**). Another good source of information is the National Park Service office at **Great Falls Tavern Visitor Center,** 11710 MacArthur Blvd., Potomac, MD (📞 **301/299-3613**). At this 1831 tavern, you can see museum exhibits and a film about the canal; there's also a bookstore on the premises. The park charges an entrance fee, $5 per car, $3 per walker or cyclist.

In Georgetown, the **Georgetown Information Center,** 1057 Thomas Jefferson St. NW (📞 **202/653-5190**), can also provide maps and information.

Hiking any section of the flat dirt towpath or its more rugged side paths is a pleasure (and it's free). There are picnic tables, some with barbecue grills, about every 5 miles on the way to Cumberland, beginning at **Fletcher's Boat House** (📞 **202/244-0461**), which is about 3¼ miles out of Georgetown and is a good place to rent bikes or boats or to purchase bait, tackle, and a fishing license. Enter the towpath in Georgetown below M Street via Thomas Jefferson Street. If you hike 14 miles, you'll reach **Great Falls,** a point where the Potomac becomes a stunning waterfall plunging 76 feet. Or drive to Great Falls Park on the Virginia side of the Potomac.

Much less strenuous than hiking is a **mule-drawn 19th-century canal boat trip** led by Park Service rangers in period dress. They regale passengers with canal legend and lore and sing period songs. These boats depart from mid-April to early November; departure times and tickets are available at the Georgetown Information Center (see above). Both the Georgetown and Great Falls barge rides last about 1 hour and 10 minutes and cost $8 for adults, $6 for seniors over 61, and $5 for children ages 3 to 14.

Call any of the above information numbers for details on riding, rock climbing, fishing, bird-watching, concerts, ranger-guided tours, ice skating, camping, and other canal activities.

10 Especially for Kids

Who knows what kids might enjoy in Washington better than other kids? So, I asked my own children, Caitlin (15) and Lucy (10); my nieces, Sarah (13) and Annie (11), and my nephew, Nick (7), what sights in Washington they would recommend to friends and cousins visiting from out of town. Here are some of their suggestions (with translations where needed—refer to mentions in this chapter for details):

Caitlin: "I still think Georgetown is a great place for teenage girls to go, because there are lots of shops, like Betsey Johnson for the girlie type, and Abercrombie, for preps. There are tons of restaurants, not just a food court. There is a mall [Georgetown Park Mall], if you like malls, but there are also nonpreppie alternative stores, like Urban Outfitters and Commander Salamander. You can also walk down to the harbor with friends or family and take a boat ride [see "Organized Tours, By Boat," in following section] for an hour or so."

Sarah: "You can have brunch at the Kennedy Center [see "Dining at Sightseeing Attractions," in chapter 6] and then go see a show, or walk around and look at the Potomac and buy souvenirs. The brunch is really cool, because the buffet is in the kitchen, so you go in and get the food (which is really good), from the kitchen and then go and sit down in the dining room, where there are a lot of windows with great views."

Annie: "I like going to the National Geographic Museum. One exhibit I especially liked was about Eskimos and Alaska. There's a booth at the museum, where you can get your picture taken with the cover of a National Geographic magazine in the background. When the picture comes out it looks like your face is on the cover of the National Geographic magazine."

Lucy: "I like going to the Kennedy Center because they always have activities and shows for children and adults. Like this year, I saw *The Shakespeare Stealer* with my friend Genevieve; it was in a small theater and there were a lot of surprises in the scenes." Another year, I saw *Annie Get Your Gun,* which was a funny musical about a girl who acted like a boy and loved trouble. The actress had a good voice and I liked all the songs, especially one called "Anything You Can Do, I Can Do Better."

Nick: "Go to the MCI Center and see the Capitals [Washington's ice hockey team] or the Wizards [Washington's men's basketball team] play. It's exciting to watch the games and they sell really good pizza at the MCI Center."

For more ideas, consult the Friday "Weekend" section of the *Washington Post,* which lists numerous activities (mostly free) for kids: special museum events, children's theater, storytelling programs, puppet shows, video-game competitions, and so forth. Call the Kennedy Center, the Lisner, and the National Theatre to find out about children's shows; see chapter 9 for details. Also read the write-up of Discovery Theater, within the Smithsonian's Arts & Industries Building, earlier in this chapter.

I've checked out hotels built with families in mind in chapter 5's "Family-Friendly Hotels"; that hotel pool may rescue your sanity for an hour or two. The "Organized Tours" and "Outdoor Activities" sections below may also be your saving grace when you've either run out of steam or need a jump-start to your day.

FAVORITE CHILDREN'S ATTRACTIONS

Check for special children's events at museum information desks when you enter. As noted within the listings for individual museums, some children's programs are also great fun for adults. I recommend the programs at the **Corcoran Gallery of Art,** the **Folger Shakespeare Library,** the **Phillips,** and the **Sackler Gallery** in particular. (The gift shops in most of these museums have wonderful toys and children's books.) Call ahead to find out which programs are running. Here's a rundown of the biggest kid-pleasers in town (for details, see the full entries earlier in this chapter):

- **National Air and Space Museum** (p. 187): Spectacular IMAX films (don't miss), planetarium shows, missiles, rockets, and a walk-through orbital workshop.
- **National Museum of Natural History** (p. 191): A Discovery Room just for youngsters, an insect zoo, shrunken heads, and dinosaurs, and the IMAX theater showing 2-D and 3-D films.

- **National Museum of American History** (p. 190): The butterfly garden, the original Star Spangled Banner, Archie Bunker's chair, and an old-fashioned ice-cream parlor.
- **Federal Bureau of Investigation** (p. 199): Gangster memorabilia, crime-solving methods, espionage devices, and a sharpshooting demonstration.
- **Bureau of Engraving & Printing** (p. 198): Kids enjoy looking at immense piles of money as much as you do.
- **National Zoological Park** (p. 193): Pandas! Kids always love a zoo, and this is an especially good one.
- **Ford's Theatre & Lincoln Museum and The House Where Lincoln Died** (p. 203 and 206, respectively): Booth's gun and diary, the clothes Lincoln was wearing the night he was assassinated, and other such grisly artifacts. Kids adore the whole business.
- **Washington Monument** (p. 178): Easy to get them up there, hard to get them down. If only they could use the steps, they'd be in heaven.
- **Lincoln Memorial** (p. 179): Kids know a lot about Lincoln and enjoy visiting his memorial. A special treat is visiting after dark (the same goes for the Washington Monument and Jefferson Memorial).

11 Organized Tours

ON FOOT

Tour de Force (© 703/525-2948; www.atourdeforce.com) is historian and raconteur Jeanne Fogel's 18-year-old company. She offers a variety of walking and bus tours around the city, revealing little-known anecdotes and facts about neighborhoods, historic figures, and the most visited sites. Fogel's tours are custom designed for groups, not individuals. Call for rates.

TourDC, Walking Tours of Georgetown, Dupont Circle & Embassy Row (© 301/588-8999; www.tourdc.com) conducts 90-minute ($12) walking tours of Georgetown, telling about the neighborhood's history up to the present and taking you past the homes of notable residents.

Guided Walking Tours of Washington ☞ (© 301/294-9514; www.dcsight seeing.com) offers 2-hour walks through the streets of Georgetown, Adams-Morgan, and other locations, guided by author/historian Anthony S. Pitch. Inquire about private tours. Rates are $10 per person, $6 for seniors and students.

BY BUS

TOURMOBILE   Best-known and least expensive, **Tourmobile Sightseeing** (© 888/868-7707 or 202/554-5100; www.tourmobile.com) is a good choice if you're looking for an easy-on/easy-off tour of major sites. The comfortable red, white, and blue sightseeing trams travel to as many as 24 attractions (the company changes its schedule and number of stops, depending on whether sites are open for public tours), as far out as Arlington National Cemetery and even Mount Vernon. Tourmobile is the only narrated sightseeing shuttle tour authorized by the National Park Service. The company offers a number of different tours, including the most popular **American Heritage Tour,** which stops at 21 sites on or near the National Mall and at three sites in Arlington Cemetery. (Again, the number of stops may be fewer than 21, if regularly scheduled stops, like the White House, are not open for public tours due to increased security.) Normally, stops include the memorials and Washington Monument, Union Station, the National Gallery, most of the Smithsonian museums (National Air & Space, National Museum of American History, National Museum of Natural

History, and the Arts & Industries Building/Hirshhorn Museum), the Capitol, and several other locations. In Arlington Cemetery, the bus stops at the Kennedy grave sites, the Tomb of the Unknowns, and Arlington House.

You simply hop on a Tourmobile at any of the locations, paying the driver when you first board the bus (you can also purchase a ticket at the booth at the Washington Monument or inside the Arlington National Cemetery Visitor Center, or, for a small surcharge, order your ticket in advance from Ticketmaster at ℭ 800/551-SEAT). Along the route, you may get off at any stop to visit monuments or buildings. When you finish exploring each area, just show your ticket and climb aboard the next Tourmobile that comes along. The buses travel in a loop, serving each stop about every 15 to 30 minutes. One fare allows you to use the buses for a full day. The charge for the American Heritage Tour is $18 for anyone 12 and older, $8 for children 3 to 11. For Arlington Cemetery only, those 12 and older pay $5.25, children $2.50. Children under 3 ride free. Buses follow figure-eight circuits from the Capitol to Arlington Cemetery and back. Well-trained narrators give commentaries about sights along the route and answer questions.

Though heated in winter, these trams are not air-conditioned in summer, and though the windows stay open, they can get hot and uncomfortable. Readers also report that Tourmobiles, being the largest trams, take a long time to load and unload passengers, which can be frustrating to those anxious to see the sights.

Tourmobiles operate daily year-round, except Christmas. From June 15 to Labor Day, they ply the Mall between 9am and 6:30pm. After Labor Day, the hours are 9:30am to 4:30pm. In Arlington Cemetery, October through March, they start at 9:30am and end at 4:30pm; April through September, the hours are from 8:30am to 6:30pm.

Tourmobile also operates round-trip tours to **Mount Vernon** (see chapter 10) and to the **Frederick Douglass National Historic Site Tour** (June 15–Labor Day). Call Tourmobile or access the website for further information and rates for these and other tours.

OLD TOWN TROLLEY   Old Town Trolley tours (ℭ 202/832-9800; www. oldtowntrolley.com) offer fixed-price, on-off service as you travel in a loop around the city. You can purchase your ticket at the booth at Union Station, or board without a ticket and purchase it en route. (One exception is the Lincoln Memorial stop. The National Park Service does not allow any tour bus service other than Tourmobile to solicit business on its lands, which means you must have a prepaid ticket to board an Old Town Trolley at the Lincoln Memorial.) Buses operate daily from 9am to 5:30pm year-round. The cost is $24 for adults, $12 for children 4 to 12, free for children under 4. The full tour, which is narrated, takes 2 hours (if you never get off), and trolleys come by every 30 minutes or so. Old Town Trolley tours cost more but stop at certain hotels, like the Capital Hilton and the JW Marriott, and travel to neighborhoods, like Georgetown, and attractions away from the Mall, like the National Geographic Society.

MARTZ GRAYLINE L'IL RED TROLLEY TOURS   Martz Grayline Tours (ℭ 202/289-1995; www.graylinedc.com) operates these red trolleys in the same fashion as Tourmobile and Old Town Trolleys, providing on-and-off service for a fixed price ($28 for adults, $14 for children) as the trolley travels around the city, stopping at more than 25 sites. Trolley stops overlap with those of the other companies, and include stops at hard-to-reach destinations, like Adams-Morgan.

BY BOAT

Since Washington is a river city, why not see it by boat? Potomac cruises allow sweeping vistas of the monuments and memorials, Georgetown, the Kennedy Center, and other Washington sights. Read the information below carefully, since not all boat cruises offer guided tours.

Some of the following boats leave from the Washington waterfront and some from Old Town Alexandria:

Spirit of Washington Cruises, Pier 4 at Sixth and Water streets SW (© **866/ 211-3811** or 202/554-8000; www.spiritcruises.com; Metro: Waterfront), offers a variety of trips daily, including evening dinner, lunch, and brunch, and moonlight dance cruises, as well as a half-day excursion to Mount Vernon and back. Lunch and dinner cruises include a 40-minute high-energy musical revue. Prices range from $29.95 to $43.95 for a lunch excursion and from $53.95 to $82.95 for a dinner cruise, drinks not included. Call to make reservations.

The *Spirit of Washington* is a luxury climate-controlled harbor cruise ship with carpeted decks and huge panoramic windows designed for sightseeing. There are three well-stocked bars on board. Mount Vernon cruises are aboard an equally luxurious sister ship, the *Potomac Spirit.*

Potomac Party Cruises (© **703/683-6076;** www.dandydinnerboat.com) operates *The Dandy* and *Nina's Dandy,* both climate-controlled, all-weather, glassed-in floating restaurants that run year-round. Lunch, evening dinner/dance, and special charter cruises are available daily. You board both vessels in Old Town Alexandria, at the Prince Street pier, between Duke and King streets. Trips range from $33 for a 2½-hour weekday lunch cruise to $80.50 for a 3-hour Saturday dinner cruise.

Odyssey III (© **800/946-7245;** www.odysseycruises.com) was designed specifically to glide under the bridges that cross the Potomac. The boat looks like a glass bullet, with its snub-nosed port and its streamlined 240-foot-long glass body. The wraparound see-through walls and ceiling allow for great views. Like *The Dandy,* the *Odyssey* operates all year. You board the *Odyssey* at the Gangplank Marina, on Washington's waterfront, at Sixth and Water streets SW (Metro: Waterfront). Cruises available include lunch, Sunday brunch, and dinner excursions, with live entertainment provided during each cruise. It costs $37 for a 2-hour weekday lunch cruise and $88 for a 3-hour Saturday dinner cruise.

The **Potomac Riverboat Company** ⨍ (© **703/548-9000;** www. potomacriverboatco.com) offers three narrated tours April through October aboard the *Matthew Hayes,* on a 90-minute tour past Washington monuments and memorials; the *Admiral Tilp,* on a 40-minute tour of Old Town Alexandria's waterfront; and the *Miss Christin,* which cruises to Mount Vernon, where you hop off and reboard after you've toured the estate. You board the boats at the pier behind the Torpedo Factory in Old Town Alexandria, at the foot of King Street; or, for the Washington monuments and memorials tour, Georgetown's Washington Harbour. *Matthew Hayes* tickets are $16 for adults, $8 for children ages 2 to 12; *Admiral Tilp* tickets are $8 for adults, $5 for children ages 2 to 12; and *Miss Christin* tickets are $26 for adults, $13 for children ages 6 to 10, and include admission to Mount Vernon. A concession stand selling light refreshments and beverages is open during the cruises.

The **Capitol River Cruise's** *Nightingale I* and *Nightingale II* (© **800/405-5511** or 301/460-7447; www.capitolrivercruises.com) are historic 65-foot steel riverboats that can accommodate up to 90 people. The *Nightingale's* narrated jaunts depart Georgetown's Washington Harbour every hour on the hour, from

11am to 9pm, April through October. The 50-minute narrated tour travels past the monuments and memorials as you head to National Airport and back. A snack bar on board sells light refreshments, beer, wine, and sodas; you're welcome to bring your own picnic aboard. The price is $10 per adult, $5 per child ages 3 to 12. To get here, take the Metro to Foggy Bottom and then take the Georgetown Metro Connection Shuttle or walk into Georgetown, following Pennsylvania Avenue, which becomes M Street. Turn left on 31st Street NW, which dead-ends at the Washington Harbour complex.

A BOAT ON WHEELS   Old Town Trolley also operates the **DC Ducks** (© 202/832-9800; www.dcducks.com), which feature unique land and water tours of Washington aboard the *DUKW,* an amphibious army vehicle (boat with wheels) from World War II that accommodates 30 passengers. Ninety-minute guided tours aboard the open-air canopied craft include a land portion taking in major sights—the Capitol, Lincoln Memorial, Washington Monument, White House, and Smithsonian museums—and a 30-minute Potomac cruise. Tickets can be purchased inside Union Station at the information desk; you board the vehicle just outside the main entrance to Union Station. There are departures daily during tour season (Mar–Oct); hours vary, but departures usually follow an 11am and 1 and 3pm schedule. Tickets cost $25 for adults, $13 for children 5 to 12, free for children under 5.

BY BIKE

Bike the Sites, Inc. ✿ (© 202/966-8662; www.bikethesites.com) offers a more active way to see Washington. The company has designed several different biking tours of the city, including the popular Capital Sites Ride, which takes 3 hours, covers 55 sites along an 8-mile stretch, and costs $40 per adult, $30 per child 12 and under. Bike the Sites provides you with a 21-speed Trek Hybrid bicycle fitted to your size, bike helmet, handlebar bag, water bottle, light snack, and two guides to lead the ride. Guides impart historical and anecdotal information as you go. The company will customize bike rides to suit your tour specifications.

12 Outdoor Activities

The Washington area offers plenty of opportunities for outdoor activities. See "Parks & Gardens," earlier in this chapter for complete coverage of the city's loveliest green spaces.

Joggers can enjoy a run on the Mall or along the path in Rock Creek Park.

Rent a bike at **Fletcher's Boat House,** Reservoir and Canal roads (© 202/ 244-0461; www.fletchersboathouse.com), or **Thompson's Boat Center,** 2900 Virginia Ave. at Rock Creek Parkway NW (© 202/333-4861 or 202/333-9543; www.guestservices.com/tbc. Metro: Foggy Bottom, with a 10-min. walk); both Fletcher's and Thompason's rent bikes from about late March to November. At **Big Wheel Bikes,** 1034 33rd St. NW, right near the C&O Canal just below M Street (© 202/337-0254), you can rent a bike year-round, Tuesday through Sunday. If you need suggested routes or want company, check out Friday's *Washington Post* "Weekend" section listing cycling trips. Rock Creek Park has an **11-mile paved bike route** ✿ from the Lincoln Memorial through the park into Maryland. Or you can follow the bike path from the Lincoln Memorial and go over the Memorial Bridge to pedal to Old Town Alexandria and to Mount Vernon (see chapter 10 for details). On weekends and holidays, a large part of Rock Creek Parkway is closed to vehicular traffic. The C&O Canal and the Potomac parks, described earlier in "Parks & Gardens," also have extended bike paths. A new 7-mile path, the **Capital Crescent Trail,** takes you from Georgetown to the suburb of Bethesda, Maryland, following a former railroad track that parallels the Potomac River for part of the way and passes by old trestle bridges and pleasant residential neighborhoods.

Thompson's Boat Center and **Fletcher's Boat House** (see above for both addresses and phone numbers) also rent boats (of course), following the same schedule as their bike rental season, basically March to November. Thompson's has canoes, kayaks, and rowing shells (recreational and racing), and is open for boat and bike rentals daily from 6am to 8pm. Fletcher's is right on the C&O Canal, about 3¼ wonderfully scenic miles from Georgetown. The same family has owned it since 1850! In addition to renting bikes and canoes, Fletcher's also sells fishing licenses, bait, and tackle. Fletcher's is accessible by car (west on M St. to Canal Rd.) and has plenty of free parking.

From late March to mid-September, you can rent **paddleboats** ⚓ on the north end of the Tidal Basin off Independence Avenue (☎ **202/479-2426**). Four-seaters rent for $16 an hour; two-seaters are $8 an hour. You can rent boats daily from 10am to about an hour before sunset.

Hikers will be happy to know about Washington's numerous **hiking paths.** The C&O Canal offers 184½ miles; Theodore Roosevelt Island has more than 88 wilderness acres to explore, including a 2½-mile nature trail (short but rugged); and Rock Creek Park boasts 20 miles of hiking trails (maps are available at the Visitor Information Center or Park Headquarters).

If you're coming to Washington in winter, you can go **ice skating** on the C&O Canal (call ☎ **301/299-3613** for information on ice conditions), as long as you bring your own skates. For a really fun experience, head to the **National Gallery Sculpture Garden Ice Rink** ⚓, on the Mall at Seventh Street and Constitution Avenue NW (☎ **202/289-3360**), where you can rent skates, twirl in view of the sculptures, and enjoy hot chocolate and a sandwich in the Pavilion Café, right next to the rink. Another outdoor rink where you can rent skates is **Pershing Park,** at 14th Street and Pennsylvania Avenue NW (☎ **202/737-6938**).

If you're here in summer and your hotel doesn't have a pool, you might consider one of the neighborhood pools run by the District's Department of Parks and Recreation. These include a large outdoor pool at 25th and N streets NW (☎ **202/727-3285**); and the Georgetown outdoor pool at 34th Street and Volta Place NW (☎ **202/282-2366**). Keep in mind that these are likely to be crowded.

Tennis lovers will have a hard time finding public courts in Washington. **East Potomac Park** has nine tennis courts, including five indoors (☎ **202/554-5962**). Fees vary with court surface and time of play; call for details. **Montrose Park** (p. 202), right next to Dumbarton Oaks in Georgetown has several courts available for free on a first-come, first-served basis; but they're often in use.

8

Shopping

Shopping may not be the reason that brings you to Washington, but once you're here, trust me, you're going to shop. You need to buy a little something for the folks at home, don't you? And what about for yourself—don't you want a unique memento to help you remember this trip for all eternity?

Besides, good shopping opportunities await you everywhere. Georgetown, whose streets are lined with stores, is a shopaholic's dream, while each of the District's other neighborhoods has its own assorted boutiques and emporiums. (See "Great Shopping Areas," below.) Ronald Reagan Washington National Airport and Union Station are, in fact, shopping malls masquerading as an airport and a train station. Each of the Smithsonian museums and just about every other tourist attraction in and around Washington has its own on-site gift shop (see the box titled "Museum Shopping" on p. 241). Even if you don't have time for a day devoted to shopping, you can still hit each site's gift shop on the way out; prices aren't cheap, but the finds can be novel.

Avowed shopper or not, you owe it to yourself to pop into a neighborhood store or two while you're here, if only for the sightseeing factor: Visit the shops where locals go, and you get a glimpse of people and how they live in that particular place.

Finally, if you just really hate the thought of spending time in a store, but still desire a souvenir, you can return home and shop D.C. online. The Smithsonian museums and many Washington landmarks and attractions have shopping pages on their websites (see chapter 7 for individual Web addresses).

1 The Shopping Scene

Washington-area stores are usually open daily from 10am to 5 or 6pm Monday through Saturday, with one late night (usually Thurs) when hours extend to 9pm. Sunday hours are usually from noon to 5 or 6pm. Exceptions are the malls, which are open late nightly, and antiques stores and art galleries, which tend to keep their own hours. Play it safe and call ahead if there's a store you really want to get to.

Sales tax on merchandise is 5.75% in the District, 5% in Maryland, and 4.5% in Virginia.

Most gift, arts, and crafts stores, including those at the Smithsonian museums, will handle shipping for you; clothes stores generally do not.

If you're a true bargain hunter, scope out the *Washington Post* website (**www. washingtonpost.com**) in advance of your trip to see which stores are having sales. Once you get to the *Post*'s home page, hit "Entertainment" at the top of your screen, click on "Shopping," and then click on "Sales and Bargains," a column that's updated weekly.

GREAT SHOPPING AREAS

Union Station   The only legitimate shopping area on Capitol Hill, Union Station has more than 100 specialty shops, selling jewelry, apparel, and gifts, and more than 45 eateries.

Downtown   The area bounded east and west by 7th and 14th streets NW, and north and south by New York and Pennsylvania avenues NW, is in a frenzy of development. Stores here include the tony Chanel Boutique, located within the Willard Inter-Continental Hotel's courtyard; and the Shops at National Place, a four-level mall whose stores include Casual Corner, and Filene's Basement. Look for the huge Borders bookstore at 14th and F streets NW, in the grand old Garfinckel's Building. Hecht's, at 12th and G streets, continues as the sole department store downtown. Metro: Metro Center.

Adams-Morgan   Centered on 18th Street and Columbia Road NW, Adams-Morgan is a neighborhood of ethnic eateries and nightclubs interspersed with the odd secondhand bookshop and eclectic collectibles stores. It's a fun area for walking and shopping. Parking is possible during the day but impossible at night. Closest Metro: You have two choices: Woodley Park–Adams Morgan, then walk south on Connecticut Ave. NW until you reach Calvert Street, cross Connecticut Ave. and follow Calvert Street across the bridge until you reach the junction of Columbia Road NW and 18th Street NW. On Saturday, you can catch the no. 98 Adams Morgan–U Street Link shuttle bus, which departs every 15 minutes from the Woodley Park station and takes you to Adams-Morgan. With a Metrorail transfer from the Woodley Park Metro station, the cost is 25¢; with no transfer, you pay $1.10. Second choice: Dupont Circle; exit at Q Street NW and walk up Connecticut Avenue NW to Columbia Road NW.

Connecticut Avenue/Dupont Circle   Running from the mini–Wall Street that is K Street north to S Street, Connecticut Avenue NW is a main thoroughfare, where you'll find traditional clothing at Brooks Brothers, Talbots, and Burberry's; casual duds at The Gap and Liz Claiborne; discount items at Filene's Basement and Hit or Miss; and haute couture at Rizik's. Closer to Dupont Circle are coffee bars and neighborhood restaurants, as well as art galleries; funky boutiques; gift, stationery, book, and record shops; and stores with a gay and lesbian slant. Metro: Farragut North at one end, Dupont Circle at the other.

Georgetown   Georgetown is the city's main shopping area. In the heart of the neighborhood, stores line Wisconsin Avenue and M Street NW, and they also fan out along side streets from the central intersection. You'll find both chain and one-of-a-kind shops, chic as well as thrift. Sidewalks and streets are almost always crowded, and parking can be tough. Weekends, especially, bring out all kinds of yahoos, who are mainly here to drink. Visit Georgetown on a weekday morning, if you can. Weeknights are another good time to visit, for dinner and strolling afterward. Metro: Foggy Bottom, then catch the bright blue Georgetown Metro Connection bus, which runs every 10 minutes, takes only a few minutes to reach Georgetown, and costs 25¢ with a Metrorail transfer, or 50¢ without a transfer. Metrobuses (the no. 30-series: 30, 32, 34, 36) travel through Georgetown from different parts of the city. Otherwise, consider taking a taxi. If you drive, you'll find parking lots expensive and tickets even more so, so be careful where you plant your car.

Upper Wisconsin Avenue Northwest   In a residential section of town known as Friendship Heights on the D.C. side and Chevy Chase on the Maryland side (north of the U.S. Naval Observatory and west of Rock Creek Park) is a quarter-mile shopping district that extends from Saks Fifth Avenue at one end to Sur La Table at the other. In between lie Lord & Taylor, Neiman Marcus, and Hecht Company department stores; a bevy of top shops, such as Tiffany's and Versace; two malls, the totally redone Mazza Gallerie and its younger-but-now-older-looking sister, the Chevy Chase Pavilion; and several stand-alone staples, such as Banana Republic. The street is too wide and traffic always too snarled to make this a fun place to stroll, although teenagers do love to loiter here. Drive here if you want; the Hecht's store parking lot offers 2 hours of free parking with validation. Or Metro it; the strip is right on the Red Line, with the "Friendship Heights" exits leading directly into each of the malls and into Hecht's.

Old Town Alexandria   Old Town, a Virginia neighborhood beyond National Airport, is becomingly increasingly like Georgetown, warts (heavy traffic, crowded sidewalks, difficult parking) and all. Old Town extends from the Potomac River in the east to the King Street Metro station in the west, and from about First Street in the north to Green Street in the south, but the best shopping is in the center, where King and Washington streets intersect. Weekdays are a lot tamer than weekends. It's always a nice place to visit, though; the drive alone is worth the trip. See chapter 10, "Side Trips from Washington, D.C.," for full coverage of Alexandria. Metro: King Street, then hop on a blue and gold DASH bus and pay $1 to reach the heart of Old Town.

2 Shopping A to Z

ANTIQUES

A few miles north of the city is not too far to go for the good deal or true bonanza you're likely to discover on **Antique Row.** Some 40 antiques and collectible shops line Howard Avenue in Kensington, Maryland, offering every sort of item in a wide variety of styles, periods, and prices. If you don't drive or catch a cab, you'll have to take the Metro and two buses. From Dupont Circle, board an L2 bus and get a transfer from the driver. Ask him to tell you when you reach the transfer point for the L8 bus. When you reach that juncture, board the L8 bus and ask to be let off at Connecticut and Knowles avenues. Howard Avenue is 1 block north of Knowles.

Antiques-on-the-Hill   A Capitol Hill institution since the 1960s, this place sells silver, furniture, glassware, jewelry, porcelain, and lamps. 701 North Carolina Ave. SE. (*C*) 877/509-3772 or 202/543-1819. Metro: Eastern Market.

Brass Knob Architectural Antiques   When early homes and office buildings are demolished in the name of progress, these savvy salvage merchants spirit away saleable treasures, from chandeliers to wrought-iron fencing. 2311 18th St. NW. (*C*) 202/332-3370. www.thebrassknob.com. Metro: Woodley Park or Dupont Circle. There's a second location across the street called the **Brass Knob's Back Doors Warehouse,** 2329 Champlain St. NW ((*C*) 202/265-0587).

cherry   This is an antiques store, all right, but as its name suggests, a little offbeat. Expect affordable eclectic furnishings and decorative arts, and lots of mirrors and sconces. 2603 P St. NW. (*C*) 202/342-3600. Metro: Dupont Circle, then a 10–15-min. walk.

Cherub Antiques Gallery   The Cherub Antiques Gallery specializes in Art Nouveau and Art Deco, art glass (signed Tiffany, Steuben, Lalique, and Gallé), Liberty arts and crafts, and Louis Icart etchings. 2918 M St. NW. (*C*) 202/337-2224. Metro: Foggy Bottom, then take the Georgetown Metro connection.

Gore-Dean   Though its offerings include some American pieces, the store specializes in 18th- and 19th-century European furnishings, decorative accessories, paintings, prints, and porcelains. Recently added are a lampshade shop, garden shop, and framing studio. 1525 and 1529 Wisconsin Ave. NW. ℂ **202/625-1776.** www.gore-dean.com. Metro: Foggy Bottom, then take the Georgetown Metro Connection.

Michael Getz Antiques   Sharing the premises with the Cherub Antiques Gallery (see above), this shop sells American, English, and continental silver; porcelain lamps; and many fireplace accessories. 2918 M St. NW. ℂ **202/338-3811.** Metro: Foggy Bottom, then take the Georgetown Metro Connection.

Millennium   This is antiques shopping for the TV generation, where anything made between the 1930s and the 1970s is considered collectible. The shop works with 18 dealers; stock changes weekly. Funky wares run from Bakelite to Heywood-Wakefield blond-wood beauties to used drinking glasses. 1528 U St. NW. ℂ **202/483-1218.** Metro: U St.–Cardozo.

Old Print Gallery   This gallery carries original American and European prints from the 17th through the 19th century, including political cartoons, maps, and historical documents. It's one of the largest antique print and map shops in the United States. 1220 31st St. NW. ℂ **202/965-1818.** www.oldprintgallery.com. Metro: Foggy Bottom, then take the Georgetown Metro Connection.

Susquehanna Antiques   This Georgetown store specializes in American, English, and European furniture, paintings, and garden items of the late 18th and early 19th centuries. 3216 O St. NW. ℂ **202/333-1511.** www.susquehannaantiques. com. Metro: Foggy Bottom, then take the Georgetown Metro Connection.

ART GALLERIES

Art galleries abound in Washington, but are especially prolific in Dupont Circle and Georgetown, and along Seventh Street downtown.

For a complete listing of local galleries, get your hands on a copy of **"Galleries,"** a monthly guide to major galleries and their shows; the guide is available free at many hotel concierge desks and at each of the galleries listed in the publication.

DUPONT CIRCLE

For all galleries listed below, the closest Metro stop is Dupont Circle.

Affrica   Authentic and traditional African masks, figures, and artifacts. The gallery's clients include major museums and private collectors from around the world. 2010 R St. NW. ℂ **202/745-7272.** www.affrica.com.

Anton Gallery   Expect to find contemporary American paintings, as well as sculpture, functional ceramics, and prints. Anton represents national and international artists. 2108 R St. NW. ℂ **202/328-0828.** www.antongallery.com.

H. H. Leonards' Mansion on O Street   Not an art gallery in the usual sense, H. H. Leonards' Mansion consists of three Victorian town houses joined together and decorated throughout with more than 5,000 antiques and artworks, in styles ranging from Art Deco to avant-garde. H's place is also her home, a special-events spot, and a luxurious B&B to boot. (See the review in chapter 5.) 2020 O St. NW. ℂ **202/496-2000.** www.omansion.com. Open by appointment only.

Kathleen Ewing Gallery   This gallery features vintage and contemporary photography. 1609 Connecticut Ave. NW. ℂ **202/328-0955.** www.kathleenewinggallery.com.

GEORGETOWN

For all the galleries listed below, the closest stop is Foggy Bottom, with a transfer to the Georgetown Metro Connection bus to get you the rest of the way.

Addison/Ripley Fine Art   This gallery represents both nationally and regionally recognized artists, from the 19th century to the present; works include paintings, sculpture, photography, and fine arts. 1670 Wisconsin Ave. NW. ℂ 202/338-5180. www.addisonripleyfineart.com.

Govinda Gallery   This place generates a lot of media coverage, since it often shows artwork created by famous names and features photographs of celebrities. In 2002, the gallery's exhibits included Doug Kirkland's photographs of Marilyn Monroe and Kate Simon's photos of Bob Marley. 1227 34th St. NW. ℂ 202/333-1180. www.govindagallery.com.

Guarisco Gallery, Ltd.   Its display of 19th- and early-20th-century paintings, watercolors, and sculptures by the likes of Camille Pissarro, T. Robinson, and H. Lebasque make this gallery as much a museum as a shop. 2828 Pennsylvania Ave. NW (in the courtyard). ℂ 202/333-8533. www.artnet.com/guarisco.html.

Spectrum Gallery   A cooperative venture since 1966, in which 30 professional Washington-area artists, including painters, potters, sculptors, photographers, collagists, and printmakers, share in shaping gallery policy, maintenance, and operation. The art is reasonably priced. 1132 29th St. NW (just below M St.). ℂ 202/333-0954. www.spectrumgallery.org.

SEVENTH STREET ARTS CORRIDOR

A couple of these galleries predate the renaissance taking place in this downtown neighborhood. To get here, take the Metro to either the Archives/Navy Memorial (Blue–Orange Line) or Gallery Place/Chinatown/MCI Center (Red–Yellow Line) stations.

406 Art Galleries   Several first-rate art galleries, some of them interlopers from Dupont Circle, occupy this historic building, with its 13-foot-high ceilings and spacious rooms. The first floor of the building is a furniture store, so keep going to the next level. Look for the **David Adamson Gallery** (ℂ 202/628-0257; www.artnet.com/davidadamsongallery.html), probably the largest gallery space in D.C., with two levels featuring the works of contemporary artists, like locals Kevin MacDonald and Renee Stout, and national artists KiKi Smith and William Wegman. The **Touchstone Gallery** (ℂ 202/347-2787; www.art-smart.com/touchstone) is a self-run co-op of 36 artists who take turns exhibiting their work; and the **Eklektikos Gallery of Art** (ℂ 202/783-8444; www.eklektikos.com) represents regional, national, and international artists. 406 7th St. NW, between D and E sts.

Zenith Gallery   Across the street from the 406 Group, Zenith shows diverse works by contemporary artists, most American, about half of whom are local. You can get a good deal here, paying anywhere from $50 to $50,000 for a piece. Among the things you'll find are annual humor shows, neon exhibits, realism, abstract expressionism, and landscapes. 413 7th St. NW. ℂ 202/783-2963. www.zenith gallery.com.

BOOKS

Washingtonians are readers, so bookstores constantly pop up throughout the city. An increasingly competitive market means that chain bookstores do a brisk business, even though D.C. can claim more general-interest independent bookstores than any other city. Here are my favorite bookstores in general, used, and special-interest categories. *Note:* Websites for chain bookstores are for the chain itself, not individual stores.

GENERAL

Barnes & Noble   This wonderful three-story shop has sizable software, travel book, and children's title sections. A cafe on the second level sometimes hosts concerts. 3040 M St. NW. ℂ 202/965-9880. www.barnesandnoble.com. Metro: Foggy Bottom, then take the Georgetown Metro Connection shuttle. Other area locations include 555 12th St. NW (ℂ 202/347-0176) and 4801 Bethesda Ave., in Bethesda, Maryland (ℂ 301/986-1761).

B. Dalton   This is an all-purpose bookstore, heavy on the bestsellers and carrying magazines, too. Union Station. ℂ 202/289-1724. www.barnesandnoble.com. Metro: Union Station. There's another location in Chevy Chase Pavilion (ℂ 202/686-6542). See entries under "Malls" for more information about these locations.

Borders   With its overwhelming array of books, records, videos, and magazines, this outpost of the expanding chain has taken over the town. Many hardcover bestsellers are 30% off. The store often hosts performances by local musicians. 1800 L St. NW. ℂ 202/466-4999. www.borders.com. Metro: Farragut North. Other Borders stores in the District include 5333 Wisconsin Ave. NW (ℂ 202/686-8270), in upper northwest D.C.; and 600 14th St. NW (ℂ 202/737-1385).

Bridge Street Books   A small, serious shop specializing in politics, poetry, literature, history, philosophy, and publications you won't find elsewhere. Bestsellers and discounted books are not its specialty. 2814 Pennsylvania Ave. NW. ℂ 202/965-5200. Metro: Foggy Bottom, then take the Georgetown Metro Connection shuttle.

Chapters, A Literary Bookstore   Chapters is strong in new and backlisted fiction (no discounts, though), and is always hosting author readings. Tea is always available, and on Friday afternoons they break out the sherry and cookies. 1512 K St. NW. ℂ 202/347-5495. www.chaptersliterary.com. Metro: McPherson Square or Farragut North.

Kramerbooks & Afterwords Café *(Finds*   The first bookstore/cafe in Washington, maybe in this country, this place has launched countless romances. It's jammed and often noisy, stages live music Wednesday through Saturday evenings, and is open all night weekends. Paperback fiction takes up most of its inventory, but the store carries a little of everything. No discounts. 1517 Connecticut Ave. NW. ℂ 202/387-1400; www.kramers.com. Metro: Dupont Circle.

Olsson's Books and Records.   This 30-year-old independent, quality bookstore chain has about 60,000 to 70,000 books on its shelves. Members of its helpful staff know what they're talking about and will order books they don't have in stock. Some discounts are given on books, tapes, and CDs, and their regular prices are pretty good, too.

Besides this location, there are two other Olsson's bookstores in the District: at 418 Seventh St. NW (ℂ 202/638-7610), at 12th and F streets NW (ℂ 202/347-3686), and at 1307 19th St. NW (ℂ 202/785-1133). In the suburbs are five other Olsson's: in Bethesda, Maryland, at 7647 Old Georgetown Rd. (ℂ 301/652-3336); in Old Town Alexandria, Virginia, at 106 S. Union St. (ℂ 703/684-0077); in Arlington, Virginia, at 2111 Wilson Blvd. (ℂ 703/525-4227) and at 1735 N. Lynn St. (ℂ 703/812-2103); and at National Airport (ℂ 703/417-1087). The stores on 7th Street, in Alexandria, and on Wilson Boulevard in Arlington each have a creditable cafe, known for its loungy atmosphere, made-in-house selections, and artistic crowd. 12th and F sts. NW (℃ 202/347-3686), www.olssons.com. Metro: Metro Center.

Politics and Prose Bookstore   This is a two-story shop in a residential part of town. A devoted neighborhood clientele helped move this shop, book by book, across the street to larger quarters in 1990 (it's expanded again since then). It has vast offerings in literary fiction and nonfiction alike and an excellent, ever-expanding children's department. The shop hosts author readings nearly every night of the year. A warm, knowledgeable staff will help you find what you need. Downstairs is a cozy coffeehouse. Staff-recommended books are 20% off; otherwise discounts are available only to members. 5015 Connecticut Ave. NW. ℃ 202/ 364-1919. www.politics-prose.com. Metro: Van Ness–UDC, and transfer to an "L" bus to take you the ¾ mile from there.

Trover Shop   The only general-interest bookstore on Capitol Hill, Trover specializes in its political selections and its magazines. The store discounts 30% on the *Washington Post* hardcover fiction and nonfiction bestsellers. 221 Pennsylvania Ave. SE. ℃ 202/547-BOOK. www.trover.com. Metro: Capitol South.

OLD & USED BOOKS

Booked Up   An antiquarian bookstore (owned by author Larry McMurtry) in Georgetown, specializing in travel and literature. You can stumble upon some true collector's items here. 1204 31st St. NW. ℃ 202/965-3244. Metro: Foggy Bottom, then take the Georgetown Metro Connection shuttle.

Idle Time Books   This dusty, two-story treasure trove of used books in Adams-Morgan is strong on politics. It also sells postcards, greeting cards, and used records and newspapers. 2410 18th St. NW. ℃ 202/232-4774. www.abebooks.com/ home/idletime. Metro: Woodley Park–Zoo or Dupont Circle.

Second Story Books   If it's old, out of print, custom bound, or a small-press publication, this is where to find it. The store also specializes in used CDs and vinyl, and has an interesting collection of antique French and American advertising posters. 2000 P St. NW. ℃ 202/659-8884. www.secondstorybooks.com. Metro: Dupont Circle.

SPECIAL-INTEREST BOOKS

ADC Map and Travel Center   This newly renovated store sells street maps and atlases for the East Coast, from Philadelphia to Atlanta, and carries an extensive collection of maps and guidebooks for the entire world. Globes and atlases are also for sale. 1636 I St. NW. ℃ 800/544-2659 or 202/628-2608. www.adcmap. com. Metro: Farragut West or Farragut North.

American Institute of Architects Bookstore   This store carries books and gifts related to architecture. 1735 New York Ave. NW. ℃ 202/626-7475. Metro: Farragut West.

Back Stage   Having moved recently from its longtime Dupont Circle location, this store remains the headquarters for Washington's theatrical community, which buys its books, scripts, trades, and sheet music here. 545 8th St. SE. ℃ 202/ 544-5744. Metro: Eastern Market.

Franz Bader Bookstore   This store stocks books on art, art history, architecture, and photography, as well as exhibition catalogs. 1911 I St. NW. ℃ 202/337-5440. Metro: Farragut West or Farragut North.

Lambda Rising   It was a big deal when this gay and lesbian bookstore opened with a plate-glass window revealing its interior to passersby. Now it's an unofficial headquarters for the gay/lesbian/bi community, carrying every gay, lesbian, bisexual, and transgender book in print, as well as videos, music, and gifts. 1625 Connecticut Ave. NW. (© 202/462-6969. Metro: Dupont Circle.

National Museum of American History Giftshop   In this museum gift shop, you'll find a wonderful selection of books on American history and culture, including some for children. Constitution Ave. between 12th and 14th sts. NW. (© 202/357-1784. www.smithsonianstore.com. Metro: Federal Triangle or Smithsonian.

CAMERAS & FILM DEVELOPING

Photography is a big business in this image-conscious tourist town. A wide range of services and supplies, from inexpensive point-and-shoot cameras to deluxe German and Japanese equipment, is available at competitive prices. Some shops offer repair services and have multilingual staff.

Penn Camera Exchange   Across the street from the FBI Building, Penn Camera does a brisk trade with professionals and concerned amateurs. The store offers big discounts on major brand-name equipment, such as Olympus and Canon. Penn has been owned and operated by the Zweig family since 1953; its staff is quite knowledgeable, and its inventory wide-ranging. Their specialty is quality equipment and processing—not cheap, but worth it. 840 E St. NW. (© 202/347-5777. www.penncamera.com. Metro: Gallery Place or Metro Center. Also at 1015 18th St. NW ((© 202/785-7366).

Ritz Camera Centers   Ritz sells camera equipment for the average photographer and offers 1-hour film processing. Call for other locations; there are many throughout the area. 1740 Pennsylvania Ave. NW. (© 202/466-3470. www.ritzpix.com. Metro: Farragut West.

CRAFTS

A mano   Owner Adam Mahr frequently forages in Europe and returns with the unique handmade, imported French and Italian ceramics, linens, and other decorative accessories that you'll covet here. 1677 Wisconsin Ave. NW. (© 202/298-7200. www.amanoinc.com. Metro: Foggy Bottom, then take the Georgetown Metro Connection shuttle.

American Studio Plus   This store features exquisite contemporary handcrafted American ceramics and jewelry, plus international objets d'art. 2906 M St. NW. (© 202/965-3273. Metro: Foggy Bottom, then take the Georgetown Metro Connection shuttle.

Appalachian Spring   Country comes to Georgetown. This store sells pottery, jewelry, newly made pieced and appliqué quilts, stuffed dolls and animals, candles, rag rugs, handblown glassware, an incredible collection of kaleidoscopes, glorious weavings, and wooden kitchenware. Everything is made by hand in the United States. 1415 Wisconsin Ave. NW, at P St. (© 202/337-5780. Metro: Foggy Bottom, then take the Georgetown Metro Connection shuttle. There's another branch in Union Station ((© 202/682-0505).

Indian Craft Shop *(Finds*   The Indian Craft Shop has represented authentic Native American artisans since 1938, selling their hand-woven rugs and handcrafted baskets, jewelry, figurines, paintings, pottery, and other items. You need a photo ID to enter the building. Use the C Street entrance, which is the only one open to the public. Department of the Interior, 1849 C St. NW, Room 1023. (© 202/208-4056. Weekdays and the third Saturday of each month. www.indiancraftshop.com. Metro: Farragut West or Foggy Bottom.

The Phoenix Around since 1955, the Phoenix still sells those embroidered Mexican peasant blouses popular in hippie days; high-end Mexican folk and fine art; handcrafted sterling silver jewelry from Mexico and all over the world; clothing in natural fibers from Mexican and American designers like Eileen Fisher and Flax; collectors' quality masks; and decorative doodads in tin, brass, copper, and wood. 1514 Wisconsin Ave. NW. ✆ 202/338-4404. Metro: Foggy Bottom, then take the Georgetown Metro Connection shuttle.

Torpedo Factory Art Center Once a munitions factory, this three-story building built in 1918 now houses more than 83 working studios and the works of about 165 artists, who tend to their crafts before your very eyes, pausing to explain their techniques or to sell their pieces. Artworks include paintings, sculpture, ceramics, glasswork, and textiles. 105 N. Union St. ✆ 703/838-4565. www.torpedofactory.org. Metro: King St., then take the DASH bus (AT2, AT5, AT7) eastbound to the waterfront.

DISCOUNT SHOPPING

Discount shops in Washington are few and far between. Stores like Wal-Mart and Target are all in the far 'burbs. This list includes the best of the D.C. bunch, followed by a sampling of thrift, secondhand, and consignment stores, where inventory may be eclectic, but the prices are often low. Also check out the listing of flea markets, later in this section.

Filene's Basement *Value* This Boston-based store may have gone bankrupt at home but continues to be a hit in Washington, selling designer and famous-name clothes and accessories, and now home furnishings. 1133 Connecticut Ave. NW, downtown. ✆ 202/872-8430. www.filenesbasement.com.Metro: Farragut North. Also at 529 14th St. NW, in the Shops at National Place complex (✆ 202/638-4110), and in the Mazza Gallerie in upper northwest Washington, 5300 Wisconsin Ave. NW (✆ 202/966-0208).

Potomac Mills Mall *Value* When you're stuck in the traffic that always clogs this section of I-95, you may wonder if a trip to Potomac Mills is worth it. Believe it or not, this place attracts more visitors than any other site in the Washington area; it's the largest indoor outlet mall around, with more than 225 shops such as Saks Fifth Avenue, Nordstrom Rack, IKEA, Calvin Klein, and BCBG. 25 miles south on I-95. Accessible by car, or by shuttle bus leaving from designated places throughout the area, including Dupont Circle and Metro Center. Call ✆ 800/VA-MILLS or 703/643-1770 for information about Potomac Mills; call ✆ 703/551-1050 for information about the shuttle-bus service. www.potomacmills.com.

THRIFT/CONSIGNMENT/SECONDHAND SHOPS

Christ Child Opportunity Shop *Value* Proceeds from merchandise sales go to children's charities. Among the first-floor items—all donations—are the usual thrift-shop jumble of jewelry, clothes, shoes, hats, and odds and ends. Upstairs, higher-quality merchandise is left on consignment; it's more expensive, but if you know antiques, you might find bargains in jewelry, silver, china, quilts, and other items. Closed in August. 1427 Wisconsin Ave. NW. ✆ 202/333-6635. Metro: Foggy Bottom, then take the Georgetown Metro Connection shuttle.

Secondhand Rose *Value* This upscale second-floor consignment shop specializes in designer merchandise. Creations by Chanel, Armani, Donna Karan, Calvin Klein, Yves Saint-Laurent, Ungaro, Ralph Lauren, and others are sold at about a third of the original price. A stunning Scaasi black-velvet and yellow-satin ball gown might go for $400 (from $1,200 new); Yves Saint-Laurent pumps in perfect condition can be had for as little as $45. Everything is in style, in season, and in excellent condition. Secondhand Rose is also a great place to shop for gorgeous furs, designer shoes and bags, and costume jewelry. 1516 Wisconsin Ave. NW, between P St. and Volta Place. ℂ 202/337-3378. Metro: Foggy Bottom, then take the Georgetown Metro Connection shuttle.

Secondi Inc.   On the second floor of a building right above Starbucks is this high-style consignment shop that sells women's clothing and accessories, including designer suits, evening wear, and more casual items, with nothing older than 2 years. 1702 Connecticut Ave. NW. ℂ 202/667-1122. Metro: Dupont Circle.

FARMER'S & FLEA MARKETS

Alexandria Farmers' Market   The oldest continuously operating farmers' market in the country (since 1752), this market offers the usual assortment of locally grown fruits and vegetables, along with delectable baked goods, cut flowers, and plants. Open Saturday mornings from 5 to 9:30am. 301 King St., at Market Square in front of the city hall, in Alexandria. ℂ 703/838-4770. Metro: King St., then take the DASH bus (AT2, AT5, AT7) eastbound to Market Square.

Dupont Circle FreshFarm Market *(Kids*   Fresh flowers, produce, eggs, and cheeses are for sale here. The market also features kids' activities and guest appearances by chefs and owners of some of Washington's best restaurants: Bis, Vidalia, Restaurant Nora, Tosca, and 1789. Held Sundays from 9am to 1pm, April through December. On 20th St. NW, between Q St. and Massachusetts Ave., and in the adjacent Riggs Bank parking lot. ℂ 202/331-7300. Metro: Dupont Circle, Q St. exit.

Eastern Market *(Value*   This is the one everyone knows about, even if they've never been here. Located on Capitol Hill, Eastern Market is an inside/outside bazaar of stalls, where greengrocers, butchers, bakers, farmers, artists, craftspeople, florists, and other merchants sell their wares on weekends. Saturday morning is the best time to go. On Sunday, the food stalls become a flea market. Tuesday through Saturday 7am to 6pm, Sunday 9am to 4pm. 225 7th St. SE, between North Carolina Ave. and C St. SE. ℂ 202/546-2698. Metro: Eastern Market.

Georgetown Flea Market *(Finds*   Grab a coffee at Starbucks across the lane and get ready to barter. The Georgetown Flea Market is frequented by all types of Washingtonians looking for a good deal—they often get it—on antiques, painted furniture, vintage clothing, and decorative garden urns. Nearly 80 vendors sell their wares here. Open year-round on Sunday from 9am to 5pm.

The school recently converted part of its parking lot into an athletic field, sending another 50 of its original 100 vendors to set up at a new location: Georgetown Flea Market at U Street, 1345 U St. NW, which is open every Saturday and Sunday from 9am to 5pm. In the Hardy Middle School parking lot bordering Wisconsin Ave., between S and T sts. NW. Metro: Foggy Bottom, then take the Georgetown Metro Connection shuttle.

Montgomery County Farm Woman's Cooperative Market   Vendors set up inside every Saturday year-round from 7am to about 3:30pm to sell preserves, homegrown veggies, cut flowers, slabs of bacon and sausages, and mouthwatering pies, cookies, and breads; there's an abbreviated version on Wednesday. Outside, on Saturday and Wednesday, are flea-market vendors selling rugs, tablecloths, furniture, sunglasses—everything. 7155 Wisconsin Ave., in Bethesda. ℂ 301/652-2291. Metro: Bethesda.

FASHION

See also "Discount Shopping," above, and "Shoes," later in this section.

CHILDREN'S CLOTHING

One-of-a-kind children's stores don't do well in downtown Washington. But if your youngster has spilled grape juice all over his favorite outfit and you need a suitable replacement, you can always head to **Hecht's** (p. 227) or to the nearest **Gap Kids:** in Georgetown at 1266 Wisconsin Ave. NW. (℃ **202/333-2411**) or at 2006 Pennsylvania Ave. NW (℃ **202/429-8711**). Also check out these two stores:

April Cornell *(Kids* Too precious for words, this store is for girls only (and their moms), selling lots of pretty, flowing, flowery dresses, plus linens and nightgowns. 3278 M St. NW. ℃ 202/625-7887. www.aprilcornell.com. Metro: Foggy Bottom, then take the Georgetown Metro Connection shuttle.

Kid's Closet *(Kids* Its storefront display of cute kids' clothes stands out among the bank and restaurant facades in this downtown block; inside are clothes and accessories mostly with brand names like Osh Kosh and Little Me. 1226 Connecticut Ave. NW. ℃ 202/429-9247. Metro: Dupont Circle.

MEN'S CLOTHING

Local outlets of **Banana Republic** are at Wisconsin and M streets in Georgetown (℃ **202/333-2554**) and F and 13th streets NW (℃ **202/638-2724**). **Eddie Bauer** has stores at 3040 M St. NW (℃ **202/342-2121**) in Georgetown, or on Wisconsin Avenue NW in Friendship Heights (℃ **202/686-9930**).

Beau Monde This boutique sells mostly Italian-made clothes, in all the latest styles, including suits, sports coats, ties, slacks, shirts, and accessories. International Square, 1814 K St. NW. ℃ 202/466-7070. Metro: Farragut West.

Britches of Georgetowne See where Washington men go for that straight-laced look. Britches sells moderately priced to expensive dress apparel, both designer wear and from its own label. Its sportswear selections are more extensive than in the past. 1247 Wisconsin Ave. NW. ℃ 202/338-3330. www.britchesusa.com. Metro: Foggy Bottom, then take the Georgetown Metro Connection shuttle. Also at 1776 K St. NW (℃ 202/347-8994).

Brooks Brothers Brooks sells traditional men's clothes, as well as the fine line of Peal's English shoes. This store made the news as the place where Monica Lewinsky bought a tie for President Clinton. It also sells an extensive line of women's clothes. 1201 Connecticut Ave. NW. ℃ 202/659-4650. www.brooksbrothers.com. Metro: Dupont Circle or Farragut North. Other locations are at Potomac Mills (p. 234), at National Airport (℃ 703/417-0602), and at 5500 Wisconsin Ave., in Chevy Chase, MD (℃ 301/654-8202).

Burberry's Here you'll find those plaid-lined trench coats, of course, along with well-tailored but conservative English clothing for men and women. Hot items include cashmere sweaters and camel's hair duffel coats for men. 1155 Connecticut Ave. NW. ℃ 202/463-3000. Metro: Farragut North.

Thomas Pink For those who like beautifully made, bright-colored shirts, this new branch of the London-based high-end establishment should please. The store also sells ties, boxer shorts, women's shirts, cufflinks, and other accessories. 1127 Connecticut Ave. NW (inside the Mayflower Hotel). ℃ 202/223-5390. www.thomaspink. com. Metro: Farragut North.

Urban Outfitters For the latest in casual attire, from fatigue pants to tube tops. The shop has a floor of women's clothes, a floor of men's clothes, as well as housewares, inflatable chairs, books, cards, and candles. 3111 M St. NW. ℭ 202/342-1012. www.urbn.com. Metro: Foggy Bottom, then take the Georgetown Metro Connection shuttle.

WOMEN'S CLOTHING

Washington women have many more clothing stores to choose from than men. Stores selling classic designs dominate, including **Ann Taylor,** at Union Station (ℭ **202/371-8010**), 1720 K St. NW (ℭ **202/466-3544**), 600 13th St. NW (ℭ **202/737-0325**), and Georgetown Park, 3222 M St. NW (ℭ **202/338-5290**); and **Talbots,** at 1122 Connecticut Ave. NW (ℭ **202/887-6973**) and Georgetown Park, 3222 M St. NW (ℭ **202/338-3510**). Beneath their modest apparel, however, Washington women like to wear racy **Victoria's Secret** lingerie—you'll find stores in Union Station (ℭ **202/682-0686**) and Georgetown Park (ℭ **202/965-5457**), as well as at Connecticut and L streets NW (ℭ **202/293-7530**).

See "Men's Clothing," immediately above, for locations of Banana Republic, Eddie Bauer, Brooks Brothers, and Urban Outfitters.

Hip boutiques and upscale shops proliferate as well:

all about jane   The independent-minded will enjoy pawing through the animal print, plaid, tweed, and colorful fashions that are making this newcomer a success in Adams-Morgan. 2438½ 18th St. NW. ℭ 202/797-9710. www.allaboutjane.net. Metro: Woodley Park, then a 20-min. walk.

Betsey Johnson   New York's flamboyant flower-child designer personally decorated the bubble-gum pink walls in her Georgetown shop. Her sexy, offbeat play-dress-up styles are great party and club clothes for the young and the still-skinny young at heart. 1319 Wisconsin Ave. NW. ℭ 202/338-4090. www.betseyjohnson.com. Metro: Foggy Bottom, then take the Georgetown Metro Connection shuttle.

Betsy Fisher   A walk past the store is all it takes to know that this shop is a tad different. Its windows and racks show off whimsically feminine fashions by new American designers. 1224 Connecticut Ave. NW. ℭ 202/785-1975. www.betsyfisher.com. Metro: Dupont Circle.

Chanel Boutique   A modest selection of Chanel's signature designs, accessories, and jewelry, at immodest prices. 1455 Pennsylvania Ave. NW, in the courtyard of the Willard Inter-Continental Hotel. ℭ 202/638-5055. Metro: Metro Center.

Commander Salamander   Loud music, young crowd, and funky clothes. Commander Salamander has a little bit of everything, including designer items (Dolce & Gabbana for instance), some of which are quite affordable. Too cool. 1420 Wisconsin Ave. NW. ℭ 202/337-2265. Metro: Foggy Bottom, then a 25-min. walk.

French Connection   This is the only Washington-area store of the London-based chain, and good for clothes that are hip but not outrageous. 1229 Wisconsin Ave. NW. ℭ 202/965-4690. www.frenchconnection.com. Metro: Foggy Bottom, then take the Georgetown Metro Connection shuttle.

Niagara   You enter through the music store, DCCD (see "Music," later in this section), and descend a couple of steps to reach this defiantly different shop selling clothes by such designers as Colovos and Milk Fed (Sofia Coppola's company). Tiny place, big bucks. 2423 18th St. NW. ℭ 202/332-7474. Metro: Woodley Park, then a 20 min. walk.

Pirjo   Come here for the funky, baggy, and pretty creations of European designers like Marimekko, Rundholz, and Lillith. Styles range from casual to dressy. Pirjo sells elegant jewelry to boot. 1044 Wisconsin Ave. NW, in Georgetown. (C) 202/337-1390. www.pirjos.com. Metro: Foggy Bottom, then take the Georgetown Metro Connection shuttle.

Rizik Brothers   In business since 1908, this downtown high-fashion store sells designs by Caroline Herrera, Oscar de la Renta, Geoffrey Beene, and other European and American designers. 1100 Connecticut Ave. NW. (C) 202/223-4050. www. riziks.com. Metro: Farragut North.

Saks-Jandel   This store displays elegant day and evening wear by major European and American designers—Giorgio Armani, Louis Féraud, Christian Dior, Valentino, Isaac Mizrahi (this was the site of the designer's promo for his movie, *Unzipped*), John Galliano, and many others. Saks-Jandel has an international clientele. 5510 Wisconsin Ave., Chevy Chase, MD. (C) 301/652-2250. Metro: Friendship Heights. Also at the Watergate, 2522 Virginia Ave. NW ((C) 202/337-4200).

GIFTS/SOUVENIRS
See also "Crafts," earlier in this section.

Chocolate Moose *(Finds*   My husband endears himself to me and our daughters when he brings home gifts at Valentine's Day and other occasions from this shop: chunky, transparent, red heart-shaped earrings, wacky cards, paperweight snow globes with figurines inside, candies, eccentric clothing, and other funny, lovely, and useful presents. 1800 M St. NW. (C) 202/463-0992. Metro: Farragut North.

The Left Bank   Francophiles and others will surely find something to take home from this collection of mostly French and Belgian novelties: Madeline lunch boxes, pretty yellow mugs for drinking *chocolat,* French travel posters, and porcelain figurines of beloved French cartoon characters, like Asterix and Tintin. 1627 Connecticut Ave. NW. (C) 202/518-4000. Metro: Dupont Circle.

Made in America   Union Station is full of gift shops, actually, but stop here if you want to pick up a baseball cap with a "DEA," "CIA," or "Police SWAT" insignia on its bill; White House guest towels; and other impress-the-folks-back-home items. Union Station. (C) 202/842-0540. www.americastore.com. Metro: Union Station. Or save your shopping for the airport; Made in America has 1 location at National ((C) 703/417-1782) and 2 at Dulles (Terminal B: (C) 703/572-2543; Terminal C: (C) 703/572-6058).

GOURMET GOODIES TO GO
Demanding jobs and hectic schedules leave Washingtonians less and less time to prepare their own meals. Or so they say. At any rate, a number of fine-food shops and bakeries are happy to come to the rescue. Even the busiest bureaucrat can find the time to pop into one of these gourmet shops for a movable feast.

See also "Farmer's & Flea Markets," earlier in this section.

Bread Line *(Finds*   Owner Mark Furstenberg is credited with revolutionizing bread baking in Washington. He started the Marvelous Market chain (see below), though he has since bowed out. At Bread Line, he concentrates on selling freshly baked loaves of wheat bread, flatbreads, baguettes, and more; sandwiches like the roast pork bun or the muffaletta; tasty soups; and desserts such as bread puddings, pear tarts, and delicious cookies. Seating is available. 1751 Pennsylvania Ave. NW. (C) 202/822-8900. Metro: Farragut West or Farragut North.

Dean & Deluca   This famed New York store has set down roots in Washington, in a historic Georgetown building that was once an open-air market. Though it is now closed in, this huge space still feels airy, with its high ceiling and windows on all sides. You'll pay top prices, but the quality is impressive—charcuterie, fresh fish, produce, cheeses, prepared sandwiches and cold pasta salads, hot-ticket desserts, like crème brûlée and tiramisu, and California wines. Also on sale are housewares; on site is an espresso bar/cafe. 3276 M St. NW. © **202/342-2500.** www.deandeluca.com. Metro: Foggy Bottom. There's 1 other cafe location, at 1299 Pennsylvania Ave. NW (© 202/628-8155).

Firehook Bakery   Known for its sourdough baguettes, apple-walnut bread, fresh fruit tarts, and, at its Farragut Square store, 912 17th St. NW (© **202/429-2253**), for sandwiches like smoked chicken on sesame semolina bread. 1909 Q St. NW. © **202/588-9296.** www.firehook.com. Metro: Dupont Circle. Also at 3241 M St. NW (© 202/625-6247), at 3411 Connecticut Ave. NW (© 202/362-2253) and at 2 locations in Alexandria, Virginia.

Lawson's Gourmet   Sitting at Lawson's cluster of outside tables and chairs, you'll see all of Washington pass by, from sharply dressed lawyers to bohemian artists and panhandlers. You can buy elaborate sandwiches made to order and very nice desserts, wines, breads, and salads. 1350 Connecticut Ave. NW. © **202/775-0400.** Metro: Dupont Circle. Also at 1350 I St. (© 202/789-1440), 1776 I St. (© 202/296-3200), and Metro Center, 601 13th St. NW (© 202/393-5500).

Marvelous Market   First there were the breads: sourdough, baguettes, olive, rosemary, croissants, scones. Now, there are things to spread on the bread, including smoked salmon mousse and tapenade; pastries to die for, from gingerbread to flourless chocolate cake; and prepared foods, such as soups, empanadas, and pasta salads. The breakfast spread on Sunday mornings is sinful, and individual items, like the croissants, are tastier and less expensive here than at other bakeries. The location is grand, with 18th-century chandeliers, an antique cedar bar, and a small number of tables. 1511 Connecticut Ave. NW. © **202/332-3690.** Also at 3217 P St. NW (© 202/333-2591) and 5035 Connecticut Ave. NW (© 202/686-4040).

JEWELRY

Beadazzled   The friendly staff helps you assemble your own affordable jewelry from an eye-boggling array of beads and artifacts. The store also sells textiles, woodcarvings, and other crafts from around the world. 1507 Connecticut Ave. NW. © **202/265-BEAD.** www.beadazzled.net. Metro: Dupont Circle.

Chas Schwartz & Son   In business since 1888, Chas Schwartz specializes in diamonds and sapphires, rubies and emeralds, and is one of the few distributors of Hidalgo jewelry (enameled rings and bracelets). The professional staff also repairs watches and jewelry. 1400 F St. NW, or enter through the Willard Hotel, at 1401 Pennsylvania Ave. NW. © **202/737-4757.** Metro: Metro Center. There's another branch at the Mazza Gallerie (© 202/363-5432); Metro: Friendship Heights.

Tiffany & Co.   Tiffany is known for exquisite diamonds and other jewelry that can cost hundreds of thousands of dollars. But you may not know that the store carries less expensive items as well, like $35 candlesticks. Tiffany will engrave, too. Other items include tabletop gifts and fancy glitz: china, crystal, flatware, and a bridal registry service. 5500 Wisconsin Ave., Chevy Chase, MD. © **301/657-8777.** Metro: Friendship Heights.

Tiny Jewel Box   The first place Washingtonians go for estate and antique jewelry, but the six-story store next to the Mayflower hotel sells the pieces of many designers, from Links of London to Christian Tse, as well as crystal and other house gifts. 1147 Connecticut Ave. NW. © **202/393-2747.** www.tinyjewelbox.com. Metro: Farragut North.

MALLS

Also see the listing for **Potomac Mills** on p. 234.

Chevy Chase Pavilion   This is a manageably sized mall with about 25 stores and restaurants, anchored by an Embassy Suites Hotel. The inside is unusually pretty, with three levels winding around a skylit atrium. Stores include a two-level Pottery Barn, Hold Everything, Talbots, Georgette Klinger, and Country Road Australia. The Cheesecake Factory, Starbucks, and a food court are among the dining options. 5335 Wisconsin Ave. NW. © 202/686-5335. Metro: Friendship Heights.

Fashion Center at Pentagon City   Nordstrom and Macy's are the biggest attractions in this elegant five-story shoppers' paradise. There's also the Ritz-Carlton Hotel where Ken Starr nabbed Monica Lewinsky, multiplex theaters, and a sprawling food court. Williams-Sonoma, Crate & Barrel, and Kenneth Cole are among the more than 170 shops. 1400 S. Hayes St., Arlington, VA. © 703/415-2400. www.shopsimon.com. Metro: Pentagon City.

Mazza Gallerie   A massive renovation completed in spring 2000 gave the mall a new look inside and out, added a nine-screen theater, expanded its Williams-Sonoma store, and generally revamped it. Neiman Marcus still anchors the mall, and stores like Ann Taylor and Harriet Kassman remain. 5100 Wisconsin Ave. NW. © 202/966-6114. www.mazzagallerie.net. Metro: Friendship Heights.

Pavilion at the Old Post Office   This is mainly a tourist trap with souvenir shops and a food court. Noontime concerts are a draw, as is the view of the city from the building's clock tower, 315 feet up. 1100 Pennsylvania Ave. NW. © 202/289-4224. www.oldpostofficedc.com. Metro: Federal Triangle.

Ronald Reagan Washington National Airport   Allow extra time before your flight and you can do all of your souvenir shopping here. The 100 stores include Victoria's Secret, Easy Spirit shoes, and gift shop outlets of the Smithsonian, the National Zoo, and the U.S. Capitol Historical Society. As we went to press, authorities had closed National Airport in the wake of the terrorist attack on the Pentagon. While it seems likely that National will reopen soon, it's impossible to state that with certainty, or to predict the length of its closing as of this writing. Arlington, VA. © 703/417-8600. www.mwaa.com/National.

Shops at Georgetown Park   This is a deluxe mall, where you'll see the beautiful people shopping for beautiful things. Ann Taylor, Caché, J. Crew, and Polo/Ralph Lauren are just a few of the high-end stores. Circuit City Express, Sharper Image, and Crabtree & Evelyn are here too. If you have kids, take them to FAO Schwarz or the Store of Knowledge.

An Old Town Trolley ticket booth (see chapter 7) is on the premises. There are several restaurants, including Clyde's (see p. 157 for details), gourmet emporium/cafe Dean & Deluca, and the parklike Canal Walk Café Food Court. 3222 M St. NW. © 202/298-5577. www.shopsatgeorgetownpark.com. Metro: Foggy Bottom, then take the Georgetown Metro Connection shuttle.

Shops at National Place   National Place has more than 75 specialty shops and eateries, including Casual Corner, Filene's Basement discount department store, and an international food court. 1331 Pennsylvania Ave. NW. (enter through the J. W. Marriott Hotel or at F St., between 13th and 14th sts.). © 202/662-1250. Metro: Metro Center.

Tysons Corner Center and Tysons Corner II, The Galleria   Facing each other across Chain Bridge Road, these two gigantic malls could lead to shopper's overload. Tysons Corner Center, the first and less expensive, has Nordstrom,

ⓒ Museum Shopping

Just what kinds of gifts can you find in museums, anyway? Last year, at Christmastime, I decided to find out. Shunning the malls, I turned to Washington museums and landmarks for all of my holiday shopping, and brought home a bounty of unique presents that (I'm pretty sure) everyone liked. Here's a little of what I gleaned:

The **National Museum of American History store** has an outstanding collection of books, CDs, and tapes (CDs from the Ken Burns PBS special on Jazz for one of my sisters, a CD of old baseball tunes for my 6-year-old nephew), but also a lot of junky trinkets. Look to the **Library of Congress** for beautiful stationery and unusual books (I chose a book on Bach for my aunt, a leather-bound journal for my brother-in-law), but don't buy the jewelry, which is overpriced and unattractive. The **Textile Museum shop** sells exquisite and one-of-a-kind clothes and accessories (I snagged a silk purse from Japan for one sister and a Turkish tote bag for another), but you can expect to pay a bundle. Overall, the **National Building Museum** offers the best inventory for its surprising, useful, and cleverly designed housewares and interesting games. Here I bought heavy bookends embossed with a Celtic design for my mom and a museum board game for my niece; I still regret not grabbing the Koziol plastic caterpillar CD rack.

Other things to note: The largest museum shop is at the **National Air and Space Museum** (3 floors!); and the shop at the **Smithsonian's Arts and Industries Building** carries a selection of the most popular items from all of the other Smithsonian shops.

You can check out some of the stores' merchandise online ahead of time: Point your browser to **www.smithsonianstore.com** (for the Smithsonian shops), **www.nbm.org/shop** (for the National Building Museum), and **www.loc.gov**, and click on "shops," for the Library of Congress. The Textile Museum website lists only its book titles. For the Web addresses of other museums, see their individual listings in chapter 7.

Bloomingdale's, and JCPenney, and specialty stores, such as Abercrombie & Fitch and Crabtree & Evelyn. The Galleria has Macy's, Saks Fifth Avenue, and more than 100 upscale boutiques. 1960 Chain Bridge Rd., McLean, VA. ⓒ 703/893-9400. www.shoptysons.com. Tysons Corner II, The Galleria, 2001 International Dr., McLean, VA. ⓒ 703/827-7700. www.shoptysonsgalleria.com. Metro: West Falls Church; take shuttle.

Union Station   One of the most popular tourist stops in Washington, Union Station boasts magnificent architecture and more than 120 shops, including the Ann Taylor, Jos. A. Banks, and Appalachian Spring. Among the places to eat are America, B. Smith, and an impressive food court. There's also a nine-screen movie-theater complex. 50 Massachusetts Ave. NE. ⓒ 202/289-1908. www.unionstationdc.com. Metro: Union Station.

White Flint Mall   Another Bloomingdale's, another long trip in the car or on the Metro; but once you're there, you can shop, take in a movie, and dine cheaply or well. Notable stores include Lord & Taylor, a huge Borders, Ann Taylor, and

Coach. 11301 Rockville Pike, Kensington, MD. ℂ 301/468-5777. www.shopwhiteflint.com. Metro: White Flint, then take the free White Flint shuttle, which runs every 12–15 min.

MISCELLANEOUS

Al's Magic Shop (Kids)   The drinks in our house always come with flies frozen inside the ice cubes (OK, so the flies are plastic), thanks to my daughter's last visit to this first-rate novelty store, where prestidigitator and local character Al Cohen is only too happy to demonstrate his latest magic trick or practical joke. 1012 Vermont Ave. NW. ℂ 202/789-2800. www.alsmagic.com. Metro: McPherson Square.

Fahrneys Pens, Inc.   People come from all over to purchase the finest fountain pens, or to have them engraved or repaired. In business since 1929, Fahrneys is an institution, selling Montblanc, Cross, Waterman, the best in the business. 1317 F St. NW (between 13th and 14th sts.). ℂ 800/624-7367. www.fahrneyspens. com. Metro: Metro Center.

Ginza, "Things Japanese"   Everything Japanese, from incense and kimonos to futons to Zen rock gardens. 1721 Connecticut Ave. NW. ℂ 202/331-7991. www.ginza online.com. Metro: Dupont Circle.

Hats in the Belfry   In business for 25 years now, this hat store features designer hats, floppy hats, straw hats, Panama hats, all sorts of hats, for men and women, some for children, and some handbags. Go ahead, try some on. 1237 Wisconsin Ave. NW. ℂ 202/342-2006. www.hatsinthebelfry.com. Metro: Foggy Bottom, with a 25-min. walk.

Home Rule (Value)   Unique housewares; bath, kitchen, and office supplies; and gifts cram this tiny new store. You'll see everything from French milled soap to martini glasses. 1807 14th St. NW (at S St.). ℂ 202/797-5544. www.homerule.com. Metro: U St.–Cardozo.

MUSIC

See also the listing for **Olsson's Books and Records** on p. 231.

Borders   Besides being a great bookstore, Borders offers the best prices in town for CDs and tapes, and a wide range of music. 1800 L St. NW. ℂ 202/466-4999. Metro: Farragut North. (See other locations under "Books," earlier in this chapter.)

DCCD   This store sells new and used CDs, new records, and new and used video games. Known best as Washington's independent rock record store, DCCD features in-store performances by local and national bands. 2423 18th St. NW. ℂ 202/588-1810. Metro: Woodley Park, then a 20-min. walk.

DJ Hut   Everything for lovers of hip-hop, reggae, R&B, and go-go. 2010 P St. NW, 2nd floor. ℂ 202/659-2010. Metro: Dupont Circle.

Melody Record Shop   CDs, cassettes, and tapes, including new releases, are discounted here, plus the shop always has a table of unused but not newly released CDs that sell for about $10 each. Melody offers a wide variety of rock, classical, jazz, pop, show, and folk music, as well as a vast number of international selections. This is also a good place to shop for discounted portable electronic equipment, blank tapes, and cassettes. Its knowledgeable staff is a plus. 1623 Connecticut Ave. NW. ℂ 202/232-4002. www.melodyrecords.com. Metro: Dupont Circle, Q St. exit.

Tower Records   When you need a record at midnight on Christmas Eve, you go to Tower. This large, funky store, across the street from George Washington University, has a wide choice of records, cassettes, and CDs in every category—but the prices are high. 2000 Pennsylvania Ave. NW. ℂ 202/331-2400. Metro: Foggy Bottom.

POLITICAL MEMORABILIA

Capitol Coin and Stamp Co. Inc. A museum of political memorabilia—pins, posters, banners—and all of it is for sale. This is also a fine resource for the endangered species of coin or stamp collectors. 1100 17th St. NW, Suite 503. (C) 202/296-0400. www.capitalcoin.com. Metro: Farragut North.

Political Americana This is another great place to pick up souvenirs. The store sells political novelty items, books, bumper stickers, old campaign buttons, and historical memorabilia. At 14th St. and Pennsylvania Ave. NW. (C) 202/547-1685. www.politicalamericana.com. Metro: Metro Center.

SHOES

For men's dress shoes, try **Brooks Brothers** (p. 236). There are local outlets of **Foot Locker** at Union Station ((C) 202/289-8364), 3221 M St. NW ((C) 202/333-7640); and 1331 Pennsylvania Ave. NW (the Shops at National Place) ((C) 202/783-2093). **Nine West** sells women's shoes from locations at Union Station ((C) 202/216-9490), 1008 Connecticut Ave. NW ((C) 202/452-9163); and 1227 Wisconsin Ave. NW ((C) 202/337-7256).

Comfort One Shoes Despite its unhip name, this store sells a great selection of popular styles for both men and women, including Doc Martens, Birkenstocks, and Ecco. You can always find something that actually feels comfortable. 1636 Connecticut Ave. NW. (C) 202/328-3141. www.comfortoneshoes.com. Metro: Dupont Circle. Also at 1607 Connecticut Ave. NW ((C) 202/667-5300), 3222 M St. NW ((C) 202/333-3399), and other locations.

Steve Madden The music's so loud, you may not be able to hear a word the salesperson says. This is the city's only Steve Madden location, the women's shoe store that's really popular among the college-age crowd for its chunky platforms, sandals, and thongs. 3109 M St. NW. (C) 202/342-6195. Metro: Foggy Bottom, then take the Georgetown Metro Connection shuttle.

TOYS

The museum gift shops are really your best bet for children's gifts. One other suggestion:

Flights of Fancy (Kids) Picture books, Playmobil toys, board games, and assorted other toys and amusements cram this small store. Union Station. (C) 202/371-9800. Metro: Union Station.

WINE & SPIRITS

Calvert Woodley Liquors This is a large store with a friendly staff, nice selections, and good cheeses (about 300 to choose from) and other foods to go along with your drinks. 4339 Connecticut Ave. NW. (C) 202/966-4400. Metro: Van Ness–UDC.

Central Liquor (Value) This is like a clearinghouse for liquor: Its great volume allows the store to offer the best prices in town on wines and liquor. The store carries more than 250 single-malt scotches. 917 F St. NW. (C) 800/835-7928 or 202/737-2800. Metro: Gallery Place.

MacArthur Liquor With a knowledgeable and enthusiastic staff, and an extensive and reasonably priced selection of excellent wines, both imported and domestic, this shop is always busy. 4844 MacArthur Blvd. NW. (C) 202/338-1433. www.bassins.com. Bus: D4 from Dupont Circle.

9

Washington, D.C., After Dark

Contrary to popular belief, political theater is not the only show in town. All through the day, as government officials deliberate headline-making decisions, and members of Congress strut across the C-Span stage, Washington's cultural arts professionals are also hard at work, preparing their entertainments and diversions for Washington's hardworking and weary, and for visitors like you. No matter what happens by day, by night the show must go on, and it does, in art houses, nightclubs, bars, and theaters all over town.

Washington's best nightlife venues are making their own headlines. The *Wall Street Journal* calls our Shakespeare Theatre "the nation's foremost Shakespeare company." According to the *New York Times,* Blues Alley is "the nation's finest jazz and supper club." The trade publication *Pollstar* names the 9:30 Club the country's highest

attended nightclub, and regularly rates it among the best in the U.S. Even our bars garner big attention, like Madam's Organ, which *Playboy* magazine has called one of the top 25 bars in the country; or the Henley Park Hotel's Blue Bar, which the *New York Times Sophisticated Traveler* magazine recently described as "an especially appealing outpost."

So read over the listings that follow to see which forms of entertainment most appeal. For up-to-date schedules of events, from live music and theater, to children's programs and flower shows, check the Friday "Weekend" section of the *Washington Post,* or go online, and browse the *Post*'s nightlife information at **www.washington post.com**. The *City Paper,* available free at restaurants, bookstores, and other places around town, is another good source.

TICKETS

TICKETplace, Washington's only discount day-of-show ticket outlet, has one location: in the Old Post Office Pavilion, 1100 Pennsylvania Ave. NW (Metro: Federal Triangle). Call © **202/TICKETS** (842-5387), www.ticketplace.org, for information. You must purchase the tickets in person. Enter the pavilion through its South Plaza entrance, on 12th Street NW, where you must pass through metal detectors to enter the building. On the day of performance only (except Sun and Mon; see below), you can buy half-price tickets (with cash, select debit and credit cards, or traveler's checks) to performances with tickets still available at most major Washington-area theaters and concert halls, as well as for performances of the opera, ballet, and other events. TICKETplace is open Tuesday through Saturday from 11am to 6pm; half-price tickets for Sunday and Monday shows are sold on Saturday. Though tickets are half price, you have to pay a service charge of 10% of the full face value of the ticket. TICKETplace is a service of the Cultural Alliance of Washington.

Full-price tickets for most performances in town can be bought through **Ticketmaster** (© **202/432-SEAT;** www.ticketmaster.com), if you're willing to pay a hefty service charge. Purchase tickets to Washington theatrical, musical, and other events before you leave home by going online or by calling © **800/ 551-SEAT.** Or you can wait until you get here and visit one of Ticketmaster's 18 locations throughout the city, including the TICKETplace outlet in the Old Post Office Pavilion (see above); Hecht's Department Store, 12th and G streets NW (Metro: Metro Center); George Washington University's Marvin Center, across from Lisner Auditorium, at 21st Street and H Street NW (Metro: Foggy Bottom); the DC Visitor Center in the Ronald Reagan Building, at 1300 Pennsylvania Ave. NW (Metro: Federal Triangle); and the MCI Center (Metro: Gallery Place). When you pay by credit card at TICKETplace and Ticketmaster, you have to show an ID to prove you are the credit card holder.

Another similar ticket outlet is **Tickets.com** (formerly Protix). You can order tickets by calling © **800/955-5566** or 703/218-6500, or by accessing its website at www.tickets.com.

1 The Performing Arts

Washington's performing arts scene has an international reputation. Almost anything on Broadway has either been previewed here or will eventually come here. Better yet, D.C. is home to truly excellent and renowned repertory theater troupes, and to fine ballet, opera, and symphony companies. Rock bands, headliner comedians, and jazz/folk/gospel/R&B/alternative and other musical groups make Washington a must-stop on their tours.

THE TOP THEATERS

Arena Stage   This outpost on the unattractive Washington waterfront is worth seeking out, despite its poor location. (Dine at a downtown restaurant, then drive or take a taxi here; or you can take the Metro, but be careful walking the block or so to the theater.)

Founded by the brilliant Zelda Fichandler in 1950, the Arena Stage is home to one of the oldest acting ensembles in the nation. Several works nurtured here have moved to Broadway, and many graduates have gone on to commercial stardom, including Ned Beatty, James Earl Jones, and Jane Alexander.

Arena presents eight productions annually on two stages: the **Fichandler** (a theater-in-the-round) and the smaller, fan-shaped **Kreeger.** In addition, the Arena houses the **Old Vat,** a space used for new play readings and special productions.

The 2002–03 September-to-June season includes adaptations of Thornton Wilder's first novel, *Theophilus North,* and of Molière's *The Misanthrope,* August Wilson's *Ma Rainey's Black Bottom,* Lanford Wilson's *Book of Days,* Rodgers and Hammerstein's musical *South Pacific,* and Wendy Wasserstein's *An American Daughter.* The theater has always championed new plays and playwrights and is committed to producing works from America's diverse cultures, as well as to reinterpreting the works of past masters. 1101 6th St. SW (at Maine Ave.). © 202/488-3300. www.arenastage.org. Tickets $27–$50; discounts available for students, people with disabilities, groups, and senior citizens. Metro: Waterfront.

John F. Kennedy Center for the Performing Arts   This 30-year-old theater complex strives to be not just the hub of Washington's cultural and entertainment scene, but a performing arts theater for the nation. Don't expect cutting-edge productions, but do look here for top-rated performances by the best ballet, opera, jazz, modern dance, musical, and theater companies in the

Washington, D.C., After Dark

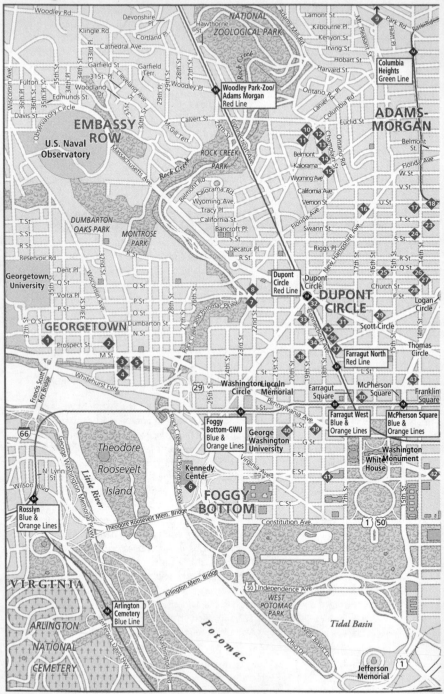

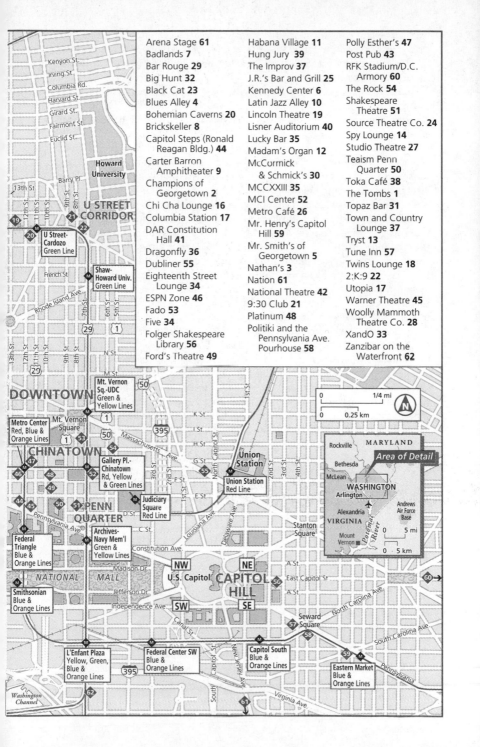

Arena Stage **61**
Badlands **7**
Bar Rouge **29**
Big Hunt **32**
Black Cat **23**
Blues Alley **4**
Bohemian Caverns **20**
Brickskeller **8**
Capitol Steps (Ronald Reagan Bldg.) **44**
Carter Barron Amphitheater **9**
Champions of Georgetown **2**
Chi Cha Lounge **16**
Columbia Station **17**
DAR Constitution Hall **41**
Dragonfly **36**
Dubliner **55**
Eighteenth Street Lounge **34**
ESPN Zone **46**
Fado **53**
Five **34**
Folger Shakespeare Library **56**
Ford's Theatre **49**

Habana Village **11**
Hung Jury **39**
The Improv **37**
J.R.'s Bar and Grill **25**
Kennedy Center **6**
Latin Jazz Alley **10**
Lincoln Theatre **19**
Lisner Auditorium **40**
Lucky Bar **35**
Madam's Organ **12**
McCormick & Schmick's **30**
MCCXXIII **35**
MCI Center **52**
Metro Café **26**
Mr. Henry's Capitol Hill **59**
Mr. Smith's of Georgetown **5**
Nathan's **3**
Nation **61**
National Theatre **42**
9:30 Club **21**
Platinum **48**
Politiki and the Pennsylvania Ave. Pourhouse **58**

Polly Esther's **47**
Post Pub **43**
RFK Stadium/D.C. Armory **60**
The Rock **54**
Shakespeare Theatre **51**
Source Theatre Co. **24**
Spy Lounge **14**
Studio Theatre **27**
Teaism Penn Quarter **50**
Toka Café **38**
The Tombs **1**
Topaz Bar **31**
Town and Country Lounge **37**
Tryst **13**
Tune Inn **57**
Twins Lounge **18**
2:K:9 **22**
Utopia **17**
Warner Theatre **45**
Woolly Mammoth Theatre Co. **28**
XandO **33**
Zanzibar on the Waterfront **62**

world. The best costs the most, and you are likely to pay more for a ticket here than at any other theater in D.C.—from $12 for a children's play to more than $280 for a box seat on a Saturday night at the opera, although most ticket prices run in the $50 to $60 range.

Tip: If you want a really good, really cheap seat in the Kennedy Center's Concert Hall, try for a chorister seat. Prices vary widely, but, to give you an idea, the National Symphony Orchestra charges $25 for these seats (orchestra seats go for about $55). Each of the 63 seats is situated right behind the stage and above the orchestra. Call the regular box office number to try and reserve one of these, which are available on a night-by-night basis, that is, you can't book a whole season's worth of chorister seats. Keep in mind, though, that you'll be as much on view as the performing musicians.

But the Kennedy Center is committed to being a theater for the people, and toward that end, it continues to stage its **free concert series,** known as "Millennium Stage," which features daily performances by area musicians and sometimes national artists each evening at 6pm in the center's Grand Foyer. (You can check out broadcasts of the nightly performances on the Internet at www.kennedy-center.org/millennium.) During the summer, the Ken-Cen adds Millennium Stage performances every Wednesday at noon on the steps of the Library of Congress's Thomas Jefferson Building. The Friday "Weekend" section of the *Washington Post* lists the free performances scheduled for the coming week; the daily "Style" section lists nightly performances under "Free Events," in the "Guide to the Lively Arts" column. Also call about "pay what you can" performances, scheduled throughout the year on certain days, for certain shows.

The Kennedy Center is actually made up of six different national theaters: the Opera House, the Concert Hall, the Terrace Theater, the Eisenhower Theater, the Theater Lab, and the American Film Institute (AFI) theater. While the Opera House undergoes renovation throughout 2003, the **Washington Opera** (www.dc-opera.org) performs instead at the Daughters of the American Revolution's (DAR) Constitution Hall (see description under "Smaller Auditoriums," below). The 2002–03 schedule includes productions of Verdi's *Aida,* Mozart's *Don Giovanni,* and Beethoven's *Fidelio.* Tickets often sell out before the season begins. The **National Symphony Orchestra** presents concerts in the Concert Hall from September to June.

Among the other productions coming to one of the Kennedy Center stages in 2003 are the International Ballet Festival, performances by the Royal Shakespeare Company, the musical *Oklahoma!,* and Andrew Lloyd Weber's *Tell Me on a Sunday*. The **Theater Lab** continues by day as Washington's premier stage for children's theater and by night as a cabaret (now in its 16th year) hosting *Shear Madness,* a comedy whodunit (all tickets $32).

These are just a smattering of Kennedy Center offerings. At the southern end of New Hampshire Ave. NW and Rock Creek Pkwy. ℭ 800/444-1324 or 202/467-4600 for tickets and information. www.kennedy-center.org. 50% discounts are offered (for most attractions) to students, seniors 65 and over, people with permanent disabilities, enlisted military personnel, and persons with fixed low incomes (call ℭ 202/416-8340 for details). Garage parking $10. Metro: Foggy Bottom (though it's a fairly short walk, there's a free shuttle between the station and the Kennedy Center, departing every 15 min. 9:45am–midnight, Mon–Sat, noon–midnight Sun). Bus: 80 from Metro Center.

National Theatre The luxurious Federal-style National Theatre is the oldest continuously operating theater in Washington (since 1835) and the third oldest in the nation. It's exciting just to see the stage on which Sarah Bernhardt, John Barrymore, Helen Hayes, and so many other notables have performed. The 1,672-seat National is the closest thing Washington has to a Broadway-style playhouse. Oddly enough, the famous theater went without a subscription series for nearly a decade. The 2001–02 season finally put one in place, bringing star-studded hits from Broadway, starting with *The Full Monty* and continuing with *Contact, Mamma Mia,* and *Saturday Night Fever.* (The 2002–03 season was still being negotiated as this book was being researched.)

One thing that has never flagged at The National is its commitment to offering free public-service programs: Saturday-morning children's theater (puppets, clowns, magicians, dancers, and singers) and Monday-night showcases of local groups and performers September through May, plus free summer films. Call ℭ **202/783-3372** for details. 1321 Pennsylvania Ave. NW. ℭ **202/628-6161,** or 800/447-7400 to charge tickets. www.nationaltheatre.org. Tickets $30–$75; discounts available for students, seniors, military personnel, and people with disabilities. Metro: Metro Center.

Shakespeare Theatre Try and snag tickets to a play here, for the productions are reliably outstanding. Season subscriptions claim many of the seats and the plays almost always sell out, so if you're interested in attending a play here, you'd better buy your tickets now. This internationally renowned classical ensemble company offers five plays, usually three Shakespearean and two modern classics each September-to-June season. The 2002–03 season includes *The Winter's Tale, Much Ado About Nothing, Richard III, The Silent Woman* (by Ben Jonson), and Ibsen's *Ghosts.* This is top-level theater, with superb acting.

The company also offers one admission-free 2-week run of a Shakespeare production at the Carter Barron Amphitheater in Rock Creek Park. 450 7th St. NW (between D and E sts.). ℭ **202/547-1122.** www.shakespearetheatre.org. Tickets $14.50–$64, $10 for standing-room tickets sold 1 hr. before sold-out performances; discounts available for students, seniors, and groups. Metro: Archives–Navy Memorial or MCI Center/Gallery Place.

SMALLER THEATERS

Some of Washington's lesser-known theaters are gaining more recognition all the time. Their productions are consistently professional, and sometimes more contemporary and innovative than those you'll find in the more acclaimed theaters. The **Source Theatre Company,** 1835 14th St. NW, between S and T streets (ℭ **202/462-1073;** www.sourcetheatre.org), is Washington's major producer of new plays. Joy Zinoman, the artistic director of the **Studio Theatre,** 1333 P St. NW, at 14th Street (ℭ **202/332-3300;** www.studiotheatre.org), showcases interesting contemporary plays and nurtures Washington acting talent; the 2002–03 season marks the theater's 25th anniversary. The **Woolly Mammoth Theatre Company,** in the Kennedy Center's AFI Theater (ℭ **202/393-3939;** www.woollymammoth.net), offers as many as six productions each year, specializing in new, offbeat, and quirky plays. (These are temporary quarters until construction of its new 250-seat state-of-the-art facility, at Seventh and D sts. NW, in downtown Washington is complete—probably not until 2004.)

In addition, I highly recommend productions staged at the **Folger Shakespeare Library,** 201 E. Capitol St. SE (ℭ **202/544-7077;** www.folger.edu). Plays take place in the library's Elizabethan Theatre, which is styled after the inn-yard theater of Shakespeare's time. The theater is intimate and charming, the theater company is remarkably good, and an evening spent here guarantees an absolutely marvelous experience. The 2002–03 season brings to the stage Shakespeare's *Love's Labour's Lost* and *Twelfth Night,* and Maxwell Anderson's *Elizabeth* *the Queen.* The Elizabethan Theatre is also the setting for musical performances, lectures, readings, and other events.

Finally, there's **Ford's Theatre,** 511 10th St. NW, between E and F streets (℡ **202/347-4833;** www.fordstheatre.org), the actual theater where, on the evening of April 14, 1865, actor John Wilkes Booth shot President Lincoln. Though popular among Washingtonians for its annual holiday performance of Dickens's *A Christmas Carol,* Ford's stages generally mediocre presentations, usually intertwined with American history themes.

INDOOR ARENAS & OUTDOOR PAVILIONS

When Madonna, U2, the Rolling Stones, or the Backstreet Boys come to town, they usually play at one of the huge indoor or outdoor arenas. The 20,600-seat **MCI Center,** 601 F St. NW, where it meets Seventh Street (℡ **202/628-3200;** www.mcicenter.com), in the center of downtown, hosts plenty of concerts and also is Washington's premier indoor sports arena (home to the NBA Wizards, the WNBA Mystics, the NHL Capitals, and Georgetown NCAA basketball). Less convenient and smaller is the 10,000-seat **Patriot Center** at George Mason University, 4500 Patriot Circle, Fairfax, VA (℡ **703/993-3000;** www. patriotcenter.com).

Largest of the outdoor venues is the **Robert F. Kennedy Memorial Stadium,** 2400 E. Capitol St. SE (℡ **202/547-9077;** www.dcsportscommission.com), the erstwhile home of the Washington Redskins (they now play at the new FedEx Field stadium in Landover, Maryland). The stadium continues as an outdoor event facility, packing crowds of 55,000-plus into its seats for D.C. United (men's) and Washington Freedom (women's) soccer games, concerts, and all-day music festivals.

The **Nissan Pavilion at Stone Ridge,** 7800 Cellar Door Dr., off Wellington Road in Bristow, VA (℡ **800/455-8999** or 703/754-1288 for concert information; www.nissanpavilion.com), has a capacity of 22,500 seats (10,000 under the roof, the remainder on the lawn), is 25 minutes from the Beltway, and features major acts varying from classical to country. The action is enhanced by giant video screens inside the pavilion and on the lawn.

During the summer, there's quality entertainment almost nightly at the **Merriweather Post Pavilion,** 10475 Little Patuxent Pkwy., just off Route 29 in Columbia, Maryland (℡ **410/730-2424;** www.mppconcerts.com), about a 40-minute drive from downtown D.C. There's reserved seating in the open-air pavilion (overhead protection provided in case of rain) and general-admission seating on the lawn (no refunds for rain) to see such performers as Nine Inch Nails, Joni Mitchell, Blink 182, The Cure, No Doubt, Jimmy Buffett, and Britney Spears. If you choose the lawn seating, bring blankets and picnic fare (beverages must be bought on the premises).

My favorite summer setting for music is **Wolf Trap Farm Park for the Performing Arts,** 1551 Trap Rd., Vienna, Virginia (℡ **703/255-1868;** www.wolf trap.org). The country's only national park devoted to the performing arts, Wolf Trap, 30 minutes by car from downtown D.C., offers performances by the National Symphony Orchestra (it's their summer home), and has hosted Lucinda Williams, Shawn Colvin, Lyle Lovett, The Temptations, Ani DiFranco, and many others. Performances take place in the 7,000-seat Filene Center, about half of which is under the open sky. You can also buy cheaper lawn seats on the hill, which is sometimes the nicest way to go. If you do, arrive early (the lawn opens 90 min. before the performance) and bring a blanket and a picnic dinner—it's a tradition. Wolf Trap also hosts a number of very popular **festivals.** The park features a daylong Irish music festival in May; the Louisiana Swamp Romp Cajun Festival and a weekend of jazz and blues in June; and the International Children's Festival each September.

The **Carter Barron Amphitheater,** 16th Street and Colorado Avenue NW (© 202/426-0486), way out 16th Street, is in Rock Creek Park, close to the Maryland border. This is the area's smallest outdoor venue, with 4,250 seats. Summer performances include a range of gospel, blues, and classical entertainment. The shows are usually free, but tickets are required. You can always count on Shakespeare: The **Shakespeare Theatre Free For All** takes place at the Carter Barron usually for 2 weeks in June, Tuesday through Sunday evenings; the free tickets are available the day of performance only, on a first-come, first-served basis (call © 202/334-4790 for details). The 2002 Free For All featured *The Two Gentlemen of Verona.*

SMALLER AUDITORIUMS

A handful of auditoriums in Washington are really fine places to catch a performance. The smallest, most clublike auditorium is the 350-seat **Barns of Wolf Trap,** 1635 Trap Rd., Vienna, VA (© 703/938-2404), which is just up the road from Wolf Trap Farm Park. From late fall until May, the schedule features jazz, pop, country, folk, bluegrass, and chamber musicians. This is the summer home of the Wolf Trap Opera Company, which is the only entertainment booked here May through September.

DAR Constitution Hall, on 18th Street NW, between C and D streets (© 202/628-4780; www.dar.org), is housed within a beautiful turn-of-the-20th-century beaux arts–style building and seats 3,746. Its excellent acoustics have supported an eclectic (and I mean eclectic) group of performers: Sting, the Buena Vista Social Club, John Hiatt, the Count Basie Orchestra, the Los Angeles Philharmonic, Lil Bow Wow, Ray Charles, Trisha Yearwood, Nina Simone, and the O Brother Where Art Thou? tour.

In the heart of happening U Street, the **Lincoln Theatre,** 1215 U St. NW (© 202/328-6000; www.thelincolntheatre.org), was once a movie theater, vaudeville house, and nightclub featuring black stars like Louis Armstrong and Cab Calloway. The theater closed in the 1970s and reopened in 1994 after a renovation restored it to its former elegance. Today the theater books jazz, R&B, gospel, and comedy acts, and events like the D.C. Film Festival.

At the 1,500-seat **Lisner Auditorium,** on the campus of George Washington University, 21st and H streets NW (© 202/994-1500; www.lisner.org), you always feel close to the stage. Bookings sometimes include musical groups like Siouxsie and the Banshees, comedians like "Weird Al" Yankovic, monologist Spalding Gray, and children's entertainers like Raffi, but are mostly cultural shows—everything from a Pakistani rock group to the Washington Revels' annual romp at Christmas.

The **Warner Theatre,** 1299 Pennsylvania Ave. NW, with the entrance on 13th Street, between E and F streets (© 202/783-4000; www.warnertheatre. com), opened in 1924 as the Earle Theatre (a movie/vaudeville palace) and was restored to its original, neoclassical-style appearance in 1992 at a cost of $10 million. It's worth coming by just to see its ornately detailed interior. The 2,000-seat auditorium offers year-round entertainment, alternating dance performances (from Baryshnikov to the Washington Ballet's Christmas performance of *The Nutcracker*) and Broadway/off-Broadway shows (*Cabaret, Lord of the Dance,*

Godspell) with headliner entertainment (Sheryl Crow, Natalie Merchant, Wynton Marsalis).

2 The Club & Music Scene

If you're looking for a more interactive, tuneful night on the town, Washington offers hip jazz clubs, lively bars, warehouse ballrooms, places where you sit back and listen, places where you can get up and dance, even a roadhouse or two. If you're looking for comic relief, Washington can take care of that, too (the pickings are few but good).

Many nightspots wear multiple hats. For example, the Black Cat is a bar and a dance club, offering food and sometimes poetry readings. So I've listed each nightspot according to the type of music it features. The details are in the description.

The best nightlife districts are Adams-Morgan; the area around U and 14th streets NW, a still-developing district, where it's best to stay on or close to U Street; the Seventh Street NW corridor near Chinatown and the MCI Center; and Georgetown. If you don't mind venturing into the suburbs, you should know about Arlington's hot spots (see the "Arlington Row" box on p. 264). As a rule, while club-hopping—even in Georgetown—stick to the major thoroughfares and steer clear of deserted side streets.

The best source of information about what's doing at bars and clubs is *City Paper,* available free at bookstores, movie theaters, drugstores, and other locations.

Washington's clubs and bars tend to keep their own hours; best to call ahead to make sure the place you're headed is open.

COMEDY

In addition to these two comedy venues, the **Warner Theatre** (see "Smaller Auditoriums," above) also features big-name comedians from time to time.

The Capitol Steps *(Moments* This musical political satire troupe is made up of former Congressional staffers, equal-opportunity spoofers all, who poke endless fun through song and skits at politicians on both sides of the aisle, and at government goings-on in general. You might catch former president Clinton crooning "Livin' Libido Loca," or U.S. Attorney General John Ashcroft bellowing "Glory Glory Paranoia." Washingtonians have been fans since the Steps got

---

Fun Fact Washington Walk of Fame

If you're going to the Warner Theatre, or are walking by (it's in the heart of downtown), be sure to check out the sidewalk in front of its 13th Street entrance, between E Street and Pennsylvania Avenue NW. Entertainers who have performed here since the theater reopened in 1992 have signed stone "pavers," and these individual blocks, bearing both a signature and a gold star, are on view in the concrete walkway. Look for the signatures of Frank Sinatra, Tony Bennett, Liza Minnelli, Shirley MacLaine, David Copperfield, B. B. King, Mikhail Baryshnikov, Chris Rock, and about 100 others. You'll notice that some performers added their own flourishes: Bonnie Raitt wrote "No Nukes" on hers; Tommy Tune imprinted the soles of his tap shoes in the pavement.

started in 1981. Since then, the troupe has performed more than 5,000 shows and released more than 22 albums, including the latest, "When Bush Comes to Shove." Shows take place in the Amphitheater, on the concourse level of the Ronald Reagan Building and International Trade Center, at 7:30pm Friday and Saturday. 1300 Pennsylvania Ave. NW (in the Ronald Reagan Bldg.). ℂ 202/312-1555. www. capsteps.com. Tickets $31.50. Metro: Federal Triangle.

The Improv   The Improv features top performers on the national comedy club circuit as well as comic plays and one-person shows. *Saturday Night Live* performers David Spade, Chris Rock, and Adam Sandler have all played here, as have comedy bigs Ellen DeGeneres, Jerry Seinfeld, and Robin Williams. Shows are about 1½ hours long and include three comics (an emcee, a feature act, and a headliner). Show times are 8:30pm Sunday through Thursday, 8 and 10:30pm on Friday and Saturday. The best way to snag a good seat is to have dinner here (make reservations), which allows you to enter the club as early as 7pm Sunday through Thursday or after 6:30pm Friday and Saturday. The Friday and Saturday 10:30pm show serves drinks and appetizers only. Dinner entrees (nothing higher than $9.95) include prime rib, sandwiches, and pasta selections. You must be 18 to get in. 1140 Connecticut Ave. NW (between L and M sts.). ℂ 202/296-7008. www.dcimprov.com. Cover $12 Sun–Thurs, $15 Fri–Sat, plus a 2-drink minimum (waived if you dine). Metro: Farragut North.

POP/ROCK/RAVE/ALTERNATIVE

The Birchmere Music Hall and Bandstand   Worth the cab fare from downtown, if you're a fan of live music by varied, stellar performers, such as Garth Brooks, Jonatha Brooke, Jerry Jeff Walker, Crash Test Dummies, Shawn Colvin, Joe Sample, John Hiatt—I could go on and on. The Birchmere is unique in the area for providing a comfortable and relatively small (500-seat) setting, where you sit and listen to the music (there's not a bad seat in the house) and order food and drinks. The Birchmere got started more than 25 years ago, when it booked mostly country singers. The place has expanded over the years and so has its repertoire; there are still many country and bluegrass artists, but also folk, jazz, rock, gospel, and alternative musicians. The menu tends toward American favorites, such as nachos and burgers; I can recommend the pulled-pork barbecue sandwich and the chili. 3701 Mount Vernon Ave., Alexandria, VA. ℂ 703/549-7500. www.birchmere.com. Ticket prices range from $16.50–$45. Take a taxi or drive.

Black Cat   This comfortable, low-key club draws a black-clad crowd to its concert hall, which features national, international, and local indie and alternative groups. The place is made for dancing, accommodating more than 600 people. Adjoining the hall is the Red Room Bar, a large, funky, red-walled living-roomy lounge with booths, tables, a red-leather sofa, pinball machines, a pool table, and a jukebox stocked with a really eclectic collection. A college crowd collects on weekends, but you can count on seeing a 20- to 30-something bunch here most nights, including members of various bands who like to stop in for a drink. Black Cat also hosts film screenings, poetry readings, and other quiet forms of entertainment in its ground floor room called "Backstage," and serves vegetarian food in its smoke-free cafe. Say hello to owner Dante Ferrando while you're here and to his dad, Bobby, who mans the kitchen. The Red Room Bar is open until 2am Sunday through Thursday, and until 3am Friday and Saturday. Concerts take place 4 or 5 nights a week, beginning at about 8:30pm (call for details). 1811 14th St. NW (between S and T sts.). ℂ 202/667-7960. www.blackcatdc.com. Cover $5–$15 for concerts; no cover in the Red Room Bar. Metro: U St.–Cardozo.

Tips Metro Takes You There

Recognizing that Washingtonians are keeping later hours these days, Metro not only keeps its trains running until 2am on weekends, but has also inaugurated special shuttle service to Adams-Morgan (home to lots of nightclubs, but no Metro stations).

Here's what you do: Take the Metro to the Red Line's Woodley Park–Adams-Morgan Station or to the Green Line's U St.–Cardozo Station, and hop on the no. 98 Adams-Morgan–U St. Link Shuttle, which travels through Adams-Morgan, between these two stations, after 6pm daily, except on Saturday, when service starts at 10am. The U Link Shuttle operates every 15 minutes and costs only 25¢ with a transfer from Metrorail, or $1.10 without a transfer.

Eighteenth Street Lounge   This place maintains its "hot" status. First you have to find it, and then you have to convince the bouncer to let you in. So here's what you need to know: Look for the mattress shop south of Dupont Circle, then look up. "ESL" (as those in the know call it) sits above the shop, and hangs only a tiny plaque at street level to advertise its existence. Wear something exotic and sexy. If you pass inspection, you may be surprised to find yourself in a restored mansion (Teddy Roosevelt once lived here) with fireplaces, high ceilings, and a deck out back. Or maybe you'll just get right out there on the hardwood floors to dance to acid jazz, hip-hop, reggae, or Latin jazz tunes spun by a deejay. 1212 18th St. NW. ✆ 202/466-3922. Cover $10–$20 Thurs–Sat; no cover Sun–Wed. Metro: Dupont Circle or Farragut North.

5   This small, three-level space is a reincarnation of what used to be the Garage, a live-music venue. 5 is a deejay-driven dance club, aiming to capture some of the late-night crowd who are too wired to go home. Open Wednesday through Sunday nights, with music starting after 10pm. 1214-B 18th St. NW. ✆ 202/331-7123. Cover $5–$15. Metro: Dupont Circle or Farragut North.

Metro Café   The Metro holds about 100 people in a room with a big stage, an L-shaped bar, red-velvet curtains, and tall ceilings. Acts range from live hip-hop and local rock bands to artist-specific themed dance events, with DJs spinning music by one group all night long, Depeche Mode, maybe, or Prince. The club attracts all ages, everyone in black. The Metro holds its own by featuring different entertainment every night, presenting short plays, poetry readings, improvisational comedy, as well as diverse kinds of music. Open nightly after 7pm. 1522 14th St. NW (between P and Q sts.). ✆ 202/588-9118. www.metrocafe.net. Cover $5–$15. Metro: McPherson Square.

Nation   This concert/dance space has separate areas for live music, dance music, and lounging, and a three-tiered outdoor patio. This is primarily a Gen-X mecca (though some performers attract an older crowd). It's also D.C.'s largest club, accommodating about 2,000 people a night. The Pet Shop Boys and Pink are among the groups to have performed here recently. But Nation is best known for its dance parties. Friday is "Buzz" night, when those 19 and older come here to rave to deejay-spun house, trance, techno and other music. Thursday is Goth night for those addicted to psytrance and darkwave music, black leather and eyeliner. Saturday is given over to a gay dance party called "Velvet." The game room and state-of-the-art lighting/laser/sound systems are a plus. The Nation is in a pretty bad neighborhood, so make sure you have good directions to get there; the building itself is very secure. 1015 Half St. SE (at K St.). ℂ 202/554-1500. www. nationdc.com. Cover $7–$30. Metro: Navy Yard.

9:30 Club Housed in yet another converted warehouse, this major live-music venue hosts frequent record-company parties and features a wide range of top performers. You might catch Sheryl Crow, Simple Minds, The Clarks, Luna, The Tragically Hip, Lucinda Williams, or even Tony Bennett. It's only open when there's a show on, which is almost every night (but call ahead), and, obviously, the crowd (as many as 1,200) varies with the performer. The sound system is state of the art and the sight lines are excellent. There are four bars: two on the main dance-floor level, one in the upstairs VIP room (anyone is welcome here unless the room is being used for a private party), and another in the distressed-looking cellar. The 9:30 Club is a standup place, literally—there are few seats. 815 V St. NW (at Vermont Ave.). ℂ 202/265-0930. www.930.com. Metro: U St.–Cardozo, 10th St. exit.

Platinum Housed in a great old building that still has its original marble floor, sweeping staircase, and high ceilings, this nightclub is the exclusive domain of the young and good-looking who like to dance. Music is described as progressive, but it's really just contemporary disco played by deejays. Four levels, three dance floors, a VIP lounge, smoke machines, balconies, high-tech sound systems—it's all here. 915 F St. NW. ℂ 202/393-3555. www.platinumclubdc.com. Cover $10, $15 after midnight Sat. Metro: MCI Center–Gallery Place.

Polly Esther's This is a three-dance-clubs-in-one emporium with '70s disco music (think the Village People, ABBA, the BeeGees) blaring from the sound system on the "Polly Esther's" dance floor, '80s tunes by artists like Madonna and Prince playing in the "Culture Club," and current radio hits blasting throughout "Club Expo." Decor for each floor matches the music of that era, so, for instance, you'll see such artifacts as a John Travolta memorial and Brady Bunch memorabilia in the Polly Esther's club. Open Thursday through Saturday. 605 12th St. NW. ℂ 202/737-1970. www.pollyesthers.com. Cover $7 Thurs, $8 Fri, $10 Sat. Metro: Metro Center.

State Theatre This is another club that's located outside the city ("7 minutes from Key Bridge") and not near a Metro station, but it offers reasonably priced live shows featuring great local and national bands (and lots of names from the past, such as Jefferson Starship and Dave Mason). This relatively small hall (holds 800) was once a movie house, and its renovation has endowed it with a superb sound system and good sightlines. The theater has a dance floor, and seats 160 at tables and another 200 theater style in the balcony, with everyone else standing. It's first come, first served for the seats, so if you really want one, get here by the time the box office opens at 6:30pm, if not earlier. The State offers a full menu and bar; table dwellers pay an extra $7.50 minimum per person for food. Most people don't mind standing, since the music featured is pretty danceable. Dr. John, Marcia Ball, Beausoleil, The Radiators, and Blame It on Jane are some of the acts you might catch here. 220 N. Washington St., Falls Church, VA. ℂ 703/237-0300. www.thestatetheatre.com. Tickets cost anywhere from $11–$33, depending on the act. Metro: East Falls Church, with a 4-min. cab ride from there.

2:K:9 Not far from the 9:30 Club is this huge and grandiose two-level nightspot with a concrete dance floor, a VIP lounge, two raised cages where

🕐 D.C. Boogie

Dance clubs used to be hard to find in Washington, but now they pro-liferate. Salsa, swing, rave, rock, disco, freak . . . you name it, it's hap-pening here. Strictly speaking, many dance spots are not "clubs," but restaurants, bars, or concert halls that feature live or recorded music on certain days or at certain times. But so what? The choices are there and varied. So read on, and then put on your dancing shoes and get on out there.

For clubs not already listed within this chapter, I've provided an address and phone number; otherwise, refer back to full entries within the main text to find out information.

For dinner and romantic dancing in the old-fashioned way, you might want to try the **Blue Bar** at the Henley Park Hotel, 926 Massa-chusetts Ave. NW (📞 **202/638-5200**), a delightful cocktail lounge with live jazz and dancing Friday and Saturday nights; or the **Melrose Bar,** at the Park Hyatt Hotel, 1201 24th St. NW (📞 **202/955-3899**), for din-ner and swing dancing to live jazz Friday and Saturday nights.

Latin jazz continues to be popular in Washington and one of the best places to salsa and merengue is Adams-Morgan's **Habana Village,** which is open Wednesday through Saturday evenings, with salsa les-sons offered Wednesday through Friday and tango lessons on Satur-day. Other choices include **Latin Jazz Alley,** also in Adams-Morgan, **Zanzibar** on the Waterfront, and **Lucky Bar,** near Dupont Circle.

Adams-Morgan, in general, is a convenient neighborhood to travel if you're in a dancing mood. Among the top spots are **Chief Ike's Mambo Room,** 1725 Columbia Rd. NW (📞 **202/332-2211**), where dance maniacs of all ages and races rock out to a mix of DJ tunes, hip-hop to R&B; and **Madam's Organ,** which is technically not a dance club, but becomes one pretty quickly when its excellent live jazz, blues, or R&B musicians take the (tiny, windowfront) stage—the place gets so packed that you'll probably end up dancing where you stand.

Just south of Adams-Morgan and Dupont Circle lies DC's hottest club, the **Eighteenth Street Lounge.** Known as "ESL," the club is so hip, it scarcely announces itself. (Look for a tiny bronze plaque.) The two-level club keeps its dance floors dark, and crowded with fashionably dressed men and women moving to the deejay-driven acid jazz, hip-hop, and instrumental reggae tunes.

Dance venues, where the emphasis is on live bands playing current music, include **Madam's Organ, Black Cat, Metro Café, IOTA,** in Arling-ton (see the "Arlington Row" box later in this chapter, for more selec-tions there), and **State Theatre,** in Falls Church. Alas, the live rock-dance scene is a category that remains woefully underrepre-sented in Washington.

Most places offer deejay-spun dance music. In addition to those mentioned above, you might consider the swank **2:K:9** (a Studio 54 for the millennium); the waterfront **Zanzibar,** for choices ranging from alternative to hip-hop; **Polly Esther's** for '80s retro; and **Nathans,** for a combination of international, Euro, and Top 40.

women dancers undulate, a bar, and a deejay booth. And that's just the first floor. The second floor features live acts and fake snow-generating machines. If it sounds all too Studio 54-ish, it may be because one of that legendary club's designers had a hand in the design here. Put on your funkiest outfit to dance to hip-hop, techno beats, and international sounds. Open Thursday through Saturday. 2009 8th St. NW. ⓒ 202/667-7750. Cover $10–$15 after 9pm. Metro: U St.–Cardozo.

JAZZ & BLUES

A calendar of jazz gigs for these and other clubs is posted at **www.dcjazz.com**, including free performances, such as those at the **Four Seasons Garden Terrace lounge**, 2800 Pennsylvania Ave. NW (ⓒ 202/342-0444), where a pianist plays jazz standards Thursday through Saturday nights.

Blues Alley   Blues Alley, in Georgetown, has been Washington's top jazz club since 1965, featuring such artists as Nancy Wilson, McCoy Tyner, Sonny Rollins, Wynton Marsalis, Rachelle Ferrell, and Maynard Ferguson. There are usually two shows nightly at 8 and 10pm; some performers also do midnight shows on weekends. Reservations are essential (call after noon); since seating is on a first-come, first-served basis, it's best to arrive no later than 7pm and have dinner. Entrees on the steak and Creole seafood menu are in the $15 to $22 range, snacks and sandwiches are $5.25 to $10, and drinks are $5.35 to $9. The decor is classic jazz club: exposed brick walls, beamed ceiling, and small, candlelit tables. Sometimes well-known visiting musicians get up and jam with performers. 1073 Wisconsin Ave. NW (in an alley below M St.). ⓒ 202/337-4141. www.bluesalley. com. Cover $16–$40, plus $7 food or drink minimum, plus $1.75 surcharge. Metro: Foggy Bottom, then take the Georgetown Metro Connection Shuttle.

Bohemian Caverns   Rising from the ashes on the very spot where jazz greats such as Duke Ellington, Billie Holiday, and so many others performed decades ago, Bohemian Caverns hopes to establish that same presence and host today's jazz stars. The club's decor is cavelike, as it was in the '20s. Musicians you might catch here include Shirley Horn, Nap Turner, and Esther Williams. The Caverns is also a restaurant, whose entrees are named after jazz legends and start at $18.50. You should dress up to come here. 2001 11th St. NW (at U St). ⓒ 202/299-0801. Cover $10–$20, but as much as $50 for someone like Shirley Horn, plus a $12 minimum for food or drinks. Metro: U St.–Cardozo.

Columbia Station (Value)   This fairly intimate club in Adams-Morgan showcases live blues and jazz nightly. The performers are pretty good, which is amazing, considering there's no cover. Columbia Station is also a bar/restaurant, with the kitchen usually open until midnight, serving pastas, seafood, and Cajun-influenced cuisine. 2325 18th St. NW. ⓒ 202/462-6040. No cover but a 2-drink or dinner-order minimum (about $8–$10). Metro: U St.–Cardozo or Woodley Park–Zoo–Adams-Morgan and catch the U Link Shuttle.

Madam's Organ Restaurant and Bar (Finds)   This beloved Adams-Morgan hangout fulfills owner Bill Duggan's definition of a good bar: great sounds and sweaty people. The great sounds feature One Night Stand, a jazz group, on Monday; bluesman Ben Andrews on Tuesday; bluegrass with Bob Perilla and the Big Hillbilly Bluegrass Band on Wednesday; and the salsa sounds of Patrick Alban and Noche Latina on Thursday, which is also Ladies' Night. On Friday and Saturday nights, regional blues groups pack the place. The club includes a wide-open bar decorated eclectically with a 150-year-old gilded mirror, stuffed fish and animal heads, and paintings of nudes. The second-floor bar is called Big Daddy's Love Lounge & Pick-Up Joint, which tells you everything you need to know. Other points to note: You can play darts, and redheads pay half-price for drinks. For what it's worth, *Playboy's* May 2000 issue named Madam's Organ one of the 25 best bars in America. Food is served, but I'd eat elsewhere. 2461 18th St. NW. ℂ 202/667-5370. www.madamsorgan.com. Cover $3–$7. Metro: U St.–Cardozo or Woodley Park–Zoo–Adams-Morgan and catch the Adams-Morgan/U St. Link Shuttle.

Mr. Henry's Capitol Hill   Almost every Friday night, at 8:30pm, Mr. Henry's features a jazz group—maybe the Kevin Cordt Quartet, who play on the second floor of this cozy restaurant. There's no cover, but it's expected that you'll order something off the menu (perhaps a burger or gumbo). Mr. Henry's has been around for at least 30 years and has always attracted a gay and lesbian clientele, though it's a comfortable place for everyone. 601 Pennsylvania Ave. SE. ℂ 202/546-8412. No cover but 2-drink minimum. Metro: Eastern Market.

Twins Lounge   In mid-June 2001, Twins moved from its longtime location on the outskirts of town to this much more vital area. This intimate jazz club offers live music every night. On weeknights, you'll hear local artists (open mike on Wed); weekends are reserved for out-of-town acts, such as Bobby Watson, Gil Scott Heron, and James William. Sunday night is a weekly jam session attended by musicians from all over town. The menu features American, Ethiopian, and Caribbean dishes. The age group of the crowd varies. 1344 U St. NW. ℂ 202/234-0072. www.twinsjazz.com. Cover $10–$20, with a $10 minimum. Metro: U St.–Cardozo.

Utopia   Unlike most music bars, the arty New York/SoHo–style Utopia is serious about its restaurant operation. A moderately priced international menu features entrees ranging from lamb couscous to blackened shrimp with Creole cream sauce, not to mention pastas and filet mignon béarnaise. There's also an interesting wine list and a large selection of beers and single-malt scotches. The setting is cozy and candlelit, with walls used for a changing art gallery show (the bold, colorful paintings in the front room are by Moroccan owner Jamal Sahri). The eclectic crowd here varies with the music, ranging from early 20s to about 35, for the most part, including South Americans and Europeans. There's live music each night it's open, with Thursday always featuring live Brazilian jazz and Wednesday the bluesy jazz singer Pam Bricker. There's no real dance floor, but people find odd spaces to move to the tunes. 1418 U St. NW (at 14th St.). ℂ 202/483-7669. No cover, but minimum drink/food charge of $15 per person. Metro: U St.–Cardozo.

INTERNATIONAL SOUNDS

Chi Cha Lounge *Finds*   You can sit around on couches, eat Ecuadoran tapas, and listen to live Latin music, which is featured Sunday through Wednesday. Or you can sit around on couches and smoke Arabic tobacco through a 3-foot-high arguileh pipe. Or you can just sit around. This is a popular neighborhood place. 1624 U St. NW. ℂ 202/234-8400. www.chi-cha.com. Cover $15 (minimum). Metro: U St.–Cardozo.

Habana Village   This three-story nightclub has a bar/restaurant on the first floor, a bar/dance floor with deejay on the second level, and a live music space on the third floor. Salsa and merengue lessons are given Wednesday through Saturday evenings, $10 per lesson. Otherwise, a deejay or live band plays danceable Latin jazz tunes. 1834 Columbia Rd. NW. ℂ 202/462-6310. Cover $5 Fri–Sat after 9:30pm (no cover for women). Metro: U St.–Cardozo or Woodley Park–Zoo–Adams-Morgan, and catch the Adams-Morgan/U St. Link Shuttle.

ⓒ Late-Night Bites

If your stomach is grumbling after the show is over, the dancing has ended, or the bar has closed, you can always get a meal at one of a growing number of late-night or all-night eateries.

In Georgetown, the **Bistro Francais,** 3128 M St. NW (ⓒ **202/338-3830**), has been feeding night owls for years; it even draws some of the area's top chefs after their own establishments close. Open until 4am, the Bistro is thoroughly French, serving steak frites, omelets, and patés.

On U Street, **Ben's Chili Bowl,** 1213 U St. NW (ⓒ **202/667-0909**), serves up chili dogs, turkey subs, and cheese fries until 4am on Friday and Saturday nights.

Adams-Morgan has several late-night dining options, including the all-night **Diner,** 2453 18th St. NW (ⓒ **202/232-8800**), which serves some typical (eggs and coffee, grilled cheese) and not-so-typical (a grilled fresh salmon club sandwich) diner grub. Down the street, the **18th and U Duplex Diner,** 2004 18th St. NW (ⓒ **202/265-7828**), also offers comfort food, like macaroni and cheese, or burgers, until 4am.

Finally, in Dupont Circle, stop in at **Kramerbooks & Afterwords Café,** 1517 Connecticut Ave. NW (ⓒ **202/387-1400**), for big servings of everything, from quesadillas to french fries to French toast. The bookstore stays open all night on weekends, and so does its kitchen.

Latin Jazz Alley   This Adams-Morgan hot spot is another place to get in on Washington's Latin scene. At the Alley, you can learn to salsa and merengue Wednesday through Saturday nights; each lesson is $5 for beginners, $10 for intermediate dancers. The club features live Brazilian music Thursday nights, 10pm to 1am. Friday and Saturday nights, from about 10pm to 2am, a deejay plays Latin jazz. Dinner is served until midnight. 1721 Columbia Rd. NW, on the 2nd floor of the El Migueleno Cafe. ⓒ 202/328-6190. $5–$10 for salsa dance lessons; 2-drink minimum. Metro: U St.–Cardozo or Woodley Park–Zoo–Adams-Morgan and catch the Adams-Morgan/U St. Link Shuttle.

Zanzibar on the Waterfront   One day Washington will get its act together and develop the waterfront neighborhood in which you find Zanzibar. In the meantime, this area is pretty deserted at night, except for a handful of restaurants and Arena Stage. It really doesn't matter, though, because inside the nightclub you're looking out at the Potomac. Yes, this is a club with actual windows. In keeping with current trends, Zanzibar has lots of couches and chairs arranged just so. A Caribbean and African menu is available, and you can dine while listening to both live and deejay music. Every night brings something different, from jazz and blues to oldies. Wednesday is salsa night, with free lessons from 7 to 8pm, though a cover still applies: $5 to get in before 10pm and $10 after. An international crowd gathers here to dance or just hang out. 700 Water St. SW ⓒ 202/554-9100. www.zanzibar-otw.com. Cover typically $10 (more for live shows). Metro: Waterfront.

GAY CLUBS

Dupont Circle is the gay hub of Washington, D.C., with at least 10 gay bars within easy walking distance of one another. Here are two from that neighborhood and one located near the White House; also refer back to **Nation** (p. 254), whose Saturday night "Velvet" party is a gay event, and to **Mr. Henry's** (p. 258), whose live jazz on Friday night pleases every persuasion, though the restaurant itself has long been a popular spot for gays and lesbians.

Badlands Twenty-seven years old and still going strong, Badlands is a favorite dance club for gay men. In addition to the parquet dance floor in the main room, the club has at least six bars throughout the first level. Upstairs is the Annex bar/lounge/pool hall, and a show room where karaoke performers commandeer the mike Friday night. 1415 22nd St. NW, near P St. ℂ **202/296-0505.** www. badlandsdc.com. Sometimes a cover of $3–$10, depending on the event. Metro: Dupont Circle.

Hung Jury For the D.C. lesbian insider. Though the address is H Street, you reach this club via an alley off 19th Street. To enter the blue door, you must be a woman or be accompanied by a woman, but Hung Jury welcomes everyone—gays, straights, men, and women. Inside the club is a large dance floor, two bars, a lounge, and a pool table. Open Friday and Saturday nights. 1819 H St. NW. ℂ **202/785-8181.** Cover $5–$10. Metro: Farragut West.

J.R.'s Bar and Grill This casual and intimate all-male Dupont Circle club draws a crowd that is friendly, upscale, and very attractive. The interior—not that you'll be able to see much of it, because J.R.'s is always sardine-packed—has a 20-foot-high pressed-tin ceiling and exposed brick walls hung with neon beer signs. The big screen over the bar area is used to air music videos, showbiz sing-alongs, and favorite TV shows. Thursday is all-you-can-drink for $7 from 5 to 8pm; at midnight, you get free shots. The balcony, with pool tables, is a little more laid back. Food is served daily, until 5pm Sunday and until 7pm all other days. 1519 17th St. NW (between P and Q sts.). ℂ **202/328-0090.** www.jrsdc.com. No cover. Metro: Dupont Circle.

3 The Bar Scene

Washington has a thriving and varied bar scene. But just when you think you know all the hot spots, a spate of new ones pop up. Travel the triangle formed by the intersections of Connecticut Avenue, 18th Street, and M Street, in the Dupont Circle neighborhood, and you'll find the latest bunch. (The triangle is also a nightclub mecca—see the writeups for the Eighteenth Street Lounge and 5, in the Club & Music Scene section of this chapter.)

If you're in the mood for a sophisticated setting, seek out a bar in one of the nicer hotels, like **the Jefferson, the Willard,** or **the St. Regis** (see chapter 5 for more information and suggestions). If you want a convivial atmosphere and decent grub, try establishments that are equal parts restaurant and bar. Refer to chapter 6 for details about **Clyde's, Old Ebbitt Grill,** and **Old Glory.**

Finally, if you appreciate strikingly whimsical décor in an intimately loungy setting, where drinks bear names like Sin on the Rocks, or Blue Nirvana, and the menu offers exquisitely prepared "small plates" of fine food, than you are right in step with Washington's latest trend. Check out Bar Rouge, the Topaz Bar, and Toka Café, included in this section.

Bar Rouge Hopping, popping Bar Rouge lies just inside the Hotel Rouge (see chapter 5), but also has its own entrance from the street—you must pass under the watchful eyes of the stone Venuses arrayed in front to reach it. As acid jazz or modern international music pulses throughout the narrow room, a large flat-screen monitor on the back wall of the bar presents evolving visions of flowers blooming, snow falling, and other photographically engineered scenes. The place is full of attitude-swaggering patrons tossing back drinks with names like Sin on the Rocks and Love Gun. A lucky few have snagged seats on the white leather-cushioned barstools at the deep red mahogany bar. Others lounge on the 20-foot-long tufted banquette and munch on little dishes of scallop ceviche sopapillas, roasted pumpkin ravioli, and other Latin-inspired tastings served by waitresses in patent leather go-go boots and seductive black attire. Bar Rouge aims to be a scene, and succeeds. But be forewarned: If it looks crowded, you'll probably want to go elsewhere. 1315 16th St. NW (at Massachusetts Ave. and Scott Circle). ℂ 202/232-8000. Metro: Dupont Circle.

Big Hunt   This casual and comfy Dupont Circle hangout for the 20- to 30-something crowd bills itself as a "happy hunting ground for humans" (read: meat market). It has a kind of *Raiders of the Lost Ark*/jungle theme. A downstairs room (where music is the loudest) is adorned with exotic travel posters and animal skins; another area has leopard skin-patterned booths under canvas tenting. Amusing murals grace the balcony level, which adjoins a room with pool tables. The candlelit basement is the spot for quiet conversation. The menu offers typical bar food, and the bar offers close to 30 beers on tap, most of them microbrews. An outdoor patio lies off the back pool room.

   Note: This place and the Lucky Bar might be the perfect antidotes to their exclusive neighbors down the block, the Eighteenth Street Lounge, Dragonfly, and MCCXXIII. If you're rejected there, forget about it and come here. 1345 Connecticut Ave. NW (between N St. and Dupont Circle). ℂ 202/785-2333. Metro: Dupont Circle.

Brickskeller *Value*   If you like beer and you like choices, head for Brickskeller, which has been around for nearly 40 years and offers about 800 beers from around the world. If you can't make up your mind, ask one of the waiters, who tend to be knowledgeable about the brews. The tavern draws students, college professors, embassy types, and people from the neighborhood. Brickskeller is a series of interconnecting rooms filled with gingham tableclothed tables; upstairs rooms are open only weekend nights. The food is generally okay—and the burgers are more than okay, especially the excellent Brickburger, topped with bacon, salami, onion, and cheese. 1523 22nd St. NW. ℂ 202/293-1885. No cover. Metro: Dupont Circle or Foggy Bottom.

Champions of Georgetown   Smells like beer. This is a sports bar where sports fans, athletes, and Georgetown University students like to hang out. Champions lies at the end of an alley off Wisconsin Avenue—be careful at night. The two-story bar is a clutter of sports paraphernalia, with TV monitors airing nonstop sporting events. Conversation has two themes: sports and pickup lines. Champions is often packed and doesn't take reservations; in the evening, you can expect to wait for a table, so arrive early. 1206 Wisconsin Ave. NW (just north of M St.). ℂ 202/965-4005. Metro: Foggy Bottom, then hop on the Georgetown Metro Connection shuttle.

Dragonfly   Expect to wait on line to get in here and the other hip clubs along this stretch of Connecticut Avenue. Dragonfly is a club, with music playing, white walls glowing, white-leather chairs beckoning, and people in black vogueing. And Dragonfly is a restaurant, with serious aspirations to please sushi-lovers. But Dragonfly is not a dance club, so put on your cool clothes but leave your dancing shoes at home. 1215 Connecticut Ave. NW. ℂ 202/331-1775. Metro: Dupont Circle or Farragut North.

The Dubliner   This is your typical old Irish pub, the port you can blow into in any storm, personal or weather-related. It's got the dark-wood paneling and

Value Cheap Eats: Happy Hours to Write Home About

Even the diviest of bars puts out some free nibbles to complement your drink—peanuts or pretzels at the very least. And good-value promotions are increasingly popular at area bars and nightclubs, such as **Whitlow's on Wilson** in Arlington (see the "Arlington Row" box on p. 264), where you can chow down on a half-price burger every Monday night. A step above these are certain fine restaurants and hotels around town that set out gourmet food during happy hour, either for free or an astonishingly low price. Here are three that even Washingtonians may not know about:

In the bar area only, **McCormick & Schmick's**, 1652 K St. NW, at the corner of 17th Street NW (© 202/861-2233), offers a choice of giant burger, fried calamari, quesadillas, fish tacos, and more, for only $1.95 each. The offer is good Monday through Friday from 3:30 to 6:30pm, Monday through Thursday from 10:30pm to midnight, and Friday and Saturday from 10pm to midnight. Friendly bartenders make you feel at home as they concoct mixed drinks with juice they squeeze right at the bar (the drinks, alas, are not discounted).

Teaism Penn Quarter, 400 8th St. NW (© 202/638-6010), which is near the MCI Center, the FBI Building, the National Gallery, and nightspots, features happy hour Thursday and Friday from 5:30 to 7:30pm, with free hors d'oeuvres like Thai chicken and Indian curries, Asian noodle salads, sticky white rice, green salad—make a meal of it! Drinks are not discounted, but they are unusual: sakes, Asian beers, gingery margaritas, and the like.

The clubby, mahogany-paneled **Town and Country Lounge**, in the Renaissance Mayflower Hotel, 1127 Connecticut Ave. NW (© 202/347-3000), is the setting weeknights from 5:30 to 7:30pm for complimentary cocktail-hour hors d'oeuvres that change from night to night: slices of roast beef on toasts, chicken/beef fajitas, pastas, and so on. Here, you also have the pleasure of watching the personable bartender Sambonn Lek at work, whether mixing drinks or performing magic tricks. Drinks are regular price.

tables, the etched- and stained-glass windows, an Irish-accented staff from time to time, and, most importantly, the Auld Dubliner Amber Ale. You'll probably want to stick to drinks here, but you can grab a burger, grilled chicken sandwich, or roast duck salad; the kitchen is open until 1am. The Dubliner is frequented by Capitol Hill staffers and journalists who cover the Hill. Irish music groups play nightly. In the Phoenix Park Hotel, 520 N. Capitol St. NW, with its own entrance on F St. NW. © 202/737-3773. www.dublinerdc.com. Metro: Union Station.

ESPN Zone   This is not a date place, unless your date happens to be Anna Kournikova. It's three levels of sports mania, in the form of interactive sports games, a restaurant, 200 televisions throughout the place tuned to sporting events, a bar area, and the most popular attraction, the Screening Room. This last venue offers a giant 16-foot video screen flanked by six 36-inch screens, each showing a different event. Seats with special headphones are arrayed in front of the screen, and you control what you listen to. 555 12th St. NW. ℭ **202/783-3776.** www.espnzone.com. Metro: Metro Center.

Fadó   Another Irish pub, but this one is Ireland as theme park. It's gotten a lot of attention since its opening in 1998, partly because it was designed and built by the Irish Pub Company of Dublin, which shipped everything—the stone for the floors, the etched glass, the milled wood—from Ireland. The pub has separate areas, including an old Irish "bookstore" alcove and a country cottage bar. Authentic Irish food, like potato pancakes, is served with your Guinness. *Fadó,* Gaelic for "long ago," doesn't take reservations, which means that hungry patrons tend to hover over your table waiting for you to finish. 808 7th St. NW. ℭ **202/789-0066.** www.fadoirishpub.com. Metro: Gallery Place–Chinatown.

Lucky Bar   Lucky Bar is a good place to kick back and relax. But, in keeping with the times, it also features free salsa dance lessons on Monday night. Sometimes the music is live, but mostly it's courtesy of a deejay. Other times the jukebox plays, but never so loud that you can't carry on a conversation. The bar has a front room overlooking Connecticut Avenue and a back room decorated with good-luck signs, couches, hanging TVs, booths, and a pool table. Lucky Bar is known in the area as a "soccer bar," with its TVs turned to soccer matches going on around the world; during the month-long 2002 World Cup playoffs, the bar received permission from the D.C. Alcoholic Beverage Control Board to open at 7am and start selling alcohol at 8am each day (later on Sun) of the championship. 1221 Connecticut Ave. NW. ℭ **202/331-3733.** Metro: Dupont Circle or Farragut North.

MCCXXIII   This is about as swank and New York as Washington gets: hipsters lined up at the velvet rope, a dress code (but really an excuse for the doorman to decide whether you measure up for admittance), outrageously high prices (drink and food charges are written in Roman numerals, so some people are taken aback when settling up), a soaring ceiling and opulent interior, beautiful women servers who purr at you, and more beautiful people milling about. 1223 Connecticut Ave. NW. ℭ **202/822-1800.** www.1223.com. Cover, for men only, $10 after 10pm. Metro: Dupont Circle or Farragut North.

Mr. Smith's of Georgetown   Mr. Smith's bills itself as "The Friendliest Saloon in Town," but the truth is that it's so popular among regulars, you're in danger of being ignored if the staff doesn't know you. The bar, which opened about 31 years ago, has a front room with original brick walls, wooden seats, and a long bar, at which you can count on finding pairs of newfound friends telling obscene jokes, loudly. At the end of this room is a large piano around which customers congregate each night to accompany the pianist. An interior light-filled garden room adjoins an outdoor garden area. 3104 M St. NW. ℭ **202/333-3104.** www.mrsmiths.com. Metro: Foggy Bottom, then take the Georgetown Metro Connection shuttle.

Nathans   Nathans is in the heart of Georgetown. If you pop in here in midafternoon, it's a quiet place to grab a beer or glass of wine and watch the action on the street. Visit at night, though, and it's a more typical bar scene, crowded with locals, out-of-towners, students, and a sprinkling of couples in from the 'burbs. That's the front room. The back room at Nathans is a civilized, candlelit restaurant serving classic American fare. After dinner on Friday and Saturday, this room turns into a dance hall, playing deejay music and attracting the 20-somethings Friday night, an older crowd Saturday night. 3150 M St. NW (at the corner of Wisconsin Ave.). ℭ **202/338-2600.** Metro: Foggy Bottom, then take the Georgetown Metro Connection shuttle.

Arlington Row

As unlikely as it seems, one of the hottest spots for Washington nightlife is a stretch of suburban street in Arlington, Virginia. I'm talking about a section of Wilson Boulevard in the Clarendon neighborhood, roughly between Highland and Danville streets. For years, people referred to this area as "Little Vietnam," for the many Vietnamese cafes and grocery stores that have flourished here. Now some are calling it "the new Adams-Morgan," as some pretty good nightclubs and several well-reviewed restaurants have joined the still-strong Vietnamese presence.

Let's get one thing straight: It isn't Adams-Morgan. Adams-Morgan is urban, ethnic, and edgy, full of the requisite black clothes, body piercings, colorful hair, tattoos, and bad attitudes. Arlington Row is a lot tamer, attracting, so far anyway, a crowd of all ages, usually dressed for comfort. You don't feel like your presence has to make a statement. Certainly, the clubs are more accessible: Metro stops are nearby, parking is easier, streets are safer, and clubs front the streets with picture windows and aren't as exclusive.

But I wouldn't recommend that you visit Arlington Row if it weren't for one key element: the music. It's live, it's good (most of the time), and it's here almost nightly. So take the Metro to the Clarendon stop and walk down Wilson, or drive up Wilson from Key Bridge, turn left on Edgewood Road or another side street, and park on the street. Then walk to these spots, all of which serve food:

The smallest of the bunch, **Galaxy Hut,** 2711 Wilson Blvd. (© 703/ 525-8646; www.galaxyhut.com), is a comfortable bar with far-out art on the walls and a patio in the alley. Look for live alternative rock most nights. No cover.

Politiki and the Pennsylvania Ave. Pourhouse   This welcome addition to the more traditional pubs along this stretch of Capitol Hill has two themes going. Its first floor plays on a Pittsburgh theme (honoring the owner's roots), displaying Steeler and Penguin paraphernalia, and drawing Iron City drafts from its tap and pierogis from the kitchen. Downstairs is a tiki bar: Think Scorpion Bowl and piña colada drinks, pupu platters, and hula dancer figurines. The basement has pool tables, a bar, and a lounge area (behind beaded curtains); the street level has booths and a bar; and the top floor occasionally features live music, dance lessons, and a promised Don Ho night. Now's your chance to wear your Hawaiian shirt. 319 Pennsylvania Ave. SE. © 202/546-1001. Metro: Capitol South.

Post Pub *Value*   This joint fits into the "comfortable shoe" category. Situated across from the offices of the *Washington Post,* the pub gets busy at lunch, grows quiet in the afternoon, and picks up again in the evening. Post Pub has two rooms furnished with old-fashioned black banquettes, faux wood paneling, mirrored beer insignias, jukeboxes, cigarette machines, and a long bar with tall stools. There are different happy-hour specials every night, like the 5 to 9pm Friday "Anything Absolut," which offers drinks made with Absolut vodka for $2.75 each. The food is homey and inexpensive (under $10) fare like onion rings,

At **IOTA**, 2832 Wilson Blvd. (© **703/522-8340**; iotaclubandcafe.com), up-and-coming local bands take the stage nightly in a setting with minimal decor (cement floor, exposed brick walls, and a wood-beamed ceiling); there's a patio in back. There's live music nightly. If there's a cover, it's usually $8 to $15.

Whitlow's on Wilson, 2854 Wilson Blvd. (© **703/276-9693**; www.whitlows.com), is the biggest spot on the block, spreading throughout four rooms, the first showcasing the music (usually blues, with anything from surfer music to rock thrown in). The place has the appearance of a diner, from Formica table–booths to a soda fountain, and serves retro diner food. (Mon half-price burger nights are a good deal.) The other rooms hold coin-operated pool tables, dartboards, and air hockey. Cover is usually $3 Thursday through Saturday after 9pm.

Clarendon Grill, 1101 N. Highland St. (© **703/524-7455**; www.cgrill.com), wins a best decor award for its construction theme: murals of construction workers, building materials displayed under the glass-covered bar, and so forth. Music is a mix of modern rock, jazz, and reggae. Cover is $3 to $5 Wednesday through Saturday.

Now, get in your car, hop the Metro, or get out your rambling shoes to visit one other place, about a mile south of this stretch of Wilson:

Rhodeside Grill, 1836 Wilson Blvd. (© **703/243-0145**; www.rhodeside grill.com), 3 blocks from the Courthouse Metro stop, is a well-liked American restaurant on its first floor. The rec-room-like bar downstairs features excellent live bands playing roots rock, jazz funk, Latin percussion, country rock, reggae—you name it. Cover averages $5 or more Thursday through Saturday starting at 9:30pm.

sandwiches, and chicken parmigiana. 1422 L St. NW (between Vermont and 15th sts.). © 202/628-2111. Metro: McPherson Square.

The Rock The Rock has the best location a sports bar could hope for, across the street from the MCI Center. The three-floor bar fills a former warehouse, its decor a montage of preexisting exposed pipes and concrete floors, TV screens, pool tables, and sports memorabilia. The most popular spot is the third floor, where the pool tables and a cigar lounge are located. In good weather, folks head to the rooftop bar. 717 6th St. NW. © 202/842-7625. www.soccer-nation.com. Metro: MCI Center/Gallery Place.

Spy Lounge You enter this cool bar through the Felix Restaurant (see chapter 6 for a review), and that's because Alan Popowsky owns them both. The Spy attempts a modern European feel, with metal stools and white walls, and builds upon a spy theme, showing scenes from James Bond movies continually on its TV screens. Popowsky keeps the place from getting too crowded, or riffraffy, by allowing only a certain number of people in at a time (and only those who are dressed attractively). 2406 18th St. NW. © 202/483-3549. Metro: U St.–Cardozo or Woodley Park–Zoo–Adams-Morgan, and catch the Adams-Morgan/U St. Link Shuttle.

Toka Café Toka is small, underground, and upscale, affecting a hip New York look, with its sleek decor of white walls and brushed steel accents, aluminum bar stools and glass-topped bar. Toka pursues an NYC ambience, too, requiring no dress code, but catering to a crowd that can afford its pricey cocktails, like the $9 signature drink, the "Tokatini" (orange vodka and Cointreau), and who enjoy bites of fancy food, such as crab croquettes or grape leaves stuffed with duck confit. (Toka is both a restaurant and bar.) Patrons overwhelmed the small space when Toka first opened in 2002; like Topaz and Rouge (see write-ups in this section), Toka works best when it's not crowded. 1140 19th St. NW. © 202/429-8652. Metro: Dupont Circle or Farragut North.

The Tombs Housed in a converted 19th-century Federal-style home, the Tombs, which opened in 1962, is a favorite hangout for students and faculty of nearby Georgetown University. (Bill Clinton came here during his college years.) They tend to congregate at the central bar and surrounding tables, while local residents head for "the Sweeps," the room that lies down a few steps and has red-leather banquettes.

Directly below the upscale 1789 restaurant (see chapter 6 for a review), the Tombs benefits from 1789 chef Riz Lacoste's supervision. The menu offers burgers, sandwiches, and salads, as well as more serious fare. 1226 36th St. NW. © 202/337-6668. Cover sometimes on Tues or Sun nights, never more than $5. Metro: Foggy Bottom, then take the Georgetown Metro Connection shuttle into Georgetown.

Topaz Bar This is Bar Rouge's sister (they are owned and managed by the same companies) and also lies within a hotel, The Topaz. The decor here emphasizes cool sensuality, hence the Philippe Starck bar stools, blue velvet settees, zebra-patterned ottomans, and leopard-print rugs. A lighting scheme fades into and out of colors: blue to pink to black, and so on. Everyone here is drinking the Blue Nirvana, a combo of champagne, vodka, and a touch of blueberry liqueur—a concoction that tends to turn your tongue blue, by the way. The Topaz Bar serves small plates of delicious Asian-inspired tastes, like shrimp and pork dumplings and stir-fry of sea scallops. 1733 N St. NW. © 202/393-3000. Metro: Dupont Circle or Farragut North.

Tryst This is the most relaxed of Washington's lounge bars. The room is surprisingly large for Adams-Morgan, and it's jam-packed with worn armchairs and couches, which are usually occupied, no matter what time of day. People come here to have coffee or a drink, get a bite to eat, read a book, meet a friend. The place feels almost like a student lounge on a college campus, only alcohol is served. 2459 18th St. NW. © 202/232-5500. www.trystdc.com. Metro: U St.–Cardozo or Woodley Park–Zoo–Adams-Morgan and catch the Adams-Morgan/U St. Link Shuttle.

Tune Inn *(Finds* Capitol Hill has a number of bars that qualify as institutions, but the Tune Inn is probably the most popular. Capitol Hill staffers and their bosses, apparently at ease in dive surroundings, have been coming here for cheap beer and greasy burgers since it opened in 1955. (All the longtime Capitol Hillers know that Fri is crab cake day at the Tune Inn, and they all show up.) 33½ Pennsylvania Ave. SE. © 202/543-2725. Metro: Capitol South.

XandO Popular from the start, XandO (pronounced "zando") is a welcoming place in the morning for a coffee drink, and even more inviting for a cocktail later in the day. Men: You'll see a lot of cute women hanging out here, drawn perhaps by the make-your-own s'mores and other delicious desserts. XandO also serves sandwiches and soups. The music is loud; the decor a cross between bar and living room. 1350 Connecticut Ave. NW. © 202/296-9341. Metro: Dupont Circle, 19th St. exit. Also at 1647 20th St. NW, at Connecticut Ave. NW (© 202/332-6364), and 301 Pennsylvania Ave. SE (© 202/546-3345).

10

Side Trips from Washington, D.C.

On the other side of the Potomac River from Washington, D.C., within an easy drive, bike ride, sail, or jaunt on the Metro, is Old Town Alexandria, a charming waterfront village full of historic attractions, good restaurants and shops, lively bars and nightclubs, and streets for strolling. If you'd like a break from Washington proper, head here. Old Town is a mere 8 miles from the District, and worth a closer look.

Better yet, make a day of it, and set your sights on George Washington's estate and gardens, Mount Vernon,

which is just another 8 miles beyond Alexandria. Plan to visit Mount Vernon first, then stop in Old Town on your return. But don't expect to find these spots any less crowded than the capital's attractions; their unique appeal, suburban locations, and proximity to downtown make them popular to local tourists and out-of-towners alike.

If you'd like to explore farther afield, consider picking up a copy of *Frommer's Virginia* or *Frommer's Maryland & Delaware*.

1 Mount Vernon

Only 16 miles south of the capital, George Washington's Southern plantation dates from a 1674 land grant to the president's great-grandfather.

ESSENTIALS

GETTING THERE If you're going by car, take any of the bridges over the Potomac River into Virginia and follow the signs pointing the way to National Airport/Mount Vernon/George Washington Memorial Parkway. You travel south on the George Washington Memorial Parkway, the river always to your left, passing by National Airport on your right, continuing through Old Town Alexandria, where the parkway is renamed "Washington Street," and heading 8 miles farther, until you reach the large circle that fronts Mount Vernon.

You might also take a bus or boat to Mount Vernon. These bus and boat tour prices include the price of admission to Mount Vernon.

Tourmobile buses (© 202/554-5100; www.tourmobile.com) depart daily, mid-June through Labor Day only, at 10am, noon, and 2pm from Arlington National Cemetery and the Washington Monument. The round-trip fare is $25 for adults, $12 for children 3 to 11 (free for children under 3). You must reserve your space in person at either Arlington Cemetery or the Washington Monument at least 30 minutes in advance. **Gray Line** bus tours (© 202/289-1995) go to Mount Vernon daily, leaving from the bus's terminal at Union Station at 8am and returning by 1pm. The cost is $28 per adult and $14 per child.

(*Fun Fact* **The George Washington Memorial Parkway**

Though few people realize it, the George Washington Memorial Parkway is actually a national park. The first section was completed in 1932 to honor the bicentennial of George Washington's birth. The parkway follows the Potomac River, running from Mount Vernon, past Old Town and the nation's capital, ending at Great Falls, Virginia. Today, the parkway is a major commuter route leading into and out of the city. Even the most impatient driver, however, can't help but notice the beautiful scenery and views of the Jefferson and Lincoln memorials and the Washington Monument that you pass along the way.

The Spirit of Washington Cruises' (© **202/554-8000;** www.spiritcruises. com) *Potomac Spirit* leaves from the Washington waterfront every day except Monday, from mid-March to mid-October at 8:30am, returning by 3pm; cost is $30.95 per adult, $20.95 per child (ages 7–11; younger children free). The Potomac Riverboat Company's (© **703/684-0580** or 703/548-9000; www. potomacriverboatco.com) *Miss Christin* operates Tuesday through Sunday May through August (weekends only from mid-Mar to Apr and Sept–Oct), departing at 12:15pm for Mount Vernon from the pier adjacent to the Torpedo Factory, at the bottom of King Street in Old Town Alexandria, and costing $26 per adult, $13 per child (ages 6–10; free for children under 6).

See the section on "Organized Tours," in chapter 7 for further details about Tourmobile, Gray Line, and boat tours to Mount Vernon. These trips generally allow you about 2 hours to tour the estate, which is adequate for most people.

If you're in the mood for exercise in a pleasant setting, rent a **bike** (see the box called "Biking to Old Town Alexandria & Mount Vernon" on p. 275 for rental locations and other information).

Finally, it is possible to take **public transportation** to Mount Vernon by riding the Metro to the Yellow Line's Huntington station and proceeding to the lower level, where you catch the Fairfax Connector bus (no. 101) to Mount Vernon. The connector bus is a 20-minute ride and costs 50¢. Call © **703/339-7200** for schedule information.

TOURING THE ESTATE

Mount Vernon Estate and Gardens If it's beautiful out, and you have the time, you could easily spend half a day or more soaking in the life and times of George Washington at Mount Vernon. The centerpiece of a visit to this 500-acre estate is a tour through 14 rooms of the mansion, whose oldest part dates from the 1740s. The plantation was passed down from Washington's great-grandfather, who acquired the land in 1674, eventually to George in 1754. Washington proceeded over the next 45 years to expand and fashion the home to his liking, though the American Revolution and his years as president kept Washington away from his beloved estate much of the time.

What you see today is a remarkable restoration of the mansion, displaying many original furnishings and objects used by the Washington family. The rooms have been repainted in the original colors favored by George and Martha. There's no formal guided tour, but attendants stationed throughout the house and grounds provide brief orientations and answer questions; when there's no line, a walk-through takes about 20 minutes. You can also rent an audio tour for

$3 that provides a 40-minute plantation overview narration. Maps of the property are available at the entrance, including an adventure map for children.

But don't stop there. After leaving the house, you can tour the outbuildings: the kitchen, slave quarters, storeroom, smokehouse, overseer's quarters, coach house, and stables. A 4-acre exhibit area called "George Washington, Pioneer Farmer" includes a replica of Washington's 16-sided barn and fields of crops that he grew (corn, wheat, oats, and so forth). Docents in period costumes demonstrate 18th-century farming methods. At its peak, Mount Vernon was an 8,000-acre working farm, reminding us that, more than anything, Washington considered himself first and foremost a farmer.

A museum on the property exhibits Washington memorabilia, and details of the restoration are explained in the museum's annex; there's also a gift shop. You'll want to walk around the grounds (especially in nice weather) and see the wharf (and take a 30-min. narrated excursion on the Potomac, offered seasonally, Tues–Sun), the slave burial ground, the greenhouse, the lawns and gardens, and the tomb containing George and Martha Washington's sarcophagi (24 other family members are also interred here). Public memorial services are held at the estate every year on the third Monday in February, the date commemorating Washington's birthday; admission is free that day. (This is also the site's busiest day, with an average of 17,000 people descending upon the place.)

Mount Vernon belongs to the Mount Vernon Ladies' Association, which purchased the estate for $200,000 in 1858, from John Augustine Washington, great-grand-nephew of the first president. Without the group's purchase, the estate might have crumbled and disappeared, for neither the federal government nor the Commonwealth of Virginia had wanted to buy the property when it was earlier offered for sale.

Today more than a million people tour the property annually. The best time to visit is off-season; during the heavy tourist months (especially in spring), avoid weekends and holidays if possible, and arrive early year-round to beat the crowds.

Southern end of the George Washington Memorial Pkwy. (mailing address: P.O. Box 110, Mount Vernon, VA 22121). © **703/780-2000.** www.mountvernon.org. Admission $9 adults, $8.50 seniors, $4.50 children 6–11, free for children under 6. Apr–Aug daily 8am–5pm; Mar and Sept–Oct daily 9am–5pm; Nov–Feb daily 9am–4pm.

DINING & SHOPPING

Mount Vernon expanded its dining and shopping services in 2001. The new **gift shop** is now twice its former size, offering a wider range of books, children's toys, holiday items, Mount Vernon private-labeled food and wine, and Mount Vernon licensed furnishings.

A **food court** replaces the old cafeteria-style snack bar and features indoor and outdoor seating and a menu of baked goods, deli sandwiches, coffee, grilled items, Pizza Hut pizza, and Mrs. Fields cookies. You can't **picnic** on the grounds

---

Tips Special Activities at Mount Vernon

There's an ongoing schedule of events at Mount Vernon, especially in summer. These might include tours focusing on 18th-century gardens, slave life, colonial crafts, or archaeology; and, for children, hands-on history programs and treasure hunts. Call to find out whether anything is on during your visit.

of Mount Vernon, but you can drive a mile north on the parkway to Riverside Park, where there are tables and a lawn overlooking the Potomac.

Meanwhile, the Mount Vernon Inn restaurant is still the option I'd recommend.

Mount Vernon Inn AMERICAN TRADITIONAL   Lunch or dinner at the inn is an intrinsic part of the Mount Vernon experience. It's a quaint and charming colonial-style restaurant, complete with period furnishings and three working fireplaces. The waiters are all in 18th-century costumes. Be sure to begin your meal with the homemade peanut and chestnut soup (usually on the lunch menu). Lunch entrees range from colonial turkey "pye" (a sort of Early American quiche served in a crock with garden vegetables and a puffed pastry top) to a 20th-century–style burger and fries. There's a full bar, and premium wines are offered by the glass. At dinner, tablecloths and candlelight make this a more elegant setting. Choose from soups (perhaps broccoli cheddar) and salads, entrees such as Maryland crab cakes or roast venison with peppercorn sauce, homemade breads, and dessert (like whiskey cake or English trifle).

Near the entrance to Mount Vernon Estate and Gardens. (C) 703/780-0011. Reservations recommended for dinner. Lunch main courses $5.50–$8.50; dinner main courses $13–$24; fixed-price dinner $15. AE, DISC, MC, V. Mon–Sat 11am–3:30pm and Sun 11am–4pm; daily 5–9pm.

2 Alexandria

Founded by a group of Scottish tobacco merchants, the seaport town of Alexandria was born in 1749 when a 60-acre tract of land was auctioned off in half-acre lots. Colonists came from miles around, in ramshackle wagons and stately carriages, in sloops, brigantines, and lesser craft, to bid on land that would be "commodious for trade and navigation and tend greatly to the ease and advantage of the frontier inhabitants." The auction took place in Market Square (still intact today), and the surveyor's assistant was a capable lad of 17 named George Washington. (Market Square, by the way, is the site of the oldest continually operating farmers' market in the country; go there on a Sat between 5 and 9:30am and you'll be participating in a 254-year-old tradition.)

Today, the original 60 acres of lots in George Washington's hometown (also Robert E. Lee's) are the heart of Old Town, a multimillion-dollar urban renewal historic district. Many Alexandria streets still bear their original colonial names (King, Queen, Prince, Princess, Royal—you get the drift), while others, like Jefferson, Franklin, Lee, Patrick, and Henry, are obviously post-Revolutionary.

In this "mother lode of Americana," the past is being restored in an ongoing archaeological and historical research program. And though the present can be seen in the abundance of shops, boutiques, art galleries, and restaurants that capitalize on the tourist traffic, it's still easy to imagine yourself in colonial times by listening for the rumbling of horse-drawn vehicles over cobblestone (portions of Prince and Oronoco streets are still paved with cobblestone); dining on Sally Lunn bread and other 18th-century grub in the centuries-old Gadsby's Tavern; and learning about the lives of the nation's forefathers during walking tours that take you in and out of their houses.

ESSENTIALS

GETTING THERE   Old Town Alexandria is about 8 miles south of Washington. If you're driving, take the Arlington Memorial or the 14th Street Bridge to the George Washington Memorial Parkway south, which becomes Washington Street in Old Town Alexandria. Washington Street intersects with King

Old Town Alexandria

Alexandria Black History Resource Center **1**
Carlyle House **6**
Christ Church **3**
Friendship Firehouse **12**
Gadsby's Tavern Museum **4**
Lee-Fendall House **2**
The Lyceum **11**

Market Square **5**
Old Presbyterian Meeting House **10**
Ramsay House Visitors Bureau **7**
Stabler-Leadbeater
  Apothecary Museum **9**
Torpedo Factory/
  Alexandria Archaeology **8**

Street, Alexandria's main thoroughfare. Turn left from Washington Street onto one of the streets before or after King Street (southbound left turns are not permitted from Washington St. onto King St.) and you'll be heading toward the waterfront and the heart of Old Town. If you turn right from Washington Street onto King Street, you'll find an avenue of shops and restaurants. You can obtain a free parking permit from the Visitors Association (see below), or park at meters or in garages.

The easiest way to make the trip may be the Metro's Yellow and Blue lines to the King Street station. From the King Street station, you can catch an eastbound AT2, AT5, or AT7 blue-and-gold DASH bus (✆ **703/370-DASH**), marked either "Old Town" or "Braddock Metro," which will take you up King Street. Ask to be dropped at the corner of Fairfax and King streets, which will put you right across the street from Ramsay House, the visitor center. The fare is $1 most of the time, but free weekends, from Friday evening through Sunday night. Or you can walk into Old Town, although it's about a mile from the station into the center of Old Town.

The town is compact, so you won't need a car once you arrive.

VISITOR INFORMATION The **Alexandria Convention and Visitors Association,** located at Ramsay House, 221 King St., at Fairfax Street (✆ **800/ 388-9119** or 703/838-4200; www.funside.com), is open daily from 9am to 5pm (closed Jan 1, Thanksgiving, and Dec 25). Here you can obtain a map/self-guided walking tour and brochures about the area; learn about special events that might be scheduled during your visit and get tickets for them; and receive answers to any questions you might have about accommodations, restaurants, sights, or shopping. The association supplies materials in five languages.

If you come by car, get a free 1-day parking permit here for any 2-hour meter for up to 24 hours; when you park, put money in the meter to cover yourself until you post your permit. The permit can be renewed for a second day.

ORGANIZED TOURS Though it's easy to see Alexandria on your own by putting yourself in the hands of colonial-attired guides at the various attractions, you might consider taking a comprehensive walking tour.

Weather permitting, **Doorways to Old Virginia** (✆ **703/548-0100**) conducts "Legend, Folklores, and Ghosts" tours April through mid-November at 7:30 and 9pm Friday and Saturday, 7:30pm only on Sunday. This 1-hour tour departs from Ramsay House and costs $6 for adults, $4 for children ages 7 to 12, free for children under 7. You purchase tickets from the guide.

Alexandria Tours (✆ **703/329-1122**) offers 1½-hour architectural and history tours April through fall, weather permitting, leaving from the visitor center at 10:30am every day but Sunday, when it leaves at 2pm. The tour costs $10 per person (free for age 6 and under) and you pay the guide when you arrive at the visitor center.

CITY LAYOUT Old Town is very small and laid out in an easy grid. At the center is the intersection of Washington Street and King Street. Streets change from North to South when they cross King Street. For example, North Alfred Street is the part of Alfred north of King Street. Guess where South Alfred Street is.

SPECIAL EVENTS

Two organizations publish helpful calendars of key Alexandria events: the **Alexandria Convention and Visitors Association** (✆ **800/388-9119** or 703/ 838-4200; www.funside.com), which covers Alexandria at large; and the City

(Tips) Patriot Pass & Block Tickets

Money-saving tickets are on sale at the **Ramsay House Visitor Center.** A **Patriot Pass "Plus" ticket,** costing $26 for an adult, $14 for children ages 11 to 17, admits you to the Carlyle House, Gadsby's Tavern Museum, Lee-Fendall House, and the Stabler-Leadbeater Apothecary. It also reserves your place on a guided walking tour of Old Town, as well as a ride aboard the *Admiral Tilp* riverboat that cruises the Potomac River along the Alexandria waterfront. The Plus ticket can save you about $7 per adult and $8 per child. Unfortunately, it can be hard to coordinate the timed tours of the historic sights and the scheduled departures of the walking tour and boat excursion within the framework of a single day. The Plus ticket makes the most sense if you're staying more than 1 day. Also available are regular Patriot Pass tickets, which include everything that the Plus ticket does, except for the walking tour; tickets are $19 for adults and $9 for children.

If you're here just for the day, you can still save money by buying a **block ticket** for admission to Gadsby's Tavern Museum, the Carlyle House, and the Stabler-Leadbeater Apothecary Shop. The ticket, which can also be purchased at any of the buildings, costs $9 for adults, $5 for children ages 11 to 17, free for children under 11. The savings come to about $1.50 per adult, $1 per child.

---

of Alexandria's **Office of Historic Alexandria** (✆ 703/838-4554; www.ci. alexandria.va.us/oha), which focuses on the historic sights. You can call and ask for information to be mailed to you, or access their separate and continually updated websites. Event highlights include:

January   The **birthdays of Robert E. Lee and his father,** Revolutionary War Colonel "Light Horse Harry" Lee, are celebrated together at the Lee-Fendall House the third Sunday of the month. The party features period music, refreshments, and house tours.

February   Alexandria celebrates **George Washington's Birthday,** on Presidents' Weekend, which precedes the federal holiday, usually the third Monday in February. Festivities typically include a colonial costume or black-tie banquet, followed by a ball at Gadsby's Tavern, a 10-kilometer race, special tours, a Revolutionary War encampment at Fort Ward Park (complete with uniformed troops engaging in skirmishes), the nation's largest George Washington Birthday Parade (50,000–75,000 people attend each year), and 18th-century comic opera performances.

March   On the first Saturday in March, King Street is the site of a popular **St. Patrick's Day Parade.**

April   Alexandria celebrates **Historic Garden Week in Virginia** with tours of privately owned local historic homes and gardens the third Saturday of the month.

June   The **Red Cross Waterfront Festival,** the second weekend in June, honors Alexandria's historic importance as a seaport and the vitality of its Potomac shoreline today with a display of historic tall ships, ship tours, boat rides and races, nautical art exhibits, waterfront walking tours, fireworks, children's games, an arts and crafts show, food booths, and entertainment. Admission is charged.

July   Alexandria's birthday (its 254th in 2003) is celebrated with a concert performance by the Alexandria Symphony Orchestra, fireworks, birthday cake, and other festivities. The Saturday following the Fourth of July.

September   Chili lovers can sample "bowls of red" at the **Hard Times Chili Cookoff** in Waterfront Park. Contestants from almost every U.S. state and territory compete, and for an admission charge of a few dollars, you can taste all their creations. Proceeds go to charity. Fiddling contests, jalapeño-eating contests, and country music are part of the fun. Late September.

October   October is Arts Month in Alexandria, and celebrations include the **Alexandria Arts Safari,** which takes place on the first Saturday in October and features archaeological and arts tours, and interactive events all over Old Town. Free.

   Halloween Walking Tours take place toward the end of October. A lantern-carrying guide in 18th-century costume tells you about Alexandria's ghosts, graveyards, legends, myths, and folklore as you tour the town and graveyards. Call the visitor center for information.

November   There's a **Christmas Tree Lighting** in Market Square the Friday after Thanksgiving; the ceremony, which includes choir singing, puppet shows, dance performances, and an appearance by Santa and his elves, begins at 7pm. The night the tree is lit, thousands of tiny lights adorning King Street trees also go on.

December   Holiday festivities continue with the **Annual Scottish Christmas Walk** on the first Saturday in December. Activities include kilted bagpipers, Highland dancers, a parade of Scottish clans (with horses and dogs), caroling, fashion shows, storytelling, booths (selling crafts, antiques, food, hot mulled punch, heather, fresh wreaths, and holly), and children's games. Admission is charged for some events.

   The **Historic Alexandria Candlelight Tour,** the second week in December, visits seasonally decorated historic Alexandria homes and an 18th-century tavern. There is colonial dancing, string quartets, madrigal and opera singers, and refreshments, too. Purchase tickets at the Ramsay House Visitor Center.

   There are so many holiday-season activities that the Visitors Association issues a special brochure about them each year. Pick one up to learn about decorations, workshops, walking tours, tree lightings, concerts, bazaars, bake sales, craft fairs, and much more.

WHAT TO SEE & DO

Colonial and post-Revolutionary buildings are Old Town Alexandria's main attractions. My favorites are the Carlyle House and Gadsby's Tavern Museum, but they are all worth a visit.

   Except for the Alexandria Black History and Resource Center, whose closest Metro stop is the Braddock Street station, and Fort Ward, to which you should drive or take a taxi, these sites are most easily accessible via the King Street Metro station.

   Old Town has hundreds of charming boutiques, antiques stores, and gift shops selling everything from souvenir T-shirts to 18th-century reproductions. Some of the most interesting are at the sites, but most are clustered on King and Cameron streets and their connecting cross streets. A guide to antiques stores is available at the Visitors Association. Also see chapter 8, which includes some Alexandria shops.

> ### *Moments* Biking to Old Town Alexandria & Mount Vernon
>
> One of the nicest ways to see Washington is on a bike ride in Virginia. It's true: Rent a bike at Fletcher's Boat House or some other location listed under "Outdoor Activities" in chapter 7, then hop on the pathway that runs along the Potomac River, heading toward the monuments and the Arlington Memorial Bridge. In Washington, this is the Rock Creek Park Trail; once you cross Memorial Bridge (near the Lincoln Memorial) into Virginia, the name changes to the Mount Vernon Trail, which, as it sounds, is a straight shot to Mount Vernon.
>
> As you tool along, you have a breathtaking view of the Potomac and of Washington's grand landmarks: the Kennedy Center, Washington Monument, Lincoln Memorial, Jefferson Memorial, the National Cathedral off in one direction, and the Capitol off in the other.
>
> Of course, this mode of transportation is also a great way to see Old Town Alexandria and Mount Vernon, too. The trail carries you past Reagan National Airport, via two pedestrian bridges that take you safely through the airport's roadway system. Continue on to Old Town, where you really should dismount for a walk around, a tour of some of the historic properties listed in this chapter, or some refreshment from one of the restaurants, before you proceed to Mount Vernon. The section from Memorial Bridge to Mount Vernon is about 19 miles in all.

Alexandria Black History Resource Center   In a 1940s building that originally housed the black community's first public library, the center exhibits historical objects, photographs, documents, and memorabilia relating to black citizens of Alexandria from the 18th century forward. In addition to the permanent collection, the museum presents rotating exhibits and other activities. If you're interested in further studies, check out the center's Watson Reading Room. A half hour is really enough time to spend at the center.

The center is actually on the outskirts of Old Town, and not in the best neighborhood. From here, it makes sense to walk, rather than to take the Metro or even a taxi, into Old Town. Have a staff person point you in the direction of Washington Street, where you will turn right and be only 2 blocks from the Lee-Fendall House, at Oronoco and Washington streets (see below).

638 N. Alfred St. (at Wythe St.). © 703/838-4356. Free admission (donations accepted). Tues–Sat 10am–4pm; Sun 1–5pm. Metro: Braddock Rd. From the station, walk across the parking lot and bear right until you reach the corner of West and Wythe sts., where you'll proceed 5 blocks east along Wythe until you reach the center.

Carlyle House   One of Virginia's most architecturally impressive 18th-century homes, Carlyle House also figured prominently in American history. In 1753, Scottish merchant John Carlyle completed the mansion for his bride, Sarah Fairfax of Belvoir, a daughter of one of Virginia's most prominent families. It was designed in the style of a Scottish/English manor house and lavishly furnished. Carlyle, a successful merchant, had the means to import the best furnishings and appointments available abroad for his new Alexandria home.

When it was built, Carlyle House was a waterfront property with its own wharf. A social and political center, the house was visited by the great men of the day, including George Washington. But its most important moment in history occurred in April 1755, when Maj. Gen. Edward Braddock, commander-in-chief of His Majesty's forces in North America, met with five colonial governors here and asked them to tax colonists to finance a campaign against the French and Indians. Colonial legislatures refused to comply, one of the first instances of serious friction between America and Britain. Nevertheless, Braddock made Carlyle House his headquarters during the campaign, and Carlyle was less than impressed with him. He called the general "a man of weak understanding . . . very indolent . . . a slave to his passions, women and wine . . . as great an Epicure as could be in his eating, tho a brave man." Possibly these were the reasons his unfinanced campaign met with disaster. Braddock received, as Carlyle described it, "a most remarkable drubbing."

Tours are given on the hour and half hour and take about 40 minutes; allow another 10 or 15 minutes if you plan to tour the tiered garden of brick walks and boxed parterres. Two of the original rooms, the large parlor and the adjacent study, have survived intact; the former, where Braddock met the governors, still retains its original fine woodwork, paneling, and pediments. The house is furnished in period pieces; however, only a few of Carlyle's possessions remain. In an upstairs room, an architecture exhibit depicts 18th-century construction methods with hand-hewn beams and hand-wrought nails.

121 N. Fairfax St. (between Cameron and King sts.). © 703/549-2997. www.carlylehouse.org. Admission $4 adults, $2 children 11–17, free for children under 11; or buy a block ticket. Tues–Sat 10am–4:30pm; Sun noon–4:30pm. Winter hours 10am–4pm.

Christ Church   This sturdy redbrick Georgian-style church would be an important national landmark even if its two most distinguished members had not been Washington and Lee. It has been in continuous use since 1773.

There have, of course, been many changes since Washington's day. The bell tower, church bell, galleries, and organ were added by the early 1800s, the "wine-glass" pulpit in 1891. But much of what was changed later has since been restored to its earlier state. The pristine white interior with wood moldings and gold trim is colonially correct. For the most part, the original structure remains, including the hand-blown glass in the windows. The town has grown up around the building that was once known as the "Church in the Woods."

> (**Tips** **Planning Note**
>
> Many Alexandria attractions are closed on Monday.

Christ Church has had its historic moments. Washington and other early church members fomented revolution in the churchyard, and Robert E. Lee met here with Richmond representatives to discuss assuming command of Virginia's military forces at the beginning of the Civil War. You can sit in the pew where George and Martha sat with her two Custis grandchildren, or in the Lee family pew.

It's traditional for U.S. presidents to attend a service here on a Sunday close to Washington's birthday and sit in his pew. One of the most memorable of these visits took place shortly after Pearl Harbor, when Franklin Delano Roosevelt attended services with Winston Churchill on the World Day of Prayer for Peace, January 1, 1942.

Of course, you're invited to attend a service (Sun at 8, 9, and 11:15am and 5pm; Wed at 7:15am and 12:05pm). There's no admission, but donations are appreciated. A guide gives brief lectures to visitors. Twenty minutes should do it here.

118 N. Washington St. (at Cameron St.). ℭ 703/549-1450. www.historicchristchurch.org. Suggested donation $5 adults, $3 children. Mon–Sat 9am–4pm; Sun 2:30–4pm. Closed all federal holidays.

Fort Ward Museum & Historic Site   A short drive from Old Town is a 45-acre museum and park that transport you to Alexandria during the Civil War. The action here centers, as it did in the early 1860s, on an actual Union fort that Lincoln ordered erected. It was part of a system of Civil War forts called the "Defenses of Washington." About 90% of the fort's earthwork walls are preserved, and the Northwest Bastion has been restored with six mounted guns (originally there were 36). A model of 19th-century military engineering, the fort was never attacked by Confederate forces. Self-guided tours begin at the Fort Ward ceremonial gate.

Visitors can explore the fort and replicas of the ceremonial entrance gate and an officer's hut. There's a museum of Civil War artifacts on the premises where changing exhibits focus on subjects such as Union arms and equipment, medical care of the wounded, and local war history.

There are picnic areas with barbecue grills in the park surrounding the fort. Living-history presentations take place throughout the year. This is a good stop if you have young children, in which case you could spend an hour or two here (especially if you bring a picnic).

4301 W. Braddock Rd. (between Rte. 7 and Seminary Rd.). ℭ 703/838-4848. www.fortward.org. Free admission. Park and museum Tues–Sat 9am–5pm; Sun noon–5pm. Donations appreciated. Call for information regarding special holiday closings. From Old Town, follow King St. west, go right on Kenwood Ave., then left on West Braddock Rd.; continue for ¾ mile to the entrance on the right.

Friendship Firehouse   Alexandria's first firefighting organization, the Friendship Fire Company, was established in 1774. In the early days, the company met in taverns and kept its firefighting equipment in a member's barn. Its present Italianate-style brick building dates from 1855; it was erected after an earlier building was, ironically, destroyed by fire. Local tradition holds that George Washington was involved with the firehouse as a founding member, active firefighter, and purchaser of its first fire engine, although research does not confirm these stories. This is a tiny place, which you can easily "do" in 20 minutes.

107 S. Alfred St. (between King and Prince sts.). ℭ 703/838-3891. Free admission. Fri–Sat 10am–4pm; Sun 1–4pm.

Gadsby's Tavern Museum 𝄞   Alexandria was at the crossroads of 18th-century America, and its social center was Gadsby's Tavern, which consisted of two buildings (one Georgian, one Federal) dating from around 1770 and 1792, respectively. Innkeeper John Gadsby combined them to create "a gentleman's tavern," which he operated from 1796 to 1808; it was considered one of the finest in the country. George Washington was a frequent dinner guest; he and Martha danced in the second-floor ballroom, and it was here that Washington celebrated his last birthday. The tavern also welcomed Thomas Jefferson, James Madison, and the Marquis de Lafayette. It was the scene of lavish parties, theatrical performances, small circuses, government meetings, and concerts. Itinerant merchants used the tavern to display their wares, and traveling doctors and dentists treated a hapless clientele (these were rudimentary professions in the 18th century) on the premises.

The rooms have been restored to their 18th-century appearance. On the 30-minute tour, you'll get a good look at the Tap Room, a small dining room; the Assembly Room, the ballroom; typical bedrooms; and the underground icehouse, which was filled each winter from the icy river. Tours depart 15 minutes before and after the hour. Inquire about living-history programs, such as "Gadsby's Time Travels," geared toward children, and "18th-Century Balls," aimed at adults who'd like to try dancing in the old-fashioned way. Cap off the experience with a meal at the restored colonial-style restaurant (see "Dining," below).

134 N. Royal St. (at Cameron St.). ✆ 703/838-4242. www.gadsbystavern.net. Admission $4 adults, $2 children 11–17, free for children under 11; or buy a block ticket. Tours Apr–Sept Tues–Sat 10am–5pm, Sun 1–5pm; Oct–Mar Tues–Sat 11am–4pm, Sun 1–4pm. Closed most federal holidays.

Lee-Fendall House Museum   This handsome Greek Revival–style house is a veritable Lee family museum of furniture, heirlooms, and documents. "Light Horse Harry" Lee never actually lived here, though he was a frequent visitor, as was his good friend George Washington. He did own the original lot, but sold it to Philip Richard Fendall (himself a Lee on his mother's side), who built the house in 1785. Fendall married three Lee wives, including Harry's first mother-in-law, and, later, Harry's sister.

Thirty-seven Lees occupied the house over a period of 118 years (1785–1903), and it was from this house that Harry wrote Alexandria's farewell address to George Washington, delivered when he passed through town on his way to assume the presidency. (Harry also wrote and delivered, but not at this house, the famous funeral oration to Washington that contained the words: "First in war, first in peace, and first in the hearts of his countrymen.") During the Civil War, the house was seized and used as a Union hospital.

Thirty-minute guided tours interpret the 1850s era of the home and provide insight into Victorian family life. You'll also see the colonial garden with its magnolia and chestnut trees, roses, and boxwood-lined paths. Much of the interior woodwork and glass is original.

614 Oronoco St. (at Washington St.). ✆ 703/548-1789. www.leefendallhouse.org. Admission $4 adults, $2 children 11–17, free for children under 11. Tues–Sat 10am–4pm; Sun 1–4pm. Call ahead to make sure the museum is open, since it often closes for special events. Tours on the hour 10am–3pm. Closed Thanksgiving and mid-Dec to Feb.

The Lyceum   This Greek Revival building houses a museum depicting Alexandria's history from the 17th through the 20th century. It features changing exhibits and an ongoing series of lectures, concerts, and educational programs.

You can obtain maps and brochures about Virginia state attractions, especially Alexandria attractions. The knowledgeable staff will be happy to answer questions. But even without its many attractions, the brick and stucco Lyceum merits a visit. Built in 1839, it was designed in the Doric temple style to serve as a lecture, meeting, and concert hall. It was an important center of Alexandria's cultural life until the Civil War, when Union forces appropriated it for use as a hospital. After the war it became a private residence, and still later it was subdivided for office space. In 1969, however, the city council's use of eminent domain prevented the Lyceum from being demolished in favor of a parking lot. Allow about 20 minutes here.

201 S. Washington St. (off Prince St.). ✆ 703/838-4994. www.alexandriahistory.org. Free admission. Mon–Sat 10am–5pm; Sun 1–5pm. Closed Jan 1, Thanksgiving, and Dec 25.

Old Presbyterian Meeting House   Presbyterian congregations have worshipped in Virginia since the Rev. Alexander Whittaker converted Pocahontas in

Jamestown in 1614. This brick church was built by Scottish pioneers in 1775. Although it wasn't George Washington's church, the Meeting House bell tolled continuously for 4 days after his death in December 1799, and memorial services were preached from the pulpit here by Presbyterian, Episcopal, and Methodist ministers. According to the Alexandria paper of the day, "The walking being bad to the Episcopal church the funeral sermon of George Washington will be preached at the Presbyterian Meeting House." Two months later, on Washington's birthday, Alexandria citizens marched from Market Square to the church to pay their respects.

Many famous Alexandrians are buried in the church graveyard, including John and Sarah Carlyle, Dr. James Craik (the surgeon who treated—some say killed—Washington, dressed Lafayette's wounds at Brandywine, and ministered to the dying Braddock at Monongahela), and William Hunter Jr., founder of the St. Andrew's Society of Scottish descendants, to whom bagpipers pay homage on the first Saturday of December. It is also the site of a Tomb of an Unknown Revolutionary War Soldier. Dr. James Muir, minister between 1789 and 1820, lies beneath the sanctuary in his gown and bands.

The original Meeting House was gutted by a lightning fire in 1835, but parishioners restored it in the style of the day a few years later. The present bell, said to be recast from the metal of the old one, was hung in a newly constructed belfry in 1843, and a new organ was installed in 1849. The Meeting House closed its doors in 1889, and for 60 years it was virtually abandoned. But in 1949 it was reborn as a living Presbyterian U.S.A. church, and today the Old Meeting House looks much as it did following its first restoration. The original parsonage, or manse, is still intact. There's no guided tour, but there is a recorded narrative in the graveyard. Allow 20 minutes for touring.

321 S. Fairfax St. (between Duke and Wolfe sts.). ℭ 703/549-6670. www.opmh.org. Free admission, but you must obtain a key from the office to tour the church. Sun services at 8:30 and 11am, except in summer, when 1 service is held at 10am.

Stabler-Leadbeater Apothecary Museum

When its doors closed in 1933, this landmark drugstore was the second oldest in continuous operation in America. Run for five generations by the same Quaker family (beginning in 1792), the store counted Robert E. Lee (who purchased the paint for Arlington House here), George Mason, Henry Clay, John C. Calhoun, and George Washington among its famous patrons. Gothic Revival decorative elements and Victorian-style doors were added in the 1840s. Today the apothecary looks much as it did in colonial times, its shelves lined with original handblown gold-leaf–labeled bottles (actually the most valuable collection of antique medicinal bottles in the country), old scales stamped with the royal crown, patent medicines, and equipment for bloodletting. The clock on the rear wall, the porcelain-handled mahogany drawers, and two mortars and pestles all date from about 1790. Among the shop's documentary records is this 1802 order from Mount Vernon: "Mrs. Washington desires Mr. Stabler to send by the bearer a quart bottle of his best Castor Oil and the bill for it."

A 5-minute audio tour will guide you around the displays. The adjoining gift shop uses its proceeds to maintain the apothecary. Allow 15 minutes.

105–107 S. Fairfax St. (near King St.). ℭ 703/836-3713 www.apothecary.org. Admission $2.50 adults, $2 children 11–17, free for children under 11; or buy a block ticket. Mon–Sat 10am–4pm; Sun 1–5pm. Closed major holidays.

Torpedo Factory

This block-long, three-story building was built in 1918 as a torpedo shell-case factory, but now accommodates some 160 professional artists and craftspeople who create and sell their own works on the premises. Here you can see artists at work in their studios: potters, painters, printmakers, photographers, sculptors, and jewelers, as well as those who make stained-glass windows and fiber art.

On permanent display are exhibits on Alexandria history provided by Alexandria Archaeology (© 703/838-4399), which is headquartered here and engages in extensive city research. A volunteer or staff member is on hand to answer questions. Art lovers could end up browsing for an hour or two.

105 N. Union St. (between King and Cameron sts. on the waterfront). © 703/838-4565. Free admission. Daily 10am–5pm; archaeology exhibit area Tues–Fri 10am–3pm, Sun 1–5pm. Closed Easter, July 4, Thanksgiving, Dec 25, and Jan 1.

ACCOMMODATIONS

It is simply not possible to find inexpensive lodging within, or close by, Old Town Alexandria. In fact, Historic Old Town proper has only one hotel inside its boundaries. That one, the **Holiday Inn Select Old Town,** 480 King St. (© 800/368-5047 or 703/549-6080; www.oldtownhis.com), and another just outside the Historic District, **Morrison House,** 116 S. Alfred St. (© 800/367-0800 or 703/838-8000; www.morrisonhouse.com), are the two I'd recommend, if you're interested in staying overnight on this side of the Potomac. Expect to pay for their fine accommodations.

Rates at the Holiday Inn range from $119 (a special rate for employees of the government or military) to $249; suites start at $400. Rooms feature 18th-century–style furnishings; king, queen, or double beds; and sitting areas. Amenities at this hotel include complimentary continental breakfast on weekdays, bike rentals, a fitness center, and an indoor pool. Ask about discounts for AAA, AARP, government, and any other groups to which you may belong.

Morrison House is an elegant small hotel recently inducted as a member into the elite Relais & Châteaux. The hotel has only 45 rooms, each appointed in high style with canopied four-poster beds, mahogany armoires, decorative fireplaces, and the like. Rates start at $175 for the smallest room off-season, and at $310 for a deluxe room in-season. Morrison House is known for its restaurant, **Elysium,** which presents award-winning contemporary American cuisine.

For other recommendations, call the **Alexandria Hotel Association** (© 800/296-1000), which will check availability and rates and book your room at one of its 20 member hotels; or the **Princely Bed & Breakfast** (© 800/470-5588; www.PrincelyBandB.com), which books lodging at 31 private Old Town homes.

DINING

There are so many fine restaurants in Alexandria that Washingtonians often drive over just to dine here and stroll the cobblestone streets.

EXPENSIVE

Geranio REGIONAL ITALIAN   Many folks think this is the best restaurant in Old Town. After a dinner in front of the log fire, a fine bottle of Chianti, an appetizer of wild mushrooms with porcini essence (or maybe the lobster polenta), entree of grilled salmon with pancetta and red-wine sauce (or maybe the osso buco), followed by dessert of tiramisu (or maybe lemon parfait), you might agree. Excellent service.

722 King St. (between Washington and Columbus sts.). © 703/548-0088. Reservations recommended. Lunch items $12–$20; dinner main courses $15–$30. AE, DC, DISC, MC, V. Mon–Fri 11:30am–2:30pm; Mon–Sat 6–10:30pm; Sun 5:30–9:30pm.

La Bergerie ⭐ CLASSIC FRENCH   This restaurant has been here forever and is ever popular. Waiters are tuxedoed and entrees are traditional, with au courant twists: lobster bisque with saffron orzo, or tournedos of tuna with onion marmalade and white beans. The owners are from the Basque region of France, so a Basque influence shows in some dishes, like the crispy cod filet with baby clams and Basquaise sauce. You'll want to dress up here.

218 N. Lee St. ⓒ 703/683-1007. www.labergerie.com. Reservations required. Lunch main courses $8–$15; dinner main courses $16–$25. AE, DC, DISC, MC, V. Mon–Sat 11:30am–2:30pm and 5:30–10:30pm; Sun 5–10pm.

MODERATE

Gadsby's Tavern COLONIAL AMERICAN   George Washington often came here to dine and dance, and this is where he reviewed his troops for the last time. Gadsby's Tavern tends toward the touristy, but it does evoke the 18th century authentically, with period music, wood-plank floors, hurricane-lamp wall sconces, and a rendition of a Hogarth painting over the fireplace (one of several).

Servers are dressed in traditional colonial attire. A strolling violinist entertains Tuesday and Wednesday nights, an "18th-century gentleman" regales guests with song and tells the news of the day (some 220 years ago). When the weather's nice, you can dine in a flagstone courtyard edged with flower beds.

The fare is adequate. It's all homemade, including the sweet Sally Lunn bread, which is baked daily. You might start with soup from the stockpot served with homemade sourdough crackers, followed by baked ham and cheese pie (a sort of Early American quiche), hot roast turkey with giblet gravy and bread-and-sage stuffing on Sally Lunn bread, or George Washington's favorite: slow-roasted crisp duckling served with fruit dressing and Madeira sauce. For dessert, try the English trifle or creamy buttermilk-custard pie with a hint of lemon. Colonial "coolers" are also available: scuppernong, Wench's Punch, and such. The Sunday brunch menu adds such items as thick slices of toast dipped in a batter of rum and spices, with sausage, hash browns, and hot cinnamon syrup. And a desserts and libations menu highlights such favorites as Scottish apple gingerbread and bourbon apple pie, along with a wide selection of beverages.

138 N. Royal St. (at Cameron St.). ⓒ 703/548-1288. Reservations recommended at dinner. Lunch/brunch items $8–$15; dinner main courses $15–$25. Half-price portions available on some items for children 12 and under. AE, DC, MC, V. Mon–Sat 11:30am–3pm; Sun 11am–3pm; daily 5:30–10pm.

Taverna Cretekou ⭐ GREEK   There aren't many truly Greek (as opposed to Mediterranean or Middle Eastern) restaurants in the Washington area, and this is undeniably the best. The Taverna has been open for more than 20 years, and is only gaining in popularity, for its traditional dishes of spanakopita and moussaka, as well as contemporary items, such as grilled red snapper with oregano and lemon, or rainbow trout stuffed with spinach and feta. The ouzo flows and, on Thursday nights, Greek music and dancing breaks out, usually ending up with diners and waiters joining the musicians.

818 King St. (at Alfred St.). ⓒ 703/548-8688. www.tavernacretekou.com. Reservations recommended. Lunch and dinner items $12–$30; Sun brunch $15.95. AE, DC, DISC, MC, V. Tues–Fri 11:30am–10pm; Sat noon–11pm; Sun brunch 11am–3pm and dinner 5–9:30pm.

INEXPENSIVE

La Madeleine FRENCH CAFE *Kids*   It may be part of a self-service chain, but this place is charming nonetheless. Its French country interior has a beamed ceiling, bare oak floors, a wood-burning stove, and maple hutches displaying crockery and pewter mugs. Its range of affordable menu items makes this a good choice for families with finicky eaters in tow.

Come in the morning for fresh-baked croissants, Danish, scones, muffins, and brioches, or a heartier bacon-and-eggs plate. Throughout the day, there are delicious salads (such as roasted vegetables and rigatoni), sandwiches (including a traditional croque monsieur), and hot dishes ranging from quiche and pizza to rotisserie chicken with a Caesar salad. After 5pm, additional choices include pastas and specials such as beef bourguignonne and salmon in dill-cream sauce, both served with a crispy potato galette and sautéed broccoli. Conclude with a yummy fruit tart or chocolate, vanilla, and praline triple-layer cheesecake with graham-cracker crust. Wine and beer are served.

500 King St. (at S. Pitt St.). ✆ **703/739-2854.** Reservations not accepted. Breakfast main courses $3.30–$6.50; lunch and dinner main courses $5–$10. AE, DISC, MC, V. Sun–Thurs 7am–10pm; Fri–Sat 7am–11pm.

South Austin Grill TEX-MEX   One of five Austin Grills in the area, this one offers the same menu, music, and ambience as other links in the chain. See p. 159 for a review of the Glover Park location.

801 King St. (at S. Columbus St.). ✆ **703/684-8969.** Reservations not accepted. Main courses $8–$15. AE, DC, DISC, MC, V. Mon–Thurs 11:30am–11pm; Fri 11:30am–midnight; Sat 11am–midnight; Sun 11am–10pm.

Union Street Public House AMERICAN/SEAFOOD   You might have to wait in line to be seated, but the line usually moves fast, since the restaurant has lots of pubby rooms. The laid-back atmosphere and comfortable decor make this a natural stop for families, groups, informal dates, and anyone who's just hopped off the bike trail to Mount Vernon. Window seats upstairs are coveted for their views of King Street. Downstairs rooms tend to emphasize the *pub* in public house—this is where singles mingle. The menu offers burgers, po' boys, oysters, fried calamari, salads, and so on.

121 S. Union St. ✆ **703/548-1785.** Reservations accepted for groups of 8 or more, except on Fri–Sat nights. Main courses $7–$20. AE, DISC, MC, V. Mon–Thurs 11:30am–10:30pm; Fri–Sat 11:30am–11:30pm; Sun 11am–10:30pm.

Appendix A:
Washington, D.C., in Depth

Two hundred and thirteen years ago, the world wondered why America had chosen this swampy locale as its capital. It took its first hundred years for Washington to evolve from bumpkin backwater status to an international hub of power, diplomacy, and beauty. Today, Washington, D.C., fully commands center stage. The terrorists who crashed a plane into the Pentagon and were foiled from crashing another plane somewhere else in the capital on September 11, 2001, did nothing to diminish Washington's place in the world—quite the contrary. Their acts served only to rally the city itself, strengthen our federal government, and renew our country's commitment to democratic ideals, for all the world to see.

And people from all over the world do come to see D.C. Tourism contributes to the bustle of this city that serves as the seat of the nation's government, as well as home to more than 572,000 people, scores of vibrant neighborhoods, countless historic landmarks and other tourist attractions, a thriving cultural and arts scene, many beautiful parks, and loads of terrific restaurants. The capital is the centerpiece of a metropolitan region that extends into the suburbs of Virginia and Maryland. This Greater Washington area has a population of 5.5 million people, making it one of the most rapidly expanding metropolitan areas, as well as the fastest growing job base, in the nation.

Just a few short years ago, Washington wasn't so attractive; visitors came to tour federal buildings, like the Capitol, the White House, and the Smithsonian museums, but stayed away from the downtown and nontouristy areas. The city's revitalization in the past few years is largely due to Mayor Anthony A. Williams, his city council, and Congresswoman Eleanor Holmes Norton, whose herculean efforts to revive the economy and provide better services around the city have encouraged developers and entrepreneurs to invest here. Their success has led Congress to contemplate handing over more control of the District to the District itself. Since D.C. is not a state, Congress oversees the city's budget and legislation. Residents elect a mayor and council, who govern the nonfederal responsibilities of the city, but Congress's micromanagement of these local issues tends to impede planning and progress. Residents also elect a delegate to Congress (Norton is the current representative), who introduces legislation and votes in committees, but who cannot vote on the House floor. This unique situation, in which residents of the District pay federal income taxes but don't have a vote in Congress, is increasingly a matter of local concern—you may notice D.C. license plates bearing the inscription "Taxation without Representation." Congresswoman Norton and others have begun to push for D.C.'s statehood or, at the very least, a true vote in Congress.

Whether or not Washington eventually wins voting rights and statehood, its dual roles as nation's capital and independent city have always been and will ever be intertwined with American history, as the following section makes clear.

History 101

A WANDERING CONGRESS It all began in 1783, when 250 Revolutionary War soldiers, understandably angered because Congress was ignoring their petitions for back pay, stormed the temporary capitol in Philadelphia to demand justice. The citizens of Philadelphia sympathized with the soldiers and ignored congressional pleas for protection; as the soldiers rioted outside, lawmakers huddled inside the State House behind locked doors. When the soldiers finally calmed down and returned to their barracks, Congress decided it would be prudent to move itself to Princeton. Lawmakers also decided they needed a capital city whose business was government and the protection thereof.

This decision to relocate was not a new one. Congress had been so nomadic during its first decade that when a statue of George Washington was commissioned in 1783, satirist Francis Hopkinson suggested putting it on wheels so that it could follow the government around. Before permanently settling in Washington, Congress convened in New York, Baltimore, Philadelphia, Lancaster, Princeton, Annapolis, York, and Trenton.

A DEAL MADE OVER DINNER When Congress proposed that a city be designed and built for the sole purpose of housing the government of the new nation, fresh difficulties arose. There was a general feeling that wherever the capital might be built, a great commercial center would blossom; therefore, many cities vied for the honor. Then, too, northerners were strongly opposed to a southern capital—and vice versa. Finally, after 7 years of bickering, New Yorker Alexander Hamilton and Virginian Thomas Jefferson worked out a compromise over dinner one night in New

Dateline

- **1608** Capt. John Smith sails up Potomac River from Jamestown; for the next 100 years, Irish-Scottish settlers colonize the area.
- **1783** Continental Congress proposes new "Federal Town"; both North and South vie for it.
- **1790** A compromise is reached: If the South pays off the North's Revolutionary War debts, the new capital will be situated in its region.
- **1791** French engineer Pierre Charles L'Enfant designs the capital city but is fired within a year.
- **1792** Cornerstone is laid for Executive Mansion.
- **1793** Construction begins on the Capitol.
- **1800** First wing of the Capitol completed; Congress moves from Philadelphia; Pres. John Adams moves into Executive Mansion.
- **1801** Library of Congress established.
- **1812** War with England.
- **1814** British burn Washington.
- **1817** Executive Mansion rebuilt, its charred walls painted white; becomes known as White House.
- **1822** Population reaches 33,000.
- **1829** Smithsonian Institution founded for the "increase and diffusion of knowledge."
- **1861** Civil War; Washington becomes North's major supply depot.
- **1865** Capitol dome completed; Lee surrenders to Grant on April 8; Lincoln assassinated at Ford's Theatre on April 14.
- **1871** Alexander "Boss" Shepherd turns Washington into a showplace, using many of L'Enfant's plans.
- **1900** Population reaches about 300,000.
- **1901** McMillan Commission plans development of Mall from Capitol to Lincoln Memorial.
- **1907** Union Station opens, largest train station in country.
- **1912** Cherry trees, a gift from Japan, planted in Tidal Basin.
- **1914** World War I begins.

York. The North would support a southern site for the capital in return for the South's assumption of debts incurred by the northern states during the Revolutionary War. As a further sop to the North, it was agreed that the seat of government would remain in Philadelphia through 1800 to allow suitable time for surveying, purchasing land, and constructing government buildings.

ENTER L'ENFANT TERRIBLE

An act passed in 1790 specified a site "not exceeding 10 miles square" to be located on the Potomac. Pres. George Washington, an experienced surveyor charged with selecting the exact site, chose a part of the Potomac Valley where the river becomes tidal and is joined by the Anacostia. Maryland gladly provided 69¼ square miles and Virginia 30¾ square miles for the new Federal District. (In 1846, Virginia's territorial contribution was returned to the state.) The District today covers about 67 square miles.

President Washington hired French military engineer Pierre Charles L'Enfant to lay out the federal city. It has since been said that "it would have been hard to find a man better qualified artistically and less fitted by temperament" for the job. L'Enfant arrived in 1791 and immediately declared Jenkins Hill (today Capitol Hill) "a pedestal waiting for a monument." He surveyed every inch of the designated Federal District and began creating his vision by selecting dominant sites for major buildings. He designed 160-foot-wide avenues radiating from squares and circles centered on monumental sculptures and fountains. The Capitol, the "presidential palace," and an equestrian statue—the last to be erected where the Washington Monument stands today—were to

- 1922 Lincoln Memorial completed.
- 1941 First plane lands at National Airport; United States declares war on Japan.
- 1943 Pantheon-inspired Jefferson Memorial and Pentagon completed.
- 1960 Population declines for first time, from 800,000 to 764,000.
- 1963 More than 200,000 March on Washington, hear Martin Luther King Jr.'s "I Have a Dream" speech supporting civil rights.
- 1971 John F. Kennedy Center for Performing Arts opens.
- 1976 Metro, city's first subway system, opens in time for bicentennial.
- 1982 Vietnam Veterans Memorial erected in Constitution Gardens.
- 1993 U.S. Holocaust Memorial Museum opens near Mall.
- 1994 Marion Barry is elected to a fourth term as mayor after serving time in prison.
- 1995 Korean War Veterans Memorial is dedicated. Pennsylvania Avenue closed to vehicular traffic in front of the White House on security grounds.
- 1997 Federal government offers aid package to save D.C. from bankruptcy. Franklin Delano Roosevelt Memorial is dedicated.
- 1998 White House beset by sex scandal. In December, the House of Representatives impeaches the president.
- 1999 Washington, D.C., inaugurates Mayor Anthony Williams. In February, the Senate acquits the president.
- 2001 While thousands protest, Pres. George W. Bush takes office in January after the most controversial election in modern U.S. history. In September, 180 people die when terrorists hijack a commercial airliner and crash it into the Pentagon.
- 2002 The city recovers from the aftermath of September 2001 terrorist attacks, rebuilds the destroyed section of the Pentagon, and imposes tighter security at federal buildings and airports. D.C. mayoral and congressional races take place.

be the city's focal points. Pennsylvania Avenue would be the major thoroughfare, and the Mall was conceived as a bustling ceremonial avenue of embassies and other distinguished buildings.

L'Enfant's plan dismayed landowners who had been promised $66.66 per acre for land donated for buildings, while land for avenues was to be donated free; of the 6,661 acres to be included in the boundaries of the federal city, about half would comprise avenues and the 2-mile-long Mall.

A more personable man might have won over the reluctant landowners and commissioners, inspiring them with his dreams and his passion, but L'Enfant exhibited only a peevish and condescending secretiveness that alienated one and all. A year after he had been hired, L'Enfant was fired. Congress offered him $2,500 compensation for his year of work, and James Monroe urged him to accept a professorship at West Point. Insulted, he spurned all offers, suing the government for $95,500 instead. He lost and died a pauper in 1825. In 1909, in belated recognition of his services, his remains were brought to Arlington National Cemetery. Some 118 years after he had conceived it, his vision of the federal city finally had become a reality.

HOME NOT-SO-SWEET HOME   In 1800, government officials (106 representatives and 32 senators) arrived according to schedule, ready to settle into their new home. What they found bore little resemblance to a city. "One might take a ride of several hours within the precincts without meeting with a single individual to disturb one's meditation," commented one early resident. Pennsylvania Avenue was a mosquito-infested swamp, and there were fewer than 400 habitable houses. Disgruntled Secretary of the Treasury Oliver Wolcott wrote his wife, "I do not perceive how the members of Congress can possibly secure lodgings, unless they will consent to live like Scholars in a college or Monks in a monastery." The solution was a boom in boardinghouses.

Abigail Adams was dismayed at the condition of her new home, the presidential mansion. The damp caused her rheumatism to act up, the main stairs had not yet been constructed, not a single room was finished, and there were not even enough logs for all the fireplaces. And since there was "not the least fence, yard, or other convenience," she hung the presidential laundry in the unfinished East Room. To attend presidential affairs or to visit one another, Washington's early citizens had to drive through mud and slush, their vehicles often becoming embedded in bogs and gullies—not a pleasant state of affairs, but one that would continue for many decades.

There were many difficulties in building the capital. Money, as always, was in short supply, as were materials and labor, with the result that the home of the world's most enlightened democracy was built largely by slaves. And always, in the background, there was talk of abandoning the city and starting over somewhere else.

REDCOATS REDUX   Then came the War of 1812. At first, fighting centered on Canada and the West—both too far away to affect daily life in the capital. (In the early 1800s, it was a 33-hr. ride from Washington, D.C., to Philadelphia—if you made good time.) In May 1813, the flamboyant British Rear Admiral Cockburn sent word to the Executive Mansion that "he would make his bow" in the Madisons' drawing room shortly. On August 23, 1814, alarming news reached the capital: The British had landed troops in Maryland. On August 24, James Madison was at the front, most of the populace had fled, and Dolley Madison created a legend by refusing to leave the president's mansion without Gilbert Stuart's famous portrait of George Washington. As the British neared her gates, she calmly wrote a blow-by-blow description to her sister:

"Our kind friend, Mr. Carroll, has come to hasten my departure, and is in a very bad humour with me because I insist on waiting until the large picture of

General Washington is secured, and it requires to be unscrewed from the wall. This process was found too tedious for these perilous moments; I have ordered the frame to be broken, and the canvas taken out; it is done. . . . And now, dear sister, I must leave this house, or the retreating army will make me a prisoner in it, by filling up the road I am directed to take."

When the British arrived early that evening, they found dinner set up on the table (Dolley had hoped for the best until the end), and, according to some accounts, ate it before torching the mansion. They also burned the Capitol, the Library of Congress, and newly built ships and naval stores. A thunderstorm later that night saved the city from total destruction, while a tornado the next day added to the damage but daunted the British troops.

It seemed that the new capital was doomed. Margaret Bayard Smith, wife of the owner of the influential *National Intelligencer,* privately lamented, "I do not suppose the Government will ever return to Washington. All those whose property was invested in that place, will be reduced to general poverty. . . . The consternation about us is general. The despondency still greater." But the *Intelligencer* was among the printed voices speaking out against even a temporary move. Editorials warned that it would be a "treacherous breach of faith" with those who had "laid out fortunes in the purchase of property in and about the city." To move the capital would be "kissing the rod an enemy has wielded."

Washingtonian pride rallied and the city was saved once again. Still, it was a close call; Congress came within nine votes of abandoning the place!

In 1815, leading citizens erected a brick building in which Congress could meet in relative comfort until the Capitol was restored. The Treaty of Ghent, establishing peace with Great Britain, was ratified at Octagon House, where the Madisons were temporarily ensconced. And Thomas Jefferson donated his own books to replace the destroyed contents of the Library of Congress. Confidence was restored and the city began to prosper. When the Madisons moved into the rebuilt presidential mansion, its exterior had been painted gleaming white to cover the charred walls. From then on, it would be known as the White House.

THE CITY OF MAGNIFICENT INTENTIONS   Between the War of 1812 and the Civil War, few people evinced any great enthusiasm for Washington. European visitors in particular looked at the capital and found it wanting. It was still a provincial backwater, with Pennsylvania Avenue and the Mall remaining muddy messes inhabited by pigs, goats, cows, and geese. Many were repelled by the slave auctions openly taking place in the backyard of the White House. The best that could be said—though nobody said it—was that the young capital was picturesque. Meriwether Lewis kept the bears he captured during his 4,000-mile expedition up the Missouri in cages on the president's lawn. Native American chiefs in full regalia were often seen negotiating with the white man's government. Matching them in visual splendor were magnificently attired European court visitors.

The only foreigner who praised Washington was Lafayette, who visited in 1825 and was feted with lavish balls and dinners throughout his stay. Charles Dickens gave the city the raspberry in 1842:

"It is sometimes called the City of Magnificent Distances, but it might with greater propriety be termed the City of Magnificent Intentions. . . . Spacious avenues, that begin in nothing and lead nowhere; streets, miles long, that only want houses, roads, and inhabitants; public buildings that need but a public to be complete; and ornaments of great thoroughfares, which only lack great thoroughfares to ornament—are its leading features."

Tobacco chewing and sloppy senatorial spitting particularly appalled him:

"Both houses are handsomely carpeted, but the state to which these carpets are reduced by the universal disregard of the spittoon with which every honorable member is accommodated, and the extraordinary improvements on the pattern which are squirted and dabbled upon it in every direction, do not admit of being described. I will merely observe, that I strongly recommend all strangers not to look at the floor; and if they happen to drop anything . . . not to pick it up with an ungloved hand on any account."

But Dickens's critique was mild when compared with Anthony Trollope's, who declared Washington in 1860 "as melancholy and miserable a town as the mind of man can conceive."

A NATION DIVIDED   During the Civil War, the capital became an armed camp. It was the principal supply depot for the Union Army and an important medical center. Parks became campgrounds, churches became hospitals, and forts ringed the town. The population doubled from 60,000 to 120,000, including about 40,000 former slaves who streamed into the city seeking federal protection. More than 3,000 soldiers slept in the Capitol building, and a bakery was set up in the basement. The streets were filled with the wounded, and Walt Whitman became a familiar figure, making daily rounds to comfort the ailing soldiers. In spite of everything, Lincoln insisted that work on the incomplete Capitol be continued. "If people see the Capitol going on, it is a sign we intend the Union shall go on," he said. When the giant dome was finished in 1863 and a 35-star flag was flown overhead, Capitol Hill's field battery fired a 35-gun salute, honoring the Union's then 35 states.

There was joy in Washington and an 800-gun salute in April 1865, when news of the fall of the Confederacy reached the capital. The joy was short-lived, however. Five days after Appomattox, President Lincoln was shot at Ford's Theatre while attending a performance of *Our American Cousin*. Black replaced the festive tricolored draperies decorating the town, and Washington went into mourning.

The war had enlarged the city's population while doing nothing to improve its facilities. Agrarian, uneducated ex-slaves stayed on, and poverty, unemployment, and disease were rampant. A red-light district remained, the parks were trodden bare, and tenement slums mushroomed within a stone's throw of the Capitol.

LED BY A SHEPHERD   Whereas L'Enfant had been aloof and introverted, his glorious vision was not forgotten, finally being implemented 70 years later by Alexander "Boss" Shepherd, a swashbuckling and friendly man. A real estate speculator who had made his money in a plumbing firm, Shepherd shouldered a musket in the Union Army and became one of Gen. Ulysses S. Grant's closest intimates. When Grant became president, he wanted to appoint Shepherd governor, but blue-blooded opposition ran too high. Washington high society considered him a parvenu and feared his ambitions for civic leadership. In response, Grant named the more popular Henry D. Cooke (a secret Shepherd ally) governor and appointed Shepherd vice president of the Board of Public Works. No one was fooled. Shepherd made all the governor's decisions, and a joke went around the capital: "Why is the new governor like a sheep? Because he is led by A. Shepherd." He became the official governor in 1873.

Shepherd vowed that his "comprehensive plan of improvement" would make the city a showplace. But an engineer he wasn't—occasionally, newly paved streets had to be torn up because he had forgotten to install sewers. But he was a first-rate politician who knew how to accomplish his goals. He began by hiring an army of laborers and starting them on projects all over town. Congress would have had to halt work on half-finished sidewalks, streets, and sewers throughout the District in order to stop him. It would have been a mess. The press liked and supported the colorful Shepherd; however, people forced out of their homes because they couldn't pay the high assessments for improvements hated him. Between 1871 and 1874, he established parks, paved and lighted the streets, installed sewers, filled in sewage-laden Tiber Creek, and planted more than 50,000 trees. He left the city bankrupt—more than $20 million in debt. But he got the job done.

L'ENFANT REBORN   Through the end of the 19th century, Washington continued to make great aesthetic strides. The Washington Monument, long a truncated obelisk and major eyesore, was finally dedicated in 1885. Pennsylvania Avenue was becoming the ceremonial thoroughfare L'Enfant had envisioned, and important buildings were completed one after another. Shepherd had done a great deal, but much was still left undone. In 1887, L'Enfant's "Plan for the City of Washington" was resurrected. In 1900, Michigan Senator James McMillan— a retired railroad mogul with architectural and engineering knowledge— determined to complete the job L'Enfant had started a century earlier. A tireless lobbyist for government-sponsored municipal improvements, he persuaded his colleagues to appoint an advisory committee to create "the city beautiful." At his personal expense, McMillan sent this illustrious committee—landscapist Frederick Law Olmsted (designer of New York's Central Park), sculptor Augustus Saint-Gaudens, and noted architects Daniel Burnham and Charles McKim—to Europe for 7 weeks to study the landscaping and architecture of that continent's great capitals. Assembled at last was a group that combined L'Enfant's artistic genius and Shepherd's political savvy.

"Make no little plans," counseled Burnham. "They have no magic to stir men's blood, and probably themselves will not be realized. Make big plans, aim high in hope and work, remembering that a noble and logical diagram once recorded will never die, but long after we are gone will be a living thing, asserting itself with ever growing insistency."

The committee's big plans—almost all of which were accomplished— included the development of a complete park system, selection of sites for government buildings, and the designing of the Lincoln Memorial, the Arlington Memorial Bridge, and the Reflecting Pool (the last inspired by Versailles). They also got to work on improving the Mall; their first step was to remove the tracks, train sheds, and stone depot constructed there by the Baltimore and Potomac Railroad. In return, Congress authorized money to build the monumental Union Station, whose design was inspired by Rome's Baths of Diocletian.

Throughout the McMillan Commission years, the House was under the hostile leadership of Speaker "Uncle Joe" Cannon of Illinois, who, among other things, swore he would "never let a memorial to Abraham Lincoln be erected in that goddamned swamp" (West Potomac Park). Cannon caused some problems and delays, but on the whole the committee's prestigious membership added weight to their usually accepted recommendations. McMillan, however, did not live to see most of his dreams accomplished. He died in 1902.

By the 20th century, Washington was no longer an object of ridicule. The capital was coming into its own as a finely designed city of sweeping vistas studded with green parks and grand architecture. Congress's 1899 mandate limiting building heights in downtown Washington ensured the prominence of landmarks in the landscape. As the century progressed, the city seamlessly incorporated additional architectural marvels, including the Library of Congress, Union Station, and the Corcoran Gallery, which were all built around the turn of the century; several more Smithsonian museums and the Lincoln Memorial were completed in 1922. A Commission of Fine Arts was appointed in 1910 by President Taft to create monuments and fountains, and, thanks to Mrs. Taft, the famous cherry trees presented to the United States by the Japanese in 1912 were planted in the Tidal Basin.

During the Great Depression in the 1930s, FDR's Works Progress Administration (WPA) put the unemployed to work erecting public buildings and artists to work beautifying them. By the 1930s, too, increasing numbers of automobiles—nearly 200,000—were traversing Washington's wide avenues, joining the electric streetcars that had been in use since about 1890.

Washington's population, meanwhile, continued to grow, spurred by the influx of workers remaining after each of the world wars. In 1950, the city's population reached a zenith of more than 800,000 residents, an estimated 60% of whom were black. At the same time that Washington was establishing itself as a global power, the city was gaining renown among African Americans as a hub of black culture, education, and identity. From the 1920s to the 1960s, Washington drew the likes of Cab Calloway, Duke Ellington, and Pearl Bailey, who performed at speakeasies and theaters along a stretch of U Street called the Black Broadway. (The reincarnated "New U," as it is dubbed, now attracts buppies, yuppies, and restless youth to its nightclubs and bars.) Howard University, created in 1867, distinguished itself as the nation's most comprehensive center for the higher education of blacks. And when the Civil Rights movement gained momentum throughout the country in the 1960s and 1970s, Washington's large black presence (nearly 75% of the city's overall population) and activist spirit were instrumental in furthering the cause.

On August 28, 1963, black and white Washingtonians joined the ranks of the more than 200,000 who "Marched on Washington" to ensure passage of the Civil Rights Act. It was at this event that Rev. Martin Luther King Jr. delivered his stirring "I Have a Dream" speech at the Lincoln Memorial, where 41 years earlier, during the memorial's dedication ceremony, black officials were required to stand and watch from across the road, segregated from the whites. When King was assassinated on April 4, 1968, rioting erupted here as it did in many cities around the country.

Ever since, black and white Washingtonians have continued to thrash out race relations in a city whose population has stabilized at 572,000, about 60% of which now is African American, including the city's mayor and congressional representative. Mayor Anthony A. Williams, whose first term in office has just ended, and Congresswoman Eleanor Holmes Norton, who has just completed her sixth term in office, have focused their efforts on improving the city, each fighting tirelessly for their constituency. (At this writing, the results of the 2002 mayoral and congressional race were not in.) Residents continue to feel upbeat about their city.

Washington, the federal city, proceeds apace, adding more jewels to its crown. In 1989, renovation of the city's magnificent Union Station was completed. Architect Daniel Burnham also designed the palatial City Post Office Building, which, in 1993, became part of the Smithsonian complex as the National Postal Museum. The same year saw the opening of the U.S. Holocaust Memorial Museum, adjoining the Mall. In 1995, the Korean War Veterans Memorial was dedicated. Washington's fourth presidential monument—and the first in more than half a century—was dedicated in May 1997, to honor Franklin Delano Roosevelt; it is the first memorial in Washington designed to be totally wheel-chair accessible. The Women in Military Service Memorial, next to Arlington Cemetery, was inaugurated in October 1997, followed, in June 1998, by a Civil War memorial recognizing the efforts of African-American soldiers who fought for the Union.

The year 2003 will see the opening of a huge, new convention center and a City Museum of Washington (across the street from the convention center), and the dedication of the World War II Memorial on the National Mall. Coming in 2004: the opening of the Smithsonian's National Museum of the American Indian, on the National Mall.

If the city's optimism about its prosperity and growth was profoundly shaken by the terrorist attacks of September 11, 2001, it has been restored in the months since. The economy has rebounded with a vengeance, and tourists are returning to Washington in greater numbers than ever. Security procedures may always be a little more involved now than before the attacks, and some federal buildings, or parts of federal buildings may remain closed to the general public—at this writing, the White House is open only to school group tours, for example. But today, as always, the capital of the United States gladly welcomes visitors from around the world to town.

Appendix B:
Useful Toll-Free Numbers
& Websites

AIRLINES

Air Canada
✆ 888/247-2262
www.aircanada.ca

Airtran Airlines
✆ 800/247-8726
www.airtran.com

American Airlines
✆ 800/433-7300
www.aa.com

American Trans Air
✆ 800/435-9282
www.ata.com

British Airways
✆ 800/247-9297
✆ 0345/222-111 or 0845/77-333-77
  in Britain
www.british-airways.com

Continental Airlines
✆ 800/525-0280
www.continental.com

Delta Air Lines
✆ 800/221-1212
www.delta.com

Frontier Airlines
✆ 800/432-1359
www.frontierairlines.com

JetBlue
✆ 800/538-2583
www.jetblue.com

Midwest Express
✆ 800/452-2022
www.midwestexpress.com

Northwest Airlines
✆ 800/225-2525
www.nwa.com

Southwest Airlines
✆ 800/435-9792
www.southwest.com

United Airlines
✆ 800/241-6522
www.united.com

US Airways
✆ 800/428-4322
www.usairways.com

Virgin Atlantic Airways
✆ 800/862-8621 in continental U.S.
✆ 0293/747-747 in Britain
www.virgin-atlantic.com

CAR-RENTAL AGENCIES

Alamo
✆ 800/227-8367
www.goalamo.com

Avis
✆ 800/331-1212 in continental U.S.
✆ 800/TRY-AVIS in Canada
www.avis.com

Budget
✆ 800/527-0700
www.budget.com

Dollar
✆ 800/800-4000
www.dollar.com

Enterprise
© 800/325-8007
www.enterprise.com

Hertz
© 800/654-3131
www.hertz.com

National
© 800/CAR-RENT
www.nationalcar.com

Rent-A-Wreck
© 800/535-1391
www.rentawreck.com

Thrifty
© 800/367-2277
www.thrifty.com

MAJOR HOTEL & MOTEL CHAINS

Best Western International
© 800/528-1234
www.bestwestern.com

Clarion Hotels
© 800/CLARION
www.clarionhotel.com
    or www.hotelchoice.com

Comfort Inns
© 800/228-5150
www.hotelchoice.com

Courtyard by Marriott
© 800/321-2211
www.courtyard.com
    or www.marriott.com

Days Inn
© 800/325-2525
www.daysinn.com

Doubletree Hotels
© 800/222-TREE
www.doubletree.com

Econo Lodges
© 800/55-ECONO
www.hotelchoice.com

Fairfield Inn by Marriott
© 800/228-2800
www.marriott.com

Hampton Inn
© 800/HAMPTON
www.hampton-inn.com

Hilton Hotels
© 800/HILTONS
www.hilton.com

Holiday Inn
© 800/HOLIDAY
www.basshotels.com

Howard Johnson
© 800/654-2000
www.hojo.com

Hyatt Hotels & Resorts
© 800/228-9000
www.hyatt.com

ITT Sheraton
© 800/325-3535
www.starwood.com

Marriott Hotels
© 800/228-9290
www.marriott.com

Motel 6
© 800/4-MOTEL-6
www.motel6.com

Quality Inns
© 800/228-5151
www.hotelchoice.com

Radisson Hotels International
© 800/333-3333
www.radisson.com

Ramada Inns
© 800/2-RAMADA
www.ramada.com

Red Carpet Inns
© 800/251-1962
www.reservahost.com

Red Lion Hotels & Inns
© 800/547-8010
www.hilton.com

Red Roof Inns
© 800/843-7663
www.redroof.com

Residence Inn by Marriott
℃ 800/331-3131
www.marriott.com

Rodeway Inns
℃ 800/228-2000
www.hotelchoice.com

Super 8 Motels
℃ 800/800-8000
www.super8.com

Travelodge
℃ 800/255-3050
www.travelodge.com

Wyndham Hotels and Resorts
℃ 800/822-4200 in continental U.S.
and Canada
www.wyndham.com

Index

See also Accommodations and Restaurant indexes, below.

FROMMER'S® COMPLETE TRAVEL GUIDES

Alaska
Alaska Cruises & Ports of Call
Amsterdam
Argentina & Chile
Arizona
Atlanta
Australia
Austria
Bahamas
Barcelona, Madrid & Seville
Beijing
Belgium, Holland & Luxembourg
Bermuda
Boston
Brazil
British Columbia & the Canadian
  Rockies
Budapest & the Best of Hungary
California
Canada
Cancún, Cozumel & the Yucatán
Cape Cod, Nantucket & Martha's
  Vineyard
Caribbean
Caribbean Cruises & Ports of Call
Caribbean Ports of Call
Carolinas & Georgia
Chicago
China
Colorado
Costa Rica
Denmark
Denver, Boulder & Colorado
  Springs
England
Europe
European Cruises & Ports of Call
Florida

France
Germany
Great Britain
Greece
Greek Islands
Hawaii
Hong Kong
Honolulu, Waikiki & Oahu
Ireland
Israel
Italy
Jamaica
Japan
Las Vegas
London
Los Angeles
Maryland & Delaware
Maui
Mexico
Montana & Wyoming
Montréal & Québec City
Munich & the Bavarian Alps
Nashville & Memphis
Nepal
New England
New Mexico
New Orleans
New York City
New Zealand
Northern Italy
Nova Scotia, New Brunswick &
  Prince Edward Island
Oregon
Paris
Philadelphia & the Amish Country
Portugal
Prague & the Best of the Czech
  Republic

Provence & the Riviera
Puerto Rico
Rome
San Antonio & Austin
San Diego
San Francisco
Santa Fe, Taos & Albuquerque
Scandinavia
Scotland
Seattle & Portland
Shanghai
Singapore & Malaysia
South Africa
South America
South Florida
South Pacific
Southeast Asia
Spain
Sweden
Switzerland
Texas
Thailand
Tokyo
Toronto
Tuscany & Umbria
USA
Utah
Vancouver & Victoria
Vermont, New Hampshire &
  Maine
Vienna & the Danube Valley
Virgin Islands
Virginia
Walt Disney World® & Orlando
Washington, D.C.
Washington State

FROMMER'S® DOLLAR-A-DAY GUIDES

Australia from $50 a Day
California from $70 a Day
Caribbean from $70 a Day
England from $75 a Day
Europe from $70 a Day

Florida from $70 a Day
Hawaii from $80 a Day
Ireland from $60 a Day
Italy from $70 a Day
London from $85 a Day

New York from $90 a Day
Paris from $80 a Day
San Francisco from $70 a Day
Washington, D.C. from $80 a Day

FROMMER'S® PORTABLE GUIDES

Acapulco, Ixtapa & Zihuatanejo
Amsterdam
Aruba
Australia's Great Barrier Reef
Bahamas
Berlin
Big Island of Hawaii
Boston
California Wine Country
Cancún
Charleston & Savannah
Chicago
Disneyland®
Dublin
Florence

Frankfurt
Hong Kong
Houston
Las Vegas
London
Los Angeles
Los Cabos & Baja
Maine Coast
Maui
Miami
New Orleans
New York City
Paris
Phoenix & Scottsdale

Portland
Puerto Rico
Puerto Vallarta, Manzanillo &
  Guadalajara
Rio de Janeiro
San Diego
San Francisco
Seattle
Sydney
Tampa & St. Petersburg
Vancouver
Venice
Virgin Islands
Washington, D.C.

FROMMER'S® NATIONAL PARK GUIDES

Banff & Jasper
Family Vacations in the National
  Parks
Grand Canyon

National Parks of the American
  West
Rocky Mountain

Yellowstone & Grand Teton
Yosemite & Sequoia/ Kings Canyon
Zion & Bryce Canyon

FROMMER'S® MEMORABLE WALKS

Chicago
London

New York
Paris

San Francisco
Washington, D.C.

FROMMER'S® GREAT OUTDOOR GUIDES

Arizona & New Mexico
New England

Northern California
Southern New England

Vermont & New Hampshire

SUZY GERSHMAN'S BORN TO SHOP GUIDES

Born to Shop: France
Born to Shop: Hong Kong,
  Shanghai & Beijing

Born to Shop: Italy
Born to Shop: London

Born to Shop: New York
Born to Shop: Paris

FROMMER'S® IRREVERENT GUIDES

Amsterdam
Boston
Chicago
Las Vegas
London

Los Angeles
Manhattan
New Orleans
Paris
Rome

San Francisco
Seattle & Portland
Vancouver
Walt Disney World®
Washington, D.C.

FROMMER'S® BEST-LOVED DRIVING TOURS

Britain
California
Florida
France

Germany
Ireland
Italy
New England

Northern Italy
Scotland
Spain
Tuscany & Umbria

HANGING OUT™ GUIDES

Hanging Out in England
Hanging Out in Europe

Hanging Out in France
Hanging Out in Ireland

Hanging Out in Italy
Hanging Out in Spain

THE UNOFFICIAL GUIDES®

Bed & Breakfasts and Country
  Inns in:
  California
  Great Lakes States
  Mid-Atlantic
  New England
  Northwest
  Rockies
  Southeast
  Southwest
Best RV & Tent Campgrounds in:
  California & the West
  Florida & the Southeast
  Great Lakes States
  Mid-Atlantic
  Northeast
  Northwest & Central Plains

Southwest & South Central
  Plains
  U.S.A.
Beyond Disney
Branson, Missouri
California with Kids
Chicago
Cruises
Disneyland®
Florida with Kids
Golf Vacations in the Eastern U.S.
Great Smoky & Blue Ridge Region
Inside Disney
Hawaii
Las Vegas
London

Mid-Atlantic with Kids
Mini Las Vegas
Mini-Mickey
New England and New York with
  Kids
New Orleans
New York City
Paris
San Francisco
Skiing in the West
Southeast with Kids
Walt Disney World®
Walt Disney World® for Grown-ups
Walt Disney World® with Kids
Washington, D.C.
World's Best Diving Vacations

SPECIAL-INTEREST TITLES

Frommer's Adventure Guide to Australia &
  New Zealand
Frommer's Adventure Guide to Central America
Frommer's Adventure Guide to India & Pakistan
Frommer's Adventure Guide to South America
Frommer's Adventure Guide to Southeast Asia
Frommer's Adventure Guide to Southern Africa
Frommer's Britain's Best Bed & Breakfasts and
  Country Inns
Frommer's Caribbean Hideaways
Frommer's Exploring America by RV
Frommer's Fly Safe, Fly Smart
Frommer's France's Best Bed & Breakfasts and
  Country Inns
Frommer's Gay & Lesbian Europe

Frommer's Italy's Best Bed & Breakfasts and
  Country Inns
Frommer's New York City with Kids
Frommer's Ottawa with Kids
Frommer's Road Atlas Britain
Frommer's Road Atlas Europe
Frommer's Road Atlas France
Frommer's Toronto with Kids
Frommer's Vancouver with Kids
Frommer's Washington, D.C., with Kids
Israel Past & Present
The New York Times' Guide to Unforgettable
  Weekends
Places Rated Almanac
Retirement Places Rated

Booked seat 6A, open return.

Rented red 4-wheel drive.

Reserved cabin, no running water.

Discovered space.

With over 700 airlines, 50,000 hotels, 50 rental car companies and 5,000 cruise and vacation packages, you can create the perfect getaway for you. Choose the car, the room, even the ground you walk on.

Travelocity.com
A Sabre Company
Go Virtually Anywhere.